LIMITS TO FRIENDSHIP

LIMITS

TO

FRIENDSHIP

THE UNITED STATES AND MEXICO

Robert A. Pastor

and

Jorge G. Castañeda

ALFRED A. KNOPF · NEW YORK

1988

THIS IS A BORZOI BOOK
PUBLISHED BY ALFRED A. KNOPF, INC.

Published in the United States by Alfred A. Knopf, Inc.,
New York, and
simultaneously in Canada by Random House of Canada
Limited, Toronto. Distributed
by Random House, Inc., New York.

Library of Congress Cataloging-in-Publication Data
Pastor, Robert A.
Limits to friendship.
Bibliography: p.
Includes index.
1. United States—Relations—Mexico. 2. Mexico—
Relations—United States. I. Castañeda, Jorge.
II. Title.
E183.8M6P23   1988   303.4'8273'072   88-45325
ISBN 0-394-55840-5

Manufactured in the United States of America
First Edition

For
Margy
and
Miriam, Javiera, Carlos Miguel, and Jorge Andrés
for helping us to appreciate
the differences

CONTENTS

PREFACE AND ACKNOWLEDGMENTS

Toward the end of his career, Matías Romero, one of Mexico's most effective ambassadors to the United States, reflected on the relationship between the two countries: "My experience . . . has shown me that there are prejudices on both sides, growing out of want of sufficient knowledge of each other, which could be dispelled, and by so doing, a better understanding secured." Nearly one hundred years later, the formula for securing a better understanding has still not been found; indeed, misunderstandings between the two nations have probably grown more numerous and intractable.

This book is born of the same aspiration as Romero's but it is tempered by the knowledge garnered from one hundred years of experience. Our purpose is to dispel misperceptions that each nation has of the other and to try to learn why they emerge. Both of us are students of our nations' foreign policies and have been involved in making policy. When the opportunity arose to study U.S.-Mexican relations from the other side, we seized it in order to analyze our two countries' problems and fashion, when possible, some solutions.

In August 1985, Robert Pastor and his family left Washington, D.C. for Mexico City and settled in the home of Jorge G. Castañeda, who took his family to Washington. As a Fulbright professor, Pastor taught at El Colegio de México, one of Mexico's leading universities specializing in international relations. For a year, Pastor and his family traveled throughout the country, and he updated, expanded, and revised the picture of Mexico he had acquired as a result of his previous studies, trips, and experience as Director of Latin American and Caribbean Affairs on the National Security Council from 1977 to 1981. He lived in Mexico during a time of change and serious problems—the contest for political power in the north, the earthquake in September 1985, and the plunge of oil prices in early 1986.

At the same time, Castañeda began a twenty-month appointment at the Carnegie Endowment for International Peace in Washington, doing research on U.S.-Mexican relations, writing, and speaking to audiences across the United States. He developed some new ideas and discarded others acquired during previous stays in the United States, the period when he advised the Mexican government on international affairs, and his tenure as professor at the National University of Mexico. While in Washington, he was able to observe closely a serious deterioration in the U.S.-Mexican relationship from a perspective different from his accustomed one.

Each of us considers the other a nationalist, a firm advocate of his nation's interests and purpose. After numerous conversations with each other and friends, we judged that there was a compelling need to take a fresh look at the binational relationship. On the basis of our experience and knowledge before we "traded places" and what we learned during our time in each other's country, we decided to write a book that would shed new light on the rapidly changing ties and the new tensions between the two nations.

The shared conviction of the importance of the relationship led us to organize our thoughts and develop our analyses in a joint effort. Our point of departure was the same: each nation is becoming increasingly important to the other. We also agreed that the best method of describing the relationship was to reflect it: by writing the book together but separately.

During our time in each other's country and especially as we wrote the book, our views evolved. We identified misperceptions in the relationship and recognized the importance of differing interests that were often at the base of those misperceptions. We replayed old arguments and developed new ones. This book is the result of that process. We emerged from the writing with a better understanding and more respect for our differences.

The format of the book reflects our judgment that the best way to describe the present state of U.S.-Mexican relations, and perhaps contribute to improving the management of those relations, was to look at them from both sides. This led us to write a book in which each of us offered his perspective from his side of the border. Although our differences of opinion are present throughout the book, we judged that the reader would benefit by a specific description of some of the major disagreements in our respective introductions. Needless to say, this initial statement of differences should be placed in the context of our respect for each other's point of view.

In order to enhance the reader's sensitivity to the differences between the United States and Mexico, we have occasionally presented the prevailing, mainstream view of each of our nations on an issue even though we might personally not share it. In particular, Pastor has sought to explain and occasionally to defend policies of the U.S. government even when he might not agree with a specific policy. In such cases, our purpose is to provide a sharper, more accurate focus on disagreements than if we had described our own views.

Despite differences on the many issues separating the two nations, we still agree on some conclusions and recommendations. These conclusions in the last chapter will seem meager only if read before the rest of the book. Except for that chapter, we do not attempt or wish to present a common or even compatible view of the bilateral relationship. The two nations have disparate interests; their perspectives are divergent and often contradictory. This reality should be reflected in any effort to achieve a serious understanding of the two neighbors. A negotiated solution between two sides of markedly different interests often represents the lowest common denominator. If the alternative to such a compromise is conflict, war, poverty, or pollution, then such an outcome is obviously desirable. But we thought that such a compromise—as one would see in a negotiated report by an American* and a Mexican— would contribute less to understanding the relationship than the use of contrasting lenses through which both nations view similar problems, challenges, and aspirations.

The scholar's goal, which motivates us, is different from that of the statesman. The statesman seeks agreement, sometimes at the expense of truth; he ignores differences, directing both sides to concentrate on what they have in common. The scholar seeks the truth, sometimes at the expense of agreement; he ignores the banal and concentrates on helping both sides to understand why and how they disagree. In the long term, we believe that the relationship between our two nations is more likely to improve if both nations recognize why they differ than if we pretend the differences are only the product of transient errors or misperceptions.

It might also be worth mentioning what this book is not. It is not a

---

*"American" refers to citizens of the United States. We use the term reluctantly because it really should apply to all the people of North and South America, including Mexicans. However, because no other single word could substitute, "American" will be used in the narrower sense. "Mexican-Americans" will refer to Americans of Mexican origin, and "U.S.-Mexican," to the two countries or governments.

history of U.S.-Mexican relations, or a detailed report or set of position papers on each of the issues that presently concern both nations. Nor is it a book about Mexico. While we have written about each country, we have tried to focus more on the relationship between the two than on the internal problems or policies of each.

In the course of thinking about these issues and writing this book, we have accumulated many debts. Robert Pastor appreciates the efforts of his students at El Colegio de México to teach him how young Mexicans think about themselves, their nation, and especially the United States. To his colleagues there, to the Fulbright program, and to Emory University, Bob gratefully acknowledges advice and support. Jorge G. Castañeda is deeply grateful to the Carnegie Endowment for International Peace for the unique opportunity it offered him. He is also indebted to the National University of Mexico, which allowed him to extend his sabbatical year and prolong his stay in the United States.

The list of those on both sides of the border who have helped us with their advice, comments, and encouragement is a lengthy one. We are both indebted to the following people who read parts or all of the manuscript: Adolfo Aguilar Zinser, Francisco Javier Alejo, Theodore Balberyszski, José Carreño, Jorge Castañeda, Rodolfo de la Garza, Juan del Aguila, K. Mathea Falco, Ira Lieberman, Abraham Lowenthal, Jennifer McCoy, David McCreery, Carlos Monsiváis, Tommie Sue Montgomery, Alan Riding, Linda Robinson, Jeffrey Rosensweig, Andrés Rozenthal, Marlise Simons, Susan Socolow, Gabriel Szekeley, Roger Toll, Viron P. Vaky, and John Womack, Jr. In addition, José Madrazo, Francine Mizell, and B. J. Morris provided much needed research assistance. Diane Diaz offered secretarial support, and Stephen Mann's technical expertise permitted our two computers to speak the same language.

Our thanks also go to Gerry McCauley, our literary agent. Ashbel Green at Knopf deserves a special note of gratitude. He not only endured our endless debates but settled them with an Olympian wisdom that was instantly recognized and accepted by both of us.

Our most unpayable debt, however, must go to our wives and families, whom we dragged to faraway places and who supported us in their way. While the two of us worked hard to learn about each other's country, our families reminded us of the limits of our good intentions, and in doing so, the essence of U.S.-Mexican relations.

May 1988
Atlanta, Georgia
Mexico, D.F.

LIMITS TO FRIENDSHIP

INTRODUCTION

—

Robert A. Pastor

It has almost become a cliché for Americans to stress Mexico's importance and to be self-critical for having ignored that important country for so long. Like most clichés, this one contains some truth, but that is not the reason it is repeated. Americans have learned that to get Mexicans to listen to them, they must first prove they are listening to Mexico. Proof comes in a pledge of respect and a confession of past errors.

U.S. government officials, who have long understood the importance of Mexico, repeat this cliché at regular intervals. Americans who live in the Southwest do not need to be told of Mexico's growing significance; they feel it every day, and the wiser ones convey that feeling to their Mexican neighbors. Aspiring politicians herald Mexico either to win support among Mexican-Americans or to display credentials as modern statesmen.

To comprehend the relationship, however, it would be more accurate to realize that for most Americans outside the government and the Southwest, many things matter more than Mexico. Americans, like most other people, are mainly concerned with their own problems. At times, of course, Americans yield to the demands of a complex world, but no country can claim the undivided attention of the United States except at moments of tragedy or crisis. And when that crisis passes, U.S. attention shifts to the next one. For those nations, like Mexico, that are permanently preoccupied with the United States, the lack of attention is disconcerting at best.

Because Americans receive most of their news from television, their attention span sometimes resembles that of an average four-year-old; often, it is as constructive. This may explain why Mexicans are uncertain whether they would like more attention from the United States or less. Whether the United States should give more, less, sustained, or better attention, however, is not the issue; it is simply a barometer for measuring the difficulty of the relationship. The issue is whether the two governments can devise a more effective way to manage their relationship for the benefit of both peoples.

The problem is that the relationship has not changed as much as the two countries. Three changes in the United States are particularly pertinent to its relationship with Mexico. In the late 1970s, the United States was compelled to acknowledge its dependence on foreign petroleum just as Mexico discovered vast reserves of oil and natural gas. Oil has proven both a blessing and, as its price fell, a curse for Mexico. But it has also given the Mexican nation a certain weight and power that has caused the United States to look at it differently.

The second change is partly the result of the first. By 1980, Mexico had become the third-largest trading partner of the United States, ahead of England, Germany, and France. With Canada as the largest U.S. trading partner, North America emerged as a trading community of great promise. The United States will not abandon its global commitments or withdraw into an illusory "Fortress America," but because of the decline of the U.S. economy in relation to Europe and Japan and the increasing difficulty of negotiating globally, the United States will look more to its two neighbors to experiment with new trading and investment arrangements. For reasons that will be described in this book, a formal North America Free Trade Area is likely to be rejected by Mexico as regularly as it is proposed by the United States, but at the same time, trade and investment will increase, and new attitudes about a broader region will eventually take root.

The third change in the United States is the most profound: the increasing presence and influence of Mexicans—both citizens and migrants. The rate of growth of the U.S. population dropped precipitously since 1960 just as immigration from the Third World rose. The pressure to get into the United States has become so extreme that when Congress opened up special places for 10,000 new immigrants in 1986, over one million people applied. Mexico has been the largest source by far of legal and illegal migration to the United States, and the rate of increase has been stunning. U.S. Census reports show that the Mexican-origin population in the United States increased by nearly three times since 1970, from 4.2 million in 1970 to 11.8 million people in 1987.

A sign of the effect of this new migration is that the Mexican-American "minority" has become the majority in important sections of the Southwest—particularly in the fast-growing mega-states of California and Texas. Mexican-Americans may be the long-missing catalyst in the American melting pot. In many communities in the Southwest, the presence of Mexican-Americans has melted together ethnic groups like Poles, Jews, Irish, and sometimes even blacks into a new undifferentiated mass called "Anglos."

The dependence on foreign oil, the emergence of a North American trading area, and the presence of Mexican-Americans have changed the way the United States looks at itself and at Mexico, but the changes in Mexico have been far more important in altering U.S. perceptions. Since 1950, Mexico's population has more than tripled to about 85 million people. Its gross domestic product expanded more than fivefold to nearly $200 billion in 1986, and its energy reserves and external debt have risen from insignificance to a level that is among the world's highest. As its economic and social weight has increased, Mexico's political foundation has begun to buckle. If Mexico were split by revolution, the United States would not be able to escape the consequences. Today, excepting the Soviet Union for strategic reasons and Japan for financial ones, Mexico probably has a greater capacity to affect the United States than any other country.

The implications of these changes have not yet been fully absorbed by either country, but the repetition of the cliché of Mexico's importance is a sign that the United States has started to pay attention and listen to Mexico. Listening, however, is not communicating. The continued incapacity of both nations to communicate remains the most difficult challenge and the key to more effective management of the relationship.

While serving in the government, I worked on virtually every issue in inter-American relations, but the one set of problems that always left me frustrated were those related to Mexico. I soon learned that my frustration was widely shared in the U.S. government. After returning to academe, I decided to look for an answer to a question that lingered in my thoughts: Why is it more difficult for U.S. officials to deal with their Mexican counterparts, even those with advanced degrees from U.S. universities, than with any other officials in Latin America, even

Cuban intelligence operatives who have had no contact with the United States for more than twenty years?

The question is at the center of this book. It is in the interests of the United States to help Mexico develop. This is a far cry from U.S. interests in Cuba. Why then is it so hard to reach agreement with Mexico? Much of my research has sought to understand the relationship between the United States and smaller, poorer nations on its periphery. These relationships are sometimes described as between the dominant and the dominated, but that simple characterization is misleading. It underestimates the strength of sovereignty, the ability of weaker governments to resist the influence of more powerful ones. The description also overlooks U.S. interests in its neighbors' development. For these reasons, the actual relationship is sometimes the opposite of what it appears, with Washington deferring to the weaker nation even as the weaker one protests U.S. interference. This pattern of interaction confuses not only the observer but both nations. Mexico is the largest and one of the most developed nations in the Caribbean Basin, but it is also the most preoccupied with the United States. Therefore, instead of using its relative strength to escape from this dependent relationship, Mexico is caught. And no relationship is more convoluted and difficult to fathom than that between the United States and Mexico.

One clue to unlocking the riddle of the relationship can be found in the cross-perceptions between strong, successful individuals and those who are weak and poor. The successful tend to attribute success or failure to an individual's traits or behavior and underestimate the effect of luck and external factors. They tend to exaggerate their own generosity and be irritated by the lack of gratitude in the recipient. The weak and poor are more likely to attribute their lack of success to the "system" than to themselves; they see the rich as demanding and selfish. The disadvantaged seek recognition and respect, and the more affluent seldom give it because they rarely see that need. Similarly, in the relationship, few Americans think they dominate Mexico, whereas most Mexicans do. Most Americans think they're helpful; few Mexicans do. Still, although some Americans do not hear the plaints of the disadvantaged or those who feel dominated, others hear the voices of the voiceless, and still others speak for them. Mexico's voice is therefore heard in the United States; whether the United States responds sympathetically is another question—one that I try to address in this book.

I had initially intended to detach myself from the recurring arguments that have ricocheted between Mexico and the United States and to comment as a dispassionate academic. But my co-author's arguments sometimes evoked from me the same kind of response that Mexico's posture has often evoked from the United States. Mexico's proclivity to blame its problems on the United States is frustrating when it is not infuriating. My co-author engages in this exercise less and is one of the leaders of a new generation in being more critical of the Mexican political and economic system than most Mexicans. His analysis and view of the relationship is more subtle and sophisticated than what one generally hears from the political establishment. He is more likely to see "coincidences" in American behavior where most Mexicans see intricate U.S. conspiracies aimed at destabilizing Mexico. Still, there is an unmistakable undercurrent in his argument that U.S. policy is at the base of Mexico's predicament or, at least, chipping at it.

In the pursuit of its interests in Mexico, the United States has sometimes contributed to political divisions, extracted more wealth than it invested, and exerted its disproportionate weight to persuade Mexico to change its policies. At other times, the United States has tried to help Mexico develop, lent support to the government when it was unstable, and been responsive to Mexico's concerns. As the United States has come to recognize its neighbor's importance and vulnerability, it has tried to refrain from being harmful and tried harder to be helpful. In the post–World War II period, the United States still has not been as helpful to Mexico as it should have been, but it is one thing to blame Americans for not helping enough; it is quite another thing to hold past U.S. transgressions responsible for current problems.

Although the purpose of the book is to describe each nation's views of the other, occasionally we leap the boundary separating our two nations—he, to impute the motives of Americans; I, to explain Mexico's problems, which are at the center of the relationship. (America's problems are at the relationship's edge.) To understand whether American perceptions of Mexico's problems are accurate or merely projections of the U.S. national experience, I have sometimes had to analyze those problems. I must also acknowledge that I have consciously tried to reflect the approach of the United States, which is stronger and more assertive of its interests in Mexico than Mexico is in the United States. My trespassing in this book, however, had the same effect on my co-author as U.S. policy generally has on Mexico: it made him suspicious and angry with U.S. arrogance. And the Mexican reaction, in turn, provokes Americans, who take offense when accused of trying to dominate, hurt, or exploit Mexico. We tend to see ourselves as just trying to be helpful, whether or not that is the case. Thus, we have replicated the relationship in this book.

A colleague of mine at El Colegio de México and one of the country's finest scholars on U.S.-Mexican relations once asked me to explain the

Carter administration's human rights policy. After I completed my answer, he had a puzzled look on his face. The reason was that he simply had no frame of reference for understanding that the United States could do anything moral or altruistic in the world. Many of Mexico's elite look at the United States through a lens that filters out positive acts by Americans and magnifies slights or negative acts.

Most Americans accept, although they rarely admit, that their foreign policy has its realpolitik dimension, but they also believe that an idealistic theme runs through the likes of the Marshall Plan, the Alliance for Progress, and the human rights policy. Americans feel that those who ignore that moral dimension are unfair, and those who view it as just a façade covering a dominating or aggressive impulse are unfriendly or hostile. Indeed, part of the problem in the relationship originates in the idealistic self-image of Americans, which is partly accurate, but which few Mexicans believe. Ironically, misunderstandings seem to occur more frequently when the United States defines its principal interests as helping Mexico.

Most Americans believe that the United States serves its interest when it aids Mexico, but many Mexicans are influenced by the view that one nation's development can only be purchased at the expense of another nation. Mexicans are therefore distraught to hear Americans talk of Mexico's interests because they are certain that Americans are only concerned about their own interests and that the two sets of interests are incompatible. Americans are nonplussed to hear Mexicans describe mutual interests as clashing. Both immediately suspect ulterior motives.

The Americans who can deal with Mexicans best are generally those who have either the least or the most contact with Mexico. Those with little knowledge of Mexico travel there with the friendliness of a tourist. Those with the most experience accept and enjoy Mexico for its differences. Those with a moderate amount of contact—the mainstream American—are generally irritated by the barriers to a better relationship erected and maintained by Mexican resentment. Americans cannot understand why a neighbor would want to set limits on friendship. This reaction is as natural to the American as the suspicion of U.S. motives is to the Mexican.

The heart of U.S. concerns in Mexico is its political stability. While I try to avoid this subject in the book, we have agreed to use this introduction to state our differences, and so I will offer a word about this issue. Since World War II, the United States has been relaxed about Mexico largely because of its stability, but the political system there is now being questioned, and this is making Mexico nervous and the United States anxious.

The first question every U.S. reporter asks when he arrives in Mexico is whether a revolution is coming. No one with any knowledge of Mexico feels comfortable with the question, and indeed, many people find themselves answering it differently from week to week. The Mexican political elite have a standard response to the question, which they offer after winking at the reporter's naïveté: "Mexico can't have a revolution because it already had one." The most interesting answer that I heard in Mexico came from a taxicab driver who failed to wink but did complete the establishment's thought: "Mexico can't have a revolution because Mexico already had a revolution, and we know from experience that revolutions do not make things better."

It is easy to predict the emergence of a new political system, but hard to know when that will occur, what it will look like, and whether it can be born without violence. During this period of political transition in Mexico, Washington is torn as to how to respond, partly because it suspects it has little influence and partly because it is uncertain which path is more likely to permit peaceful change. Violence might occur if the governing Institutional Revolutionary Party (PRI) continues to maintain its political hegemony, or it might result if the PRI relaxes its control and permits other parties to take power. Sometimes, riots come from hopelessness, the belief that access to power is blocked and the system won't change; and sometimes, instability comes from the first glimmer that change is possible. This uncertainty together with the Mexican political system's complexity ought to serve as a stop sign for Americans who think about prescribing political solutions.

Manuel Talamás Comandari has the passion of a revolutionary and a cause—genuinely free elections. He is also the Bishop of Chihuahua. In a meeting with me and a PRI friend of mine, on the eve of the elections in Chihuahua in July 1986, the bishop turned his wrath on his countrymen: "Governments change power in every country but Mexico. How can you explain that? The problem in our country is that one party has been in power for fifty-seven years, and it won't listen to the people or give them or other parties a chance to be elected. This is the moment for democracy." The bishop did not let up for nearly two hours. During that time, he returned time and again to the importance of free elections, but he also talked about the need for free education ("the government imposes its own vision of history, which excludes the Church") and freedom of the press (he would like a radio station). In answer to a question from my friend, the bishop accepted the need for a new "national program" that would respond to the concerns of alienated groups.

When we left the meeting, I felt that the bishop and the people he represented would never relent until the government respected the vote, but my friend from the PRI had heard an entirely different message. He said that the bishop's acceptance of the idea of a "national program" meant that all he really wanted was for the PRI to respond to the Church's concerns. The problem in his mind was that the PRI had done a poor job negotiating with the bishop, but the churchman's concerns could be satisfied within the existing system. "That is our political culture," he said. It occurred to me that our sharply divergent interpretations of the same meeting was a metaphor for the frequent misunderstandings between our two nations. I was projecting my nation's heritage of political competition onto an alien Mexican landscape that had a different heritage based, in the period since their revolution, on the politics of unity.

And yet, after a year in Mexico, I was less certain about the depth of the roots of the differences between the two national experiences. My original view of Mexico's politics had been deeply influenced by Octavio Paz's writings about his country's political culture and by Alan Riding's refinement of the same idea. But during the year spent in Mexico, I was struck by the widespread disillusionment with the same political culture. References to "political culture" seemed to have become the property of the PRI, a justification for maintaining a system that the nation had outgrown. Most of my students and many intellectuals and leaders began to question PRI's monopoly on power, and looked to refashion the political system to permit real choice.

"Choice" was the issue of the 1986 election in Chihuahua, and it foreshadowed the 1988 presidential election, which showed the growing power of the opposition. Mexico now sits at a crossroads. If it follows the traditional path, the PRI would negotiate a new "national program" and widen its umbrella to cover Cuauhtemoc Cárdenas's followers. A second path would mean respect for the vote and the emergence of multiparty democracy. If Mexico took this path, the PRI would accept the loss of governorships and eventually even the federal government. The PRI prefers the first path; the question is whether the rest of Mexico will follow.

What is to be done? The U.S. dilemma in Mexico follows from three simple propositions. First, instability in Mexico would probably have more serious consequences for the United States than instability in any other country. This is another, more precise way of saying Mexico is important to the United States.

Second, there is no country in the world which is more sensitive to U.S. efforts to influence it than Mexico, and no country as successful in resisting American influence. If the United States is too direct or heavy-handed, it is likely to evoke the opposite of what it wants. If the United States is subtle and indirect, Mexico is likely nonetheless to misinterpret U.S. motives and erect a wall around a decision to keep out U.S. influence.

Third, the United States is a congenital problem solver. Americans believe that every problem has a solution, and if it's a serious problem, Americans will not quit until they have found one. As Mexico's problems expand in number and severity, American politicians will rediscover Mexico and "solve" its problems. Throughout the history of U.S.-Mexican relations, Americans repeatedly proposed solutions; few stopped to ask why Mexico had not yet responded to the previous ones.

Together, the three propositions mix to become an explosive compound. If riots occur in Mexico, causing migration, capital flight, radicalism, and chronic violence and instability, U.S. citizens will undoubtedly be harmed and border states will be adversely affected. The pressures in the United States to solve Mexico's problem will build—as they did during the Revolution and the administration of William Howard Taft. Sensible Americans will understand that U.S. involvement can only worsen the situation, but the chances are that those calling for the President to do something will greatly outnumber those proposing patience.

Projecting their national experience, Americans are likely to believe that the twin sources of Mexico's problem are state control of the economy and the lack of democracy. The state's heavy involvement in the economy is inefficient and inhibits private initiative; the lack of democracy precludes accountability. Americans assume that the only way to minimize corruption and abuse of power is to vote politicians out of office at regular intervals. To Americans, the solution, therefore, will seem as simple as the problem: Open the economy and respect the vote. Genuine democracy would have the added benefit of giving Mexicans a sense of self-esteem, thus making possible a more mature relationship with the United States.

Nonetheless, the United States should not get involved in Mexico's political debate; indeed, it should stay as far from it as it can. This is the dilemma: Democracy is central to Mexico's ability to change peacefully. While many in Mexico know that Washington supports democracy, no Mexican wants to be told that by the United States. The American system is pragmatic and assertive; it is seldom patient, and yet that is what is needed in the future.

Americans can be helpful in this difficult transition toward a more open economic and political system, but only indirectly. The United States can assist Mexico on debt, market access, and other economic issues. But in political matters, Washington should cross its fingers and respect Mexico's ability to decide for itself.

In this book, I have tried to reflect the exuberance and expansiveness of Americans and the impatience and frustration they often feel in dealing with Mexico. It is not difficult to articulate these traits, as they are natural to me. But my own views of the best way to approach Mexico are different. I believe the United States needs to temper these traits because they reinforce Mexico's defensiveness and make the relationship more difficult. Instead, the United States should stress patience, tolerance, and respect. In the long run, they will yield more rewards than more traditional behavior.

INTRODUCTION

Jorge G. Castañeda

It is often said that the United States should pay more attention to Mexico. Perhaps—but maybe Mexico should pay less attention to the United States. The United States plays too large a role in my country's life, domestic and international. In economic matters, in cultural and psychological terms, and even in the field of foreign policy, the American presence is overwhelming. It obsesses Mexico, drives us to distraction, and despite the evident advantages of contiguity, makes everything more difficult.

The only way for Mexico to improve its relations with the United States is to make them less important. In marked contrast to the situation in the United States—the only way to better American ties with Mexico is to give them the importance they deserve—we are increasingly acknowledging in Mexico that the shortest distance between two points is not a straight line. The road to better links with the United States leads south, not north. Only by firmly anchoring our ties to Latin America will we ever achieve the balance so necessary to stable relations with our northern neighbor.

If the administration of President Miguel de la Madrid can claim any foreign policy successes, it is to have begun to redirect Mexico's attention

toward South America. Thanks to the convergence of several factors—
the debt crisis, which hit every country simultaneously, the emergence
of democratic governments in most of South America, the negative
reaction provoked throughout the continent by Ronald Reagan's policy
in Central America—Mexico has more in common with the hemisphere
than before.

For now, Mexico's refocusing to the south has scarcely gone beyond
rhetoric. Economic complementarities exist, but they are difficult to
identify or encourage. Years of neglect, suspicion, and mistrust on all
sides create obstacles which may in turn take years to overcome. But the
first steps have been taken; a new course has been set, and Mexico has
finally begun to realize that there is life south of the Panama Canal.

Until these promising transformations materialize, though, the United
States will continue to play the dominant role in Mexico's outlook and
relations with the rest of the world. The only way for my country ever
to reduce the American factor's weight is to understand it and persuade
the United States that better ties mean lesser ties. However, this book is
mostly about relations between Mexico and the United States as they are,
rather than as they should be. Its purpose is to analyze the conflictive
coexistence of two neighbors at the close of the twentieth century.

Our perspective is still molded by the clashing forces of economic
integration and nationalism, contiguity and asymmetry. Since Mexico
came forth as a nation in the nineteenth century, we have been buffeted
by the pull of economic integration with the United States and the
opposing push of the nation's emerging, defensive nationalism, as strong
as ever, of the 1988 election. It has been torn between the obvious attraction of contiguity with the world's wealthiest and most powerful nation
and the ensuing resistance provoked by the prevailing asymmetry between a rich country and its neighbor, still desperately poor.

Today both trends have reached a watershed. Integration and the tug
of proximity have in fact already entered a new phase, as Mexico proceeds with the changes in its economy currently underway. It looks as
if the present direction of the nation's economic course in the coming
years will continue: a greater opening to the rest of the world, and
especially the United States, in trade, investment, and technology.

Mexican nationalism is also at a crossroads. During the last century,
it helped forge a nation which had little to hold it together. Our oft
misunderstood and always perplexing nationalism has been crucial in the
country's history. It contributed to create the political and ideological
climate in which an industrial base and modern infrastructure could be
built rapidly. Behind the walls—never impenetrable—erected against
foreign influence and presence, the country was transformed at dizzying

speed from a rural, illiterate, backward, and largely peasant nation to the predominantly urban, literate, middle- and working-class society it is today.

Until the late 1960s the immense majority of the country's population shared both the nationalism and the cause it symbolized—Mexico's development. Though this ideal implied sacrifices and development had its limitations, nationalism was the object of a national consensus. It was perceived, at least tacitly, as a modernizing force by most of our people.

The 1968 student movement, which left hundreds dead but brought tens of thousands into the street in protest against the undemocratic nature of the political system, marked the end of that consensus. The previous agreement within Mexican society concerning the purpose of the country's nationalism began to crumble. The end of Mexico's forty-year-old economic miracle in 1982 brought the preceding era of nationalist consensus to a close. But the nationalism itself did not subside.

What many observers have hailed or lamented as the decline of the country's acute sense of national identity—expressed through the "Americanization" of Mexican culture and urban society, capital flight, indifference or opposition to the political system, support for a greater opening to the world—is a loss of direction, not the end of the road. We are no less nationalistic, our people no more pro-American than before. But our nationalism is presently seeking new goals and new causes to espouse.

The old causes are losing their currency. The majority of Mexico's urban, literate population, while far from affluent, has benefited from the nation's economic boom. It is no longer willing to accept the arguments that were once implicitly acknowledged, and rejects the notion, held both by Mexican defenders of the status quo and by its American detractors, that consumption patterns and tastes imply a political and national choice. These Mexicans do not see their nationalism endangered by the food they eat, the clothes they wear, or where they keep their money. They may not be entirely right in their assessment, yet it seems evident that this is where they stand.

The alternatives to the past which have appeared thus far—defending the national currency, the political system, or the abstract principles theoretically embodied in the Central American conflict—ring hollow to many Mexicans. Either they sound demagogic and hypocritical or they lean too far to the left for a population which considers itself middle of the road or left of center. These formal expressions of Mexican nationalism do not seem to be perceived by a majority of Mexico's urban, emerging middle classes as a modernizing factor in national life.

If most Mexicans embraced that nationalism in the recent past and made it part of the national psyche, this was because we saw it as *the* modernizing force of Mexico. The solution to the current disenchantment must then be sought in the same domain. The enduring nationalism of the Mexican people, which has inevitably been directed at the United States, will only translate anew into policies and political convictions—as it did from 1917 to the mid-1970s—if it again becomes, and is perceived as, a fundamentally modernizing factor of Mexican history. For now, the nation's intellectuals and politicians have not discovered a way to bring about the necessary *aggiornamento* of Mexican nationalism. But this incapacity should not be construed as a sign of extinction of the ideological themes which have sustained us as a nation for over a century.

If there is one lesson to be drawn from the stunning strength shown by the nationalist left in the 1988 elections for the presidency, it lies precisely in the currency and vigor of these ideological friends. But the Cárdenas effect was also a symptom of a possible solution to the nationalism-modernization enigma: perhaps the country chose to transform an old-school, nationalist personal icon into the standard bearer of its clamor for democratization, equating nationalism, democracy and modernity in a totally unexpected fashion.

Economic modernization and efficiency cannot move mountains, much less masses. From a strictly economic point of view it may seem encouraging—possibly even praiseworthy—that wages in the *maquiladora* or in-bond industry along the U.S.-Mexican border are virtually the lowest of their kind in the world. It is hardly possible, however, to proclaim with pride that Mexico is moving forward, now that salaries have fallen to less than a quarter of what they are in South Korea, below half what they are in sweatshops of Hong Kong, and less than 50 percent what they are in the Jamaican tropics. Mexico faces an undeniable problem in this regard. We are still in search of the right combination of nationalism and economic development, economic reality and the mobilizing myths that inspire an entire people.

Double but separate authorship evidently implies individual responsibility and frequent discord on many issues. These will be apparent in the text itself and need no underlining or explanation. But some disagreements are more important and conceptual than others.

In my opinion, Robert Pastor's chapters underestimate the strength and currency of Mexican nationalism, particularly in its anti-American bent. Even the modern Mexican middle classes continue to harbor deep feelings of resentment and even anger at the United States. Their penchant for American lifestyles and products should not be mistaken for an ebbing of traditional suspicion and hostility toward the United States.

Similarly, the fact that, until the 1988 presidential elections, this sentiment was not translated into a clear-cut political inclination—on the left of the political spectrum—in no way diminishes its topicality.

Too many motives for this negative feeling remain in modern Mexico, and in contemporary American attitudes toward Mexico and its people. Less racism and discrimination against Mexicans of all ages, classes, and origins in the United States, and more respect for Mexico as a nation, have still not erased the reasons for holding a grudge against the United States. I think my co-author underrates the strength of this sentiment.

I also believe that Pastor's chapters give insufficient credence to the continued resiliency and persisting, though unquestionably weakened, legitimacy of the Mexican political system. It is far from being above suspicion or beyond criticism with regard to to its anti-democratic nature and practices, or in relation to the waning support it enjoys among the nation's inhabitants. But too many Mexican and American critics have mistakenly confused their own desires for its transformation with the real possibilities of change. The system no longer delivers the goods it once did: economic growth has vanished since 1981. And the country has changed: mechanisms which functioned adequately with widespread acceptance among the population are clearly obsolete—and in dire need of modification.

Yet nothing guarantees—and actually there are many signs to the contrary—that a more democratic Mexico would be less progressive, nationalistic, or anti-American. There is a tendency to identify Mexican nationalism with a discredited and unrepresentative elite, and moderate, mature, and responsible views and policies—in particular toward the United States—with a repressed and silent civil society thirsting for closer ties with the United States. There is a grain of truth in this, but not much more. The overwhelming success encountered by the left-of-center nationalistic candidacy of Cuauhtémoc Cárdenas in the 1988 presidential election—roughly 30 percent of the national vote, first place in Mexico City, second place nationwide—was a striking confirmation of this fact.

Finally, I have a methodological disagreement with my colleague. He has chosen to express openly and frequently his opinions about my country; I have chosen to do so rarely about his. Now and then, I will venture a point of view as to why the United States acts the way it does in relation to Mexico, but the instances are few and far between. In contrast to my co-author, who has strayed over the border, I have limited the scope of my analysis to the Mexican side of the bilateral relationship.

My reasons for proceeding in this fashion do not involve high principles or nationalistic self-righteousness. Many Americans (and other foreigners) have written penetrating studies, essays, histories, and novels about Mexico. It is my belief, though, that the American reader wants to hear about the Mexican perspective from a Mexican author. My contribution to this book lies in my knowledge of my own country, and only marginally in my knowledge of the United States; I believe Robert Pastor's contribution lies in his knowledge of his country, not of mine.

Had I thought differently, I would have developed throughout my chapters a number of reflections about the traits of the American national character which have often made relations with the United States a trying experience for my country and many others. I had the good fortune of observing the Reagan era in U.S. foreign policy from the ideal vantage point, at an ideal time: Washington, D.C., from 1985 to 1987. Like many of my countrymen and fellow Latin Americans, I arrived in the United States, despite my previous periods spent living there, with a number of ideas regarding the coherence and purpose of American policy toward Mexico and Latin America in general. I frequently disagreed with the procedures and goals of that policy, but thought it possessed a certain underlying logic.

My residence in Washington convinced me that while there was nearly always more coherence and logic to American policy toward Mexico and Latin America than most U.S. analysts claim, there is generally far less method than we tend to believe south of the Rio Grande. The reasons for this are precisely those American traits which make dealing with the United States in the international area as frustrating as it is.

If I had chosen to venture north of the border in my chapters, I would have dwelt on the difficulties that the United States' lack of a sense of history, due to the virtual absence of any common national history, creates for nearly every nation in its relations with the United States. A slender history makes for a short memory, which in turn implies that every negotiation, conflict, tension, or disagreement takes place in a vacuum: the United States' interlocutors must start over every time. There are no historical precedents, and the experience of the past is not a relevant consideration or, less still, a valid argument.

I would have stressed the problem which numerous foreign diplomats, statesmen, and observers have always encountered when dealing with the United States: the extent to which the unaccountability of the American political system in the field of foreign affairs makes life with the United States frequently intractable. The fact that in the design and implementation of foreign policy the President can escape responsibility for the actions of the federal bureaucracy, the Congress, or the courts is nerve-racking at best, and more often conducive to tensions in international relations.

Whether the rest of the world sides with the Congress and sees in it a reassuring, moderating counterweight to the folly of an extremist administration, as was the case during the Vietnam War and the Reagan years, or whether the Congress becomes a powerful or insurmountable obstacle to an administration's sound intentions (the Panama Canal Treaties or the Salt II Agreement), the issue is always the same. Each entity ducks behind the other, and the buck rarely stops anywhere, but rather keeps shifting in an institutional shell game. The traditional American responses—this is how democratic systems operate; this is how the U.S. political system functions—are either false or beg the question: if that is the way the system works, perhaps it is time to change it.

Finally, I would have emphasized the difficulties that emanate directly from the contradiction that exists between the United States' overwhelming wealth, power, and influence in the modern world and its provincialism and incapacity to see itself for what it is: a world power, with interests and responsibilities throughout the globe, which cannot be subjected to the provincial, idealistic, and often naïve considerations which determine American foreign policy. Realism and an accurate assessment of the balance of forces in any one area at any one time, together with drawing the appropriate conclusions from that assessment, are the way traditional superpowers, previously known as empires, manage their foreign affairs. Despite recurrent exceptions, the United States has yet to come to terms with its status in the world; by the time it does, it may no longer have the status it has held since 1945.

No book on such a complex subject can aspire to be all-encompassing. From the Mexican perspective, I have tried to cover the main areas, to update traditional fields of research and knowledge, and perhaps explore new or emerging regions of the bilateral relationship. But many zones remain *terra incognita.* The networks which professionals—doctors, engineers, dentists, accountants, scientists, and businessmen—from both nations are developing represent the most important missing link. A lot is happening which we know little about, beyond official ties and previous well-known "people to people" bonds. If there are fertile fields of research in U.S.-Mexican relations, these new networks should certainly be at the top of the list.

Likewise, a number of policy conclusions could be drawn from the main thrust of many arguments. If my principal line of reasoning implies that Mexico today is caught in a cross fire between its history and traditional nationalism and the powerful forces of economic integration pulling it toward the United States, the questions are obvious.

What does economic integration—formal and informal—mean? Throughout the sections on the Mexican perspective it should be taken to mean, first, the high and growing concentration of Mexico's trade, financial flows (debt and foreign investment), transfers of technology, tourism, and international economic relations in general with the United States. Second, it signifies the increasingly unimpeded, unfettered, though perhaps not free, legal and illicit flows of goods and services, capital and people, ideas and information, between the two nations.

Should Mexico resist integration? Or should it manage, govern, and administer that integration, with full awareness of its inevitability? Should Mexico negotiate that integration—that is, attempt to squeeze every last concession from the United States in exchange for steps which are unavoidable but which it could delay, complicate, or combat at every stage? Should Mexico try to get more from the process of integration and put less into it?

There are no clear-cut answers to these questions. Nonetheless, this book hopes to frame them in the proper context, enabling others to give their responses and, of course, giving each author's replies, either directly or obliquely. If it fulfills any of these challenges, if it serves any of these purposes, it will have contributed to a better understanding of Mexico's future and the United States' role in it. A role which will be important but not decisive: the United States cannot solve Mexico's problems; only time and the Mexican people can.

PART I

—

BARRIERS

1

SHAPING MINDS AND ATTITUDES

The Mexican Mind

—

Jorge G. Castañeda

On March 3, 1947, one hundred years after the fall of Chapultepec Castle to American troops, Harry S Truman became the first President of the United States to visit Mexico City. During his stay, steeped in the symbolism of reconciliation, Truman stood guard at the old monument—just beneath the castle—to Mexico's "Child Heroes," a group of cadets who, a century before, leaped to their deaths from the overlooking parapets wrapped in Mexican flags. As General Winfield Scott's invading army approached Chapultepec in September 1847, the cadets preferred to die rather than surrender their national banner to the American invader.

Truman brought with him some battalion flags captured by Scott's soldiers and returned them to Mexican President Miguel Alemán, hoping to turn a new leaf in the two nations' relationship. In his welcoming remarks Alemán also spoke of the War of 1847. In line with Truman's gestures, and the presumed new era of cooperation in Mexican-American relations ushered in by World War II, Mexico's first civilian President since the Revolution of 1910 made a statesmanlike reference to the events of 1847: "The greatness of history never lies in eternalizing the past."[1] Observers on both sides of the border viewed the presidential encounter as a milestone on the road to a new, "more mature" Mexican interpretation of the two nations' common history. Mexico, it seemed, was finally letting the dead bury their dead and putting the tragic and painful history of its relations with the United States behind it.

In fact, this was anything but a transformation and really nothing more than a fleeting episode in Mexico's long struggle to achieve a perception of its past truly shared by all its people. In 1986, nearly forty years later, as Texas commemorated the one hundred and fiftieth anniversary of its secession from Mexico, a Texan congressional delegation— as well as Ambassador John Gavin and House of Representatives Majority Leader Jim Wright—appealed to the President of Mexico to allow the insignia flown by the New Orleans Grays at the Alamo to leave Mexico on loan. For over a century the flag had lain in the vaults of the same castle beneath whose shadows Truman and Alemán vowed to let bygones be bygones. Following the traditional Mexican aphorism—attributed to Benito Juárez—for dealing with the United States: "Say yes, but never say when," Mexican authorities responded: "The flag cannot be loaned now because of restoration. Neither can a photo be taken. They are restoring it and it is going to take a considerable length of time."[2]

Nations can be judged by the way they mourn their dead and read and write their history. Mexico's history is a subject of disagreement among our own people, not to mention historians, writers, and intellectuals of different political persuasions. But there is far more convergence on some aspects than others. Over the last several decades, a consensus has begun to emerge in Mexico concerning its relations with the United States, a tremendously important chapter of the nation's past. But that consensus is in many ways only skin deep, not extending to every corner of Mexican society.

Because of the traumatic nature of the events of that past, only slowly has Mexico—a divided country in many respects—been able to forge a unified vision of the turbulent and tragic history which we share with the United States. With time, events perceived so differently when viewed from opposite sides of the border have come to be seen on the Mexican side with growing, though not unanimous, accord. True, the vision clouds up if more recent events are considered. But the desire to build and conserve a Mexican consensus is present even in that more disputed focus, shaping the way millions of Mexican children today learn our nation's history.

The unified idea of the past has not arisen alone and spontaneously from the ashes of defeat and invasion, territorial losses and perceived humiliation. As in most countries, oral traditions passed on from parent to child are of great importance. In Mexico, however, massive public elementary education, based since 1960 on free and compulsory text-books, has played a key role in achieving an increasingly homogeneous vision of the nation's origins and evolution. As Mexico's most respected social critic, Carlos Monsiváis, has phrased it: "Elementary education has been the basis for the country's unification and the main vehicle for its nationalist impulse."[3]

Today there are fifteen million Mexican children under the age of twelve in school. They all learn about their country's geography, history, and culture from the same social science textbook. Theirs is the first generation whose parents are also largely literate, having attended the same public school system and studied similar textbooks. Although there has never been unanimous support in Mexico for the standard textbook, it has gradually become a fixture of Mexican life precisely for the reasons which have made it anathema to its enemies and critics: it propagates a common, government-determined vision of the nation's past and present, its cultural and sexual mores, its system of values, and its place in the world.

In 1960, when the standard textbook's first edition was drafted, the effort was met with stiff opposition from the right wing, the Church, and the business community, particularly from the north. And when a sec-ond, revised edition was drawn up in 1972–73 under the outspokenly nationalistic and culturally broad-minded administration of Luis Echeverría, the debate over the book's ideological, cultural, and even sexual content, as well as its very existence, turned into a pitched battle between the country's political factions. Opponents of the new edition were attacked as "traitors to the fatherland," and its advocates were accused of wanting to annex Mexico to the Soviet Union, or at the very least to Cuba.

The heightened passions were understandable. In a country where almost half the population is under fifteen, the stakes are high in the struggle for school-age children's hearts and minds. Historical references are remarkably recurrent and significant in contemporary Mexico. The version of the country's past handed down to its children is of great political import. If the United States is a country of lawyers and respect for legal scripture, because as Arthur M. Schlesinger, Jr., has written, Americans are "an essentially historyless people,"[4] then Mexico might well be the mirror opposite. Laws have been rhetorically worshipped, "obeyed but not complied with," yet history and its lessons have tradi-tionally been revered. Similarly, and this is clearly reflected in the differ-ences between Mexico's schoolbooks and their U.S. equivalents, the Mexican outlook is more universal, less ethnocentric. In history, geography, and other fields, Mexican textbooks devote more space and attention to events and trends abroad, and far less to purely domestic matters, than U.S. textbooks do.

The content of the 1972–73 edition of the textbook, still in circulation today, is a far cry from the Alemán-Truman honeymoon of more than forty years ago. The description it gives of Mexico's trials in its not so peaceful coexistence with our northern neighbor fulfills a decisive function in forming the vision of history which an immense majority of Mexico's schoolchildren will grow up with and remember. This role is not exclusive, or the same for all sectors of society; other factors also count, and children in private elementary schools are less influenced by it. Children's worldviews are not identical to what they are taught in the classroom. Adults' conceptions of the world, their country and its history, are not shaped only by what they learned at the youngest of ages.

This perhaps is more true in Mexico than elsewhere. Mexican children are extraordinarily sensitive to family influence, because of the strength and role of the family in Mexican society, as in most of Latin America. But like their U.S. counterparts, our children are also subjected to massive doses of television and comics, mostly of American origin or inspiration. When foreign observers of Mexico are struck by the contrast between most Mexicans' generally not hostile individual attitudes toward Americans and the strong nationalism present in textbooks, historical lore, and contemporary ideology, they are simply perceiving this split influence. School and the traditional family pull in one direction, modern-day television and "culture" in another, sometimes opposite, sometimes parallel direction.

The first mention of Mexican-American relations in the standard textbook appears in the fourth-grade social science manual. The initial reference is to the Texan secession of 1836.

> Some North Americans had obtained permission to settle in Texas, which then belonged to Mexico. Afterward they became dissatisfied with the Mexican government and became independent. . . . In order to subdue them, Santa Anna ventured forth with an army which arrived in desperate shape. . . . He emerged victorious in the first battles against the Texans, but was taken prisoner at San Jacinto. The lack of arms and money made it impossible to reconquer Texas. Since most of the population was of North American origin, in 1845 Texas became part of the United States.[5]

The account of this initial U.S.-Mexican encounter is even-handed. Although some secondary-school history books narrate differently the episode of the Alamo, for example, referring to "Mexican soldiers' heroism" and "Texans' greater resources and better arms," there is barely a chauvinistic flavor to it.

The standard textbook description of the Texan secession keeps its distance from many Mexican historians who stress American President Andrew Jackson's backing for the Texan cause. Nor does the textbook version dwell on the expansionist sentiment present at the time in the United States or on the links between the Texan secession and the upcoming American invasion of Mexico, which would lead to the loss of more than half the country's territory. The next mention of U.S.-Mexican relations in the fourth-grade schoolbook comes precisely in reference to that invasion.

According to Mexican children's history books, the nation was in poor shape on the eve of the war.

> The country was functioning poorly. Almost no one paid taxes, and the national government was unable to pay its employees or its army. Debts, conflicts, and insecurity were on the rise. . . . There were not enough doctors and health problems were increasing dramatically.[6]

Once again, the historians charged with educating Mexico's future generations provide an accurate description, painfully honest in acknowledging that the Mexican nation-state did not yet truly exist as a working entity. This view becomes explicit as the account of the war gets underway.

> Since many Mexicans blamed the country's ills on the central government, in 1847 a Federalist Constitution was once again put into force. The union of Texas with the United States and the North Americans' desire to take over New Mexico and California, which belonged to Mexico, led to their invasion of our country.[7]

Having established the historical record, the standard textbook makes an intellectually straightforward attempt to place the facts in a broader context. An effort is made to have Mexico's fourth-graders understand the reasons for the debacle by emphasizing the domestic aspects of Mexico's travail: "Mexicans were divided. Some thought that in order to raise money to defend the country, the Church's properties . . . should be sold off; others did not agree."[8] There are no instances of "gringo-bashing," and the sparse references to North American ambition and expansionism are sober, even understated.

The school manual stresses that the real roots of the nation's defeat lay in the still embryonic nature of its existence. The "moral" of the story is all the more effective, and the subdued description bears witness to one of the reasons why Mexican nationalism endures: the facts speak for themselves. Consequently, the schoolbook concludes its tale of those troubled times with a brief explanation and a simple warning:

> Many Mexicans had not realized what they were, but for the first time they felt Mexican in the face of the enemy, and they understood the importance of national unity. The country's situation was heartrending. . . . This entire period was confused and sad, but the Mexican nation was being formed and the road was a hard one.[9]

The true message the textbook's authors wished to convey with regard to the last century's defeat lies in these sentences. The message is simply that Mexico is lost, easily falling prey to American domination, when it is divided. When we forget our nationalism, the nation's very existence is in danger. This precept has been toned down over the years, but remains ever-present. The first edition of the standard textbook, published in 1960, was much more explicit than the more recent version in this regard. It quite openly—and rather demagogically and moralistically—preached: "The invasion of Mexico is an experience which we should never forget: the unity of all Mexicans is indispensable, for through domestic peace comes progress, and through progress, the strength needed to protect ourselves from ambition and injustice."[10]

For a country with extraordinarily strong regional, ethnic, and social divisions, whose origin lies in the eventually successful but extremely painful absorption of the conquerors by the conquered, this is a powerful message. Transmitted from generation to generation, through education and tradition, its updating, or modernization, has proved exceedingly difficult; many in Mexico today consider so-called more mature interpretations of the nation's history a thinly disguised form of national treason. They argue that there is literally no foolproof way of knowing when the process of nation-forming has come to term and when these more mature views will no longer jeopardize a still unfinished gestation. In the last analysis, if one takes the view of Mexican nationalism which millions of Mexican children are exposed to, and which many Mexican adults end up adopting, there are indeed no guarantees that the same cause—lack of a national identity—will not produce the same effect—national disintegration.

. . .

Needless to say, the dramatic events of the last century do not constitute the only chapter of conflict with the United States in Mexico's schoolbooks. The next significant example comes in the context of the Revolution of 1910. This is still a fundamental reference point for contemporary political debates and issues, and though it may be ever less relevant to modern Mexico, the nation's foremost institutions all date from the Revolution and its aftermath.

As every Mexican schoolchild knows, the Revolution began when a northern landowner, Francisco I. Madero, decided to challenge Porfirio Díaz in the 1910 presidential elections. Díaz had been in power for over thirty years, and was not quite convinced he should leave office. Electoral fraud, a call to arms, and massive social discontent arising from the dictator's economic policies finally drove him from power and catapulted Madero to the presidency. The growing reluctance of broad sectors of Mexican society to accept the massive presence of foreign—and particularly American—holdings in Mexico was an important factor in the *ancien régime*'s downfall. Millions of acres of land, railroads, banks, utilities, and oil and mineral resources were all in foreign hands.

Immediately after Díaz's departure, though, problems emerged, and by early 1913 the old dictator's allies, as well as many sectors of the army, were plotting against Madero. In this context, the standard textbook describes the next major episode of overt American involvement in Mexican affairs. As history comes closer, Mexico's focus becomes sharper:

> General Victoriano Huerta was among those [who refused to give up the privileges they held before the Revolution]. With the complicity of the United States' ambassador in Mexico, he betrayed Madero's trust and had him murdered in February 1913. Madero's assassination produced indignation throughout the country and soon a popular movement against Huerta developed. . . . The United States took advantage of these circumstances to directly intervene in Mexico to protect its economic interests; with that purpose, in 1914 United States' troops occupied the port city of Veracruz.[11]

Mexico's younger generations thus learn almost as soon as they can read that the United States has actively interfered in Mexican affairs, not only in the nineteenth century but also as recently as the Revolution. It has done so, according to compulsory textbooks used in most Mexican classrooms today, among other things by having one of its envoys in Mexico conspire to assassinate our national heroes. Hence it should come as no surprise that the activities of contemporary American ambassadors arouse the suspicion and fears that they do. When a classically arrogant American envoy like John Gavin, who represented the Reagan administration in Mexico from 1981 to 1986, adopts a high-profiled and outspoken stance, he inevitably provokes negative reactions in many sectors of Mexican society. Every Mexican under forty has learned from the standard textbook that Henry Lane Wilson, Gavin's predecessor in 1913, actually did what Gavin was only accused or suspected of doing years later.

But according to the standard textbook, the United States not only conspired in Mexico through its envoys. It also meddled in Mexican affairs by sending troops and occupying parts of the nation far removed from the border, in its heartland. It did so for less than honorable, in fact illegitimate motives, acting in defense of what were base economic interests from the Mexican perspective as well as long-standing privileges and inequalities against which the Revolution was fought. The picture Mexican schoolchildren perceive is that the United States intrudes in matters which are none of its business, and does so on the wrong side.

The standard textbook has an ambiguous status in Mexico today. It continues to be a source of debate between the Church, the private sector, and the conservative political parties on the one hand, and the state and its secular and progressive defenders on the other. In many parochial and private schools, the standard textbook is set aside and other manuals are used. This is accepted practice: it is sufficient for the Ministry of Education books to be formally in the curriculum for these schools to remain on the right side of the law.

Disagreements over the textbooks' content and very existence will probably endure as long as they are used. And they undoubtedly will continue to be used, since if there is one issue on which the existing Mexican political system will not yield willingly—or at all—it is surely this one. Public education in Mexico carries overwhelming political and ideological clout, from children's perceptions to the strength of the 750,000-member PRI-affiliated teachers' union. So much so that when an optional standard textbook for high schools was drawn up in 1988, it rekindled many of the debates of its elementary school predecessor.

There is no standard compulsory textbook for middle and secondary schools. *Private* junior high schools follow rather conservative texts, whereas the Ministry of Education tends to recommend more progressive books for the *public* schools under its jurisdiction. Yet the private school books are not necessarily less nationalistic in their account of U.S.-Mexican history. Mexican conservatism has always possessed a denominationally sectarian, nationalistic anti-American streak: Americans are not in the main Catholics, and Mexico gets into trouble when non-Catholics are allowed a free rein in the country's affairs.[12] Many nineteenth-century conservatives were convinced that only Catholics are truly Mexican, true Mexicans are all Catholic, and Mexico's only authentic friends are necessarily Catholic. This belief has a dated ring to it today, even for the religious right, but at least through the 1940s it was widely shared.

Ever since the nineteenth century's conflicts over the Church's landholdings, the country's leaders have faced the daunting task of limiting the power of the Church in a massively Catholic nation. From the Cristero War in the 1920s through Pope John Paul's visit to Mexico in 1979, this attempt has given rise to unending tensions. The Reforma period in the 1850s was a watershed: a majority of the nation's population has supported the struggle to curb the Church's influence ever since. But the dissenting minority has always been a large and vocal one.

Education is part of this problem, and by no means a minor part. The country has faced continuing difficulties in coming to terms with the secular nature of the state and state-sponsored, compulsory public education in a highly religious country. Needless to say, the problem is not resolved, nor will it be soon. But as in so many other areas, Mexican society has reached an understanding with itself on this matter over the years.

There are differences between the broad thrust of most secondary school textbooks and the standard elementary school manual.[13] Regarding the War of 1847, for example, some junior high school accounts do not simply explain American behavior; they tend to justify it, or in some extreme cases to apologize for it and discreetly criticize Mexican intransigence. These history books suggest that Mexico should have known that it was going to lose, and might have saved a lot of blood and trouble—as well as possibly obtaining a better deal—if it had sold California and the other real estate in question instead of going to war over it. Mexican adolescents are taught that the authorities of the time turned down—perhaps intransigently—a series of American proposals.

Likewise, several textbooks commonly used in both public and private secondary schools suggest that perhaps U.S. involvement in the Mexican Revolution and particularly Woodrow Wilson's occupation of Veracruz were not entirely selfish. These accounts imply that American intervention on this occasion was essentially altruistic: the United States simply sought democracy in Mexico and an end to the Huerta dictatorship. But even these stress the unacceptable nature of U.S. intervention, both then and now, whatever its motives or purposes. The focus might seem paradoxical, yet it is not untypical of Mexican nationalist sentiments. On the one hand, Wilson is portrayed as being on the right side: against the Victoriano Huerta dictatorship responsible for Madero's death. Yet by taking sides at all, the United States automatically puts those who resist it in a more favorable light. Thus in some accounts, Huerta even emerges as a patriot struggling against American interference.

The historical points made by secondary school textbooks concerning the effects of Woodrow Wilson's policy in Mexico may not be, strictly speaking, false. But their version of events differs dramatically from those in the standard elementary school textbooks, which traced the origins of this particular American intervention in Mexican affairs to the protection of American economic interests. Indeed, few Mexican historians and scholars—and undoubtedly few Mexicans in all walks of life— would accept that American interference in our domestic matters has ever been unselfish or well-intentioned. The nuances separating these viewpoints are all the more significant. Consequently, in order to bridge them, the Mexican political establishment has unanimously concluded that what counts is not the motive or purpose of American interference, but its very fact: no intervention is acceptable. This axiom of Mexican policy toward the United States, however, is not always taken for granted by other sectors of Mexican society.

A recent example illustrates this paradox. In early 1986, on the eve of the World Cup soccer championship in Mexico, the government was confidentially informed by Ambassador John Gavin that U.S. intelligence had uncovered a plot by guerrillas from El Salvador to infiltrate commandos into the country and disrupt the upcoming sports spectacular. The Reagan administration offered to help Mexico deal with the supposed threat. Notwithstanding serious concern in governing circles over the risks of terrorist incidents during the World Cup, and despite the generalized perception of President Miguel de la Madrid's government as the least anti-American administration in the last twenty-five years, the authorities refused to act on or even acknowledge Gavin's warning.

Hidden and ignoble American motives were immediately suspected. The subsequent closing of the U.S. Embassy Visa Section in Mexico City for several months because of "lack of guarantees for the safety of applicants from terrorist attacks" (according to the State Department), as well as Mexico's own investigations, confirmed the initial suspicions. There was no terrorist plot, no infiltration, and no U.S. assistance required. But this only became apparent after the fact and Mexico's first reaction was classically circumspect: if the United States expresses a desire to intervene in Mexican affairs, whatever the ostensible and declared motivation, Mexico should refuse first and ask questions later. Yet if the episode had been made public at the time, significant sectors of Mexican public opinion would have criticized the authorities for not taking American views seriously.

This discord concerning the United States and Mexico's relations with it also affects scholarly works on the history of Mexican-American ties. As a result of its right-of-center leanings, the *General History of Mexico,* coordinated by the late Daniel Cosío Villegas and published originally in four volumes in 1976 by El Colegio de México, is perhaps more in tune with Mexico's present-day ruling elite and accordingly is the best example of a more academic Mexican view of the two nations' common history. It is widely used in Mexican high schools, both public and private, as well as in the first years of college.

Josefina Zoraida Vázquez, the author of the chapter devoted to the Texan secession and the American invasion, and probably Mexico's premier historian of this period—she was also one of the co-authors of the standard elementary textbook—provides a balanced and detailed characterization of the events which made both episodes and their outcome inevitable.[14] Vázquez adopts the consensus view that the overriding cause of Mexico's debacle during the first thirty years of independence was the unfinished nature of our nationhood and institutions.

The noteworthy facets of this well-documented and sophisticated analysis of the U.S.-Mexican conflict lie in the statements it makes about the situation in Texas and the United States. Vázquez underlines the fact that Mexico lost Texas because of the sheer force of settler demographics and that American meddling and ambitions were just catalysts. By pointing out that in 1832 only 3,400 of a total of 24,700 inhabitants of Texas were Mexican, the historian concludes that the facts speak for themselves.

Similarly, she acknowledges that many settlers were initially opposed to annexation, if only because the United States had a less liberal land distribution policy than Mexico's or than an independent Texas would have permitted. Moreover, the author suggests that after the 1836 secession, Mexico might have been better off accepting the advice of Mexican as well as British leaders to recognize Texan independence in exchange for a commitment not to pursue annexation to the United States.[15] The question of whether this would have altered the final outcome is not explored by Vázquez.

The Colegio de México book emphasizes the domestic factors in the United States which led to the American invasion of Mexico in 1846–47. It stresses the importance of the "Calvinist sense of mission and predestination" in American thought, as well as the lasting effects of the "lack of roots characteristic of a society of immigrants." A concluding sentence sheds light on how Mexican historians view the United States' past, and perhaps even the present or future:

> The faith in the American Constitution as a formula for perfect government would provide a justification for expansionism, through the slogan of "extending the area of liberty," that is to say, extending American institutions in order to save those poor forsaken souls who did not know them and were bound by the chains of tyranny. Not all Americans realized the irony involved in the fact that in many cases—such as the case of Texas—the extension of the area of liberty was also an extension of the area of slavery.16

This is possibly a consensual vision of Mexican intellectuals' and politicians' vision of the United States as a somewhat pretentious, probably conceited, and often hypocritical nation that perceives only those aspects of its own actions deemed worthy of its own mythology. Whether on the subject of Texan independence or today's "war on drugs," many Mexicans tend to accentuate the darker aspects of American life, those which the United States itself often refuses to acknowledge in its dealings with its southern neighbor.

As in the case of Texas's separation from Mexico, Josefina Zoraida Vázquez hints that in the negotiations over California and New Mexico preceding the 1847 invasion, the Mexican position was not entirely sound. In any case, it was incomprehensible to Americans, who

> did not understand Mexican stubbornness, whereby in spite of their need for money, [the Mexicans] refused to sell uninhabited land, which they would lose anyway. But in addition to the conviction on the part of [Mexico's] Presidents concerning the impossibility of selling "national patrimony," there existed a strong feeling of national pride which felt a near obligation to respond with arms to multiple American insults.17

A similar lack of understanding is widespread among bankers and investors today who do not understand how Mexico, strapped for capital and technology, refuses to modify its legislation on foreign investment. Now as in the nineteenth century, the answer lies not in economic irrationality or ignorance, but in the fact that such choices are always made and placed in a wider context. Wisely or not, the question in 1846 was not a dollars-and-cents, cash-flow issue; nor is the present problem one of setting the most advisable *economic* limits to foreign investment and foreign trade in Mexico. What is at stake is the perception by Mexican leaders and significant sectors of Mexican public opinion of the effects of certain decisions on our *viability* as a *nation:* selling California and New Mexico a century and a half ago, or permitting foreign investment in the Mexican oil and petrochemical industry today, for example.

Mexico cannot boast that it has always made the right decision, and sometimes, as events of the last century show, appearances may indicate that it made the wrong one. But the same modern and mature viewpoint expressed in the *General History* nevertheless concludes that "in spite of the costly losses, the country overcame the perils of disintegration, and the deep pessimism and traumatic experiences which it went through awakened the national consciousness."[18] This may be a rationalization, but the statement is not entirely untrue: the selling of half the nation's territory in the nineteenth century would have spared Mexican and American lives, but might have sealed Mexico's fate as a nation. Sonora, Chihuahua, and Baja California would have gone the way of California, New Mexico, and the other territories ceded in the Treaty of Guadalupe Hidalgo, as demanded even after the war by the expansionist party in the U.S. Senate and in President James Polk's entourage. Fighting and losing proved to be a better deal than selling and perhaps losing far more.

This is not the only lesson which the *General History* draws from its overview of the history of U.S.-Mexican relations. In her study of American involvement in the Mexican Revolution and particularly the 1914 occupation of Veracruz, Berta Ulloa, one of Mexico's leading authorities in her field, takes a dim view of Woodrow Wilson's true motives for interfering in Mexican matters:

> Wilson . . . adopted a "moralist" policy [toward Mexico] with imperialist ambitions. . . . The last stage, . . . which began in February of 1914, was the one in which Wilson's interventionist ambitions took form. With the pretext of an incident in Tampico, he ordered the armed occupation of the port of Veracruz. . . . Wilson's policy was rejected by Venustiano Carranza and by the Mexican people, and in addition did not achieve Huerta's resignation.[19]

From Ulloa's perspective, Wilson's reasons for intervening in Mexican affairs were far from altruistic. As in the elementary school textbook, this historian comes down squarely on the side of self-interested and not particularly well-intentioned causes for Wilson's Mexican adventure. As the dictator Huerta was about to fall, the United States began discussing the future with Venustiano Carranza, who already wielded about as much presidential authority as was possible in Mexico during those turbulent times. Yet Wilson continued to defend short-term American business interests. In any case, whatever Wilson's underlying motives were, the author stresses that Carranza rejected American support for his attempts to overthrow Huerta. He emerges as a statesman who preferred to bide his time and reach power on his own terms, instead of owing Huerta's departure—and his own accession to the presidency—to American pressure. In the historian's words:

> Carranza let Wilson know that his government had offended Mexico and damaged the Constitutionalists' chances. . . . He insisted that basic legal principles had been notoriously violated, that the long-lasting presence of the troops was an unjustified invasion, that [he] would never accept the support of a foreign invasion to ensure [his] victory, and that [he] did not believe that the sole purpose of Wilson's policy was to remove Huerta. . . . Wilson's compulsion to intervene in Mexico's internal affairs led him to order the occupation of Veracruz, a warlike act against the people which contradicted his claims of friendship, and which did not fulfill his goals. The immediate Mexican reaction was armed defense and to forget differences in the face of the common enemy, the United States.[20]

These are the strongest statements made in the entire analysis. Regardless of Wilson's motives, given Carranza's refusal to accept American aid in removing Huerta from power, the issue was whether internal differences among Mexican factions should be set aside in the face of foreign hostility or intervention. In addition, Mexicans had to choose whether to accept foreign help for their domestic endeavors or to reject it, no matter how disinterested it appeared to be, nor how noble the cause.[21] Carranza's reply to the first question was categorical—he continued to combat Huerta even while American troops patrolled Veracruz—and so was his answer to the second one. The precedent has remained valid.

In nearly all domestic conflicts in modern Mexico, the winning side—since the Revolution, the government side—has raised the specter of national disintegration due to foreign intervention. As in most countries, it has maintained that whenever the nation is threatened by external danger, domestic strife should take second place or, better still, be eliminated. But unlike elsewhere, the constant and powerful reality of foreign interference has lent substantial credibility to the threat of intervention. On those occasions when the Mexican left, and later the right, did not accept the principle of stifling domestic dissent because of the ever-present danger of American interference, the price was high. The absence of any significant political opposition in Mexico until the mid-1980s was partly due to this phenomenon: too many opponents of the establishment have, often for the right reasons, committed the mistake of underestimating the widespread fear—well founded or not—of a new era of foreign involvement in Mexican matters.

Largely because of this fear, there has been little disagreement concerning the illegitimate nature of support from abroad for domestic purposes. The conviction that Carranza acted correctly in refusing Wilson's embrace is widely shared, and it has served its purpose of discouraging any break with this tradition. Under no circumstances is foreign assistance for internal politics deemed legitimate even today, though there is a tendency to acknowledge that Carranza's situation was somewhat exceptional. Woodrow Wilson *did* want to get rid of Huerta and *did* contribute to his downfall. This permitted Carranza to reject Wilson's overtures, claiming that Huerta's eventual departure was due exclusively to his struggle. Carranza thus owed nothing to the United States.

American support in Mexican politics today continues to be more of a liability than an advantage. In Mexico, as elsewhere, the "kiss of death" syndrome exists and cannot be countered by claims of historical inaccuracy. The fact that our revolutionaries and Presidents have traditionally sought some backing from the United States—if only by seeking safe haven on American soil or American arms—does not dissipate the perilous political connotations of an American embrace. It is simply one more illustration of the seemingly contradictory attitude that Mexico has toward U.S. involvement in its politics—simultaneously rejecting its intervention and seeking its backing.

These feelings may be changing today. Increasingly, right-of-center groups and politicians in the north of the country and in Mexico City are seeking out and receiving aid and encouragement from Mexicans in the United States and from American sympathizers. Yet the conservative National Action Party (PAN) militants who in 1986 sought to enlist U.S. Senator Jesse Helms's backing for their struggle were roundly condemned by all sectors of Mexican opinion, including their own party. Public opinion polls published in the Mexico City daily *Excelsior* weeks after the Senate hearings on Mexico chaired by Helms showed a high degree of anti-American feeling among those questioned: 47 percent said their "opinion" of the United States had worsened over the past five years; 60 percent felt that the United States was a disagreeable or unpleasant neighbor, and 59 percent considered it to be an "enemy coun-try."[22] The Helms hearings undoubtedly contributed to the extreme views held by many Mexicans.

Dissident groups on the left are also more frequently resorting to the foreign press to further their political aims. Human rights and civic associations are calling on institutions like Amnesty International to redress their grievances. The PAN recently took its claims of electoral fraud to the Organization of American States and the Inter-American Human Rights Court. As the Mexican economy opens up to the rest of the world, the nation's traditional definitions of what constitutes unac-ceptable intervention from abroad is changing, and will continue to do so.

But the foundations on which those definitions ultimately rest—that is, the way in which we Mexicans have obtained our knowledge of our country's history, and the importance we attach to the history of Mex-ico's relations with the United States—will probably change less quickly, if at all. That is perhaps the way it should be: every nation needs a common vision of its past, of its glories and its shames. It has taken Mexico many years to acquire one; it should not be relinquished or tampered with if it has served the nation well. Most Mexicans believe it has.

The American Mind

—

Robert A. Pastor

A fifth-grade student in DeKalb County, Georgia, studies U.S. history from a textbook that captures the nation's exuberance in its title, *America! America!* Mexico is mentioned in only five events, and this amounts to less than eight of 752 pages. The longest reference is about "winning Texas" and the U.S.-Mexican war in a section called "From Sea to Shining Sea."

The book draws a picture of the United States as a nation "of new opportunities and endless possibilities" propelled by a divinely inspired "manifest destiny . . . to bring progress and democracy to all of North America." In the path of this drive west, Mexico learned, as students would learn, that "the United States was on the move, and nothing . . . could stop it."[1] The Texan war for independence and the war against Mexico are not seen within the context of U.S. relations with Mexico or even with Latin America. In U.S. history texts, Mexico is a way station on the purposeful trek of the United States across the continent.

There are no standard national history texts in the United States; the very idea would evoke protests, anxiety, or disbelief among jealously independent school districts. The distrust of federal authority that remains an important leitmotif of the American political character is per-

haps most evident in the field of education. Local communities strenu-
ously resist federal efforts to encroach upon or restrict local autonomy.

Yet despite this tradition of local independence, social science textbooks reveal a remarkable degree of homogeneity across the nation.
Frances FitzGerald analyzed these textbooks and found that they "differ
from one another . . . not much more than one year's crop of Detroit's
sedans."[2] Local communities in the United States reject the idea of a
national text but unconsciously choose from a small number of similar
textbooks. This is due to a commercial response to a national market,
but it also reflects a common national experience. The homogeneity is
also possible because the textbooks are not perceived as vehicles of a
partisan interpretation of U.S. history.

The United States has been described by one journalist as nine separate
"nations [that] look different, feel different, and sound different from
each other."[3] And yet these separate "nations" educate their children
with the same television programs and similar textbooks. Only four
states—Texas, California, Florida, and North Carolina—require publishers to include a special appendix on their state. The publishers accede
to this request from the first two states because of the size of the market
and from the latter two because their local districts all purchase the same
book. Except for those appendices, all students in the United States study
their history from similar textbooks.[4]

The U.S. texts both reflect and influence their nation's character. If
Mexico's self-concept has been derived partly from its defeat by the
United States, the national identity of the United States has been influenced more by its victories. The implicit instruction of U.S. textbooks
is to stimulate initiative and inspire ambition and confidence in Americans as individuals. The lesson that American youth should draw from
its history is to be proud, optimistic, and confident in the nation's future.
Each generation passes to the next its task of moving the nation forward
and keeping the story of the United States a success. Mexico's place in
U.S. books is small.

In 1895, Theodore Roosevelt, who would become President six years
later, and Henry Cabot Lodge, a senator from Massachusetts, tried to
divert America's attention from internal development to new global
horizons. To prepare youth for a role on the world stage, the two of them
wrote a book, *Hero Tales from American History*. Their stated purpose
was to tell stories in a way that instilled in Americans "manly qualities
. . . of patriotism, and of lofty adherence to an ideal [that] are essential
to the well-being of a masterful race."[5]

One of the stories was about the Alamo, described as "one of the most resolute and effective fights ever waged by brave men against overwhelming odds in the face of certain death." That essay, which was written by Roosevelt, describes the war of Texan independence as resulting from the jealousy of Mexicans who could not accept the brave, hardworking American settlers. In an effort to suppress Yankee ingenuity, according to Roosevelt, the Mexican General Antonio López de Santa Anna "invaded Texas" and committed "dreadful atrocities." Davy Crockett, Jim Bowie, and other heroes who defended the Alamo were described as "men of iron courage and great bodily powers," but their numbers were too few and Santa Anna was merciless. Their heroism, however, inspired their compatriots to defeat Mexico at the battle of San Jacinto.

By the 1980s, after two very popular movies, North Americans still remembered the Alamo, but the new textbooks replaced Roosevelt's zeal with some balance and the righteousness with some sensitivity. From *America! America!* the fifth-grader in 1988 did not learn whether the Mexicans or the American settlers were to blame for Texas's war for independence. Instead, the war is described as a result of cultural and political differences between English-speaking Protestants from the United States and Spanish-speaking Catholic Mexicans. The Mexicans said that North Americans could settle in the vacant northern part of their country if they would accept certain conditions—for example, converting to Catholicism. The settlers accepted the conditions in principle, but not in practice, and a new Mexican leader, General Santa Anna, changed some of the rules. Santa Anna tried to raise taxes, centralize power in Mexico City, and restrict further immigration. In response to these decisions, the settlers revolted.[6]

Even in this fifth-grade textbook, students learned that the war was not a clear-cut struggle between right and wrong, since the settlers had slaves and Mexico theoretically had abolished slavery in 1829. But the enduring, subliminal point of the war was the inequality of the struggle: a few settlers were able to defeat a large army. North Americans were the underdog—a role the United States savors. That is why the most celebrated and remembered battle of the war was the Alamo even though it was a defeat. The text inflates the numbers and rounds them off, describing the odds as daunting—"200 courageous fighters held off about 5,000 Mexican soldiers for twelve days." The Alamo symbolized even more sharply than Sam Houston's surprise victory at San Jacinto the determination of a nation with a destiny.

The "Child Heroes" of Mexico play somewhat the same role in Mexican history as the Alamo heroes play for the United States, but with an important difference. The Mexicans took their own lives, reflecting a fatalism that is prevalent in Mexico but absent from U.S. history books.

In contrast, the Americans never gave up. Not only did they defy their fate to triumph in spirit, but the settlers also achieved a practical goal, giving Sam Houston time to recruit volunteers to stop the Mexican army. In short, the lesson of the war, like that of the history book, was that "nothing could stop America."

In more advanced grades, the American picture of the war becomes grayer. U.S. high school students learn, for example, that part of the reason that Santa Anna tried to reassert control over the northern part of his country was that he suspected, with justification, that the North Americans harbored aspirations for independence.[7] His decisions, however, made his fears come true, a self-fulfilling pattern that was not unique to Mexicans.

The student also learns that northern and southern states disputed whether the fruits of western expansion would be slave or free states, and that this division, in turn, inhibited further expansion. In 1836, all but 61 of 6,000 Texas settlers voted for annexation to the United States. Andrew Jackson wanted to annex Texas, but he did not ask Congress to do that because he judged it would divide the country and could provoke a war with Mexico.[8] The overall message of the high school texts is that the responsibility for the Texan war was shared, and the settlers overcame great odds to win. As in the elementary texts, the emphasis was on the heroism of the Americans, not on the weakness or villainy of the Mexicans.

In the case of the U.S.-Mexican war, the causes of the war and the conduct of the United States are described in a straightforward way by American history texts, although the interpretation and the level of detail vary according to the age of the student and the bias of the historian. Our fifth-grader learns that Sam Houston allowed Santa Anna to return to Mexico after he accepted and signed two treaties, one recognizing the independence of Texas and the second accepting the Rio Grande as the border. The Mexican general subsequently renounced both treaties and threatened war if the United States annexed Texas. James K. Polk did not share Jackson's fear of a war with Mexico, and campaigned in 1844 for the presidency as an expansionist Democrat. Before his election, the Senate rejected a treaty that would annex Texas, but afterward Congress sensed the shift in the public mood and approved the annexation by majority vote in a joint resolution. Mexico then broke diplomatic relations, and Polk sent John Slidell to negotiate the purchase of California and New Mexico. Mexico would not receive Slidell, let alone negotiate with him.

Impatient with Mexico's intransigence, Polk then ordered General Zachary Taylor to march his troops to the Rio Grande, the southern border of the new state of Texas. After Mexican troops fired on Taylor's, Polk asked Congress on May 11, 1846, to declare war. Within two years, American troops captured California and General Winfield Scott controlled Mexico City. On February 2, 1848, the Treaty of Guadalupe Hidalgo was signed. Mexico accepted the Rio Grande as the southern boundary of Texas and ceded New Mexico and California to the United States for $15 million.

In the secondary school texts, North American students learn that Polk was prepared to go to war if Mexico would not sell California or settle the Texas boundary dispute. Polk was therefore preparing a declaration of war when news arrived that Taylor's forces had been attacked by Mexico.[9] More advanced texts indicate that "Polk baited Mexico into war" in order to acquire California. In addition, the debates within both countries are given more attention. Within Mexico, a "revolution" on January 1, 1846, brought to power a new government that was "spoiling for a fight against the United States."[10] Within the United States, the more bellicose side also won, albeit without a revolution. The South and West supported the war, but the northern states viewed it as an expansionist conspiracy of slave owners. The Whig-dominated legislature of Massachusetts denounced it as a war of conquest.

How was Mexico portrayed in these histories? Santa Anna was "unscrupulous" for having deceived the United States on three separate occasions. Allan Nevins and Henry Steele Commager, two of America's foremost historians, describe the Mexican government as "inefficient, corrupt, and tyrannical."[11] Although Americans prevailed in most of the battles, they fought hard against larger Mexican armies. The main theme of the histories of the war, however, was not that the United States was an underdog. Nor did historians argue that the United States was right.

Most historians recognize that the war was one of conquest, but only a few dwell on this facet. Some note that the conquest of weaker neighbors was the rule in international relations, not the exception; what was unique was that the United States acquired only the northern part rather than all of Mexico, and paid for it, an unusual act for a victorious imperialist. These are all digressions, however. The principal theme of the histories of the war is summed up in the concluding comment that the treaty with Mexico "almost completed American expansion across the continent."[12] For students of American history, the war is not viewed as against Mexico, but rather as completing the expansion of the Republic.

Between the war and the Revolution of 1910, many important events in Mexico and in its relationship with the United States pass unrecorded in the fifth-grade text. In the 1860s, Mexico was occupied by France, initiall' with the aid of Spain and Great Britain. After the Civil War, the United States helped Mexico to liberate itself, and then both nations embarked on thirty years of economic modernization. Porfirio Díaz, who ruled Mexico during most of this time, invited foreign investors, and about half were Americans. The fifth-grader then learns that the Mexican Revolution began with the overthrow of Díaz and that U.S. businessmen tried to prevail upon their government to intervene in Mexico to protect their interests. But the American people did not want to go to war, and "through their labor unions, church groups, and the newspapers," they persuaded the Senate to pass a resolution calling for a peaceful settlement of the differences with Mexico.[13] There is no mention of the landing of troops at Veracruz, but the section on the Mexican Revolution is entitled "Intervening in Latin America," and it includes a reference to the U.S. intervention in Nicaragua at that time.

In secondary school texts, in less than one page, American students learn of the "civil war" in Mexico and the events surrounding the landing of the marines in Veracruz. There is no mention of U.S. "complicity" in the death of Francisco Madero. More advanced history books report that U.S. Ambassador Henry Lane Wilson conspired with reactionary generals—Huerta and Félix Díaz—to overthrow Madero, but he did so in contravention of instructions he received from the U.S. Department of State, and there is no evidence that he was either aware of or conspired in the murder of Madero.[14] The ambassador's behavior was condemnable, but he was acting on his own against government policy during a transition between Presidents. President Woodrow Wilson was so horrified by the coup and the murder that he refused to recognize the Huerta government.

The major issue for the United States was how to respond to the violence and continued threats to U.S. citizens and property. Although Woodrow Wilson's sympathies were with the Constitutionalist forces of Venustiano Carranza, he first adopted an attitude of "watchful waiting." Then he tried unsuccessfully to mediate between the two sides. In April 1914, in response to a purported insult, and also to prevent the delivery of a shipment of arms from Germany to Huerta's forces, the marines landed in Veracruz. Huerta's followers fought the marines, and there were casualties on both sides, but this event and a subsequent mediation helped the Constitutionalists to ease Huerta out of power.[15]

U.S. history books report both the chaos of Mexico's revolution and the pressures on Washington to protect American citizens and property. Beyond that, some historians stress the restraint of the Wilson administration; some, its arrogance and intervention. The intervention at Veracruz is the first event in the history texts in which the United States related to Mexico as a complex nation rather than as a challenge to U.S. ambitions.

The Mexican Revolution and U.S. intervention are brief episodes in American history. President Wilson's sympathy for the Revolution and his attempt to unseat Huerta are viewed as well intentioned but contradictory, and to some historians, simply hypocritical. U.S. history books, particularly modern ones, are not reticent about criticizing the nation's impatience, insensitivity, or interventionism.

Contemporary views of Mexico are most sharply highlighted when placed in front of earlier history books. Each generation interprets the past in a different light with a different purpose. History does not change, but the collective memory of a nation evolves as contemporary events increase the importance of some past events and render others less relevant.

In her study of U.S. history textbooks of the nineteenth and twentieth centuries, Frances FitzGerald was astonished to find how much both the style and the content changed. More startling is the rapidity with which modern interpretations change. In the nineteenth century, major changes in history books were visible every generation; in the first half of the twentieth, every decade; in the last two decades, every three years.[16] Nineteenth-century historians, according to FitzGerald, were deeply biased against all foreigners, but especially Spanish, who were described by one scholar, Jedidiah Morse, as "naturally weak and effeminate."[17] Textbooks tended to list prejudices and stereotypical negative traits of Latin Americans. Only in the 1920s did FitzGerald detect the first signs of a readiness to recognize Latin America's contributions to the world.

During World War II, the American Council on Education established a committee to analyze the inter-American content in textbooks in various fields in order to try to improve understanding of Latin America.[18] The committee found "no evidence of conscious and perverted antagonism toward Latin America—no effort on the part of any group willfully to distort the story of inter-American relations." But it did identify some racial prejudices, a "Kiplingesque condescension," and a tendency to stress the political and military aspects of the relationship more than the economic and cultural dimensions.[19] The report concluded that the quantity and quality of scholarship on Latin America had improved over the previous quarter century, but more progress was needed.

As part of its study, the committee analyzed how various history texts described the U.S.-Mexican war. To its surprise, the committee found that the books had become so sympathetic to the Mexican point of view that the typical reader might "be led to take a critical view of the American position and to acquire a tolerance, if not complete approval, of Mexican acts."[20] This conclusion reflected a combination of the historians' detachment and the committee's wartime patriotism.

The debate between isolationists and internationalists that had long divided the nation was resolved by World War II. The lesson drawn in postwar textbooks was unequivocal: peace and prosperity depended on a sustained international role for the United States. Reflecting this prevailing view, U.S. texts encouraged a new generation to think internationally.

More profound change in American life and its textbooks came in response to the civil rights movement in the 1960s, the Vietnam War, and the new wave of immigration from Latin America and Asia beginning in the late 1960s. Textbooks began to acknowledge the racism in American society, the interventionism of American foreign policy, and the changing character of the nation. Students were encouraged to view other cultures as different rather than deficient. U.S. history books no longer began with the discovery of America in 1492 but rather with the migration from Asia 25,000 years before. Sections were included on the Aztec and Mayan civilizations and the various Indian tribes that inhabited North America before the Europeans arrived. The new books redefined the national identity of the United States to incorporate Mexican and other Third World immigrants, and these peoples were viewed more sympathetically than ever before.[21]

All of these changes are evident in the texts used by today's students. American history is still a success story, but the texts also strive to be balanced and fair. Conflicts are portrayed as having multiple causes. Blame is apportioned to both sides. The new relativism and willingness to acknowledge past mistakes is not an exhibition of weakness or guilt, as some critics contend; rather it is a combination of an old optimism and a new sensitivity.

Each country's history is organized around different fears and focused on different horizons. The three cases that are at the center of this chapter—Texan secession, the U.S. invasion, and intervention in Veracruz—are Mexico's traumas, and indeed, the United States uses different terms to describe the first two. If the United States shared Mexico's fear, we would have noted the conspiracies of Mexican ambassador Matías Romero in the 1860s to unseat Abraham Lincoln and oust Secretary of State William Seward,[22] or focused on the Zimmermann telegram from Germany in 1917, offering Mexico the territory taken by the United States in the nineteenth century in exchange for an alliance with Germany in World War I. But these incidents, which could arouse American mistrust of Mexico, either are footnotes in U.S. history books or omitted altogether.

Part of the reason for the different emphasis is simply that the United States is a world power for which Mexico plays a peripheral role, while Mexico is preoccupied with maintaining its independence from the United States. American leaders view the Soviet Union and world Communism as primary threats, but they are worried that the American people are more preoccupied by domestic concerns. Reflecting a widespread elite concern, U.S. histories in the postwar period have tried to discredit isolationism and encourage each generation to remain involved in the world.

History sits differently on the two countries. In Mexico, it is like a block of granite, inhibiting movement. In the United States, it is like a rolling stone. In Mexico, the past "lives." Mexicans are justly proud of their heritage, the great Mayan and Aztec civilizations, the colonial buildings, but they are more pessimistic about the future. In contrast, Americans take pride in their newest building, the latest invention, the most recent success. The past motivates; it does not slow the future in the United States.

Beginning in the late 1970s, the sheer quantity of information on Mexico that has washed into the United States has been tidal in its dimensions. Like most cultural "invasions," the one from Mexico has not been imposed; it has been embraced in its many forms—from consumer products, like Dos Equis beer, to the increasing use of the Spanish language, to new restaurant chains like Taco Bell, to sports figures like Fernando Valenzuela. Newspaper and television coverage of Mexico has also increased sharply in recent years, and since 65 percent of the population is said to receive its foreign news from television, one should not underestimate the influence of TV in shaping the popular view of Mexico.[23]

Whether television and tacos have had more influence than textbooks on the way Americans think about Mexico is impossible to determine, but the contemporary U.S. image of Mexico is discernible from an analysis of public opinion polls. The predominant image that Americans have of Mexico is friendly and sympathetic, but very concerned. In a Harris Survey in August 1986, Americans—by the substantial margin of 75 to 18 percent—felt a genuine affinity for Mexico.[24] In public opinion surveys in 1978, 1982, and 1986 conducted by Gallup for the Chicago Council on Foreign Relations, Americans were asked how favorably they viewed various countries in the world. Mexico was consistently ranked among the top five. It was viewed more favorably than any other Third World country, and since 1982 Americans have felt "warmer" to Mexico than even to Israel.[25] This feeling is based partly on proximity and direct experience. In a 1986 survey, 48 percent of those who responded said that they had visited Mexico. The only foreign country Americans visited more often was Canada; only 37 percent had been in Europe.[26]

Americans view Mexico as very important in itself and as compared with other countries. The Harris Survey found that 93 percent of the American people believe that a "stable, reliable, and friendly" neighbor is important for the United States. In all the surveys of the Chicago Council on Foreign Relations, Americans recognized that they had a "vital interest" in Mexico. This appreciation increased sharply between 1978 and 1982, probably as a result of the Mexican oil boom and increased press attention. In 1978, 60 percent of the U.S. public and 90 percent of a sample of national leaders indicated that the United States had a vital interest in Mexico, which was ranked fifteenth of twenty-four countries in the "vital interest" category.[27] By 1982, 74 percent of the American public and 98 percent of the elite believed that the United States had a vital interest in Mexico—the seventh most important country of twenty-two. Those figures remained stable in 1986.

In the 1982 Council survey, the public was asked whether the United States would be threatened if a Communist government came to power in each of six countries. Of those countries, which included France, Iran, and Saudi Arabia, Mexico stimulated the most concern, with 61 percent of the public and 70 percent of the elite viewing it as "a great threat," as compared, for example, with 31 percent of the public and 37 percent of the elite viewing a Communist government in France as "a great threat."

The importance that Americans attach to Mexico stems not only from the fear of a threat, but also from a recognition of the interdependence of the two economies. When asked whether economic problems in Mexico affect the United States, 77 percent said that they did and only 19 percent disagreed.[28] Other surveys indicate that four out of five Americans think that illegal immigration from Mexico is a serious problem for the United States, and three out of four believe that the drug flow from Mexico is a major reason for the U.S. drug problem.[29]

The principal themes of the two nations' history books resonate in the public opinion polls. Americans feel close to Mexico, but they sense that these feelings are not reciprocated. While 83 percent of Americans are friendly toward the Mexican people, only 52 percent believe that the Mexican government is friendly toward the United States. One-third of Americans feel that the Mexican government is *not* friendly to the United States. This is surprisingly high for a neighbor, but if anything, it probably underestimates the actual negative attitudes of Mexican government officials toward the United States. Similarly, while 93 percent of Americans feel it is important to have "a stable, reliable, and friendly neighbor," 53 percent of Americans do *not* believe that the Mexican government is such a neighbor.[30]

Americans like Mexico, and they are certain that Mexico is important to the United States, but they are extremely uneasy about whether the country can solve its problems. In a series of questions, 52 to 63 percent of Americans said that current problems of drugs, debt, corruption, and illegal immigration demonstrate that there is something "seriously wrong with the way Mexico is being run."[31] An extensive survey by Yankelovich Clancy Shulman asked some blunt questions about U.S. attitudes toward Mexico in July 1986. If the responses, which were embarrassingly direct, had been statements by U.S. senators rather than a poll, they might have caused a diplomatic incident. Sixty-nine percent of Americans indicated that they thought the source of Mexico's problems was that it was "poorly governed" while 8 percent thought it was "well governed." Sixty-five percent believe there is a lot of political corruption in Mexico; only 16 percent think there is not much corruption.[32]

The analysis is clear, but Americans are uncertain what policy the United States should pursue toward Mexico. A *Time* poll indicated that more than half of Americans think the government should not increase foreign aid to Mexico. In another poll, Americans split as to whether the United States should give priority to Mexico over other needy countries. Finally, 54 percent agreed that the United States should pressure Mexico to have free elections as a way to solve its problems, while 41 percent disagreed with that prescription.[33]

These disparate views are not surprising in a nation as vast and diverse as the United States. One cannot speak of a single U.S. view of Mexico, but in trying to understand contemporary American feelings about Mexico, it might be useful to visualize two interacting sides of the American mind. One side of America is proud of its history and accomplishments, and another side is supportive of our friends and sympathetic to the underdog. The first side defends the United States in any international dispute, and the second is more willing to listen to the other side, and if that other side is relatively poor and weak, to defend that position even against their government.

Some groups and individuals reside permanently on one side or the other. Some on the right, for example, believe that the United States is without fault and the other party to a dispute is always wrong. Some on the left think that the United States has been mostly or all wrong in its foreign policies. Most educated Americans, however, are probably influenced by both tendencies; they are both proud of the United States and sympathetic to smaller, poorer nations.

The two tendencies are evident in the debates in Congress and on editorial pages of the major newspapers. In a content analysis of thirty-one newspaper and guest editorials on Mexico in *The New York Times* from 1983 through 1986, there were roughly an equal number of articles that were critical of Mexico's policies (thirteen) and critical of U.S. policy toward Mexico (twelve). The other six articles did not blame one side or the other.[34] Reflecting the two sides of the American mind, the *Times* opened its pages to the U.S. view of Mexico's problems first, and then, to the Mexican view of U.S. criticisms. About one-third of the guest editorials between 1984 and 1986 were written by Mexicans, who lectured Americans: "Don't Push Mexico" and "Enough Mexico-Bashing." Editorials of the *Times* agreed that Senator Jesse Helms should "Stop Bullying Mexico," and then appropriately, with the other hand, criticized the electoral fraud in Chihuahua in "Mexico Bashes Itself."[35] For the most part, Mexican views are integrated into the public debate in the United States. This is sometimes because some Americans view U.S. policy as many Mexicans do: as dominating and oppressive; and sometimes Mexicans themselves are invited to state Mexico's position.

Some, like former U.S. ambassador to the United Nations Jeane Kirkpatrick, confuse the American tradition of openness to different views with weakness, and sympathy for poorer neighbors with a "blame America first" perspective. Such a characterization is equivalent to the Mexican dismissal of a U.S. view, but in the more open debate in the United States, Kirkpatrick's opinion misses the point. The debate in the United States is not between pro- and anti-American positions but between those who accept Washington's definition of U.S. interests and those who would favor an alternative definition.

In some ways, the U.S. debate is a reflection of the international negotiation. When U.S. policy is partly an accommodation to the other side's position and interests, it is also a smooth blending of the two sides of the American mind—of pride in the United States and respect for others. Other times, in response to events or changes in the world, one tendency will prevail in the collective mind of America. For several years after the détente with the Soviet Union initiated by Richard Nixon, the United States was more relaxed about its own security and more open and interested in the views of Third World nations. After the Soviet invasion of Afghanistan and the Iranian seizure of U.S. hostages, the more aggressive, less tolerant tendency of America was ascendant.

The tendency that prevails in the U.S. approach to Mexico depends on international events, but also on Mexico's policies and statements and the deepening appreciation of Mexico's importance to the United States. This last factor has served in the last decade to temper the more aggressive side of the United States. Mexicans may not be aware of this because as they listen to the debate between the two sides of the American mind, they tend to pay most attention to the strident voices arguing for a more assertive posture, and discount the calmer voices calling for a more respectful approach. At the end of the debate, however, U.S. policy is more likely to reflect a quiet compromise between these two tendencies.

It is difficult to determine the extent to which America's view of its history influences current attitudes toward Mexico. Public opinion surveys have not asked questions that would permit such a judgment; perhaps the absence of such questions is an unintended confirmation that history plays a smaller role for the United States than it does for Mexico.

Nonetheless, there are times when U.S. history is awakened and becomes a contemporary issue. On a visit to Indonesia in 1962, Attorney General Robert F. Kennedy was asked about the U.S.-Mexican war by some students. He conceded that it "was not a very bright page in American history." His remarks were forgettable everywhere except in Texas, where they provoked outrage. Texas Senator John Tower condemned Kennedy for his "glaring ignorance," and the Houston District of the Veterans of Foreign Wars sent Kennedy a history of Texas along with a letter denouncing his remarks.

The Attorney General was later asked about the incident, and he explained that when he returned from Indonesia, he met with the President and Vice President Lyndon Johnson in the White House. In mock seriousness, Robert Kennedy explained that his brother "said he wasn't going to muzzle me, but from now on, all speeches on Texas should be cleared with the Vice President."[36]

It is, of course, easier for the country that won the war to make light of the history. This particular incident recaptured—albeit once over lightly—the debate within the United States on the war, with Texas fighting and Massachusetts protesting. Texas is still proud of its role, and Massachusetts apologetic. The different interpretations of this event illustrate the division in the American mind. But with the possible exception of some people in Texas and Massachusetts, most Americans do not debate history as much as they do current policy. Americans are unlikely to feel either much pride or much guilt over the fact that the U.S. expansion across the continent was at the expense of Mexico.

Free of the baggage of a past, Americans have a contemporary image of Mexico as a country that is very important to the United States and one for which they feel a fondness and affinity. It is very instructive that one of the final entries in the fifth-grade history book is a discussion of the "challenges of the 1980s," and Mexico is one of the few challenges mentioned. The book describes President Reagan's plan for a North American Accord, a vague proposal for greater cooperation among the United States, Canada, and Mexico, and says, correctly, with both sensitivity and a tinge of regret: "The Mexicans were hesitant about agreeing to this partnership."[37]

Each new proposal from the United States suffers from historical amnesia; each hesitant and suspicious response from Mexico suffers from historical paralysis.

As one explores the galaxy of problems that both separate and unite the United States and Mexico, history is not just a vision of the past. It continues to divide the two countries, but contemporary problems do not stem from interpretations of history. Nor are the problems due to historians' adjectives that excite national pride on one side and rage on the other, or the omissions and exaggerations of the events that are alternately embarrassing to one side and provocative to the other. These only tug on the margins of the issue.

The center of the problem is simply that the United States is a nation that does not feel a need to remember its past, and the Mexican government feels it cannot afford to forget it. Mexico is anxious to redeem its past while the United States is a nation that is preoccupied with forging a new future.

And yet it is precisely because the present is an interpreter, not a prisoner, of the past that history need not be a barrier in U.S.-Mexican relations. There is, in brief, nothing fixed or predetermined about the way each nation should use its history. Different generations can use it differently in the United States, but also in Mexico. There have been times, for example, when Mexican leaders seemed ready to ignore or pour water on the history, and other times when they preferred to stoke the embers.

Josephus Daniels, U.S. ambassador to Mexico from 1933 to 1942, unintentionally offers a colorful case study of the different uses of history. Daniels, a North Carolina newspaper editor and close friend of Franklin D. Roosevelt, is acknowledged in both countries as the best U.S. ambassador to have served in Mexico. He begins his memoirs with a story that shows how relations sometimes can be improved by betting on the future rather than reliving the past.

When Daniels informed his wife that President Roosevelt asked him to be ambassador to Mexico, his wife, whom he called his "best counsellor," protested strongly that he could not accept the position. Daniels was puzzled and asked why. "Don't you remember Veracruz?" she responded. "Have you forgotten that you sent the fleet to Veracruz in 1914 and as a result a number of Mexicans were killed by the Navy's landing party?"[38]

Daniels admitted: "I had forgotten all about the Veracruz expedition."

"You and Franklin Roosevelt may have forgotten about it," his wife replied, "but you may be sure the Mexicans have not forgotten. They will not receive you."

When Josephus and Addie Daniels dined later with the President, she could not help asking Roosevelt why he had appointed her husband. Roosevelt said that it was "an excellent appointment, and . . . I know he will make a great Ambassador."

Addie Daniels then asked the President, "Have you forgotten Veracruz?"

The President was silent for a moment and then said, "I had forgotten all about the Veracruz incident. Had the Chief?"

In 1914, Josephus Daniels was Secretary of the Navy in the Wilson administration and the "chief" of Franklin D. Roosevelt, who was then Assistant Secretary of the Navy. Daniels sent the order for the marines to land at Veracruz, and Roosevelt was responsible for implementing it. The action resulted in the death of 126 Mexicans and 19 Americans. In trying to understand why both he and the President had failed to recollect the incident, Daniels thought the reason was that he and Roosevelt "had believed that we were really aiding liberty-loving Mexicans to free themselves from the Huerta reign of absolutism."

Addie Daniels was right. The Mexicans did not forget Veracruz; nor did they remember it as her husband did. After newspapers reported Daniels's appointment, Mexican protesters stoned the U.S. embassy. Handbills condemned the appointment as "a slap at the Mexican people and the spitting upon the memory of the dead who defended Veracruz." The papers called on "workers, peasants, soldiers, students," everyone, to reject the appointment, but the Mexican government granted agrément—acceptance of the ambassadorial appointment—in less than one day. Dr. José Puig, the Minister of Foreign Relations, had been ambassador to Washington and knew Daniels as a man of liberal views and a friend of organized labor. Puig not only took the risk of accepting a controversial appointment with what the embassy described as "unprecedented rapidity," but he committed himself to it. He called in the Mexican press, told them of Daniels's background, and suggested that they "would be wise to let sleeping dogs lie."

Upon learning of Mexico's decision, Roosevelt dictated a telegram instructing the U.S. chargé in Mexico City to meet with Puig to express the President's personal appreciation for the prompt decision and to ask

Puig to inform his President that Roosevelt "has complete confidence in Mr. Daniels, who is an old and trusted friend and that the selection of so distinguished a national personage and close associate of the President is for the purpose of indicating the deep and friendly interest" of Roosevelt in excellent relations. Privately, and without informing the U.S. government, the Mexican government took special precautions to assure Daniels's security the moment he crossed the border.

Mexico's risk was richly rewarded. Relations between the two nations began well and, despite many serious problems in a convulsive period that could have led to conflict, remained strong throughout the Roosevelt administration. Daniels himself played a central role in developing a relatively sympathetic and tolerant U.S. policy toward the Mexican Revolution and particularly the nationalization of U.S. oil companies.

What would have happened if the Mexicans had hesitated or responded negatively to the appointment of Daniels? We do not need to speculate, because Roosevelt later confided what his reaction would have been: "If the Mexicans cannot deal with Daniels, they can have no dealings with me." If Mexico had responded negatively to the appointment, Roosevelt would have responded in the same manner, and the downward cycle of a deteriorating relationship would have begun. At the minimum, the possibility of good relations would have been lost, perhaps irretrievably during the turbulent 1930s.

History can be used to inhibit or prevent communication. If suspicions born in history cause people to see only the negative shadows of a decision or an event, past mistakes will be repeated indefinitely. But as the case of Daniels's appointment shows, history need not be a barrier. Like sleeping dogs, history could be put aside, and a good story of a Mexican risk and a generous response by the United States could be remembered.

2

INTERVENTION

From Mexico Looking Out

—

Jorge G. Castañeda

On April 22, 1983, Anthony Arredondo, the U.S. consul in Hermosillo, the capital of the border state of Sonora, hosted a supper attended by local leaders of the National Action Party (PAN), which in recent years has made important inroads in the north of Mexico, and by conservative local businessmen. Also present, and perhaps more importantly, was Archbishop Carlos Quintero Arce of Hermosillo, generally considered one of the more conservative members of the Mexican ecclesiastical hierarchy.

The dinner created a minor commotion in Mexico, which sprang from one simple problem. Through its diplomatic representatives, the U.S. government was viewed in Mexico as openly interfering in Mexican domestic politics by publicly meeting—and thus associating itself—with the conservative opposition to the government. In this way, Washington was considered to be taking sides in internal Mexican matters, and more or less conspiring against the government of President Miguel de la Madrid. At a time of growing political difficulties in Mexico, and in an area of the country where the opposition was gaining ground, representatives of the U.S. government were getting together with the pro-American opposition and with a church leader who supported it.

Later, in August 1984, Ambassador John Gavin himself went to Sonora and dined at the Hermosillo Holiday Inn with local PAN leader Carlos Amaya Rivera, Archbishop Quintero Arce, and businessmen from the area. This occurred less than a year before strongly contested state gubernatorial elections were to be held. Soon after, Gavin also traveled to Chihuahua, another northern state where the PAN was gathering strength and where forthcoming elections would severely strain the ruling party's hegemony. There, as in Sonora, Gavin met with local PAN leaders, the church hierarchy, and businessmen identified with the conservative movement, although he would also pay a call on the state governor.[1]

No amount of valid examples of symmetry or reciprocity could alter the perception held by wide circles of the Mexican political establishment—with the obvious exception of the PAN—that Gavin's and other U.S. representatives' "dinners" with the opposition were a typical illustration of heavy-handed American meddling in Mexican domestic affairs. Some objected that, after all, the Mexican ambassador to the United States met and dined freely during the Reagan years with Democratic senators and congressmen in Washington without anyone paying the least attention. Others noted that Soviet, Cuban, and more recently Nicaraguan diplomats posted in Mexico often attended public ceremonies or evening events held by left-wing political parties or groups without provoking indignation or even raised eyebrows on the part of Mexican authorities. The De la Madrid administration had privately expelled Cuban and Nicaraguan officials for going too far in their local activities, but neither the expulsions nor the activities received much attention. The difference involved the nature, size, and motives of the "intervening party."

Indeed, symmetry and the reciprocity which stems from it are almost considered profanities in Mexico when uttered in the context of the overwhelming asymmetry which underlies U.S.-Mexican relations. The fact is that, with one or two remotely conceivable exceptions, it makes no difference whom Mexican diplomats in Washington see or meet with, and their power, influence, or standing cannot be equated with that of their American counterparts in Mexico. Likewise, other than under extremely exceptional circumstances, the clout or leverage that Soviet, Cuban, or Nicaraguan envoys wield in Mexico is negligible when compared with that of their American counterparts. Because of the overpowering global asymmetry in size, power, wealth, and interests between the two countries, each item or part of the relationship is also deemed to be asymmetrical. Reciprocity is simply the diplomatic translation of symmetry: if two parties are equal, then what is valid for one is valid for the other. But when applied to official behavior—or to other matters, such as trade—in the context of Mexican-American relations, in Mexico we inevitably tend to view it as unfair, hypocritical, and detrimental to Mexican interests. When John Gavin implicitly and rhetorically questioned his critics about what was wrong with his meeting with the Mexican political opposition, he was seen as acting disingenuously. The answer was obvious: he was intervening in Mexican affairs.

Beyond anecdotes and details, the overriding reasons why Mexico views American interference in its internal affairs as illegitimate and negative are essentially historical. As outlined previously, Mexicans are taught from early on that the United States has always had designs on our country, either through direct territorial ambition or by seeking to influence our affairs to make Mexico more amenable to American interests and wishes. This same historical experience shows that nearly every time the United States has gotten involved in Mexican politics, there has generally been a domestic faction tacitly or explicitly welcoming that involvement. From the early nineteenth century through the last military rebellions of the 1930s, Mexican political groups have seemed willing to espouse American backing for their domestic endeavors, seeking American recognition, arms, or money for their own purposes. Through the 1920s, U.S. diplomatic recognition was precisely the key to obtaining arms, money, and international stature for any Mexican government.

But such American backing skews the balance of political forces because of the very size and weight of U.S. influence in Mexico. By bringing this support to bear on behalf of one political wing and against another, the United States—and its Mexican welcoming committee—tilt the playing field, making fair play well-nigh impossible for the other actors. The history of Mexican views of American intervention until 1940 is thus largely made up of recurrent, implicit pacts among Mexican political factions committing themselves to never again invite American assistance, only to have the next excluded or defeated group break the compact and do exactly what everyone had agreed not to do: reach out for American support.

Mexican distaste notwithstanding, if American involvement in the country's affairs is in favor of the "right" causes—i.e., honest elections, economic modernization, etc.—what is wrong with it? Is there a major difference between our rejection of American interference allegedly on behalf of "democracy" and rejection of supposedly similar instances of U.S. intervention by South Africa's rulers, Ferdinand Marcos in the

Philippines, or Augusto Pinochet in Chile? Are not all of these "anti-interventionist" stances simply a pretext for the perpetuation in power of an individual or a political system?

There are two responses. First, and perhaps most important, few Mexicans believe that the reasons for U.S. intervention in Latin America in the nineteenth and twentieth centuries have lain in altruistic advocacy of noble causes. Whether in reference to American intervention in Mexican affairs or in other Latin American nations (the division of Panama and Colombia at the turn of the century in order to build and own the Panama Canal; the recurrent landings of marines in Central America and the Caribbean through the 1920s and 1930s; the CIA-organized overthrow of the government of Guatemala in 1954; the U.S.-sponsored invasion of Cuba at the Bay of Pigs in 1961; the American invasion of the Dominican Republic in 1965; the CIA's activities against the Chilean government between 1970 and 1973; the contra war in Nicaragua from 1981 to the present; the invasion of Grenada in 1983), the motives for American intrusion have been viewed as far more tightly linked to the defense of *American interests* (economic in some cases, strategic or political in others) than to the pursuit of *universal values.* Certain sectors of Mexican and Latin American opinion may agree with one instance or another of U.S. intervention in defense of its interests; others may not. But few believe that what has led the United States in the past—or what will lead it in the future—to meddle in the hemisphere's internal politics is a selfless, virtuous commitment to worthy ideals.

On occasion, American interests and those ideals may theoretically coincide. But viewed from Mexico and Latin America, the historical examples of this are few and far between. Thus the question "What is wrong with American intervention if it occurs for the right reasons?" is a false one from a Mexican perspective. It *has not* occurred for the right reasons (Lincoln's support for Juárez's struggle against French intervention and Maximilian of Austria is an arguable exception) and there are scant grounds for expecting that it ever will. Great powers have traditionally needed to believe that their power and domination was exerted for a higher good; their leaders have often undertaken their mission with the utmost sincerity. But this rationale is far from convincing or self-evident to other nations, particularly those on the receiving end of great powers' foreign ambitions.

Second, the Mexican people have strong feelings with regard to the link between political reform and American intervention. A poll taken in Mexico in late 1986 showed that 63 percent of the population thought that the political system should change so that candidates of other parties could win more often. But at the same time, in reply to the question

"What is the most negative aspect of the United States?" the third trait mentioned, immediately after drug addiction and nuclear weapons, was interventionism.[2] Mexicans *do* desire a democratization of their society, but not as a result of American pressure. Consequently the United States can only make this goal more difficult to achieve, by tarnishing it and portraying those who favor it as equally favoring U.S. involvement. If a greater opening of Mexican society comes about not as a result of national efforts but rather as an outgrowth—partially or completely—of American interference, even if it was well intentioned, it probably will not prosper. Conversely, if democratization comes as a result of a truly nationalistic movement, it will take root all the more strongly.

Several factors made recent American meddling—together with conservative Mexican acquiescence or solicitation—more ominous than on previous occasions. As a general rule, the weaker it feels or actually is, the more strongly a Mexican administration will react to the perception or reality of U.S. intervention. The De la Madrid administration in 1983 and 1984 was at a delicate juncture: the economy was in poor shape; the system's credibility and legitimacy were being tested; everything contributed to its being particularly sensitive, and prone to react violently to any hint of U.S. intervention in Mexican affairs.

Since the mid-1970s two new elements contributed to greater Mexican sensitivity to U.S. interference. This was reflected in the feeling, based on the discovery of huge oil deposits, on Mexico's becoming a major oil producer and the foremost supplier of oil to the United States, and subsequently on Mexico's economic crisis, that the country had become more important to the United States than ever before. The greater Mexico's importance to the United States, the stronger the temptation for the United States to meddle, it was felt.

Moreover, the agreement among Mexican political factions not to invite U.S. support had lasted longer than on previous occasions. Precisely because of the painful memories left by American and other foreign interference during the Revolution and its aftermath—the humiliating Bucareli Agreements signed with the United States in 1923 regulating the application of the 1917 Constitution to American claims on and properties in Mexico—attempts by major political forces to overturn the government or modify the status quo with American backing petered out after the Revolution. The last significant attempt occurred in 1940, when right-wing presidential candidate General Juan Andrew Almazán, running against Manuel Avila Camacho, the governing party candidate, sought American assistance after he was declared the loser in an election which many in Mexico thought he had actually won. Amid charges and countercharges of electoral fraud, coups, and treason, Almazán fled the country, seeking President Roosevelt's backing. He did not receive it, for reasons pertaining to the world situation as well as the advice of Ambassador Josephus Daniels.

Since then and until the late 1980s, with very minor exceptions, Mexican political groups had by and large respected the unwritten rule and unsigned agreement not to seek or welcome American involvement in domestic matters. Even the government had in a sense abided by this rule, by at least formally renouncing almost all U.S. aid, and particularly by not accepting any under the Alliance for Progress program in the 1960s. Hence, when in the early 1980s John Gavin began dabbling in Mexican regional politics, and local conservative politicians accepted (or welcomed) this new development, other Mexicans had valid motives for alarm. They had all the more reason to worry since "American intervention" had acquired a new dimension.

For many Mexicans, and certainly for most politicians, intellectuals, union leaders, and journalists, the U.S. presence in our country today is overwhelming not only because of its sheer size and weight but mainly because of what we perceive as its single-mindedness and centralization. Americans tend to see little if any coordination or unity among the widely scattered, heterogeneous, and often disparate components of their country's presence—industrial corporations, banks, service firms—in Mexico. But many Mexicans see a unified U.S. economic presence in the nation, commanding some of the most important areas of the economy, monopolizing the country's foreign trade, and exercising clear leadership among the international banking community.

Similarly, instead of clearly—and perhaps naïvely—distinguishing between private U.S. individual stakes in Mexico on the one hand and American official interests and representation on the other, as many north of the border would, the prevailing view south of the border tends to stress the commonality of purpose. Mexicans often consider the relationship between U.S. business interests in Mexico and American officialdom as incestuous. Finally, a substantial portion of our political establishment, even among those who have studied or lived in the United States, does not view the American press as a distinct entity, operating at "arm's length" from the official U.S. representation in Mexico and, to a lesser extent, the local American business community.

Thus the terms "American" presence, involvement, or intervention have a precise meaning: those actions taken by or resulting from the unified, coordinated, and purposeful behavior of U.S. business interests, the U.S. government (including in many cases the Congress), and the press. Mexican officials, intellectuals, and students of the United States do not ignore the differences and even the contradictions which often exist not only among these three sectors but also within each one of them: between the banks and multinationals present in Mexico, between the executive branch and the Congress, or within the executive branch itself; between the local press in the Southwest and the larger national papers, or between local correspondents and senior editors in New York, Washington, or Los Angeles. But these strains or diverging viewpoints are always placed in the broader context of converging, overall "American interests" in Mexico, which from our perspective will always outweigh whatever real disagreements may exist. History has not disproved this conception.

The economic component of American influence in Mexico deserves an entire chapter, and the growing importance of the U.S. press in the two countries' relations will be studied in the context of nongovernmental ties between the two nations. A quick glance at the scope and characteristics of the U.S. official presence, though, is useful at this stage, if only because it can shed light on why so many Mexicans share the vision of a monolithic and overpowering American stake in Mexico.

The U.S. diplomatic mission, which includes the embassy in Mexico City and eight consulates, is the largest in the world. The embassy itself, with approximately six hundred employees, of which half are Mexican support personnel, is about the same size as the other two largest American diplomatic posts, London and Manila. In addition, the United States operates four general consulates, located in Guadalajara, Monterrey, Ciudad Juárez, and Tijuana, with a staff of between thirty-five and forty, of whom about fifteen are American. There are four smaller U.S. consulates, in Mérida, Mazatlán, Matamoros, and Hermosillo. These lesser missions, normally staffed by four or five U.S. officials and an equal number of Mexican support employees, deal mainly with routine consular matters (passports, visas, etc.) but also serve to maintain an official U.S. presence throughout Mexico. Recently, some of the smaller consulates have begun to include a Drug Enforcement Administration official among their personnel. These American missions reproduce—on a smaller scale, of course—the relationship the embassy in the capital has with the local American community: the business sector, retirees, artists, journalists. Indeed, the close ties existing in Mexico City become even tighter in smaller cities, where there are fewer Americans, who consequently seek each other out more often. The American consul in Mérida, Yucatán, for example, is perhaps more important for the local American colony than the U.S. ambassador is for the more than 100,000 American residents of Mexico City.

The embassy in Mexico City not only differs in size from other American diplomatic missions in the world. Up to twenty departments, services, or agencies have representatives in the marble compound on Paseo de la Reforma, more than at any other U.S. diplomatic mission in the world. In addition to the State Department, these include: the Department of Agriculture, the Internal Revenue Service, the Immigration and Naturalization Service, the Customs Service, the Drug Enforcement Administration, the Department of Commerce, the United States Information Agency (USIA), the Agency for International Development (AID), the Department of the Treasury, the United States Travel Service, the Graves Registration Service (which attends to the graves of Americans buried in Mexico), the Department of Defense, the Department of Justice (generally but not always FBI agents), the CIA, the Social Security Administration, and the Bureau of Alcohol, Tobacco, and Firearms.[3]

Needless to say, no other country has a similar diplomatic presence in Mexico. No wonder then, given the sprawling American economic presence and influence in Mexico and the more than one hundred accredited American foreign correspondents, that Mexicans should tend to associate these three sectors, viewing them as separate but united parts of a whole. It is not surprising either that theories of intervention and destabilization should come to mind when those sectors appear to be working in unison.

Recent events illustrate both the coincidences (which have been called uncanny) that do occur and the Mexican reaction to what inevitably appears as a hidden agenda of American interventionism. The synchronization of events is undoubtedly more relevant in explaining the Mexican vision of a monolithic U.S. influence in Mexico than for understanding American purposes. Indeed, more than the actual evidence—which is not always there—of U.S. intervention and its motives, goals, and strategy, it is often the existence of too many signs all pointing in the same direction which convinces Mexicans that the United States is once again intervening in their country's affairs. Indirect American actions persuade Mexico that the United States is after something, and this conviction often precedes the actual knowledge of what, if anything, the United States seeks.

The problem is that the same facts can fit together in different interpretations. There was, and still is, no evidence of a recent conspiracy to destabilize Mexico: no congressional investigation has delved into the matter, no revelations have been made. But it is difficult to discard out of hand, simply on the basis of logic and deduction, the possibility of some sort of hidden agenda, at least not by the highest echelons of the Reagan administration. It seems clear that the President himself and the State Department were not party to any "Mexican conspiracy."

But simple pressure in one country often appears as a campaign in another. More important, the freewheeling nature of the Reagan administration made it far from impossible for lower-level officials to formulate and implement policies without their superiors' knowledge or acquiescence. Later, the upper echelons find out, and the fallout is limited. But in the meantime, the damage is done. The description that follows should be seen in this light.

In May 1984, President Miguel de la Madrid made his first state visit to Washington. He had met previously with Ronald Reagan on two occasions: as President-elect in Tijuana–San Diego in 1982 and as President in La Paz, Baja California, in August 1983. But a certain symbolism is always involved in a Mexican head of state's first trip to the U.S. capital, and De la Madrid's team, as well as the President himself, had many reasons for wanting things to come out letter-perfect. The new President had not been able to shake the perception within the Mexican business community that the country's problems—a massive foreign debt, an economy in full recession, a discredited political system—derived partly from the government's close ties with Nicaragua and Cuba and its constant conflicts with the United States over Central America. The view was mainly held with regard to José López Portillo, De la Madrid's predecessor; yet even the new administration, despite significant changes in Mexico's Central American policy during its first year and a half in office, suffered from this interpretation. Hence, it was of the utmost importance to show the country that without caving in to the United States on Central America or other matters, Mexico was no longer picking fights with Ronald Reagan over Nicaragua and no longer suffering the consequences of poor relations with Washington.

But instead, the state visit, as well as the seemingly endless month of May, turned into a nightmare which would mark De la Madrid's entire presidency. Everything that could have gone wrong did, and the dramatic chain of events turned into the worst possible scenario for De la Madrid: the archetypal image of a U.S.-sponsored destabilization campaign against Mexico in general and the Mexican presidency in particular.

To begin with, the substantively insignificant but highly sensitive protocol aspects of De la Madrid's visit got off to a rocky start and never recovered—a sinister omen for a country and a presidency so attentive to perceptions, dignity, and the trappings of power. Rather than being received by Ronald Reagan at Andrews Air Force Base (a practice that had been discontinued long before but which the Mexican people still expected) or by Secretary of State George Shultz (as should have been the case for a state visit), De la Madrid was met by the State Department's number two man, Kenneth Dam, a rather low-level official in the view of Mexican public opinion. De la Madrid's problems with protocol did not end there. When he addressed a joint session of Congress, the President of the Senate's seat was empty: Vice President George Bush was in India.

In Mexico, as nearly everywhere else in the world, the treatment a country's leader receives abroad is considered a reflection of that country's standing; a slur, even a minor one, becomes an affair of state because it reflects on the country itself. The slights received by De la Madrid in Washington put him in a no-win situation: either the insults were deliberate and relations with the United States were thus far from friendly (sometimes a good thing in Mexican politics, but not what De la Madrid wanted to prove on that trip) or the snubs were mere coincidence. But this explanation only made things worse: if it just happened that Secretary Shultz was out of town or too busy to welcome De la Madrid off the plane, if Vice President Bush just happened to be traveling abroad, what kind of respect did Mexico and its leader command, if they were not able to ensure that coincidences of this sort not occur during a state visit to Washington?

In fact, what tinted these ultimately unimportant events in the dark hues of conspiracy were several other simultaneous, more substantive considerations. First and foremost was journalist Jack Anderson's column in the Washington *Post* the day before De la Madrid's arrival, accusing the President of having "stashed away" $162 million in a Swiss bank account. Building on the widespread belief that previous Mexican chiefs of state had illegitimately enriched themselves during their time in office, Anderson's charge, leaked, according to him, by administration officials and based on purported intelligence documents he was supposedly allowed to read, dealt a devastating blow to De la Madrid's credibility. Not necessarily in Washington, but mainly in Mexico, where whatever is published by the foreign press on our country and its leaders is almost automatically deemed true, and where such fine distinctions as the difference between a syndicated column and the editors of a newspaper which publishes it are not exactly germane to public debate. The fact that De la Madrid's associates back home proceeded to confiscate copies of that day's *Post* did not improve matters: photostats of Anderson's column circulated throughout Mexico City's government offices and residential neighborhoods. Days later, in any case, the critical weekly *Proceso* published it.

Few in a position to know believed the accusation, but public opinion probably did. Most knowledgeable Mexicans were familiar and comfortable with De la Madrid's reputation for personal integrity, and whatever his other drawbacks, doubted that he would so recklessly endanger his presidency. What troubled the Mexican political establishment was the article itself, and its source: why did someone in the Reagan administration with sufficient standing to plant evidence or with access to documents which could bestow credibility on the accusation make one or the other available to Anderson? In addition, when the Mexican presidential spokesman made an undignified demand for a certificate of good behavior from the U.S. government, all he received was a relatively noncommittal statement attributed to the Mexican desk officer at the State Department declaring that to the best of "its knowledge" Miguel de la Madrid was an honorable man. Did the leaks and innuendos represent U.S. policy toward Mexico, or did Reagan's *abrazos* and smiles constitute a truer reflection? Or both? Was this part of the same policy which led to the perceived breaches of protocol, or was it entirely coincidental?

There were several circumstantial reasons for believing that differences between Mexico and the United States on Nicaragua lay behind the incidents. Just before the visit, *Newsweek* had reported on a National Security Council document attributed to Constantine Menges, the senior NSC official in charge of Latin America, calling for increased American pressure on Mexico to change its Central American policy.[4] It was almost beside the point, from the Mexican perspective, that the proposal had finally been rejected by President Reagan and that it had probably been leaked by its detractors, rather than by its advocates.

Reagan's welcoming speech for De la Madrid on the White House lawn on May 15 was of greater relevance. Instead of stressing the positive aspects of the U.S.-Mexican relationship and the agreement between the two nations on several bilateral issues, the American President emphasized their differences on Central America. *The New York Times*'s front-page headline was symptomatic: "Blunt Talk Marks Reagan's Welcome for Mexico's Chief: Central America Is Issue."[5] Ronald Reagan stated his views on Nicaragua, Cuba, and other regional matters with his customary outspokenness and without the least consideration for Mexico's positions or sensitivities. This was later compensated for when Reagan agreed to De la Madrid's request to begin at least pro forma negotiations with the Sandinistas. But this would not become known for several weeks; in the meantime, the image of Reagan browbeating De la Madrid became engraved in many of his countrymen's minds. Some would also recall proudly how De la Madrid stood his ground, refusing to back down; but others, particularly within the private sector, would conclude—not without reason—that once again Mexico's relations with the United States had soured due to the government's siding with the Sandinistas. Never mind that De la Madrid had wanted to convey the opposite impression.

In addition to events in Washington, which all pointed in the wrong direction, the situation in Mexico was far from comforting to the Mexican leadership. On May Day, in addition to a Molotov cocktail thrown at the presidential balcony from the crowd below during the traditional parade, a serious incident had taken place on the border with Mexico's southern neighbor. A large contingent of Guatemalan army troops had penetrated deep into Mexican territory and openly attacked a refugee camp. Six refugees who had fled the Guatemalan highlands in fear of the army's terror were murdered at El Chupadero.

To make matters worse, since the beginning of the fateful month of May, there had been a violent run on the peso, which had lost one-quarter of its value in a few weeks. Mexico's urban middle classes always purchased dollars each time the future looked doubtful; on this occasion, the speculation against the currency was attributed to political uncertainty stemming from difficulties with the United States. The rumors about such difficulties were in turn fed by the plunging devaluation of the peso and De la Madrid's tribulations in Washington. But the lack of sound economic grounds for the drop in the peso's value led many to believe that the run on the national currency was anything but economically motivated, and was simply another facet of the apparent campaign against Mexico. This campaign was increasingly perceived as being orchestrated from Washington, with the concurrent financial implementation in Mexico placed in the hands of U.S. corporations and bank representatives, only too happy to quench the business community's gargantuan thirst for dollars.

The last shoe dropped on May 30 as evening descended on Mexico City. Manuel Buendía, the country's foremost journalist, whose daily column on the front page of *Excelsior*, Mexico's leading daily, was required breakfast reading for every politician, businessman, foreign diplomat, and journalist in Mexico, was shot and killed while leaving his downtown office. In a country where credit for most things which function or come out well is rightly claimed by the government, blame for disasters, man-made or natural, is squarely placed on the same government and the murder was no exception. His assassination is still unsolved, and the De la Madrid administration is still held responsible, if not for the murder, at least for not having brought its perpetrators to justice. Suspicions that the United States and in particular the CIA were involved were voiced minutes after the news of Buendía's murder, since he had frequently denounced CIA activities in Mexico and had published the names of several presumed agents and station chiefs. The U.S. embassy denied that it had anything to do with the journalist's death, despite the fact "that he was no friend of the U.S."

De la Madrid's presence at Buendía's wake lent solemnity to the occasion, and showed the government's sympathy for the journalist's widow and son, but also underscored the serious blow to the administration. And few Mexicans believed the United States had little to do with the country's springtime travail. As Héctor Aguilar Camín, the editor of *Nexos,* Mexico's leading monthly, and one of the country's most respected intellectuals, said in a widely praised essay: "Whoever Buendía's assassins may have been, the perception of troubled waters accelerated or defined matters and gave Buendía's death an extreme political connotation as part of a logic of conspiracy and destabilization which equally threatens Mexico's inert society and its immobile government."[6]

Indeed, this was a textbook case of a conspiracy theory fitting the available "evidence" perfectly, *if* one had the slightest bent for such constructions. True, each event could be individually interpreted, and the ensuing multiple, isolated, and adequate explanations could be easily accepted. In this light, the protocol mishaps were either figments of oversensitive Mexican imagination or coincidences or both. The Jack Anderson column could simply be the product of intelligence community and/or right-wing mischief with no policy implications whatsoever. The run on the peso could be interpreted as a result of overvaluation and nervousness on the part of Mexican businessmen who doubted the government's commitment to a full-fledged modernization of the economy. And Manuel Buendía's murder could easily be seen as an internal matter which just happened to have occurred at the same time as the other events. More important, the very idea of a centrally orchestrated destabilization campaign against Mexico by the government of the United States was not supported by any direct evidence and apparently made no sense.

The argument against a conspiracy was simple enough. Washington had always known that its paramount interest in Mexico was the country's stability, and the best guardian of that stability had historically been the existing political system, founded in the early 1930s. There was no alternative to that system, and in spite of the country's growing economic difficulties, little reason for the United States to tinker with mechanisms which had proved their worth over the years. Central America was sufficient cause for zealots and undercover agents to act out their fantasies, but not for undertaking a government-wide, concerted, multifaceted policy of destabilization.

But if looked at from the other side, the view of the American monolith lumbering into conspiratorial action was not farfetched. There was a motive: Central American and Nicaraguan policy, and a general (conservative) ideological dissatisfaction in Washington with the way Mexico was being governed. There was a purpose: to weaken the key institution in the Mexican political system by showing that the United States no longer considered President De la Madrid an exclusive and trustworthy interlocutor. Each American sector had its work assigned to it and performed to perfection: the press by slandering the Mexican President; the U.S. government by snubbing him and making the disagreements between the two nations explicit; finally, the American business sector in Mexico by contributing to or leading a speculative attack on the peso, with the dramatic effects that a devaluation of the currency has in Mexico.

Was this a realistic assumption or merely another instance of Mexican official paranoia and penchant for conspiracy theories? To a large extent, the "factual" answer is less relevant than the conditions leading to the presumption that there was a conspiracy afoot and that the United States was, once again, intervening in a deliberate fashion in Mexican affairs to further its own interests. Retrospectively, of course, given what we now know about Oliver North's activities and CIA Director William Casey's obsession with Mexico, the idea of a scheme to destabilize Mexico, run from the National Security Council, because Mexico did not support U.S. policy in Nicaragua is not inconceivable, especially with the hindsight provided by the Iran-contra affair.[7] Nor is it implausible that the initial steps of such an unauthorized enterprise were put in motion before the whole strategy was wiped off the drawing boards by higher and more responsible officials. While the prevailing view in Mexico was perhaps more simplistic and less nuanced, seeing obvious U.S.-wide conspiracies, Mexican officials and intellectuals had valid motives for perceiving a concerted and centrally planned offensive against the country's policies both at home and abroad. It *did* appear that the many faces of the U.S. presence in Mexico were simply the proverbial heads of the hydra.

Nor was this the first time Mexico had received striking confirmation of its views of the American behemoth: coordinated, multifaceted, and duplicitous. But in a country where almost half the population is under fifteen years of age, starting history over from scratch is a daily chore. Most Mexicans were not directly affected by this episode, other than to see corroboration that the United States and Mexico did not get along well. But many young or inexperienced officials in President De la Madrid's entourage learned that nationalistic, chip-on-the-shoulder intransigence in dealings with Mexico's northern neighbor was not an obsolete political heirloom. For years it had been Mexico's only effective strategy in an uneven struggle.

Other coincidences in later years have strengthened the worst fears of many Mexicans. In October 1986, for example, when a spate of news and events inimical to Mexican interests surfaced in the United States, few in Mexico doubted that the country's neighbor was up to its old tricks again. Two major American dailies, *The New York Times* and the Chicago *Tribune,* simultaneously ran week-long, front-page, highly critical series on Mexico. In a two-week period, the U.S. Congress passed three laws with immediate negative consequences for Mexico: the Simpson-Rodino Immigration Act, which affected Mexico more than any other country and which had languished for years in Congress; the Superfund eleven-cent oil-import fee, which affected exports of Mexican oil to the United States; and last, a congressional resolution attached to the 1986 Drug Bill, naming Mexico as a "drug-negligent" nation.

Denunciations of campaigns against Mexico flooded the Mexican press and erupted from the political establishment. President De la Madrid's administration felt compelled to draft and make public a number of official protests to the Reagan administration, the Congress, and even *The New York Times.* Again, the important point was not so much the reality of American intervention, which as before was arguable and indecipherable in regard to its motives and purposes. The key issue was the perception in Mexico that disparate and normally conflicting circles in the United States were acting in a united and highly effective fashion against Mexican interests. The De la Madrid government had little choice but to react in the intransigent and perhaps oversensitive manner in which it did, particularly in view of the fact that Ronald Reagan had been informed of the difficulties Mexico was going through and should have been more sensitive to them.

Mexico's constant preoccupation with U.S. intervention in the country's internal affairs must be seen as a form of marginal damage control. The disproportionate weight and import of American economic, cultural, and political involvement in Mexico is such an apparent mainstay of Mexican life, over which the country, its leaders, and its population have so little discernible sway, that the only possible policy or attitude becomes protest and intransigence at the margins. Precisely because only new or seemingly secondary aspects of American involvement appear to be potentially changeable or restrainable by Mexican action, those are the areas which the political debate on U.S. interference tends to center on.

When an American ambassador queried a Mexican cabinet minister about the possibility of the battleship *Iowa* docking at the port of Vera-cruz, with the resulting hundreds of marines and sailors on shore leave, the answer he got was similar to the warnings on some New York City parking signs: "Don't even think of asking." Yet at the same time Mexico has granted U.S.-dominated international financial institutions—the International Monetary Fund or the World Bank—oversight over its economy in ways which many other countries have deemed unacceptable. Foreign observers are often struck by the superficially incongruous stances of Mexican officials: protesting or inflaming public opinion about minor expressions of U.S. presence in Mexico, such as McDonald's franchises, in contrast to silence on issues of much greater significance, such as cooperation between Mexican and American intelligence forces, Drug Enforcement Administration agents illegally bearing arms in Mexico, the share of Mexico's foreign trade held by the United States (over 70 percent), or millions of border inhabitants depending on the "other side" for everything from milk to health care.

The key to the contradiction lies in a certain economy of effort regarding contention, protest, and conflict between the two nations. Regardless of the leeway that Mexico may have, and which it often underestimates, in managing its overall relationship with the United States, maneuvering room is narrow with respect to many of the basic structural features of the bilateral ties. There is very little that Mexico can realistically do in the short run and at a reasonable cost about the magnitude of its American economic links; there is nothing that Mexico can do about the border. But a great deal can be achieved at the margins, in both substance and style. Mexico can have a relatively autonomous foreign policy, it can maintain its dignity and independence by stressing atmospherics and symbols, and it can arrest *new* trends of American intrusion in its domestic matters. Mexico can seldom usually do very much about major issues, but it can achieve results by creating a serious commotion about less important, though not meaningless, questions.

Furthermore, intransigence whenever and wherever possible is not simply the only available policy; it is also the one which sends the clearest signals to all concerned. The United States becomes aware that if it transgresses or attempts to unilaterally modify traditional norms of what is and is not acceptable, Mexico will do everything it can—protests, more or less spontaneous outpourings of nationalistic outrage, difficulties in day-to-day relations—to obstruct the U.S. intent. Likewise, domestic Mexican groups and factions stand duly forewarned that violation of the demand for unity implies a cost: being branded a "traitor to the fatherland," exclusion from traditional cooptation mechanisms and government favors, banishment from the political mainstream.

Another factor argues in favor of this unwillingness to compromise. There is a traditional belief in Mexico that anything less than this unyieldingness will open the floodgates to an unending flow of American demands and interference, as well as to unfettered competition among rival Mexican factions for U.S. backing. If Mexico gives in on a minor issue, it will soon be pressured on new and more important ones. Similarly, if Mexico legitimizes some forms of "American intervention" as opposed to others which remain out of bounds, soon pressures would arise for the latter to be assimilated to the former.

In support of this, students of U.S.-Mexican relations point to the sad and frustrating paradox whereby the De la Madrid administration, by all standards the least anti-American, most conservative Mexican government in years, which included among its high-level officials the greatest number with links to the United States, is also the team which has suffered the worst relations with the United States in recent memory. There is obviously no direct, necessary link between the two facts; undoubtedly the circumstance of a highly conservative, ideologically committed administration in Washington, together with the deepening of the Mexican crisis, explains much of the deterioration in the two countries' relations. But the suspicion remains that some of Mexico's problems with the United States during the mid-1980s had to do with a willingness on the part of the De la Madrid administration to be accommodating.

Nationalistic intransigence on the margins with regard to American intervention is a policy that has served Mexico well, whether in dealing with Washington or with the ever-present temptation on the part of internal political forces to seek backing north of the border. This policy has always had its drawbacks, but these were generally manageable and minor. More recently they have become more noticeable; there is reason to believe that in the coming years the disadvantages will make the policy more unwieldy, and perhaps even unworkable. Widening domestic political competition and greater attention to Mexico in the United States are contributing to this process.

A case in point: the hearings on Mexico held by a Senate subcommittee on Western Hemisphere affairs in May and June of 1986 at the initiative and under the chairmanship of Senator Jesse Helms. The outcry in Mexico was deafening, and nearly unanimous: the government, the left, the right, the intelligentsia, and the business sector all decried the hearings themselves as well as statements made during the Senate sessions on the internal situation in Mexico. A midsize demonstration in Mexico City brought members of the PRI and the left under the same banner in public for the first time in years. In the United States, friends of Mexico and critics of the Reagan administration protested and lamented the damage to U.S.-Mexican relations which would result from Helms's "Mexico-bashing" antics.

In Mexico, though, the thrust of the criticism was directed far more at the hearings' "interventionist" tint than at what was actually said. The government's official statements stressed the illegitimacy per se of the U.S. Senate's deliberating on Mexico's internal matters.[8] Critics again suggested a hidden agenda and dubious motives on the part of the Reagan administration itself, which tried to distance itself somewhat from the proceedings, and less conservative senators. Several officials, such as Customs Commissioner William von Raab and Assistant Secretary of State for Inter-American Affairs Elliott Abrams, had used the Helms hearings to publicly air their views on Mexico.

Opinion in Mexico seemed to support its government's stance. A poll published in *Excelsior* showed that when asked whether the Senate hearings "constituted American intervention in Mexico's internal affairs," 84 percent said yes, while only 15 percent replied negatively. When queried as to the purpose of the Senate deliberations, 86 percent responded that the aim "was to subjugate the government of Mexico even more to the interests of the government of the United States." To a similar question with different replies to choose from, 26 percent answered that the hearings' goal was to "bring about changes in the Mexican government"; 31 percent thought the aim was to "modify the Mexican political system."[9]

Yet to the same extent that Helms's attempts to poison binational ties were a caricature of the worsening of Mexico's image in the United States during the previous year, our "anti-interventionist" reaction was somewhat quixotic. Precisely because real American intervention in Mexican affairs had been such a serious matter in the past, and continued to be so in the present, the question arose whether the facile equating of any American activity with "intervention" was not weakening Mexico's own brief against more serious interventions.

Indeed, it was increasingly difficult to reconcile Mexico's growing and largely fulfilled ambition to play a greater role in the world with its dramatic reluctance to be looked at or critically analyzed by foreign eyes or institutions. Granted, the authorities and most nationalist sectors of public opinion had emphatically repeated that their objection was not to foreigners delving into "private Mexican affairs," but to the fact that it was the U.S. Senate, an organ of the U.S. government, that was sitting in judgment on the country and its leaders. But the tone of the reaction, its modalities, and its thrust were so similar to reactions to other highly publicized foreign attempts to examine Mexican phenomena that the coincidence was too great to go unnoticed. Many foreigners sympathetic to Mexico's concerns and distraught over the anti-Mexican insults and latent racism present in many of Senator Helms's tirades felt that, at heart, what Mexicans were questioning was the right and ability of any non-Mexican to hold opinions and to possess legitimate curiosity with regard to our country's internal workings. This began to be viewed as an archaic and unreal attitude, incompatible with Mexico's growing stature in the world.

It appeared more and more likely that the traditional and well-grounded Mexican fear of U.S. intervention was increasingly at odds with Mexico's new role in the world and that it was being fanned by national authorities for other purposes. This was in fact the case; the Mexican government could point to a new textbook illustration of American intervention in Mexico's political affairs. This time the vehicle was U.S. congressional opinions and "concern" over the situation in Mexico, as well as the behavior of the American press.

As indicated earlier, political developments in the country's northern states had become a highly charged issue for the Mexican leadership. The reasons were easy to understand. The conservative opposition was gaining ground in the most politically sensitive region of the country. The north was the cradle of the Revolution, but was also the area of Mexico with the closest ties to the United States. It was more developed, urban, educated, and dynamic than the rest of the nation. This was where the traditional political system's growing obsolescence was most flagrant, and where the increasingly nationwide clamor for democratization was being formulated most articulately and forcefully. Hence Miguel de la Madrid's government inevitably frowned on the opposition led by the PAN in the north and had to be frankly terrified by any trace of American interference in regional politics. The fact that the government would use the perceived threat of U.S. meddling as an instrument for blunting charges and the reality of widespread electoral fraud in Coahuila (in late 1984), Sonora and Nuevo León (in mid-1985), and Chihuahua (in mid-1986) did not make that interference less dangerous. Nor did it erase the numerous hints and clues of real American involvement.

In some cases, of course, there were blatant exaggerations. In early 1985, after protesting PAN supporters and disgruntled PRI militants rioted in the border town of Frontera and in the industrial city of Monclova, both in the state of Coahuila, the local PRI bureaucracy ran a full-page paid insert in several national newspapers "protesting against the PAN invitation to the foreign press, radio, and television to intervene in national affairs,"[10] which was obviously nonsense. But there did exist a widespread belief that American groups and individuals, if not the government of the United States, were increasingly implicated in northern politics, in support of PAN candidates. Likewise, cynicism and suspicion met the American media's newfound interest in elections in states and small towns which most U.S. reporters had never heard of before, much less covered. All of this was building up through 1985 and early 1986 and came to a head with the gubernatorial elections in Chihuahua in July of that year.

In recent years the PAN had made enormous gains in the state, winning the mayoralties of the seven largest cities in the 1983 municipal elections, including Ciudad Juárez, the largest border town, across the line from El Paso, and Mexico's fifth-largest city, and Chihuahua, the state capital. The local business community, led by Eloy Vallina, the head of one of Mexico's largest industrial conglomerates, had begun to turn against the PRI and the government in 1982, when the group's bank was nationalized along with the rest of Mexico's financial institutions. The PAN candidate for governor, Ciudad Juárez mayor Francisco Barrio Terrazas, was young, charismatic, and combative, though eccentric and somewhat of a mystic. The local PRI was divided and weakened, and it looked as if the PAN could pose a serious threat to the governorship of a state for the first time in years, in any case since the Yucatán elections in 1969. The PRI had won every election for governor in the country since the 1930s.

When initial results heavily favored the official candidate, there was no dispelling the belief that widespread fraud had marred the voting. Every segment of public opinion expressed the view that the elections were fatally flawed. The local and national leaderships of Mexico's three most important left-wing political parties—the Unified Socialist Party of Mexico (PSUM), the Mexican Workers' Party (PMT), and the Revolutionary Workers' Party (PRT)—not known for their pro-PAN sympathies, all sided with the PAN in denouncing fraud and cheating. The local church, constitutionally and by tradition barred from participating in political matters, called on the faithful to boycott Sunday Mass, although eventually the Vatican forbade it from implementing this threat. Last, but certainly not least important, twenty-one public personalities, including several of Mexico's most distinguished intellectuals— writers Octavio Paz, Elena Poniatowska, and Carlos Monsiváis and painter José Luis Cuevas—issued a statement calling for new elections. Only the government of Miguel de la Madrid insisted that the PRI candidate had won cleanly.

But the specter of intervention continued to hover over the Chihuahua affair, and the authorities were able to capitalize skillfully on real instances of U.S. involvement, both tarnishing the protests and discrediting the protesters. On August 13, nearly a month after the Chihuahua vote,

De la Madrid accepted Ronald Reagan's invitation to Washington to patch things up after the Helms hearings. The day of his arrival, a conservative American group calling itself the Council for Inter-American Security, led by Francis Bouchey—with White House communications director Patrick Buchanan, ambassador to Costa Rica Lewis Tambs, and other Reagan officials on its board—paid for a full-page advertisement in the Washington *Post.* The ad reprinted the call to boycott Mass in Chihuahua and the statement of the twenty-one public personalities demanding a new vote.[11] Few things could have embarrassed De la Madrid more.

One that could have was barely averted. Several days before the Mexican President's arrival in Washington, he received implicit confirmation that his government's views of the Jesse Helms affair and congressional intrusions in Mexican affairs were not as farfetched as may have seemed. Five senators from both parties (Pete Wilson of California, Dennis DeConcini of Arizona, Phil Gramm of Texas, Paula Hawkins of Florida, and Pete Domenici of New Mexico) filed a Senate resolution urging De la Madrid to cancel the Chihuahua elections because of the reports of fraud. Here was congressional intervention at its worst: American senators not only expressing an opinion concerning a domestic Mexican issue, but pressuring the Mexican President to heed their concern. De la Madrid was able to defuse the issue and avoid a full Senate vote only by meeting with DeConcini and hearing him out on Chihuahua and other matters. But senatorial opinion had become a factor in a Mexican political equation.

Finally, during those very days, a PAN extremist was enrolling American conservative support to disrupt De la Madrid's visit and keep the pressure on the Chihuahua issue. Ricardo Villa, a former PAN congressman from the central state of Puebla, viewed by many as a zealot more than a political conservative, on the Saturday before De la Madrid arrived met at a Washington hotel with Carl "Spitz" Channel, the chairman of the American Endowment for the Preservation of Liberty. Channel, who had funded a number of pro-contra television commercials during the congressional debate on aid to the Nicaraguan counterrevolutionaries in mid-1986, and who according to press accounts had worked closely with Lieutenant Colonel Oliver North on contra fund-raising activities, had agreed to finance similar television spots against De la Madrid and the Mexican government.[12] The commercials never ran, but here again were unmistakable indications of American intrusion in Mexican political affairs.

The fact was that the thin line between American *expression of opinions* concerning Mexican matters and American *interference in those matters* was easily crossed. Whether it be the Senate, parts of the American press publishing leaks from low-level administration officials —without asking why the leaks were occurring at a particular time—or private American groups or individuals with close links to administration figures, the United States did seem to be paying more attention to and taking sides more openly in Mexican politics than it had in years. This did not diminish the validity of the opposition's charges of electoral fraud or of claims that the Mexican electoral system was rigged in favor of the PRI and the government. But the government's countercharges that there was more to elections in the north than met the eye, and that the contest was not between the PAN and the PRI but between Mexico and the United States, gained credibility because of the reality of American involvement, no matter how disperse or how trivial.

In the final analysis, Mexico has always had to cope with the reality, the threat, and the fear of U.S. intervention in its domestic affairs. First and foremost, there is the reality of U.S. interference. It has ranged from the War of 1847 to the occupation of Veracruz in 1914, from American marshals quelling riots and breaking strikes in mining areas and elsewhere in the north at the turn of the century to John Gavin's meetings with and American conservatives' sympathy for the PAN in the 1980s. This intervention is a constant of U.S.-Mexican relations, and there is little reason to hope that it will fade away or even decrease with time. Mexico is too important and the United States' interests in Mexico too large for it to resist the ever-present temptation to meddle in its internal affairs.

There is also the threat of intervention, made credible by its reality and its feasibility. Since the middle of the last century, Washington has resorted to this threat on many occasions, sometimes explicitly, sometimes with greater discretion but no less effectiveness. The United States tends to call this "legitimate retaliation," implying that the consequences of a given Mexican act would be legally and more or less automatically imposed on the U.S. government, regardless of the latter's own true wishes. This view states that if, for example, Mexico defaults on its foreign debt; if it doesn't improve its performance on drug-related matters; if it continues to vote in favor of so-called anti-U.S. resolutions at the United Nations—in a nutshell, if it acts in ways which are considered detrimental to American interests—some form of reprisal will inevitably be forthcoming. This is seen in Mexico as a threat of U.S. intervention, since its purpose lies in modifying Mexican official stances or policies in favor of Washington's interests.

Finally, there is the fear of American intervention, ever present in the

Mexican psyche, firmly grounded in a century and a half of stark reality, and often manipulated by Mexican powers that be for their own aims. The Mexican people do fear intervention, because its consequences are deeply engraved in their collective consciousness. Precisely because the fear is as pervasive as it is, the tendency to prey on it, and achieve domestic goals by invoking it, is a constant in Mexican politics. Frequently, Mexican authorities will explain their behavior by darkly implying that the alternative to their course of action was . . . American intervention. On other occasions, Mexico's leaders will insinuate that while the opposition—of the right or of the left—may ostensibly be struggling for clean elections, a freer press, or democratic labor unions, in fact it is simply the stalking horse for . . . American intervention. Few will believe the accusations, but fewer still will reject them out of hand; the consequences of being mistaken are great, and the rewards for being right are negligible.

Not every threat of American intervention becomes a reality and not all fears of interference are justified. Mexico has recurrently swung from dismissing the reality and the threat of intrusion—generally at the beginning of Mexican administrations, and certainly throughout the 1940s and 1950s—attributing both to excessive fear, to transforming every threat or fear of intervention into a looming reality. Unquestionably, Mexico has often shot from the hip and "uncovered" threats which did not exist; similarly, it has aloofly disregarded very real threats or undeniable realities of interference. Because of the high political stakes involved in distinguishing the three separate layers of fact and policy, the trap of well-intentioned confusion or the temptation of expedient deception is always present and difficult to resist. As the world and Mexico's role in it change, the only recourse for avoiding the opposite pitfalls of anachronism and self-styled "maturity" seems to lie in drawing an ever more scrupulous distinction between the reality, the threat, and the fear of American intervention in Mexico's affairs, and in giving each its true importance—not more, not less.

From the United States Looking In

Robert A. Pastor

An American tourist who stays in a hotel in the Zona Rosa of Mexico City hardly notices, but it is one of the first things that an American resident sees, and few ever adjust to it. Walls. Big, gray cinder-block walls separate houses and families, dividing the city. Lawns exist and children play in Mexico City, but mostly behind the walls.

On September 20, 1985, the day after the city was jolted by an earthquake, the Mexicans in my neighborhood went into the street to ask neighbors whether their electricity and water had also been cut off. With an American's reflex, I used the opportunity to invite some neighbors, who lived directly across the street, to our house for drinks. They accepted, and we enjoyed several hours of conversation. They had lived in the neighborhood for twelve years, but told us this was the first time they had been invited into the home of one of their neighbors.

Robert Frost captured the American unease with walls when he wrote: "Before I build a wall, I'd like to know what I was walling in or walling out." Walls can make an American claustrophobic. If one grows up with them, as Mexicans do in the capital, one takes them for granted.

Walls can protect, but they also make it difficult to know what is happening outside. You can hear footsteps from inside the walls, but you can't be sure who or what it is. The more insecure or fearful the listener, the more ominous and threatening the sounds. Shouting epithets or threats from the ramparts is one strategy for uniting the people inside and discouraging invaders, but it chases away friends and those who are neither friends nor foes. Constant vigilance also diverts attention from other problems.

When informed of the death of an eminent rival, Talleyrand, the great French statesman, was reported to have said, "I wonder what he meant by that." Soon after he arrived as ambassador to Mexico in January 1974, Joseph John Jova was struck by the similarity between the Mexican elite and the French whom they admire.[1] Both have minds that revel in conspiracies, connecting disparate facts or events, and seeing hidden meanings or a U.S. strategy where none exists. Jova was amused when he wasn't disturbed by Mexico's conspiracies because he felt the opposite problem was more serious. Instead of generating conspiracies, the U.S. government's problem was that it was chronically uncoordinated and disinterested in Mexico.

To assess whether individual actions by the U.S. government add up to a strategy, and the strategy is complemented by a conspiracy, one should start by looking at each act. The American reception of President De la Madrid in May 1984 by a low official may have been considered insulting, but the official happened to be Acting Secretary of State. Since the Secretary and the Vice President were abroad, he was actually the ranking official below the President, who does not receive state visitors at the airport. So no slight could have been intended. The Vice President did not attend De la Madrid's speech at a joint session of Congress for the same reason he was not at the airport; he was abroad. The State Department promptly denounced Jack Anderson's column about De la Madrid, and privately informed the Mexicans that it had no control over leaks or columnists, not a surprising revelation to anyone with any experience in Washington. The U.S. official noted that high officials in the Reagan administration had also been targets of Anderson's pen.

A *Newsweek* item suggested that Constantine Menges, an NSC staff member, proposed a "diplomacy master plan to convince De la Madrid and his key aides of the virtues of the Administration's fight against Communism in Central America." The article also noted that the effort was blocked successfully by the State Department and U.S. Ambassador John Gavin. Menges later explained that he was trying to encourage the State Department to make its case on Central America more often and publicly in Mexico, and that the leak to *Newsweek* was State's attempt to isolate him. It succeeded. He tried to persuade the National Security

Adviser and the President to instruct the Secretary of State to implement the directive, but neither would do it.[2]

The list could go on, but since none of these alleged acts of mischief or destabilization seems to hold up, it would be illogical to connect them into a U.S. conspiracy. Every U.S. ambassador has had to cope with Mexican conspiracy theories. Ambassador Charles Pilliod acknowledged that he was "a little puzzled" with this penchant when he first arrived in 1986.[3] Originally, he thought it was a lack of knowledge, but he soon concluded: "It is not a lack of knowledge or information; it is an ignoring of reality. . . . There is a block."

Although not responsible for these Mexican headaches, the United States did become involved in several of them as a consequence of Mexico's cry of pain and anger or call for help. The nature of that involvement, which was not always helpful, is worth examining because it sheds some light on the relationship.

The State Department, whose mission is to maintain good relations with other governments, is sometimes overly sensitive to Mexico's sensitivities. Prior to De la Madrid's arrival in Washington in May 1984, it prepared a list of all of those leaders who had been met at the airport by the Deputy Secretary of State, including the British and West German Prime Ministers. However, neither the list nor the fact that no other government would need to be consoled in such a manner mollified Mexico.

Given the very different policies of the two governments toward Nicaragua, one would have expected a tough public exchange. Ronald Reagan's statement is remarkable, however, only for its gentlemanliness. "We welcome you," Reagan said, "with the respect and admiration due to the leader of a great nation. We welcome you with the warmth and goodwill with which one greets a friend." Reagan brimmed with compliments of De la Madrid and his policies, including Mexico's participation in the Contadora Initiative. He even said that the two leaders shared the same goals in Central America, although "we do disagree . . . on the means by which to achieve our goals."[4]

A second case had an ironic twist. The controversy involving Ambassador John Gavin and the opposition began in April 1983 when Mexico City newspapers reported his dinner with PAN leaders and the archbishop in Sonora. If the Mexican government had really been upset by the news, it probably would not have been reported, particularly because the meeting did not happen. The U.S. consular officer hosted the dinner as part of his routine responsibilities to meet with political and business leaders associated with the government and the opposition; Gavin was not even in the country at the time. The story of "Gavin's dinner" was covered widely because the PRI wanted to use it to discredit the PAN for conspiring with the U.S. ambassador. The report also produced an unexpected dividend.

John Gavin viewed one of his ambassadorial missions as trying to create a "mature" relationship between the two nations. This was not possible, in his view, until a group in the PRI stopped using the United States as "a whipping boy and a scapegoat."[5] He therefore responded to virtually every charge against the United States or himself in the newspapers or by government officials. This not only placed him in an adversarial position with the Mexican media on important issues, but it also involved him in many petty disputes that a more sophisticated envoy would have ignored.

According to two of his aides, he was enraged when the newspapers criticized his meeting with PAN officials, and told them: "The PRI aren't going to tell me who to meet with. They're not going to use me as a foil." Characteristically, Gavin did not fall into the PRI's trap; he leaped into it with enthusiasm. He arranged a dinner with various party representatives in Sonora in August 1984. The PRI representatives first accepted, and then did not attend, leaving him to meet alone with the PAN. The real message of his dinner, however, was not that the United States was conspiring with the PAN, but that the PRI wanted it to appear that this was happening. The ambassador, once again, proved the unwitting accomplice.

Behind Mexico's preoccupation with U.S. intervention lies history, but also the contemporary U.S. presence in Mexico, which is sizable and visible. The products and culture produced by American transnational corporations are disseminated worldwide. Advertising, which is ubiquitous in non-Communist countries, standardizes and connects consumer habits, and the billboards attracting people to Coca-Cola, Big Macs, and the Pizza Hut are evident in Mexico. But there are grounds for asking whether the U.S. economic, cultural, or official presence in Mexico is overwhelming, united, or single-minded, and whether Mexico is exceptional.

U.S. investment in Mexico has grown from $414 million in 1950 to $9.6 billion in 1986.[6] However, the country's share of total foreign investment has declined steadily from nearly 75 percent in 1950 to 69 percent in 1975 to 60 percent in 1986. While Mexico's external debt mushroomed, the U.S. portion remained about one-quarter. In 1986, U.S. direct investment in Mexico amounted to 5 percent of Mexico's gross domestic product, which is comparable to the weight of foreign direct investment in the United States ($209 billion or 5 percent of the U.S. gross national product). In brief, the overall American economic presence in Mexico has grown in size during the last thirty years, but it has shrunk in relationship to the growth of other foreign investments and remained trivial in relationship to the whole of Mexico's economy.

Even as U.S. investment increased, the percentage of its citizens working for American corporations in Mexico declined by two-thirds between 1960 and 1977. By 1977, only half of one percent of all technical and professional staff and 5.5 percent of all managerial staff in U.S. corporations in Mexico were Americans.[7]

The size of this economic presence is insignificant when compared with Canada. In 1970, Canada had less than one-half of Mexico's population but twelve times as much U.S. investment. In 1983, Mexico had three times the population of Canada, but $7.6 billion of U.S. investment compared with Canada's $44 billion. As a percentage of Canada's gross domestic product, U.S. investment then amounted to roughly 15 percent, or three times what it is in Mexico. Canadians worry about the size and power of the American presence, but their debates on whether to limit integration are much less intense and of a wholly different character than the vitriol that stains the subject in Mexico. Part of the difference in the two countries' fears of U.S. intervention may be explained by culture and history.

The official U.S. presence is larger in Mexico than in any other country, but that fact—like the proverbial footsteps—could be interpreted in different ways. One could view the size of the embassy as an ominous sign of dominance, or as a recognition of the complexity of the relationship, or as an indication that the United States takes its relationship with Mexico seriously. Most domestic departments—for example, Agriculture, Labor, and Justice—are represented in the embassy because relations with Mexico sit at the intersection between domestic and international issues, and that is where "accidents" sometimes occur. One could also interpret the official presence as serving some of Mexico's interests too, as the largest proportion of U.S. officials are responsible for immigration and consular matters. This is particularly true of the consulates, which also help provide assistance and information to American tourists, an increasingly important source of foreign exchange for Mexico.

Americans living abroad are a diverse lot. The pensioners and some businessmen tend to live in American "ghettos," relating more to other Americans than to Mexicans. Students, researchers, consultants, and many businessmen mix more. To varying degrees, all are purveyors of an American consumer culture, but here again, their influence is insignificant compared with that of television, newspaper advertising, and Mexican migrants.

It is hard to envisage the "American presence" as a single-minded juggernaut intent on taking advantage of Mexico. The pensioners are mostly interested in living as well and as peaceably as they can on their social security checks. Students are there to learn; businessmen, to earn. Some dislike their stay, but many more enjoy living in Mexico.

American newspaper reporters generally adopt an adversarial approach in their coverage of governments. Whether they use this mind-set against the Mexican government or against U.S. policy toward Mexico depends partly on which government feeds them more and better information, who they are, and what their home editors want. It is almost impossible to discern a single perspective among the numerous correspondents who represent American publications that range across the political spectrum. Moreover, the competition among the reporters also tends to cancel out any particular bias.

Whether one judges the U.S. presence as large or small relative to the Mexican state and economy, one still needs to distinguish *presence* from *influence.* Rather than try to influence the Mexican government, most Americans try to stay out of its way.

Successful businessmen understand that they need to relate to the Mexican government like a Mexican rather than an American, only they should be even more indirect and subtle because the Mexican government's power to create problems for them is awesome and arbitrary. Businessmen all over the world try to find ways to avoid paying taxes or being regulated by government, but the skills needed in Mexico are considerable. To obtain a favorable decision on a major investment or a change in operations, businessmen often have to spend several months—sometimes years—working their way up to the top of the government, where the President himself often decides.

Most U.S. businesses are members of the American Chamber of Commerce, which raises general issues of policy through its contacts with Mexican business associations. The Chamber is also an aggressive opponent of U.S. protectionism. In September 1987, it sent a letter to 213 members of Congress arguing against provisions of the trade bill that could hurt Mexico's—and its members' own—exports to the United States. One of the Chamber's arguments was that "Mexico's economic health is crucial to overall U.S. interests."[8] In Mexico, however, American businessmen rarely try to influence general trade, tax, or investment matters because they know that that is unacceptable and that general policies are less important in Mexico than the way they are implemented.

Americans who live and work in Mexico City for any length of time have read the handwriting on the walls: be discreet; don't interfere or even think about it. Until the early 1980s, when the American Roger Toll became editor of Mexico's English-language daily newspaper, the *News* was a collage of wire service reports and tourist tidbits. Toll gradually made the paper respectable and even started probing the edges of the politically permissible. Those boundaries, which are respected by Mexican journalists, but harder for Americans to accept, were delineated for him in 1986, and the next year for his successor, Pete Hamill, by Romulo O'Farrill, the Mexican newspaper owner. Both Toll and Hamill trespassed, and both lost their jobs.

In general, the American community in Mexico is diffuse and, as a group, as deferential as Americans can be, which admittedly may still be quite aggressive as compared with most Mexicans. This does not mean that American residents lack influence, but the more astute members of the community understand that resorting to the U.S. government to influence Mexico is like using a boomerang, not a lever.

The relationship between U.S. businesses in Mexico and Washington has changed definitively during the twentieth century. Until Franklin Roosevelt's Good Neighbor Policy, the U.S. government staunchly defended its business interests in Mexico, although there were some exceptions to this rule. Woodrow Wilson angrily criticized U.S. businessmen who tried to use his administration to stop Mexico's revolution and retrieve their profits: "There are those who wish to possess Mexico, who wish to use her, who regard her people with condescension and a touch of contempt, who believe they are fit only to serve and not fit for liberty of any sort. Such men cannot and will not determine the policy of the United States."[9]

The watershed event that altered the three-sided relationship among the two governments and U.S. business was the nationalization of the petroleum industry in 1938. Washington was divided as to the appropriate response, but it was divided even further from the oil companies. During the negotiations, the companies were usually furious with Washington's position, which reflected a combination of Josephus Daniels's sensitivity to Mexico's revolution and Roosevelt's recognition of the strategic importance of a friendly frontier as World War II approached.[10]

As U.S. investments shifted after the war from the extractive industries into manufacturing, American businessmen became more flexible and adapted to Mexico's rules. In the increasingly important auto industry, for example, most corporate executives resident in Mexico wanted to keep their government out of the issues they considered important. In the end, Mexico was able to impose first its import-substitution policy and later its export-promotion strategy on the American auto companies, who initially resisted but soon adapted.[11]

Today, both the U.S. government and American businessmen understand that their effectiveness often requires them to keep some distance from the other. Foreign Service officers prefer an arm's-length relationship for professional reasons. Businessmen elect not to use the U.S. government in Mexico or to confront Mexican bureaucrats, as that is an exercise in futility if not a ticket to leave. Most Americans have learned to bargain with the Mexican government, and they have deferred to Mexico's insistence that they remain independent of the U.S. embassy.

The mere bulk of the U.S. presence does exert a pervasive, indirect influence on Mexico, but more often than not, its effect is contrary to American interests. The sense that the United States is all around serves to justify the walls. Even if the weight of the United States is small in relationship to the density of the Mexican nation or as compared with the American presence in Canada, that feeling—those footsteps—keeps the Mexicans more defensive and resistant to U.S. influence than any other country.

This is not to suggest that the United States lacks clout in Mexico, or that the Mexican government does not respond to U.S. influence. It is to say that the United States is hardly monolithic; its objectives are diverse; and the Mexican perception of the size of the U.S. presence combined with the vigorous nationalism of the country actually reduces the possibilities of influence. A U.S. President would consider himself lucky to have 10 percent of the power over events in Mexico that Mexicans seem certain that he possesses.

In the natural state of international relations, governments try to persuade each other. The United States exerts influence on Mexico in pursuit of its interests, and vice versa. There are times when Mexico will concede a point, but it will almost never do so in a manner that permits the Americans to think that they have prevailed. The United States also employs this strategy to deny Mexico the feeling that it has achieved its goal. The result is that both sides remain frustrated and upset with the other even when they succeed. This is how the two governments keep the relationship neurotic.

Another tactic that the Mexican government employs to great effect is to try to prevent the United States from pursuing a sensitive issue by denouncing "intervention." No word is used so often and so imprecisely by Mexico, and the imprecision is deliberate. For example, the Mexican criticism of the Gavin dinner was not about what was said, but about the fact that it occurred, or rather that it was supposed to have occurred. Similarly, while Senator Helms and several administration officials made insensitive and sometimes unfair accusations at the Senate hearings in June 1986, the Mexican government did not protest those statements. It simply disapproved the right of Congress to hold hearings on Mexico.

Listening to Mexican charges of U.S. "intervention," one might conclude that U.S. marines land in Mexico every third year. In fact, the United States has not intervened militarily in Mexico since its revolution. Even during this turbulent period from 1910 to 1920, Mexico was hardly an innocent and passive victim of American and European intrigues. In an excellent study of the period, Friedrich Katz described it as "a case study not only of how local rifts can be exploited for global ends, but of how global rifts can be exploited for local ends."[12] Everyone—the Mexican revolutionaries and counter-revolutionaries, the Americans, Germans, British, and French—tried to use each other for their own purposes. But in the end, the Mexicans were more effective in manipulating the foreigners than the other way around. The Europeans failed utterly; and the Americans were humiliated by Pancho Villa and helpless to prevent repeated insults and injuries to their citizens. The lesson of the Mexican Revolution was that foreign intervention is often counterproductive in that it gives the opponent a potent weapon: nationalism. Since 1920, the Mexican state has acquired stability and solidity, and the United States has grudgingly accepted limits on its ability to influence Mexican policies.

Nevertheless, the Mexican government established the National Museum of Intervention in 1981 to remind its citizens that U.S. intervention is not just a historical concern. Larry Rohter of *The New York Times* reported what the visitor first encounters: "At the entrance stands Uncle Sam, his ax raised triumphantly over a prostrate Mexico. But inside . . . the tables are turned, and it is the United States that comes under unrelenting attack."[13] The charge of "intervention" today does not reflect an obsession with history; it is a political tactic to put the United States on the defensive by claiming that the United States is trying to put Mexico on the defensive.

If one reads between the lines of the reaction to Jack Anderson's column on De la Madrid's alleged corruption, one might detect a clue to solving the riddle of Mexico's contemporary antipathy. Anderson is published on the back pages of the Washington *Post* with the comic strips because his sensational columns do attract notoriety, but few Washington leaders take him seriously. His column on De la Madrid was a typical piece, citing "classified U.S. intelligence documents" indicating that the Mexican President had "amassed a multimillion-dollar fortune since he took office." It ended with a cute remark from an "insider" that the PRI's "only rule . . . is: Don't rock the trough."[14]

Washington is inundated with newspapermen making or looking for leaks in the ship of state. An astute bureaucrat or newspaper reader can usually assess the quality of the leak and the two or three buildings or institutions that are the most likely sources. To be any more specific than that—for example, to identify the leaker—is almost always a futile task, which, nonetheless, every administration undertakes, because either it was embarrassed or some genuinely important item of national security was involved.

It appears extremely unlikely that the Anderson column came from a policy source—the NSC or State—or from the CIA. It might have come from another intelligence agency or more likely some "consultant," whose information was accepted without questions because the story of "corruption in high places" is a favorite one for Anderson. The Mexicans, of course, took the article very seriously. This was partly due to the nature of the charge and the fact that De la Madrid had been trying to cultivate an image of probity distinct from his predecessors. The Anderson column was also a cultural shock, as Mexican newspapermen do not write articles critical of their President.

The State Department knew that the Mexican government would be extremely upset, and even before hearing so, the director of the Office of Mexican Affairs tried to obtain clearances from the intelligence community to issue a statement denying the allegations. In fact, the agencies did not have any credible information on corruption by De la Madrid, but they were not prepared to say that it did not exist. The statement therefore said:

> The United States government applauds De la Madrid's commitment to addressing the issue of honesty in government. All the information available to all U.S. government agencies leads us to the firm conclusion that De la Madrid has set both a high personal and official standard in keeping with this commitment.[15]

That confirmed either that Anderson's column was not based on U.S. intelligence information or that the entire intelligence community judged Anderson's information unreliable. The statement, however, was not adequate for the Mexican government.

The conspiracy charge only conceals the real answer: the Mexican leadership does not care whether the American people or the U.S. government takes Jack Anderson seriously; they care that the Mexican people do. The standard which Mexicans use to judge whether an event

has occurred or a charge is accurate is whether a U.S. newspaper publishes it. On sensitive issues, the Mexican people do not trust the polls
or the press in Mexico or, apparently, their government. The government
would prefer to blame the Americans than to acknowledge this point.

In both the United States and Mexico, the elite and the masses are driven
by contradictory impulses. In the United States, the general public is
self-preoccupied, with little interest in the world. The U.S. elite is constantly struggling against what it perceives as a popular isolationist
impulse. Policymakers often exaggerate a threat and oversell a program.
To gain congressional support for aid to Greece and the Marshall Plan,
President Harry Truman was advised to "scare hell out of the American
people," and he did just that.

Mexico's political establishment serves as commissars interpreting
U.S. policies for the general populace and trying to limit the relationship.
During the 1980s, hundreds of meetings have been sponsored and organized by U.S. foundations and research institutes to improve understanding among Americans and Mexicans. Americans who attend these events
rarely hesitate to admit their errors, and they are frustrated when the
Mexicans agree that American policies are the problem but will not
admit to Mexican mistakes. Americans are irritated when a Mexican,
invariably a representative from the PRI or the government, tries to
inhibit his or her countrymen from saying something independent, candid, or, worse, critical of Mexico.

There are more than twenty-two major centers for Latin American
studies in the United States and almost one hundred smaller centers. In
the last decade, centers specializing in Mexico or U.S.-Mexican relations
have emerged in the Southwest and have been expanded. In contrast,
Mexico had one center that specialized in U.S. studies, and that was
discontinued after a few years. It was supported by U.S. foundations and
the Mexican government, but the latter withdrew support after the center asserted its independence. Two other institutions in Mexico are trying
to establish U.S. studies centers, but their efforts have just begun.

The difference in wealth between the United States and Mexico does
not explain sufficiently the unevenness in research institutions since Mexico does devote substantial resources to its universities. Moreover, since
the United States is much more important to Mexico than vice versa, one
would expect that Mexico would study the United States more closely.
In fact, everyone in Mexico thinks about the United States somewhat,
but almost no one thinks about it systematically, whereas in the United
States there are a good number of specialists who think systematically
about Mexico, but most people do not think about Mexico at all. This

asymmetry is reflected in the countries' different views of each other. Many Americans think that problems in Mexico can be solved simply by cooperation between the two governments, whereas more sophisticated analysts understand the limits to cooperation imposed by Mexican nationalism. Mexican conspiracy theories about the United States can be maintained because of the lack of a more detailed, subtle understanding of the way the U.S. political system works.

Both nations are deeply concerned about being taken advantage of by the other. To rally the people in Mexico against domestic and foreign rivals, all the PRI needs is a small sign either that the United States is not taking Mexico seriously or that it is trying to take advantage of Mexico. From time to time, the United States unintentionally obliges with such a sign.

The United States also does not like being used by Mexico. In the 1930s, Nelson Rockefeller and his mother commissioned a mural from Diego Rivera, the famous Mexican artist. Rockefeller knew Rivera was a Communist, but he asked him in the spirit of the Good Neighbor Policy. Pleased with a Rivera drawing which depicted John D. Rockefeller as the center of world progress, he commissioned the mural. Rivera then made a few changes—for example, putting Lenin at the center of the mural instead of John D. Rockcfeller—and as one can imagine, the point of the mural changed, from an encomium of capitalism to a paean to Communism. Needless to say, this upset the Rockefellers, but the point of the story is that what really impelled them to drape and ultimately destroy the mural were the repeated reports they heard "that the Mexicans thought [Mrs. Rockefeller] had no spirit and was permitting Rivera to put something over on her."[16]

U.S. government officials also dislike the thought that Mexico might try to put something over on them. They know, as Octavio Paz has written, that Mexicans have an image of an American as "a big overgrown fellow and something of a simpleton . . . who can be fooled."[17] When a small fellow takes a swipe at a big one, as Pancho Villa did when he crossed the border into New Mexico and killed seventeen Americans, he knows that the big fellow is going to hit back. In fact, that was Villa's goal—to provoke U.S. intervention, undermine the authority of the Carranza government, and generate nationalist support for himself. President Wilson followed the script and sent General John Pershing into Mexico on a fruitless quest to capture Villa. In a message to Congress, Wilson complained that the Mexicans went "out of their way to show disregard for the dignity and rights of" Americans, and that we were "singled out . . . for slights and affronts."[18]

Today, much of the relationship is still about "face," saving it or

offending it. Communication between both governments is severely inhibited and conflict is sometimes the result of mutual fear that the other
side is seeking unfair advantage. The modus operandi for some in Mexico
is to exaggerate the negative and neglect the positive aspects of U.S.
behavior, and to be defensive and intransigent. This reflex evokes a
negative reaction from the United States, and the two nations remain
gridlocked in an unsatisfying and unproductive relationship.

A positive relationship is possible using the same reflex. Josephus
Daniels was a successful American ambassador because he exaggerated
the positive in Mexico's behavior and placed the negative features of
Mexico in their correct perspective. On the eve of World War II, he was
aware of extensive German influence in Mexico and numerous Nazi
sympathizers among the elite. But he believed that if he behaved as if the
Nazis were about to take over, support for the United States would be
dissipated. His sincerity and positivism were reciprocated by Mexico
during those difficult years, and his ability to keep the situation in perspective served both countries.

John Gavin, on the other hand, started with a good idea—to promote
a mature relationship—but he soon became mired in responding to every
Mexican accusation and charge. Inevitably, he came to exaggerate the
negative features in the relationship and lost sight of the whole.

Repeated charges of U.S. intervention might sound as if Mexico is
trying to exclude American actors, but that is less than half the picture.
In fact, the main purpose is to exclude local rivals. By accusing local
politicians of treason for collaborating with the United States, PRI leaders seek to strip away the opposition's legitimacy and contain American
influence. Nonetheless, to judge a Mexican leader by the degree of his
anti-Americanism is another way of saying that a close relationship with
the United States is not desirable.

During the 1952 presidential election in Mexico, Adolfo Ruiz Cortines
was attacked severely, though unfairly, for having "cooperated with and
aided the American naval forces that landed in Veracruz [his home state
and residence] in 1914." According to a State Department report at the
time:

This campaign had an influence on his outlook in the early stages
of his administration. He felt under the necessity of disproving that
he was pro-American working for "Yankee interests." This caused
him to lean backwards in not supporting those who were openly
friendly to the United States and undoubtedly influenced him in
putting into his Cabinet some men who are known to be hostile to
. . . American interests and private enterprise. . . . The attack had

its origin in the Foreign Office, and our point of view was not permitted to be published.[19]

The United States kept a low profile, and waited patiently for the pendulum to swing back, which it did.

Mexico's relationship with its neighbor to the south sheds the kind of light on its relationship with the United States that one sees reflected off a mirror. Adolfo Aguilar, a Mexican scholar of Guatemala, wrote that the Guatemalan people do not consider Mexico an enemy. Nevertheless, he argues, "for reasons of their own, the dominant classes of Guatemala want to view us as a threat. Faced with their lack of secular legitimacy and their isolation from the most numerous sectors of society, they have frequently attempted to gain legitimacy and support by citing supposed Mexican aggressions." Aguilar recognizes the parallel between Mexico and the United States, but dismisses it—"such parallels can be carried too far"—too quickly.[20] The stronger power is almost always incapable of understanding the fears of the weaker one, even if a nation is both.

In the summer of 1980, Mexico was experiencing its worst drought in twenty years. Crops were lost, cattle were dying, and because the reservoirs were low, power outages were frequent throughout the country. Under daily pressure to explain why the rain had stopped, the director of Mexico's National Meteorological Service was moved to suggest that American hurricane-tracking aircraft might be responsible. "The idea," according to Christopher Dickey, the Washington *Post* reporter in Mexico City, "took off like flames through dry tinder, and for three weeks, Mexican newspapers have run daily front-page headlines" attacking the United States.[21] One researcher from the university at Guadalajara described in great detail the history of hurricanes in Mexico, and concluded that the only possible explanation for the drought was "the deliberate and effective program carried out by the United States." *Excelsior* declared in its headline: "The Hurricane Hunters Are Protecting Florida's Tourism."

The political storm over this issue was based on the presence of an airplane from the National Oceanographic and Atmospheric Administration (NOAA) that was recording the temperature and velocity of the hurricanes. The suggestion that NOAA's plane had "hijacked" Mexico's rain would have been laughable, of course, if Mexico had not taken it so seriously. The U.S. embassy therefore had to deny the charges and confirm that Mexico had approved the flights.

After making the standard swipe against the United States for its "extreme insolence, cruelty, abuse," one Mexican columnist for *Razones* finally tried to sound a note of reasonableness in the chorus of attacks: "Despite everything that has gone before, we cannot keep presenting the United States as the author of every wound we suffer or every stupidity we commit." But his was a lonely voice. At a press conference, Mexico's Foreign Minister barred any further NOAA aircraft from Mexico's airfields until a full-scale investigation was completed.

So much of the U.S.-Mexican relationship is bound up in hidden meanings in barren clouds.

PART II

—

FRICTIONS

3

FACE TO FACE

The U.S. Government

Robert A. Pastor

As Director of Latin American Affairs on the National Security Council, I was exhausted after months preparing for the President's trip to Mexico. I had worked into the early-morning hours of February 6, 1979, with Rick Hertzberg, the President's speechwriter, on the draft of an address that Carter would give before the Mexican Congress. We thought we had found a way to defuse Mexico's historical suspicion of the United States by having Carter begin his speech quoting Octavio Paz, Mexico's great poet and writer.

"For more than a century, *that* country," Paz wrote of the United States, "has appeared to our eyes as a gigantic but scarcely human reality. Smiling or angry, its hand clenched or open, the United States neither sees nor hears us, but keeps striding on, and as it does, enters our land and crushes us. It is impossible to hold back a giant. It is possible, though far from easy, to make him listen to others. If he listens, this opens the possibility of coexistence."

"My friends," Carter would then say, "I have come to Mexico to listen."

Satisfied with the speech, I drove home. A few hours later, the telephone roused me from sleep.

"This is the White House Situation Room," said the voice on the other end in the staccato style in which the military are taught to speak. "The Pentagon has just sent us a report on Mexico." I was accustomed to being awakened by reports of revolution or drug-running. "Mexico" was unusual.

The Situation Room sergeant continued his report at the same methodical clip: "A U.S. marine specialist fourth class has just been apprehended in Acapulco for raping President López Portillo's daughter."

I sat up with a start and tried to catch my breath. My sleep had been interrupted by Mexico's nightmare.

The relationship between the two peoples and nations has grown in response to powerful integrationist forces within each country and between them. In contrast, the relationship between the two governments has been retarded by the weight of history and distorted by ubiquitous symbols that are interpreted to confirm each government's worst suspicions of the other. The most gruesome three symbols in the U.S.-Mexican lexicon were all combined in the report: rape, the Mexican President's daughter, a U.S. marine.

After two days and numerous cables frantically exchanged between the White House and the U.S. embassy in Mexico City, this particular report, like most of the symbolic impediments to the relationship, was found to contain a small grain of truth wrapped inside many layers of exaggeration and fabrication. An incident occurred on an Acapulco beach involving a marine and the Mexican President's daughter. However, what happened was that the marine made a pass at the President's daughter, and her bodyguard decked him, with no apologies to the marine anthem.

If this story had been reported, it would have created the kind of incident that absorbs the time and energy of high government officials and distracts them from important problems. These incidents have little to do with the real relationship but everything to do with the way it is perceived.

The report of the marine and the President's daughter neatly symbolized some of the exotic currents that swirl around the relationship between the two governments. Most Washington officials try to show Mexico that its suspicions are groundless. That was one purpose of Carter's visit in 1979, and the reason why the White House was stunned by the report of the marine. In truth, Washington's view of Mexico is characterized more by ambivalence than antagonism, more by malaise than malice.

There is no question that the United States behaves insensitively, but it can also be hypersensitive. The swing from arrogance to deference has confused both Mexicans and Americans. Why does the United States sometimes act with great sensitivity—for example, in respecting Mexico's pace for developing its oil in the 1970s—and at other times grab at Mexico's jugular—for example, when it slowed traffic on the border in 1969 and 1985? Why is the United States sometimes impervious to Mexico's concerns—for example, on Central America—and yet at other times solicitous—for example, on Reagan's decision to attend the North-South Summit in Mexico in 1981?

To understand the relationship between the two nations, one should start with history and people. To understand the relationship between the two governments, one must begin at the top.

Summits between the Mexican and U.S. Presidents began in 1909 during the administrations of William Howard Taft and Porfirio Díaz, but they were interrupted for thirty-four years because of revolution in Mexico and world war. In 1943, Franklin Roosevelt met with Manuel Avila Camacho, and from then into 1988, eight succeeding Presidents of Mexico and seven of the United States have met each other thirty-nine times. Though Mexico is often considered a low priority for the United States, most U.S. Presidents have taken Mexico very seriously. Since 1943, the U.S. President has conferred with the Mexican head of state more often than with any other country's.

President Roosevelt privately instructed his ambassador to Mexico: "Write me often of all that goes on with you in Mexico."[1] In his memoirs, President Eisenhower cites a letter he wrote to John Foster Dulles, his Secretary of State, in June 1955: "I probably have written to you more on the subject of Mexico than any other single matter. . . . I am so earnestly of the opinion that our relations with Mexico must be a first and continuing concern of ours . . ."[2] Several close aides to Lyndon Johnson also noted his deep "emotional concerns [which] concentrated mainly on the Mexican relationship." Johnson had traveled to Mexico, taught Mexican-American students, and had a Texan's preoccupation with the stability of its neighbor.[3]

U.S. Presidents have recognized the connection between American national security and Mexico's stability. All countries must be especially sensitive to their neighbors for security reasons, although these vary with each relationship. Mexico obviously does not pose a direct security threat to the United States; the threat is potential and indirect. Instability could create the conditions for a hostile group to take power and invite a powerful adversary to defend and help Mexico in exchange for its assistance in spying on or acting against the United States.

A strategic relationship between Mexico and a U.S. rival may seem farfetched today, but before both world wars, some Mexican leaders feinted toward Germany, and during World War I, Mexico allowed German secret service agents to use it as a base of operations against the United States.[4] Even if a Mexican regime never deliberately chose to ally with America's rival, one could imagine scenarios that could lead to such an outcome. If, for example, a Mexican government deepened its relations with the Soviet Union and the United States responded provocatively, then the Mexicans might seek additional help from the Soviets to defend their regime. An analysis of why this has not happened in the past should reassure some of those who fear it in the future, but regardless of how improbable one might view this scenario, no leader in the United States can ignore it entirely. The history of the relationship is strewn with many examples of how a misunderstanding could create a situation that neither government would logically or deliberately choose.

Most nations become anxious when a neighbor builds up its armed forces; Mexico's anxiety is so acutely developed that it protests when it hears an American associate its name with the term "national security." In February 1984, General Paul Gorman, the head of U.S. Southern Command, testified before a Senate Armed Services Committee that Mexico could be "the No. 1 security problem" for the United States. A spokesman for the Mexican Foreign Ministry, Augustín Gutiérrez Canet, immediately denounced his statement as "an interference in the internal affairs of Mexico." He went further, saying that Gorman's statement "presents a danger to the security of Mexico. It is with this argument that the United States could assume the right to intervene in our country."[5]

The argument that Mexico's national security is endangered when the United States declares that its national security is jeopardized is an example of the circular illogic that often passes for communication between the two governments. Nonetheless, the State Department continued its walk around the circle by publicly disavowing Gorman's statement and characterizing it as his "personal views." To complete the farce, Gutiérrez was reprimanded for issuing a public instead of a private criticism.

What is so ironic, tragic, and yet typical is that both governments were disagreeing profoundly over how to define a fear they shared. Formulated differently, the United States fears instability, division, and the consequences of long-term poverty in Mexico, fears which presumably Mexico shares. These anxieties, together with the need to manage difficult bilateral problems and the hope of building a good relationship, are what have motivated U.S. Presidents to give a relatively consistent and high level of attention to Mexico over the years.

Donald Wyman analyzed twenty-two major disputes in U.S.-Mexican relations from 1920 to 1975.[6] Although U.S. power has always greatly exceeded Mexico's, the outcomes of these disputes reflected a rough parity, with eight coming closer to Mexico's objectives and ten coming closer to those of the United States. Nearly three-quarters of the disputes were economic, but the issues changed. Before World War II, most of them related to U.S. corporations and Mexico's laws, and Mexico tended to prevail. After the war, and the repeal of the trade agreement between the two countries, Mexico was generally unsuccessful in its effort to change U.S. trade policies, but did prevail on a number of other bilateral issues. Wyman concluded that relations in the prewar period, particularly in the 1920s, were "visibly strained" and the conflicts "easily escalated." After the war, in those areas where Mexico succeeded, this was due to "the U.S. desire, amid the trials of global leadership, to preserve political stability and to maintain an essentially cooperative relationship."

In 1976, for the first time in twenty-four years, new Presidents of the United States and Mexico came into office at the same time. Both men inherited difficult situations, although for different reasons, and both talked of moral renewal and had reputations for integrity and competence. Each hoped to restore confidence in his country and to forge a new relationship between the two nations.

Although Jimmy Carter had little international experience, he had visited Mexico several times and had an appreciation for its importance to the United States. He was the first President since Thomas Jefferson who spoke Spanish, and as a former governor of a southern state, he viewed Mexico as both a potential problem and a great economic opportunity. Therefore, he chose to invite José López Portillo as his first state visitor in February 1977, and one of his objectives was to help his counterpart restore the confidence of the international financial community in Mexico's future. Kind words by Carter helped, although not as much as the reports of Mexico's oil discoveries.

Thirty-five years after Mexican President Cárdenas nationalized the foreign oil industry in 1938, the nation had become an oil importer. The sharp rise in oil prices in the mid-1970s led PEMEX, the Mexican national oil company, to explore for more oil, and by 1976 technocrats had begun to realize that Mexico had much greater reserves than anyone had thought. López Portillo appointed a dynamic businessman and friend, Jorge Díaz Serrano, as director of PEMEX, and Díaz Serrano drafted an ambitious six-year, $15 billion investment plan to transform Mexico into one of the world's major oil producers. During López Portillo's visit, the Carter administration privately assisted Mexico in its efforts to obtain new financing.[7]

The Presidents held two pleasant days of useful talks. At the conclusion, the two governments issued a communiqué, which said, in part: "The two Presidents pledged that they would examine closely in the next few months the multiple aspects of the relations between Mexico and the United States with a view to developing policies that reflected the interrelated nature of mutual problems." This was López Portillo's formulation of the problem; Carter's proposed solution was a consultative mechanism of cabinet ministers from both governments to examine the full gamut of issues and report to the two Presidents.

Both Presidents had full agendas of problems they needed to solve, and by the time they returned to the bilateral issues, a new obstacle in the most sensitive area of all—energy—stood between them. The expansion of Mexico's oil production raised many old fears and new issues. An article in September 1977 in *Proceso,* a weekly magazine, cited an obscure American analyst speculating about U.S. intervention to protect its national security interests in Mexican energy.[8] When López Portillo decided to build a pipeline for Mexican gas to flow to the U.S. border, leftist critics assailed him for giving away the Mexican patrimony, even though the gas was then being flared.

The Carter administration was aware of Mexico's strong nationalistic feelings about its natural resources, and tried to be sensitive. When asked whether Washington would pressure Mexico to export more oil and gas, Carter diplomatically answered with a meaningless statement: the United States only wanted to buy what Mexico wanted to sell at mutually agreeable prices.[9]

After learning that U.S. gas companies had begun to negotiate with PEMEX, James Schlesinger, Carter's energy adviser and subsequently Secretary of Energy, met on June 27, 1977, with Díaz Serrano and the Secretary of National Patrimony, José de Oteyza. Schlesinger told them that the U.S. government and autonomous regulatory agencies wanted a long-term gas agreement if Mexico did, but the agencies would not approve an agreement if the price was above the Canadian figure ($2.16) and would rise with the price of #2 fuel oil. An agreement that exceeded these levels would also imperil the Carter administration's energy bill, which was its highest domestic priority.

Although it should have been self-evident, Schlesinger explained why the interests of the gas companies were different from those of the U.S. government and why the latter took precedence. The gas companies wanted to pay a high price for Mexican gas because that would allow them to circumvent domestic regulations while putting pressure on Congress to raise the domestic price. Two weeks later, after receiving reports that the Mexicans had ignored Schlesinger and accelerated their negotiations with the gas companies, Washington sent a high-level delegation to Mexico to repeat the same points and urge the Mexicans to negotiate directly with the U.S. government and not complete an agreement with the gas companies.[10]

The warnings were ignored. On August 3, 1977, Díaz Serrano signed a letter of intent with six U.S. gas companies to import immediately 50 million cubic feet per day at a price of $2.60 per thousand cubic feet. The price would be linked to the price of #2 fuel oil, exactly what Schlesinger had warned not to do. The agreement would last for six years, with the amount of gas expanding to 2 billion cubic feet a day by 1979.[11] Considering the political sensitivity of selling gas to the United States and Mexico's distrust, the decision to sign this agreement seemed to the U.S. negotiators inexplicably reckless or careless.

By coincidence, an opportunity occurred for the two Presidents to discuss the issue. Carter invited the Mexican President—along with others in the hemisphere—to attend the signing of the new Panama Canal treaties and have a private meeting. When López Portillo declined because the event was scheduled near the time of his *Informe* (the annual report) and also because he was reported to have had reservations that the treaties did not go far enough to assert Panamanian sovereignty, Carter phoned and asked him to reconsider. López Portillo said he could not come. If the meeting had occurred, the Mexican President would have been able to make Carter sensitive to the political implications of the issue, and it would have allowed Carter to explain his own political problems on energy. This opportunity was lost.

In October 1977, Senator Adlai Stevenson of Illinois, whose constituents feared higher gas prices, introduced a resolution that would preclude Export-Import Bank financing to Mexico for the pipeline "unless and until it is established that the Secretary of Energy has approved the price." His resolution provoked protests from Mexico, and he dropped it. The bank approved the credits in December, but many Mexicans, including the ambassador, continued to equate incorrectly Stevenson's resolution with the imposition of sanctions against Mexico.[12]

In December 1977, Díaz Serrano and the Minister of Foreign Relations visited Washington. They first met with Vice President Mondale, but did not raise the gas issue. The Mexicans then met with Schlesinger, whom they later accused of rejecting the agreement, but that was not within his power. Repeating what he had said before, Schlesinger suggested ways to modify the agreement so that the independent regulatory agencies might approve it, but the Mexicans had painted themselves into a corner. López Portillo, who felt exposed politically, decided not to renew the letter of intent with the gas companies. The Mexican magazine *Siempre* printed a cartoon on the cover that made him appear to be hanging from the ceiling by a paintbrush. The metaphor described how he felt the United States had treated him.

This issue, more than any other, affected López Portillo's view of President Carter and led to a deterioration of the relationship. The Mexican press blamed U.S. arrogance and intransigence, and the American press, for different reasons, also criticized the Carter administration, which did not respond to the accusations because it did not want to exacerbate the problem.[13]

Why Mexico signed the agreement despite repeated warnings by the U.S. government and the heavy political cost of rejection is not clear. Perhaps López Portillo was a victim of an ideology that believed that multinational corporations make U.S. policy. Perhaps he was a prisoner of a political system where Presidents can control any government decision, and did not understand or believe that regulatory commissions in the United States are genuinely autonomous rather than extensions of the President. He apparently did not comprehend the role of Congress, as he later described Senator Stevenson's effort as binding and intended to offend Mexico rather than as hortatory and trying to defend his constituents. Perhaps López Portillo was not fully informed about Díaz Serrano's negotiations.[14]

But, in the end, a relatively insignificant nondecision by the United States had a very important political effect in Mexico and on the relationship. The incident confirmed each government's stereotypes of the other. For Mexicans, the U.S. decision not to approve the gas agreement provided added proof of the arrogance of the United States. For North Americans, Mexico's decision to sign the gas agreement in August 1977, despite U.S. warnings, provided proof that Mexican ideology would continue to prevail over communication and produce bewildering decisions.

On August 14, 1978, Zbigniew Brzezinski, Carter's National Security Adviser, signed Presidential Review Memorandum (PRM) #41, launching the longest high-level "Review of U.S. Policies Toward Mexico" undertaken by the U.S. government. The study culminated with three cabinet-level NSC meetings that prepared the President for his trip to Mexico in February 1979.

The PRM was a list of questions for the bureaucracy—in this case, fourteen agencies—to answer. "The central objective of the review is to develop a coordinated and well-integrated approach to our relations with Mexico."[15] The State Department was designated the principal coordinator, and papers were requested on each of the main issues in the relationship as well as on their interrelationships. The Assistant Secretary of State for Inter-American Affairs, Viron Peter Vaky, chaired the interagency meetings that discussed and refined the papers for the NSC. It soon became apparent why it was so difficult for the United States to achieve a coherent, integrated policy toward Mexico. Routinely, from forty to eighty people attended the meetings, with seemingly nothing in common but that their decisions had some impact on Mexico. U.S. domestic agencies probably have as much and sometimes more influence on Mexico than the State Department, and none wants to permit either State or the White House to "interfere" with *its* policy. The essence of the President's administrative problem was to persuade the domestic agencies to be more responsive to his policies and priorities than to the agency's constituency in the country and in Congress.

The Immigration and Naturalization Service (INS) of the Justice Department was responsible for immigration. The Agriculture Department worked with farmers to define "marketing orders" that limited imports of certain kinds of Mexican vegetables and enforced health regulations on beef imports. The Treasury and Commerce departments, the International Trade Commission, and the Special Trade Representative were all responsible for some part of U.S. trade policy that directly or indirectly affected Mexico. The Department of Housing and Urban Development had an agreement with its Mexican counterpart, as did most of the agencies in the areas of science and technology. The Treasury Department was concerned about Mexico's debt and its access to the international development banks. The Defense Department, state and local governments, independent regulatory commissions—these and other agencies made policies toward Mexico, sometimes without being aware of it.

Generally, the State Department encourages the domestic agencies to be more cooperative and less abrasive in their relations with Mexico, whereas Mexico's Ministry of Foreign Relations plays exactly the opposite role, encouraging the Economic Ministries, which are more interested in reaching agreement with their U.S. counterparts, to be more difficult. Lacking domestic constituencies, both foreign affairs agencies represent their respective national interests, but by and large, the economic agencies on both sides ignore their guidance and deal pragmatically with each other, for the good of both.

The State Department views itself at the top of the vast foreign policy-making apparatus, but like Rodney Dangerfield, it complains that no one gives it any respect. The PRM papers prepared for State by each agency were either deliberately uninformative or legal briefs on behalf of the status quo. Before too long, portions of the PRM had leaked to the newspapers, and Mexicans soon leaped to conclusions about U.S. conspiracies. One official from the Mexican embassy, evidently confused by the PRM and under pressure from his government to find out more about it, called the National Security Council to ask for a copy of the top secret study.

The cabinet members of the NSC began to discuss the papers and debate the options in December 1978. The discourse on the issues revealed more clearly than anyone had planned the U.S. government view of the relationship. Virtually every discussion followed the same pattern, reflecting a collective subconscious not evident to the participants. The Secretary of State or the U.S. ambassador opened the meeting by underscoring the critical importance of Mexico to the United States: "The United States has a central interest in a stable, prosperous, and humane Mexico." There was unanimous agreement on that point, and the group turned to specific issues.

The cabinet secretary responsible for a particular issue would describe the two governments' positions and leave little doubt that either the problem was unsolvable or Mexico was at fault, uninterested, or opposed to any new initiative. The Special Trade Representative would explain how the U.S. government had done everything possible within the law to lower its trade barriers to Mexican products, but unless Mexico joined the General Agreement on Tariffs and Trade (GATT) or made some small reciprocal concession, the United States could not go any further. Moreover, he explained, and others agreed, that Mexico's development prospects were hampered more by its own than by U.S. protectionism. The Deputy Attorney General would explain that he had consulted with Mexico several times on immigration policy, but Mexico had failed to respond. The Secretary of Energy stated that Mexico had ignored his warnings about the gas agreement, and the United States did not need Mexican gas at this time. After each secretary had made his statement, the NSC would add the various positions together and conclude that only a very aggressive strategy by the United States could induce Mexico to take the kinds of steps necessary for its own good.

Just before agreeing to such a strategy, a conferee would remind the group of Mexico's strategic importance and why it is in the U.S. national interest to be helpful. The debate would resume on the high road, and a participant would ask what the United States should do. Since Mexico was uncooperative or uninterested in new ideas, the Cabinet saw no point in suggesting any. In lieu of new ideas, the administration—and its successor—proposed organizational gimmicks: a new consultative mechanism, cabinet council, "coordinator," or binational commission—a better way to manage an unmanageable relationship.

The debate on energy is instructive. Carlos Fuentes, the Mexican novelist, expressed the feelings of some Mexicans in the title of an article he wrote for the Washington *Post:* "Listen, Yankee! Mexico Is a Nation, Not an Oil Well."[16] The PRM noted that Mexico's emergence as an oil power was one of the main reasons for its increasing importance to the United States. U.S. dependence on Middle Eastern oil increased from 21 percent of its imports in 1975 to 40 percent in 1979. The prospect of rising Mexican oil production was viewed by Americans as an exceptionally positive development because it would reduce U.S. dependence, boost global oil production and thus reduce prices, and offer Mexico needed resources to invest in its development.

The issue for the U.S. government was whether to encourage Mexico to expand its oil production. The NSC consensus was that rapid development of Mexico's oil reserves might destabilize the country, and it was far more important to avoid that outcome than to reduce dependence or raise the world production. Moreover, the entire Cabinet accepted Schlesinger's point that even if the United States wanted greater production, it could not encourage Mexico to produce any more than it desired, and any efforts would be either counterproductive or misinterpreted. Therefore, the NSC concluded that the United States should be helpful if requested by Mexico—for example, by facilitating the licensing of oil drilling equipment—but state clearly that the United States respected Mexico's decision on how fast to produce its own oil. In other words, Washington judged that its interests in Mexico's gradual development were more important than its interests in reducing its dependence on Middle Eastern oil.

Instead of secretly developing a strategy to plunder Mexico's patrimony, or reduce its agricultural potential, or enforce its dependence, as various Mexican commentators suspected, the U.S. government reached an undramatic conclusion at the end of its most comprehensive policy-making exercise toward Mexico: consult first. Carter approved of this recommendation because he judged that the best way to fashion a modern and respectful relationship was to avoid making any decisions before he had an opportunity to talk with López Portillo.

More intriguing than the single conclusion—to consult—was the fact that the Cabinet dodged the two central questions of the PRM. First, how could the many issues in the relationship be organized in a mutually beneficial "package"? López Portillo had stressed the importance of constructing an integrated package, and that was the initial purpose of the PRM.[17] Why then did the U.S. government fail to answer the question?

The idea of relating issues to one another is attractive in the abstract, but it is only possible when one is negotiating issues that can be broken down into tradable components—like tariffs, aid, or missiles. At the time, the most obvious trade-off was that the United States would ignore illegal migrants in exchange for more and cheaper Mexican oil. The problem in this case, and in U.S.-Mexican relations in general, is that almost every issue has a symbolic, sovereignty component that is impossible to trade. Legally, the United States could not decide to ignore illegal migrants, and politically, Mexico could not trade its national patrimony at a price below market value.

Each issue—energy, temporary worker programs, trade—has a zero-sum, sovereignty dimension which precludes trade-offs. For example, the two governments can negotiate tariffs or quotas on individual products, but a sovereignty issue like Mexico's entrance into GATT is nonnegotiable. The sovereignty components of these issues explain why the United States never assembled a package and why Mexico never proposed one.

The second fundamental question of the PRM was whether the overall relationship should be (1) a "special relationship," whereby the United States develops more favorable trade, migration, energy policies, etc.; (2) a balanced relationship comparable to U.S. affiliations with its European allies; or (3) a special sensitivity in which global policies are tilted to take into account the great importance of Mexico.

To the general public, the concept "special relationship" is redundant at best since all relationships are "special." But to those who read symbols like astrologers read stars, the term "special relationship" is laden with meaning. At his first meeting with Carter, López Portillo criticized the idea of a special relationship, but his protest seemed directed at former Secretary of State Henry Kissinger, who had used the term in 1976 to refer to Brazil. The Carter administration thought it would eliminate the paternalism of the past merely by not using the term, and Carter therefore agreed with López Portillo, without realizing that they meant different things, and therefore did not agree at all.

A "special relationship" could mean that the United States would tilt all of its policies to give a better deal to Mexico, but the problem with that approach is that Washington would inevitably expect something—besides gratitude—in return, and Mexicans are unlikely to satisfy U.S. expectations. Alternatively, the United States could seek a Common Market or a free trade area involving the free movement of goods, investment, technology, and perhaps labor. This idea was constantly dismissed within the U.S. government during the PRM exercise because no one thought Mexico wanted it. Occasional informal communications with high-level Mexican officials confirmed this perception. The United States could also negotiate sectoral arrangements—like the U.S.-Canadian automotive pact—but again few in the government felt Mexico would be interested, and that was an accurate assessment. For all these reasons, any variation of a "special relationship" was dismissed before it was ever really proposed.

A second option—a "balanced" policy—would be to treat Mexico like England or France. The problem with that is that Mexico is a poor Third World nation that shares a long border with the United States. A wide range of U.S. domestic policies affect Mexico adversely, and problems in Mexico often affect the United States. A "balanced" approach would ignore the effects of these policies and problems and overlook the convoluted psychology that makes the relationship so difficult.

The third option—an effort to be sensitive—is selected by default. After reaching this simple answer, the hard question is whether the U.S. government can implement such a policy.

In October 1978, during the PRM deliberations, a series of newspaper articles reported that the United States was trying to seal the border by constructing a "tortilla curtain." The Mexican press accused Washington of trying to stop migration as a way to pressure Mexico to sell its oil and gas at cheaper prices.[18] López Portillo and Hispanic leaders in the United States condemned this "Berlin Wall" across the Rio Grande.

The real story, which was not covered as fully as the initial one, was that the INS decided to replace six miles of existing fence and build an additional sixteen miles at two areas of the border where the largest number of legal and illegal crossings occur. The articles were the result of an interview with the Houston contractor, who proudly explained that he had designed a fence with razor edges that could not be climbed without losing fingers and toes. The White House, needless to say, halted the fence construction, but the damaging perceptions were not so easily changed. A month later, a newspaper editor asked Carter: "Have you heard about the steel wall on the border to stop the illegal entry into the United States?" Carter restrained himself: "You mean the fence? Yes, that was a serious mistake."

The issue for the U.S. government was whether it could design a mechanism to coordinate and integrate the policies of different agencies while preventing embarrassments like the "tortilla curtain" or misunderstandings like the gas fiasco. An answer to this question would follow the summit meetings.

. . .

Carter's luckless trip to Mexico City in February 1979 set a precedent that even De la Madrid's ill-starred visit to Washington five years later could not match. Despite the most intensive preparations, and the best of intentions, almost nothing went right on the trip, except the final agreements, which the press failed to report.

It started the night before the trip. The U.S. ambassador to Afghanistan was assassinated, and Iranian "students" almost took the U.S. embassy hostage. Instead of getting a good rest, Carter, Vance, and Brzezinski worked straight through the night. If the trip had been to any other country, it probably would have been postponed. (The next year, Carter canceled a trip to Canada because of the Iranian crisis, but the consensus was that Mexico would view a postponement as an insult.) At 7 a.m., *Air Force One* flew to Mexico.

At their first meeting in 1977, the difference in style between the two Presidents was hardly noticeable. Two years later in Mexico City, those differences had begun to irritate. López Portillo enjoyed expounding on abstract issues, whereas Carter preferred to solve specific problems. Carter viewed the summit as an opportunity to adjust his policies to take account of Mexican views and make progress on the issues. He was repeatedly frustrated by his inability to elicit a comment specific enough from López Portillo to permit some progress or agreement.

The two presidential conversations on this trip occurred on consecutive days and lasted more than three hours each. At the first session, on international issues, the Presidents seemed to switch roles, with Carter expressing his support for Third World aspirations and López Portillo suggesting the need for the United States to send signals to the free world as clear and strong as those sent by the Soviet Union. López Portillo's presentation seemed almost Kissingerian in philosophy, and his aide later confirmed that Kissinger had met frequently with the Mexican President before the visit as well as afterwards.

Mexicans eat lunch in midafternoon, which meant that the Americans waited until 5:30 Washington time before they began their second meal of the day. Two hours later, after too much wine, the two Presidents rose to toast one another.

The White House press corps travels with the President and reports on his visits even though it seldom knows anything about the countries he is visiting. During a lengthy briefing for the press prior to the trip, several journalists from leading U.S. newspapers expressed dismay about the complexity of the agenda and asked U.S. officials to assist them with a "handle" for a story. As the Mexican President rose to give his toast, "handles" began to fall from the sky.

López Portillo began with a thoughtful, though complicated statement about the cultural and psychological difficulties of the relationship, but a few of his comments appeared as acidic references to the U.S. position on the gas deal. "Among permanent, not casual, neighbors, surprise moves and sudden deceit or abuse are poisonous fruits that sooner or later have a reverse effect," said the Mexican President. Occurring on the day of the kidnapping and assassination of the U.S. ambassador in Kabul and the attack on the U.S. embassy in Teheran, this comment and others reinforced the picture of a U.S. President being "lectured" and "scolded" by another Third World leader.[19]

Characteristically, whereas López Portillo stressed the differences separating the two countries, Carter chose to emphasize the number of "things in common" the two nations and Presidents shared. "We both represent great nations; we both have found an interest in archaeology . . ." He then tried to ease the tension by improvising: both were joggers and he had learned to jog in Mexico City on a previous visit, when he was "afflicted with Montezuma's revenge." The audience responded awkwardly but politely to this obvious effort to lighten the atmosphere. Few Mexicans knew the American joke, but the U.S. press described it as "maladroit" and "crude."[20]

The special irony of "the battle of the toasts," as *Time* described it, was that the main unreported points of both toasts were the significant ones. López Portillo did vent his anxieties, but he also complimented Carter as a moral man—a most unusual comment from a Mexican leader to his American counterpart: "We see in you a leader who has sought to revive the moral foundations of the political institutions of the United States." The essence of Carter's toast was to respond to those in Mexico who believed that U.S. policy aimed to contain Mexico or foster its dependency. Instead, Carter encouraged Mexico to play a leading role in international affairs even "though our two countries may not agree." On the North-South dialogue, world peace and nonproliferation, and human rights: "We welcome Mexico's advocacy of these issues."

The U.S. press coverage of the visit concentrated on the facile "handles"—Mexico's lecture and Carter's weakness—and ignored not only the broader messages of the toasts but also the significant substantive agreements reached on the second day. Ironically, the reporting influenced the meetings of the two Presidents in a way that made the coverage less accurate, the meetings more productive, and the personal relationship more strained. On the second day of meetings, López Portillo accepted direct government-to-government negotiations on natural gas. In addition, the two Presidents agreed on several projects, such as electricity exchanges on the border. They decided to improve cooperation on narcotics matters and consult on immigration. These items and others were noted in an extensive communiqué that was issued at the conclusion of the visit.

López Portillo tried to revise the image that the press had grafted onto the visit in an impromptu news conference at the airport after Carter departed. He expressed his "deep satisfaction" with the talks and with Carter's speech, which was delivered in Spanish. He described Carter's address as "the expression of a modern statesman who understands the changing world in which he lives, confronting it with moral strength and political determination." He also spoke of the agreements the two had reached, including the one on natural gas. The Mexican papers reported his remarks in full, but most of the U.S. press had departed both physically and mentally with Carter.

The image of López Portillo's "tongue-lashing" and Mexico's "macho mood" was fixed by that one exchange of toasts, and continued to influence the way that newspapers reported U.S.-Mexican affairs the next fall when the two Presidents met again in Washington to sign a natural gas agreement.[21]

The press coverage of De la Madrid's visit to Washington five years later was similar in listing the numerous insults, mistakes, and blunt exchanges suffered by the visiting President and in overlooking the agreements. The two visits seemed to reflect from the same mirror.

Although Carter did not return with a warmer feeling for López Portillo, his sense of the importance of Mexico was strengthened. He issued numerous directives to his cabinet officers instructing them to follow up on the various initiatives that had been discussed. Most importantly, on April 26, 1979, Carter sent an unprecedented memorandum to his entire Cabinet: In order to ensure that "all actions directly or indirectly affecting Mexico promote basic U.S. national interests and are consistent with our overall policy toward Mexico, I ask that each of you accord a high priority to any and all matters within your jurisdiction affecting Mexico, consciously giving good relations with Mexico a continuing high priority in your thinking and planning." Moreover, every decision should be "based on the fullest possible prior consultation."

A presidential declaration that Mexico should be given higher priority was one step; translating that intention into government-wide policies was another matter. Instead of reorganizing the entire government, Carter chose to create a new position, an ambassador-level "coordinator" who would advise him and the Secretary of State, have access to the entire Cabinet, and intervene to ensure that various agencies would consider the "Mexican dimension" before making domestic decisions.

There was no precedent for a "coordinator," and indeed that uniqueness plus the fact that it was to be held by an "ambassador" confused many about its proper role. Congressmen and Mexicans both queried as to the need for a second ambassador to Mexico, a question which showed the degree of puzzlement sowed by the idea. Actually, the Mexican ambassador to Washington should have been playing this role of persuading U.S. officials of Mexico's importance. During the Carter administration, the Mexican ambassador could even have had access to the President if he so requested, but he did not.

Indeed, this is another example of how the projection of political systems has served neither nation well. The modus operandi of the United States at home and abroad is generally open, loud, arm-twisting politics, while Mexico's way is private, discreet, and sometimes opaque bargaining. The U.S. ambassador often projects himself onto an environment that fails to appreciate that style, and similarly, the Mexican ambassador goes through normal State Department channels rather than play the political game with Congress and the press. White House officials wonder why the Mexican ambassador is so reticent, while officials in Mexico City become infuriated with the U.S. ambassador's aggressiveness.

The Carter administration decided that since U.S.-Mexican relations needed an active and strong voice in Washington overseeing the domestic departments and coordinating and integrating U.S. policy, then the U.S. government would have to develop a surrogate. That was the concept behind the coordinator. For reasons having to do with personality and politics, the idea did not achieve its promise or purpose. Instead of trying to serve as a buffer between Mexico and the U.S. political process, the new coordinator, who was a politician, often served as a megaphone pressing U.S. interests on Mexico.

But just when Washington was endeavoring to make its domestic or small decisions more sensitive to Mexico, the government of Mexico made a "small" decision that had a large impact on the United States. Before the Shah of Iran traveled to New York to receive medical treatment in October 1979, López Portillo told him he could return to Mexico when he completed treatment. Within a week of his arrival, Iranian militants seized the U.S. embassy, beginning the longest and most agonizing crisis of Carter's presidency. After undergoing chemotherapy treatments for his cancer, the Shah decided to return to Mexico, but López Portillo denied his reentry. Carter's only reference to Mexico in his memoirs was his reaction to this decision by López Portillo:

> I was outraged. The Mexicans had no diplomatic personnel in Iran, had moved all their people out of the country, and did not need Iranian oil. We'd had every assurance from them that the Shah would be welcome. They had given us no warning of their reversal; apparently the President of Mexico had simply changed his mind at the last minute. It was a serious blow.[22]

López Portillo was persuaded by his Foreign Minister that there was no reason to help the Yankees on this issue, and it would lose him support in the Third World. It was a shortsighted, serious mistake. Carter placed great importance on a person's pledge; to break one's word, especially on an issue of such political importance to Carter, was something he could not forgive. In anger, Carter asked his staff to prepare a list of decisions that would convey to López Portillo the cost of breaking his word. But in time, as his temper cooled, Carter was persuaded not to pursue this negative tack. No incident, however, affected his feelings toward the Mexican President as much or as adversely as López Portillo's decision on the Shah.

Carter entered the White House determined to improve the relationship with Mexico. By the time he left office, despite considerable effort and some success, especially in the areas of energy and science and technology, the relationship had not improved, and in some ways it had deteriorated. The personal link between the Presidents had soured badly, largely because of two avoidable incidents—the initial failure to reach a gas agreement and differences as to whether to readmit the Shah.

The change in the U.S. President in 1981 followed by a new Mexican President the next year permitted both sides to start the relationship anew. Public opinion polls in the United States suggested that Americans felt frustrated that their altruism and leadership were not appreciated; they were angry about being pushed around by small Third World nations; and they believed that their patience and restraint were being taken for weakness and passivity. Mexican leaders could only comprehend these polls in their own terms. Instead of perceiving the United States as weaker, some Mexicans believed that their neighbor might become more dangerous. President Reagan appeared to be the incarnation of the Mexican stereotype of the gringo, a "cowboy," who saw the world divided between bad and good, Communism and the free world.

Still, as a two-term border state governor, Reagan had much more contact with Mexico and understood it better than many other politicians. During his campaign, Reagan proposed a "North American Accord," an economic and military partnership between the United States and Mexico.[23] Though the idea was unrealistic, it was a sign of the importance he attached to the relationship. Before his inauguration, Reagan met with López Portillo on the border. Their meeting was surprisingly friendly. Reagan, so skilled in the use of symbols, literally extended his hand across the border and gave López Portillo a rifle as a present and received a horse in return.

Unlike that of many of his predecessors, Reagan's interest in Mexico did not diminish during his administration. He met with López Portillo four times and then with Miguel de la Madrid six times between 1981 and 1988. No U.S. President conferred as frequently with a Mexican President as Reagan, who used the get-togethers to maintain a good personal relationship.

The differences between the Carter and Reagan administrations were most evident in the change in priorities and style. The Reagan administration's highest priority in the region was to stop Communism and roll it back. Whereas the Carter administration viewed Mexican policy toward Central America as unhelpful and an irritant, the Reagan administration saw it as a formidable obstacle to achieving its objectives. Second, like most Republican regimes, Reagan's placed greater emphasis on the role of private enterprise—both domestic and foreign investment—as an engine for development. U.S. policy therefore aimed to encourage the opening of Mexico to foreign investment and to reduce the role of the state in Mexico's economy. Third, as a conservative administration, Reagan's placed greater emphasis on law enforcement, whether that related to narcotics or illegal immigration. Fourth, as a party that combined both conservative and revolutionary (or counterrevolutionary) instincts, the Republicans seemed to alternate between supporting the PRI for the sake of stability and associating with the PAN for its ideology.

Each of these differences reflects more of a shift in priorities than a change in policy. All U.S. administrations tend to oppose Communism and value private investment, law enforcement, stability, and democracy. A conservative and a liberal President differ on the weight given to each interest and the strategy to implement it.

American Presidents differ not just in their policies and priorities, but also in their management styles. Reagan's strength was to set the direction for his administration in clear, ideological terms. His weakness stemmed from his inability or disinterest in ensuring that his officials followed his approach. His policy toward Mexico reflected both his strength and his weakness, both his general desire to pursue good relations and his specific interests in Central America, private enterprise, drug control, and democracy. A fully consistent policy would have required a trade-off between good overall relations and particular interests, but most policies—and Reagan's was no different—tried to attain both.

There were many times when Reagan reassured Mexico of his desire for a good relationship while his subordinates were condemning it for corruption, leftism, or political fraud. Mexicans added up these contradictory signals and concluded that they represented a subtle conspiracy; American analysts tended to see simply confusion or incoherence. As one steps back from the details of U.S. policy, however, one can detect a coherent pattern that is more than confusion and less than conspiracy. The pattern was evident during previous administrations as well.

It helps to visualize the relationship as two lines on a graph; each has a different pattern and purpose. The first line begins in the middle and then swings up to the top and then down to the bottom of the graph. These volatile swings represent the public side of the relationship, which appears to oscillate between statements of eternal friendship and provocative actions, between Reagan's *abrazo* with De la Madrid and Senate hearings that denounce Mexico. The line never swings too high toward a good relationship; the danger is that it might swing too low and damage the overall relationship. The sharp swings are prompted by an event— the decision on the Shah, a Jack Anderson column, the Helms hearings. The weight and suspicion of the past transform these events into major problems and volatile swings.

At the same time that the relationship is buffeted by these swings, there is a second line that is steady and inches its way across the graph. This represents the slow plod of the two governments as they try to make progress on the important, but routine issues of trade, investment, border control, and narcotics. Occasionally, a particular event, such as the killing of a DEA agent, can propel these issues into a volatile swing, but more often the public's short attention span ignores the slow progress of negotiations, which are at the heart of the relationship. On February 13, 1988, after Reagan's meeting with De la Madrid in Mazatlán, George Shultz and three other members of the Cabinet briefed the press. Reporters focused on the controversial issues of drugs and Central America rather than on Shultz's comment that during the previous eighteen months, the two governments had concluded twenty-six agreements, including several on trade, civil aviation, and a mutual legal assistance treaty. These represented the slow, boring plod of the relationship.

During the Reagan administration, individual agencies pursued their own bureaucratic interests as aggressively as they thought was necessary to be effective. Sometimes Reagan supported the agency; at other times he reassured Mexico and restrained the agency. Together with his Mexican counterpart, Reagan often used their summit meetings to set the boundaries of unkindness to the relationship. Both Presidents jabbed and reassured the other simultaneously. They both had a stake in pushing specific interests, but not so hard as to jeopardize the relationship or the stability of Mexico.

Neither government lost sight of the larger picture in the relationship, as demonstrated by three events. First, when their country suspended debt payments in August 1982 and faced the prospect of default, the Mexicans discarded their traditional aloofness and approached the United States for immediate help. The Reagan administration responded by discarding its free market ideology and rapidly assembling a $9.45 billion package of aid and credits. Although U.S. banks were at risk in other debtor countries, the administration took the lead with its own funds only in the case of Mexico. The combined interests of the two nations in finding a way to help Mexico through its debt crisis led them to leap over the barriers. Necessity prevailed over ideology.

The second occasion occurred on September 19, 1985, the day Mexico City was ravaged by an earthquake. Although the relationship was then strained seriously by differences on Central America, the United States did not hesitate to offer aid. Initially, De la Madrid was unaware of the extent of the damage, and reflexively, did not respond to the offer. Mexico always has had difficulty accepting direct assistance from the United States, believing that the United States would eventually seek something in return. For that reason, it rejected both the Alliance for Progress and the Peace Corps.

Because Washington is aware of this sensitivity, and because it has a stake in Mexico's development, it has always found some indirect mechanism to channel aid to Mexico. The principal channel for the last two decades has been the World Bank and the Inter-American Development Bank, but the United States also directly provides small grants—for example, about $20 million worth of dried milk—through private voluntary organizations. All of this is done to save face while helping Mexico. Once De la Madrid realized the effect of the quake, and Ambassador Gavin accepted the need for an indirect face-saving mechanism for distributing the aid, an arrangement was worked out.

The third case is the most instructive. The Reagan administration had grown obsessed with both Nicaragua and Mexico's defense of Nicaragua. At a summit meeting in Mexicali in January 1986, Central America was practically the only issue, and there was, of course, no meeting of the minds. At the same time, Mexico was heading into the second phase of its debt crisis.

Despite the confluence of these two issues, and the fact that most Mexican newspapers perceived an orchestrated campaign by Washington to force Mexico to change its policy on Central America in exchange for help on its debt, the administration did not link the two issues. Constantine Menges, who left Reagan's NSC in 1986 for Jack Kemp's Presidential campaign, later blamed the administration's passivity for Mexico's "anti-democratic policy in Central America." He wrote that Mexico followed this policy because it was "the path of political convenience with no political or economic costs to Mexico in all the Reagan years." He was distressed to confirm that Reagan had rejected linkage.[24] This was partly for bureaucratic reasons: the Treasury Department refused to allow the State Department, which was managing Central American policy, to intrude on its debt-management jurisdiction. Treasury, once again, was instrumental in helping Mexico to arrange a $12.5 billion loan and debt-rescheduling package in 1986–87.

Bureaucratic politics, however, do not explain the whole of U.S. policy, because if Secretary of State George Shultz and Reagan had decided that Mexico's Central American policy was more important to the United States than the debt negotiations, the Treasury Department's position would have changed immediately. Rhetoric to the contrary, the overall U.S. policy was that Mexico's political stability and economic development were much more important to U.S. interests than its policy on Central America.

In 1982, the context of the relationship changed as dramatically as it had four years earlier. Mexico's oil boom, which seemed permanent and had allowed it to compete with Washington in Central America, suddenly burst. López Portillo had bet that the oil under Mexico was worth much more than the money he was borrowing. He was wrong. He was not alone in placing that wager, but the bill he left his nation was one of the worst. From 1976 to 1982, during his *sexenio,* Mexico's external debt soared from about $24 billion to over $87 billion.[25]

Mexico's economy and living standards declined precipitously. The effect on the nation's self-confidence was even more severe. Mexico changed from an assertive Third World nation to one that was intensely preoccupied by its worst economic crisis since the Great Depression. Economic weakness, combined with new political demands for change, made the regime even more sensitive than usual to real and imagined pressures from Washington. Mexico, which had feared that the United

States would exploit its new wealth, now worried it would take advantage of its new weakness.

Reagan's policy, however, reflected both a solicitousness to Mexico in ways that the administration would never consider with another government and a heavy-handedness. At the summit meeting in May 1984, which was so disappointing to De la Madrid, Reagan accepted a recommendation to send George Shultz to Managua for talks and to follow these up with a series of bilateral meetings between the United States and Nicaragua in Manzanillo, Mexico. This was not the first time that Reagan stepped out of character in response to a request from the Mexican President. He himself attended a North-South Summit in Cancún, although he rejected the idea of the Third World, and he sent Secretary of State Alexander Haig to Mexico for a private meeting with Cuba's Vice President.

On the other hand, on February 16, 1985, U.S. customs officials began to slow traffic across the entire border from Brownsville to San Ysidro. The initial stated purpose of Operation Intercept was to search for clues in the disappearance of Enrique Camarena Salazar, the DEA official who had been kidnapped in Guadalajara on February 7. Within two weeks, however, Ambassador Gavin admitted that the real reason was "to encourage the prosecution of criminal elements, including drug traffickers," by Mexico.[26]

The border functions as a kind of symbolic pulse to the relationship, and any effort by one country to choke traffic inevitably raises the blood pressure on the other side. Mexicans reacted in anger to the overt pressure. Why did the Reagan administration do it?

In 1985, Mexico became the major foreign source of heroin and marijuana and a transshipment point for cocaine. Camarena had been involved in an operation that seized large shipments, and one of the region's drug kingpins, Rafael Caro Quintero, ordered several men from the Mexican Federal Security Directorate to bring Camarena to his house, where he was tortured and then killed. Within two days, the director of the DEA flew to Guadalajara to assist in the search for Camarena, and soon realized that the local police were frustrating his efforts. On February 16, agents identified Caro Quintero at the airport. The Judicial Police tried to stop Quintero, but were prevented from doing so by the Federal Security Directorate. After nine days of trying to cope with obstacles placed in his path by Mexican Federal Security Directorate, the DEA director decided that the only way to get high-level attention was to pressure Mexico. He called the Commissioner of Customs, William von Raab, who instructed his border guards to slow traffic.

On February 20, Ambassador Gavin returned to Washington for consultations, and the next day the Mexican government lodged a formal protest against the slowdown. President De la Madrid then personally phoned President Reagan, who said he would end the border slowdown. Both agreed that the two Attorney Generals should meet soon to resolve any problems. Three days later, on February 25, the Federal Security Directorate made the first of a series of arrests. Camarena's body was discovered on March 5, and a month later the Costa Rican police, advised by the DEA, identified and arrested Quintero. The border slowdown caught the attention of the Mexican government, and although it complained, it became more active in pursuing Camarena's murderers afterwards than before. Moreover, the government's drug campaign increased demonstrably after this event, much as it had after President Nixon had ordered a similar Operation Intercept in 1969.

American officials, including the Attorney General, felt a strong loyalty to one of their men, but they also believed that the entire operation would be jeopardized unless the U.S. government threw its energy behind finding Camarena and bringing his killers to justice. Washington, however, pays a long-term price for such an overt act of pressure by confirming Mexico's resentment. Alternatives need to be found.

For the first time in fifty years, Mexico's political system emerged as an issue in the relationship. When De la Madrid was elected in 1982, he pledged "moral renovation" and greater openness in the political system, and in 1983 the PAN won a significant number of mayoralties in the northern part of the country. The American press reported on alleged PRI fraud in gubernatorial races, and the Mexican government, which had censored such reports in Mexico, accused the Americans of "intervention."

The Reagan administration was using the democratization theme to justify its support for the contras in Nicaragua, but it was pulled in two directions as to whether to relate the theme to Mexico. On the one hand, it was ideologically sympathetic to the PAN; on the other hand, it feared that pushing the PRI too hard could hurt overall relations and conceivably endanger the long-standing stability in Mexico. These two tendencies appeared to cancel each other out, leaving the United States with a vague and equivocal policy on democratization in Mexico.

Mexico's debt crisis raised the political question in the United States. Significantly, the U.S. foreign policy establishment had become so attuned to Mexico's sensitivity that only a conservative outsider like Senator Jesse Helms pursued the question. Against the wishes of the Reagan administration and the Republican leadership of the Senate Foreign Relations Committee, Helms opened Senate hearings:

> If the United States is called upon, both directly and indirectly, to bolster the faltering Mexican economy, we have the right to inquire to what extent our assistance might be stabilizing or destabilizing. . . . If Mexico wants United States help, the Mexican people have no choice, it seems to me, but to bring about fundamental political reform. . . .
>
> I would say to the Mexican government, open up your electoral process to review and inspection. . . . Mexico deserves no help from the international community until this is done. And let the press in Mexico speak with an open mind. Let all of the political parties in Mexico criticize the process and recommend reforms. . . . The Mexican government, if they expect any monetary help from the United States, must, in my judgment, give the Mexican people a chance to speak.[27]

The Helms hearings drove Mexico to distraction. The government organized demonstrations against the U.S. embassy and passed formal notes of protest to the State Department. The hearings were largely ignored in the United States, but a number of newspapers, including *The New York Times,* had articles on Mexico's reaction.

The process by which Americans make policy is often very difficult for foreigners, and many Americans for that matter, to understand. The Constitution designed a government to guarantee freedom, not to be efficient or orderly. Therefore, instead of consolidating power in the hands of the President and drawing straight lines of command, the Constitution divided power between institutions. Congress and the President share responsibility for making policy, thus guaranteeing competition while offering incentives for cooperation. As a result, there are many actors in Washington, and outside, pressing and grabbing at policy. The Constitution's essence has been implanted in the American political character that seeks, first, to accumulate power and wealth. Then, when too much power is concentrated, other institutions are activated to check, balance, and divide the new power center. Foreigners accustomed to seeing policy handed down from a single office are either confused by what they see, or they conclude that the real government is working in private, devious ways.

U.S. policy making may be difficult to comprehend, but no more so than the relationship between the United States and Mexico. The sounds and the fireworks suggest that the two governments are incapable of reaching agreement on anything, and indeed, they often appear on the verge of blows. But at the same time, middle-level officials in both governments and the people of both nations patiently make progress on one issue at a time, and they often succeed in reducing the misunderstanding between the two nations—far from the glare of the television cameras.

The two Presidents sit at the summit of the relationship and try to press specific interests while keeping everything in perspective and within the bounds of civility. They have largely succeeded in preventing any significant breakdown in the relationship in the last twenty years, but they have also failed to forge any significant breakthroughs.

Despite Mexican fears of conspiracies and destabilization, U.S. Presidents—at least for the last forty years—have seemed to understand clearly the importance of Mexico's development and stability for the United States. These are compatible interests that both nations share, but that does not mean that both governments will agree on how to pursue them. Needless to say, they have not agreed, and suspicions of each other's motives have impeded understanding. Each has been sensitive and insensitive, although infrequently at the same time. Until both nations learn to concentrate on the broader picture, they will continue to evoke the worst rather than the best in the other.

The Mexican Government

—

Jorge G. Castañeda

After leaving office, an ex-President of Mexico remarked that he could not have fulfilled his duties a single day beyond the date of his term's end. When queried as to which of the many possible and obvious reasons—constitutional, political, personal—led him to this conclusion, he replied that he had come to be so anti-American, so irritated by U.S. government behavior toward Mexico, so personally indisposed toward a number of high-level American officials, that he simply could no longer govern Mexico the way he should—on an even keel as far as relations with its northern neighbor were concerned.

This statement reflects how Mexican officials feel the country's ties with the United States should be managed. For decades now, the government's role in conducting policy toward Washington has been more the result of existing, conflicting nongovernmental forces than a decisive factor in actually shaping relations. Mexico's official policy is, despite American suspicions or wishes, much more an effect than a cause. It is the fluctuating, often erratic outcome of two broad social, historical, economic, and cultural trends: Mexican nationalism, firmly anchored in the country's history and sensitivity, as real today as ever, with its traditional suspicion and wariness of American intervention in Mexican affairs; and the powerful forces driving the two nations together through numerous forms of formal and informal economic integration. If Mexican policy toward the United States at times appears contradictory, or confusing, it is because the factors which shape its contours are extraordinarily difficult to control.

The key to understanding how Mexican authorities set the country's course in dealing with their neighbor to the north must be found in the reasons which explain why the nation's political system, despite its obvious vices and drawbacks, has lasted as long as it has. According to the vast majority of Mexico's leaders, politicians, and intellectuals, the political mechanisms created in the late 1920s and early 1930s have endured above all thanks to continuity, relative prosperity, and sovereignty, which together equal stability and survival. For some, economic growth has been the root of political stability; for others, inversely, the political system set up in the late 1920s made economic growth possible. Whichever came first, with time, both phenomena became inseparable.

Since 1928, when Alvaro Obregón was elected President for the second time and then assassinated just before taking office, every changeover of power from one President to his successor has taken place uneventfully. None has been shot, removed, or forced from office in sixty years. This contrasts remarkably with the first century of the country's independence, during which peaceful successions were a rare exception. Presidents either simply did not leave office (Porfirio Díaz held on for nearly thirty years), were overthrown or assassinated (as was the case with two of the country's three leaders after Díaz and during the Revolution: Francisco Madero and Venustiano Carranza), or never really governed. The importance of establishing a peaceful succession mechanism, whereby the nation switches leaders every six years without bloodshed or civil strife, cannot be overestimated. Its longevity is unique in Latin America and the Third World.

Similarly, the fact that after ten years of revolution, hundreds of thousands dead, and often incredible turmoil affecting nearly every individual's life, order finally returned without excessive repression, explains much of the support the emerging political system received in the late 1920s and ever since. The nineteenth century, along with the Revolution and the stark brutality of many aspects of Mexican life, instilled a fear of violence in the nation's population that still runs deep and wide.

But peaceful continuity would not have sufficed to endow the country's institutional framework with the longevity it has enjoyed. If from 1940 Mexico had not experienced an economic boom that lasted until 1982, and which despite inequalities, mismanagement, and waste improved the standard of living of the majority of its people, it is doubtful that social peace would have been maintained. A rural, illiterate, and backward nation became an urban, literate, largely working- and middle-class society in which large islands of rural destitution persist but are no longer its central features.

The national product grew at a yearly average rate of over 6 percent during those forty years—a performance no country in Latin America, and few in the entire Third World, can match. The country's inhabitants acquired a stake in a system that created jobs, delivered subsidies, provided schools and health care, and managed a growing economy. In spite of the injustice, corruption, and enduring poverty, things improved for most Mexicans, though far more for the few and far less for the many.

Prosperity, however—or in any case a better lot in life—like stability and peaceful transitions, did not solve an essential problem the nation had not solved during its first hundred years: how to stop, or at least control, the United States' misdeeds against Mexico without endangering stability or prosperity. The country's leaders had to be seen by the nation as defending Mexico's sovereignty, dignity, and very existence, but without going so far—like Pancho Villa's expedition into Columbus, New Mexico, in 1916—that its integrity became jeopardized.

Last, the Mexican political system has endured as long as it has because it has managed to create a vacuum in its wake. In the perception of the Mexican people, since the late 1920s there has been no alternative to the PRI and the governments in place. Even today, as the political system is clearly exhausted and in need of a major overhaul, the absence of an alternative continues to be one of its greatest strengths.[1]

In mid-1987, during the waning months of his honeymoon with the Mexican political establishment, the U.S. ambassador, Charles Pilliod, Jr., received a public lecture from a predictable source. Pilliod acknowledged in a speech that the United States had intervened in Mexican affairs on three occasions. Gastón García Cantú, a hypernationalist historian, whose views are not widely shared but who for several years has written a front-page column in *Excelsior,* had a different opinion:

From the end of the eighteenth century through 1918, there were 285 invasions, incidents of intimidation, challenges, bombardments of ports, and subtractions of territory out of which seven American states were carved. No people in the world have had their territory, wealth, and security as plundered by anybody as Mexico has by the United States.[2]

The terms are extreme. This dramatic version of the history of U.S.-Mexican relations may not be the one held by eighty-five million Mexicans. Nonetheless, humiliation at the hands of the United States was a constant factor in Mexican life until after the Revolution. Putting an end to it without threatening other, equally desired goals became one of the attributes which succeeding governments emerging from the Revolution deemed indispensable to their survival. The widespread perception in the country at large, regardless of momentary lapses or sectoral disagreements, is that since the early 1930s the existing political system has guaranteed the nation both dignity and the absence of major conflicts with the United States, both sovereignty—compared with the nineteenth century—and cordiality.

In managing government-to-government binational ties, Mexican authorities invariably mention the need for respect from the United States, to never appear to be caving in, giving in, or inviting in the American behemoth. At the same time, they are always careful never to go too far and overstep the bounds of the peaceful, dignified, if not enthusiastic coexistence which has prevailed in the relationship since the 1920s. This requires a never-ending, often apparently incoherent balancing act, the logic of which is only comprehensible when seen as a whole and over time.

The acrobatics involve changes of pace, different roles for different actors, and contrasting discourses for varying audiences at different moments. This is how Mexico has managed its state-to-state ties with the United States for more than a half a century. Many of the recourses, habits, and tricks have outlived their usefulness or outgrown their purpose. But they represent the tried and trusted ways of relative success, and weaning the country and its leaders from them is not an easy process.

From 1940 through the late 1960s, Mexico enjoyed a double honeymoon in its relations with its neighbor. Externally, the United States' overwhelming military and economic supremacy in the world coincided with a period during which Mexico concentrated on its industrialization and preferred to look inward. The United States would not have permitted, and Mexico did not desire, major substantive confrontation. Mexican-American ties, though not without frictions and differences, were uneventful. The Colorado River salinity dispute, with its damage to crops in northwestern Mexico, and the recovery of the Chamizal—a slice of Mexican territory whose possession had changed because of a modification in the course of the Rio Grande—were perhaps the period's most important bilateral issues.

On the internal front, foreign affairs and policy toward the United States in particular were handled in a simple, generally consensual fashion. True, substantive disagreements did occasionally surface, chiefly between the Finance and Foreign ministries, and mainly on economic issues. But even in these cases, the differences did not get out of hand, as shown by the fact that the same individual—Antonio Carrillo Flores, Finance Minister from 1952 to 1958, ambassador to the United States from 1958 to 1964, and Foreign Minister from 1964 to 1970—occupied the posts where most of the infighting was taking place. The additional fact that Carrillo Flores was strongly pro-American showed that, with minor exceptions, binational relations did not divide the political establishment.

In Mexico as in many other countries, the heart of foreign relations is the presidency. In the same way that Charles de Gaulle insisted that foreign policy was his "reserved domain" under the French Constitution of 1958, according to constitutional precepts Mexico's governmental links with the world and thus the U.S. are the President's preserve. The chief executive is not alone at the center of policy, but he is, however, ultimately responsible for whatever happens on the binational front.

During the 1940s and 1950s, decisions were not of great complexity or time-consuming or heartrending. The advantages or the downside of any given option appeared in simple, cut-and-dried terms. The President's authority and wisdom in this domain were unquestioned, and the federal bureaucracy was still sufficiently pliant for his orders to be carried out with reasonable effectiveness. Only sporadically were options brought to the National Palace, or to Los Pinos, as the presidential residence is called, in confrontational terms by the interested agencies. Rarely did two or more entities even deal with the same issues, much less hold differing viewpoints in relation to them. The federal institutions involved in policy toward the United States had their own briefs and dealt with them separately under the President's guidance. A basic consensus, laid down by the President, prevailed on how policy toward Washington should be handled.

Likewise, there were very few disagreements or even diverging viewpoints on U.S. affairs outside the government. The business community, the labor movement, the Church, even the intelligentsia, all backed official policy, with each sector emphasizing the features it liked best and ignoring those which were not to its taste. To a large extent, relations with the United States were of interest only to a few; more important, they directly and significantly affected only a limited number of inhabitants.

During this period, tensions arose due to conflicting forces which affected the country's policy and attitudes toward the U.S. This strain was managed by insulating the decisions that had potentially conflictive implications for the U.S. from the less confrontational measures, and by countering the effects of those decisions with policies running in the opposite direction. The best example was Mexico's refusal to break diplomatic relations with Cuba in the early 1960s and the ensuing tensions with Washington for most of the decade. The continuance of relations had no corollaries in other matters: Mexico supported the United States during the Cuban Missile Crisis, and did not back revolutionary movements elsewhere in the hemisphere or the Third World. More important, within the government, the Foreign Ministry's position of maintaining links with Fidel Castro's regime remained formal and limited to distant diplomatic ties.

Economic relations between Mexico and Cuba ground to a halt; tourism was discouraged and no high-level visits in either direction took place. Above all, the Ministry of the Interior and the presidency itself, through its military chief of staff, cooperated fully with U.S. agencies in watching over the Cuban embassy in Mexico City and by making life miserable for its staff. Julián López, the Cuban ambassador to Nicaragua from 1979 through the mid-1980s, still bears the scars of his treatment at the hands of the Mexican police in 1967. The embassy was regularly photographed and harassed by Mexican officials and watched closely by Americans as well. All travelers to the island, Mexican and foreign, were photographed, fingerprinted, and intimidated at the Mexico City airport. The Mexican embassy in Havana included among its staff Humberto Carrillo Colón, a Mexican journalist recruited by the CIA, sent to Havana with Mexican acquiescence, and soon caught spying by the Cubans.

In the Mexican view, all of this more than made up for the refusal to sever relations; implicitly and reluctantly, the United States accepted this quid pro quo, never going beyond diplomatic pressure and persuasion in its attempts to have Mexico comply with its desires. The policy also met with widespread agreement in Mexico, particularly within the government. The left was happy because American wishes were not acceded to and the only Cuban link to the rest of Latin America remained intact. The right understood that behind diplomatic niceties Mexico was cooperating with the United States on its Cuban policy. The Interior Ministry did not insist that the President break relations; the Foreign Ministry did not question presidential decisions involving personnel in Havana, procedures at the airport, or surveillance of the Cuban mission. Presidents Adolfo López Mateos and Gustavo Díaz Ordaz managed this delicate equilibrium well.

But the honeymoon and the intricate system of presidential fiat and balancing acts contained the germs of their own inoperativeness. The events which closed the decade also brought an end to the period of tranquillity and quiet efficiency in the government's handling of Mexican-American relations. The nostalgic days of apparent serenity and superficial understanding, both masking deep tensions, inequalities, and impositions, had passed. The country which the United States and many of Mexico's own leaders had known since World War II had changed.

The end of American hegemony, U.S.-Soviet nuclear parity, and the Vietnam War coincided with Latin American and Mexican events to conclude this stable phase in Mexican-American relations. The Cuban Revolution had a delayed effect in Mexico, but underlined the possibility of hemispheric independence and diversification, although at a cost. And Mexico was emerging from its period of developmental introspection.

The 1968 student movement shook Mexican society to its very foundations. It impugned the government's lack of nationalism, along with nearly everything else in national life. While the students' main demands concerned civil liberties and the need for democratization, by bringing out the most right-wing features of the nation's political system the movement also stressed the government's closeness to the United States. Many politicians accused the students of being Communist agitators influenced from abroad; others charged them with being part of a subversive plot to impede the celebration of the 1968 Olympic Games. The country's political establishment reached the conclusion that the system had to open up, incorporate the students, and refurbish its "revolutionary image"; it also concluded that the government's nationalist credentials had to be strengthened.

This process became identified with Mexico's next President, Luis Echeverría, paradoxically known for the hard-line, anti-Communist, far from anti-American views he espoused during the six years he served as Gustavo Díaz Ordaz's Minister of the Interior. His metamorphosis was stimulated by two important events in U.S.-Mexican relations which disturbed the serenity of previous years. One was Operation Intercept, the virtual closing of the border between the two nations by Richard Nixon in June 1969. According to the American administration, Mexico was not doing enough to combat drug traffic into the United States. From the Mexican standpoint, Nixon was seeking a scapegoat to hide his government's own impotence in the face of growing drug abuse in the United States. But the most important conclusion many Mexicans drew from the three-week slowdown at the border concerned the lack of American trustworthiness. The Díaz Ordaz regime, known for its moderate approach to the United States, was not even forewarned.

Likewise, when in August 1971 the Nixon administration without warning imposed a 10 percent duty on imports, severely affecting all countries but particularly Mexico, which sold over 70 percent of its exports to the United States, the recently inaugurated Echeverría government felt betrayed. What was the purpose of striving for close ties with the United States when it treated Mexico no differently from other countries—that is, selfishly and arrogantly? All these factors led to a revision of previous governments' belief that the country enjoyed a "special relationship" with the United States. It was never clear what this term actually meant, or what Mexico truly expected. But by early 1972 the Echeverría government decided that its predecessors had gone too far in accommodating the United States. The peace and quiet of years gone by was no longer deemed necessary, given the relative decline in U.S. power, and no longer desirable, in view of the wear which the development model on which the previous tranquillity rested was beginning to show.

From that largely implicit and subconscious decision stem a number of trends which continue to determine the Mexican government's management of bilateral affairs. The process whereby the country began to search for ways to establish its independence, diversify its foreign links, and redefine its relations with the United States coincided with a period during which international factors acquired greater relevance in domestic affairs. Ties with the United States, in particular, grew exponentially: more of the same in some cases, entirely new trends in others.

From the emergence of the border region as an entity with interests possibly different from those of the rest of the country to the growth of Mexico's foreign debt from less than $5 billion in 1970 to over $105 billion in 1988; from the previous consensus within and without official circles on policy toward the United States to growing dissension inside each administration; from presidential anger over humiliation at the hands of the United States to presidential despair over the country's apparent impotence in binational matters due to domestic factors: the 1970s and 1980s brought dramatic changes in Mexico's U.S. policy. Today's frictions and tensions have little in common with the placidity of the honeymoon years, but the former are more in tune with reality than the latter.

Today the President is still at the center of Mexico's relations with Washington, but he presides over a more complex situation. The number of federal agencies with American connections has grown dramatically; so has the importance of previously existing connections. In economic matters, because of the close ties that Mexico has been obliged to establish with the U.S. Treasury, the Federal Reserve, and most significantly the International Monetary Fund and the World Bank, the number of economic entities dealing with the United States has also increased.

The Finance Ministry nominally handles most economic negotiations, but the Programming and Budget Ministry participates in policy matters as the central economic policymaking body. The Central Bank logically is involved in those negotiations, particularly regarding monetary policy, interest rates, and new lending, while the Trade and Industrial Development Ministry, together with the Foreign Trade Bank, handles trade matters, and Nacional Financiera, the national development bank, negotiates loans. The Ministry of Energy, Mining, and State-Owned Industry also takes part in economic policy negotiations and loan negotiations; most of the industrial reconversion strategy, including privatization, is under its wing.

The Ministry of Agriculture deals with its American counterpart on issues of common concern such as sanitation and disease control. PEMEX, the national oil monopoly, sells petroleum to the U.S. Strategic Reserve, although this is also handled by the Ministry of Energy. The Ministry of Communications and Transportation negotiates airline agreements and radio frequency sharing with the United States. The Ecology and Urban Development Ministry deals with the Environmental Protection Agency on matters ranging from acid rain originating in Arizona-based copper smelters and drifting over the border to the treatment of Tijuana–San Diego sewage. The Ministry of Labor holds talks on immigration.

The growth in the agencies involved extends also to the number of officials within each ministry who deal with the United States. It is no longer rare for director generals, similar in rank and responsibility to U.S. deputy assistant secretaries, to conduct substantive, front-line negotiations with their American counterparts. If one multiplies the amount of agencies by the number of officials in each one having something to do with the United States, the total can be numbing.

Economic affairs, however, are only part of the picture, though from the Mexican perspective they are probably the most important one. The Ministry of the Interior, in charge of internal security and domestic politics, handles binational security matters. With the FBI, it takes up law enforcement questions not handled by the Attorney General's office; with the CIA it cooperates in keeping watch on Eastern bloc embassies and Latin American revolutionaries in Mexico. With the Bureau of Alcohol, Tobacco, and Firearms, it conducts negotiations on binational theft and smuggling. Terrorism and immigration are also on its binational agenda.

But to the extent that the Minister of the Interior is in charge of the government's day-to-day political management and security matters, he often becomes a privileged interlocutor on strictly political affairs for the

United States government and its ambassador. In Mexico, as in other countries where it exists, the job is considered to be of a right-wing slant, and is frequently offered to politicians with a right-wing reputation, although there have been exceptions. Since its everyday chores make its occupant a hard-liner even if he wasn't one originally, the Minister of the Interior may be chosen by the President or simply ends up being the cabinet member most able to mend fences with the United States when others have picked too many fights. President Echeverría's and President De la Madrid's respective Interior Ministers—Mario Moya Palencia and Manuel Bartlett—both played such a role, getting along reasonably well with the U.S. ambassador—Joseph John Jova in the first case, chiefly John Gavin in the second—while other cabinet officers, mainly the Foreign Minister, come to have a poor relationship with the ambassador.

The Attorney General's office also has a number of important U.S. connections, the most well-known and conflict-generating one being drug enforcement. Through the Federal Security Directorate, the Attorney General's office is the country's chief drug enforcement body and thus the United States' Drug Enforcement Administration's principal counterpart—a doubtful privilege which until 1985 it shared with the Federal Security Directorate, located at the Ministry of the Interior. It gets the merit for cooperation when things work well—between 1972 and 1983—and is the victim of drug-related "Mexico-bashing" when they don't.

Finally, the Ministry of Defense and to a minor extent the Ministry of the Navy have their own ties with the United States. While these relationships are real and varied, they have never been as intimate as those which most other Latin armed forces have enjoyed with their American colleagues. Mexico has not sent officers for extended duration to U.S. Army, Navy, or Air Force training schools, or to the counterinsurgency facilities in Panama; it has always refused even the most remote insinuation of any American military presence in Mexico. Although the size of the Mexican military mission in Washington is substantial, its main purpose is weapons and equipment procurement, rather than coordination or exchange of information.[3]

But the links are close nevertheless, and high-ranking Mexican military officers frequently visit U.S. military installations in Washington and elsewhere. The American military attachés at the embassy in Mexico are very active, and undoubtedly have contacts within the Mexican military which both governments would prefer to keep out of the public light. There is more than meets the eye to U.S.-Mexican military relations—as shown, for example, by the reports published in early 1987 about landing rights granted by the Ministry of Defense to U.S. helicopters shuttling to and from Honduras for military maneuvers.[4] But in general terms this area of government-to-government relations seems, for now, to be of minor importance.

Broadly speaking, individual agencies in the Mexican government with sectoral, technical ties to the United States reflect and sometimes represent those forces within Mexican society which are pushing for closer relations between the two countries. Above all, the entities involved in economic affairs—the Ministries of Finance, Programming and Budget, Trade and Industrial Development, the Central Bank, and to a lesser extent the Ministry of Energy, Mining, and State-Owned Industry—are the spokesmen for the forces of economic integration driving the two nations together. The officials they employ are no less patriotic or more "pro-American" than others, but their natural constituencies lead them to fulfill this function.

These are also the ministries that have the closest connections with the Mexican private sector. Although reluctant to forsake the many specific forms of state-sponsored protection with which it has been favored for several decades, the business community systematically lobbies in general terms for less conflictive relations with the United States. It insists that the government be more conciliatory with its neighbor on all issues not directly affecting its immediate interests, but that it push harder on matters of direct concern to the private sector. Its natural interlocutors in the government are by definition the economic ministries, who on occasion sympathize with the private sector's conception of Mexican-American affairs, although they may not share it entirely. In their view, the Mexican government should be more conciliatory with Washington on all noneconomic issues in order to achieve greater progress on economic matters.

The economic and financial bureaucracy can also be a vehicle for American government pressure. During most of the De la Madrid administration, the United States repeatedly tried to make Mexico shift its Central American policy. This pressure was frequently applied through the economic ministries in Mexico. Often when a Mexican cabinet member would enter into delicate economic negotiations with an American counterpart, he would receive the message: it would be so much easier to solve important economic problems between the two nations if only Mexico would stop obstructing U.S. policy in Central America. Although the Mexican official would in general reject his American colleague's interpretation, on his return to Mexico City he would dutifully inform the President, who though quite aware that most of this was bluff and that the road to economic cooperation with the United States did not run through Managua, would nonetheless have to take it into account as a point of view held by his own cabinet officers. The economic officials would also circulate the story of their Washington meetings among members of the private sector, who would accept it at face value, not so much because they believed it—although some did—as because it dovetailed with their own stance.

Despite the fact that it no longer coordinates, centralizes, or even closely follows most of the multiple negotiations and exchanges between the Mexican government and the United States, the country's Foreign Ministry plays a key role in policy toward the United States. Institutionally, it handles all government-to-government ties. Despite the bonds many government agencies on both sides of the border have directly established with each other, because of inertia a great deal of communication passes through the Foreign Ministry. The twenty-story, white marble tower in Tlatelolco engages in myriad negotiations, problems, and procedural issues as well as mountains of paperwork. Its functions range from processing import permits for American embassy staffers bringing cars in from the United States to the work of the International Boundary and Water Commission; from political matters of great importance to both nations, such as the situation in Central America, to dozens of daily diplomatic communications.

Both abroad and in Mexico, the Foreign Ministry has in recent times been considered the most leftward-oriented of Mexico's federal agencies involved in relations with the United States. There is a grain of truth in this stereotype, but not much more than that. The question is not whether Foreign Ministry officials are more to the left or more nationalistic than other sectors of the bureaucracy; it is doubtful they are. The real issue is whether the institutional role played by the Foreign Ministry drives it toward more confrontational positions, which are balanced out by other ministries, which generally fulfill more conciliatory functions.

Several simple characteristics of the Foreign Ministry's functions in U.S.-Mexican affairs explain this situation. The traditional diplomats—not always captained by one of their own[5]—form the only sector of the government, with the exception of the President, that approaches bilateral relations from a political perspective. The negotiators of an airline agreement on behalf of the Ministry of Communications and Transportation, for instance, may understand the political implications of their work, but they perceive it—correctly—as a technical task. Even the security apparatus views its form of cooperation with the United States as basically nonpolitical.

Officials from the Finance Ministry frequently handle far more delicate and important matters in Mexican-American relations than the Foreign Ministry, but they also tend to see their negotiations, confrontations, and agreements with Americans from a technical perspective: interest rates, oil prices, etc. They are no less patriotic than other officials; they are as interested in the larger picture of binational relations as their diplomatic colleagues. Nor are they less versed than the latter in American motivation, strategy, and tactics toward Mexico.

But they invariably sublimate that knowledge and plunge into their technical negotiations without placing them in the broader context of the two nations' overall relations. They do not address the political implications of a given technical agreement, be it on drug enforcement, countervailing duties, or the terms of new IMF, World Bank, and commercial bank lending. They are right in doing so: their job is to reach agreements issue by issue and leave the politics to others.

An additional explanation of the Foreign Ministry's role in binational matters derives from the fact that it is the only Mexican agency, together with the presidency, to have an across-the-board view of bilateral relations. While it is clearly incapable of keeping tabs on everything, and is often uninformed about certain contacts, it possesses a reasonably complete picture of most matters under consideration by both nations. Every other entity will inevitably judge the entire gamut of U.S.-Mexican relations by the progress—or lack of it—in its particular field. Only the Foreign Ministry, and through it the presidency, has an overall perception.

When relations in general are on a sound footing, the Foreign Ministry will in theory place particular contentious issues in the context of broader, more positive ties. It will play down the importance of the matter in hand. But given the historical trend in U.S.-Mexican affairs, the opposite situation often prevails. An individual Mexican agency, often in tandem with its American counterpart, will tend to believe, if the state of its specific relations is good, that the same holds true for the state of general relations.

More paradoxically, it will become convinced that overall relations could be as good as its particular ties with the United States, if only its example were followed. As Mexico's Secretary of Agriculture said in an interview in 1987:

I personally have maintained rather good relations with American producers and authorities in the agricultural field. Some of these relations have prospered despite political differences. And I have

dealt with my counterparts so easily and naturally that sometimes
I wonder why the hell we can't always manage things this way in
relations between Mexico and the United States.[6]

The Foreign Ministry plays the role of the spoilsport. It constantly
points out—to the President, the rest of the government, and the country
at large—that short-term appearances in, say, agricultural matters notwithstanding, overall relations are not particularly good. It is forced to
stress that the administration whose Department of Agriculture seems
to be cooperating on sanitation inspection for Mexican lemons is no
different from the one complaining to the press about corruption in
Mexico. It reminds everyone that the ambassador making a nuisance of
himself through his abrasive remarks, the Secretary of the Treasury who
steadfastly refuses to consider any innovative solutions to the debt crisis,
and the "friendly" Secretary of Agriculture belong to the same U.S.
administration.

The final reason which explains the Foreign Ministry's reputation as
a factor of contention in U.S.-Mexican relations involves its links to
society. The Foreign Office is the President's ministry. It has no real
money of its own, and no grass-roots constituency. There are no domestic interlocutors who pressure it or come running to it in search of favors
or solutions, and there is no great opportunity for public notoriety except
at the very top. But because the Foreign Ministry deals with an area
central to many Mexicans, it is the President's ministry, and the Foreign
Minister is perceived as the President's man, with scant political following or clout of his own. No Foreign Minister in modern times has been
a serious presidential contender.

Since it is the President's agency, it is also the head of a coalition whose
purpose it is to defend and promote the President's foreign policy, whatever it may be, and which is the true, though not often apparent constituency for Mexico's nationalistic foreign policy. Key components of this
coalition are the ruling party, the Congress, the majority of the country's
intellectuals, parts of the labor movement, and most of the Mexico City
press with the exception of newspapers directly linked to the business
community. Each sector plays a greater or minor role in the coalition
depending on the incumbent President's preferences. The PRI had an
important foreign affairs function during the Echeverría administration,
a highly visible role in the López Portillo regime, but virtually none with
Miguel de la Madrid, under whom the Senate enjoyed a relatively high
profile.

But in contrast to countries where those who make up a coalition hold
significant quotas of power in their own right, in Mexico the foreign

policy establishment has little weight to speak of. It represents a significant force in Mexican society only because its components are the
mouthpieces through which Mexican nationalism and suspicion, fear,
and resentment of the United States speak. The entire mechanism leaves
open the question whether this form of representation is faithful and
accurate, but the political elite believes it to be so and nothing has so far
disproved this belief. The political system works as if the foreign policy
establishment directly expressed the grass-roots nationalism embedded
in the hearts and minds of the Mexican people.

Unlike the U.S. case, this establishment constitutes the rank-and-file
support for the President's reserved domain. He does not negotiate that
support; he need not nurture or court it. The sectors which make it up
are there precisely to support the President's foreign policy, and particularly his policy toward the United States, whatever its nature. It is
worthy of support because it is the President's policy, not because of its
intrinsic merits. The support for the policy predates the policy itself,
explaining why the same individuals, groups, and political currents can
all back policies which may seem diametrically opposed. Foreign policy
is considered immutable: official pronouncements on policy toward the
United States always include apparently incongruous statements to the
effect that the nation's stance, as President De la Madrid has expressed
it, "is not influenced by issues arising out of internal political disputes
between different factions."[7]

The job of formulating the country's U.S. policy in ways that allow
the mechanisms linking it to the rest of Mexican society to function
adequately; the task of "selling" the President's policy to this disparate
coalition; the role of choosing the right terms, making the right speeches,
leaking the right information, and selecting the correct people for intimate access falls largely to the Foreign Ministry. It packages the policy,
puts it in historical perspective, and justifies the obvious twists and turns
in policy toward the United States by showing how in fact there are no
such fluctuations. Its task is to remove pressure from the President by
placing itself at least implicitly to his left, allowing him to appear above
the fray and responsive to nationalistic pressures from the ministry, the
people, and the intellectuals as well as to pro-American pressures from
the right, the business community, the Church, and other parts of his
own Cabinet.

On some occasions, this role is artificially concocted. During the
López Portillo administration, the President's three most controversial
and "left-wing" trips abroad—two to Nicaragua, one to Cuba—were all
decided by the chief executive without his Foreign Minister's knowledge,
and in the case of a February 1982 visit to Managua, against the advice

given by the minister when he learned of it. Yet López Portillo continued—correctly—to portray himself as being to the right of the Foreign Ministry, and the ministry continued to play the game of appearing to be to the left of the President.

Since 1977, presidential encounters between the two nations have become regular, mostly yearly events. Some years—1978, 1980 1985, 1987—have been skipped; during others, there have been multiple meetings, as in 1981 when López Portillo and Reagan met four times. Each time, the Mexican leader must fulfill contradictory demands. He must represent the nation as a whole: any mistake, slight, or defeat is the country's, not just his own. He must also be perceived as giving equal consideration to the views of the right and the left, of both pro-American and nationalistic forces, of economic realities and political imperatives.

Like all chiefs of state, he must address his domestic constituency, but cannot neglect or forget the importance of his foreign interlocutor and, in the case of the United States, its own constituency in Mexico. He must do so without a personal and professional staff. To this day the Mexican presidency does not have a National Security Council type of foreign affairs staff, although Presidents have had informal advisers.

He also has to cope with some of the peculiar habits recent American administrations have developed in negotiating with other nations. For reasons which have to do with American idealism and dislike for realpolitik, the United States expresses its demands in an indirect, disguised fashion. Instead of clearly stating its agenda, it often sets forth its point of view as in fact being in the other nation's interest, presenting itself as acting more out of concern for its interlocutor's well-being than out of acknowledged self-interest. This American trait returned with a vengeance under Ronald Reagan, coinciding with Mexico's economic crisis. American demands of Mexico were presented as remedies for Mexico's ills, not as concessions desired by the United States in pursuance of its own interests.

Mexico's joining GATT, changing its foreign investment legislation, protecting American intellectual property provisions, privatizing state-owned firms, cutting subsidies, or increasing drug enforcement activities were all brought up by the United States, not as concessions the United States wanted Mexico to make, but as measures which Mexico should take to solve its own problems. Even on Central America, Reagan administration pressure on Mexico to support U.S. policy was presented not as an outright demand but as something Mexico should do for its own good—to "stem the tide of Communism in Central America," which threatened stability in a way which "Mexico underestimated."

The rub, of course, is that if these policy decisions are implemented by Mexico in this context, they do not bring with them corresponding concessions on the part of the United States. Paradoxically, since the Mexican government always prefers to present its economic policy, or its position on Central America, as the result of its own initiative, and not in response to U.S. pressure, it boxed itself into a corner by accepting this very American way of viewing international relations.

During the De la Madrid administration, Mexico was not able to extract concessions from Washington in exchange for many of the policies it had embarked upon largely as a result of U.S. urging. This weakened Mexico's bargaining stance, often forcing it into one-sided agreements. Mexico must emphasize that its "best interests" are not a subject of negotiation. It is not for the United States to define what "Mexico should do for its own good." Mexico should not acquiesce in this U.S. tactic, whatever passing domestic political advantages it may entail.

In preparing for summits, the President receives briefing books and extensive advice from cabinet members involved in Mexican-American affairs. He holds cabinet meetings at which all or most of the ministers express their views, frequently at odds with each other. In the last analysis, however, he must decide alone without relying on a potentially "neutral" body whose responsibility would be to set out the parameters of each decision. If Mexico is to improve its management of international matters, it will soon have to set up some sort of staff or council to coordinate the nation's foreign affairs. The President can no longer do so on his own.

The problems inherent in this situation surfaced in mid-1986 when Mexico came close to unilaterally suspending payments on its foreign debt. Oil, which then earned 75 percent of the country's exports, had plummeted from over $25 per barrel to below $12. Mexico had received no new funds from abroad for nearly two years and was running out of cash. It seemed increasingly difficult to continue meeting yearly interest payments of almost $10 billion.

De la Madrid had to take a variety of factors into account to make his decision. The economic aspects of the issue were relatively clear, and the Finance Ministry was as knowledgeable an agency in this field as one could find anywhere. But De la Madrid knew that the economic facet of the question was only one part. Other considerations, mainly political, were involved, as were other Mexican federal entities.

How would the American government respond to a unilateral Mexican decision? The Foreign Ministry and the embassy in Washington had their views, not necessarily identical. At that very time, Jesse Helms was holding his Senate hearings, and certain mid- and high-level U.S. officials were denouncing Mexico and its government while others were supporting the De la Madrid record. Did the Helms sessions in May have anything to do with the threat De la Madrid made in February to suspend payments?

The American press was another factor. It had been highly critical of the Mexican government and political system in recent times, often paralleling right-wing American views. How would it respond to a Mexican moratorium? The agency charged with knowing the answer was the Presidential Spokesman's office, whose views on nearly everything were different from those held at the Foreign Ministry, the Mexican embassy in Washington, and the Finance Ministry. What would the domestic reaction be? Would Mexico's middle classes and private sector panic, make massive purchases of dollars, and fall prey to absurd rumors, as they had done in the past? This was the Interior Ministry's domain, but its assessment had to take into account how the U.S. embassy in Mexico would act. This in turn depended on Washington's position, the analysis of which was the Foreign Ministry's task.

The final decision was President De la Madrid's. He made it, fired his Finance Minister, who rumor had it supported a different course, and opted for prolonged negotiations to obtain fresh credits. Jesús Silva Herzog's dismissal was probably more linked to domestic political considerations, and in particular to who De la Madrid's successor would be, than to foreign debt policy, but the connections between succession politics, economic policy, and Mexican-American relations were plain to all. The Mexican chief executive got his new loans on good terms, but Mexico continued to pay huge amounts of money in debt service. Whether the United States pressured, threatened, or persuaded Mexico to follow this route—Federal Reserve Chairman Paul Volcker made a secret trip to Mexico in the thick of the decision-making process— remains unknown. The Mexican President's decision involved a great number of considerations, and virtually no institutional process for reviewing them. This was the flip side of his enormous, but terribly solitary power.

On the eve of summits, but also in general, the issue of the two nations' and governments' asymmetry tends to surface. This is most clearly reflected in the question of "who sees whom." The U.S. ambassador is received by the President almost whenever he requests an appointment; the Mexican ambassador in Washington seldom sees the Secretary of State and almost never the President or the White House Chief of Staff.

While this lack of reciprocity is not exclusive to Mexico, it often gets out of hand because it trickles down to lower levels.

Thus the Assistant Secretary of State for Inter-American affairs tends to think that since he is the senior official in the government dealing with Mexico, he should handle matters at no less than cabinet level in Mexico and should see the Mexican President whenever he considers it necessary. Other, low- or middle-level U.S. officials think along similar lines. Needless to say, although presidential emissaries are sometimes received at high levels, the possibilities of mid-level Mexican officials seeing any U.S. cabinet member are virtually nil.

But the question of asymmetry goes beyond hierarchy and protocol. It leads to the more substantive issue of "disproportionate importance," which, more than most matters, has complicated Mexico's management of its ties with the United States. Because of the tremendous differences in size, wealth, and power between the two nations, Mexico is often seriously affected by American actions which derive either from minor bureaucratic decisions or from U.S. government policy addressed to all nations but hitting Mexico harder than others.

Internally the public clamor can be deafening, since the particular U.S. policy—the 1971 10 percent import fee, the 1986 eleven-cent oil import fee, the obligation to acquire U.S. insurance in Texas for all Mexican vehicles in 1987—can have serious consequences in Mexico. Yet there is little the Mexican government can do, given that it is dealing with American acts that do not belong to the realm of U.S. policy toward Mexico or, if they do, are at a very low level, on which Mexican authorities have scant leverage. The fact that American authorities sporadically and falsely invoke this situation, pretending that a certain decision is simply bureaucratic or low-level when in fact it is not—for example, the Customs Commissioner virtually closing down the U.S.-Mexican border in February 1985—does not diminish its significance.

It is often exceedingly difficult, if not impossible, for the Mexican government to get high-level American attention on issues of great import to Mexico but of small interest to the United States. All nations suffer from this problem, yet it affects Mexico more, since the number of minor issues on its agenda with the United States is greater than for other countries. Mexico often finds itself in the frustrating situation of having no interlocutor on issues which it deems important but are insignificant to its neighbor.

In addition, the President of Mexico has to cope with an apparently minor nuisance that in fact can create serious turbulence for the government. The Mexican press, while relatively critical of the government insofar as editorials, op-ed articles, and political columns are concerned, is highly controlled with regard to hard news. This is all the more true in relation to coverage of sensitive issues; there are few more sensitive than Mexican-American relations, particularly at the presidential level. To a considerable extent, the authorities can control and regulate the information appearing in the press regarding the country's policy toward the United States. The cost of this control is high, though, since it is largely responsible for the dreadful state of press coverage of news from the United States regarding Mexico.

Fourth-rate correspondents, part-time stringers, censored copy, and wire service sourcing by the Mexican media make it possible for the government to partially control what is printed. The other side of this is that the news coming from the United States and printed in the Mexican media on Washington's policy toward Mexico, or U.S.-Mexican relations as seen in the United States, bears little relation to reality. The mechanism is a sad but well-oiled one.

A Mexican journalist is sent to Washington on special assignment or as a shoestring correspondent. His editors have to justify the expenses involved and so does the journalist. Since there is not a large number of news items concerning Mexico in the United States, the correspondent begins to invent stories, either of his own volition or under pressure from his superiors. Typically the reports have an anti-American bent, because this way the chances of obtaining front-page space are greater.

Unknown American academics are interviewed, with resulting banner headlines warning of terrible things to come for Mexico. Documents with little or no authority or circulation are quoted as if they emerged from the Oval Office. Mexican academics or politicians are then questioned as to their reaction to the spectacular (and meaningless) statements quoted from the United States. Finally the government is queried as to its views in relation to both the original story from the United States and the commentary surrounding it in Mexico.

The Foreign Ministry or the President's spokesmen know full well that in the overwhelming majority of these cases there is literally nothing to comment on or react to. Yet were they to say so, it would mean accusing the press of making things up or telling the country that the government attaches no importance to a seemingly serious situation. Neither option is acceptable, so the government is forced to adopt a stance with regard to a non-event. And the President, just before his coming meeting with the American President, is forced to act publicly as if the non-event existed, as if he was truly concerned about it, and perhaps even to promise that he will take it up with the U.S. chief of state.

Sometimes more extreme solutions can result. In July 1987 the government news agency correspondent in Washington wrote a story reporting that a De la Madrid–Reagan meeting would take place that August. The upcoming Mexican presidential succession would be high on the agenda, read the cable. The following day the Mexican presidency issued a formal denial (the story was wrong) and fired the correspondent, who was later reinstated because of union pressure. He had followed a poor tip because of the urge to make headlines, and the government had felt forced to reprimand him for creating turbulences on the eve of the presidential succession.

The President must also make a series of decisions regarding the public relations aspect of his meetings with his colleague from the United States. In some cases, he clearly prefers a so-called successful meeting, in which some formal agreements, no matter how unimportant, will be signed and presented to public opinion as evidence of success. In others, the opposite is desirable: a cool meeting with no confrontation but no warmth or effusiveness either. This option is valid for both sides.

In July 1979, for example, Ambassador Patrick J. Lucey confidentially told the Mexican government that if the two countries reached an agreement on a pricing formula under which private American companies would purchase natural gas from Mexico, Jimmy Carter would prefer that this not be linked to the visit by President López Portillo a few months later. Despite the fact that the breakdown in gas price negotiations had seriously soured Mexican-American relations just two years before, and notwithstanding the importance both nations attached to the issue, Carter's envoy told the Mexican government that for domestic political reasons the American President did not want to be associated with an agreement which would be too favorable for Mexico.

Just before a summit but in fact almost always, the Mexican government, and consequently the President, must decide how hard and how publicly the nation's case should be pushed. For obvious reasons, and mainly since the late 1970s, Mexican officials have enjoyed privileged access to the U.S. media, academia, the corporate world, and the Congress. Many sectors of American public opinion may not agree with what the Mexican government has to say, others may even have a strongly unfavorable bias against it, but most are willing to listen. In a majority of cases, however, the Mexican government has proved unwilling to be listened to.

In the past, Mexican authorities had for practical purposes limited official ties to Washington and, within the U.S. capital, to the executive branch. Although there are more than forty Mexican consulates throughout the United States—far more than any other nation has—and many American cities with large Mexican populations (not just Americans of Mexican descent), Mexican interests, or significant local interests in Mexico, the nation's leaders have traditionally preferred to deal almost exclusively with Washington. While the U.S. Congress has played an important role in U.S.-Mexican affairs since Congressman Abraham Lincoln questioned the U.S. invasion in 1847, Mexico has confined its links with the U.S. legislative branch to specific instances, on an ad hoc, private basis. The yearly, binational interparliamentary meetings are useful safety valves and have proved adequate for airing differences, but have little impact on policy.

Until ten or fifteen years ago, this strategy worked well for Mexico. With minor exceptions, most of the nation's official business with the United States could be conducted in Washington and with the executive, undeniably Mexico's best ally within the U.S. government. There was no overpowering necessity to reach out beyond Washington or to establish a long-term policy of dealing with the Congress. Until the Vietnam War and Watergate, the American presidency, together with the State Department and the NSC, was, as far as Mexico was concerned, a relatively effective interlocutor. An agreement with the executive implied a guarantee of intent and implementation. There was no need to touch other bases. Nor did it seem logical: the Mexican government works in a highly centralized fashion, and there is a natural tendency to believe every government does.

Most important, Mexican authorities have always felt that a more active, forceful, and wide-ranging presentation of Mexico's views in the United States would lead to the most dire of consequences: reciprocity. The belief is that the United States would take advantage of Mexican representatives lobbying the Congress and addressing academic groups in New England or corporate dinners in the Midwest to do the same in Mexico. The nation has felt that it would violate the principle of nonintervention by adopting a higher profile in the United States, thereby opening its flank to similar acts by the United States, against which the principle of nonintervention could no longer be invoked. Mexico would have been the first to break it.

This perspective is beginning to change in Mexico, though not always in the right direction. The De la Madrid administration hired a number of U.S. public relations and lobbying firms, the choices being of dubious judgment and success. The contracting with Michael Deaver, later convicted of influence peddling, was not the best idea the Mexican government ever had; the hiring of the Hannaford Company, formerly associated with Deaver, was carried out against the wishes of the Mexican embassy in Washington, dooming the operation to eventual failure. The contract was later rescinded and a new one was drawn up with another firm.

Despite the mistakes, there is an emerging current of opinion in Mexico convinced that the government can no longer limit its activities in the United States to Washington and the executive. Increasingly, there are calls for a more aggressive Mexican policy, which would, in a sense, take Mexico's case directly to the American people, outside the American capital and on a lasting basis. A more dynamic stance by the country's consuls throughout the United States, acting as mini-ambassadors, a more forceful presence by Mexican officials and intellectuals in the American media, and a broader national debate with regard to the difficult issue of how to deal with the Congress are some of the possible features of a new Mexican stance.

The question of broadening the Mexican government's reach in the United States leads directly to the last and possibly most important difficulty the President of Mexico must face in his meetings and dealings with the U.S. chief executive. The problem is, of course, one which every world leader has had to grapple with when dealing with the United States, at least since the early 1970s: who's in charge?

In Mexico's case, the proverbial unaccountability of the American political system—the President not controlling the separate agencies within his own executive branch, which disagree with each other, the Congress not agreeing with the President, the entire mess coming to a climax and crisis under Ronald Reagan—is made worse by the great number of federal and state-level entities involved in Mexican affairs. Furthermore, because of the domestic implications of many U.S.-Mexican issues, more members of the Congress tend to become involved in these affairs than in other routine cases.

When trying to ascertain the actual U.S. position on a given issue, the President of Mexico faces an array of divergent, incoherent, and often contradictory stances. The Mexican leader knows that his American colleague can impose his views if he commits sufficient resources, but only at a high political price. Moreover, the Mexican chief executive knows that the U.S. President can only act that way a finite number of times; at some point, his political capital with the Congress, departments, and state authorities dries up.

In the last analysis, the Mexican President is forced to make educated guesses as to those issues on which he should press for U.S. presidential action. He has to decide on which occasions his American colleague is arguing in good faith that he cannot go to the mat with the Congress and when he is simply using American Presidents' traditional excuse for inaction: "The Congress will not buy it." The seeds are sown here for one of the more serious problems in recent Mexican-American relations.

The personal relationship between the two Presidents is of great importance to Mexico, because so much depends on the correct assessment the Mexican chief executive has of his American counterpart's stance and favorable disposition toward Mexico. At the same time, the frequent meetings between the two leaders and their even more constant communication in other forms also create numerous opportunities for mistaken interpretations, feelings of deception and disappointment, which end up giving way to personal animosity, such as between José López Portillo and Jimmy Carter, or good personal chemistry, as between Miguel de la Madrid and Ronald Reagan. Political decisions, like Mexico's refusal to readmit the Shah of Iran in November 1979 or the American closing down of the border over drug disputes, are taken as personal betrayals. But one President's perception of broken trust is the other's defense of national interests, however arguable the latter may seem to his opposite number.

Excessive personal communication can often complicate matters: while obviously more effective and rapid, it can lead to uncomfortable situations. It is much more difficult to say no to the President of another country than to a lower-level official; and even among Presidents, some things are better left unsaid. The roller-coaster cycle of the Mexican President's personal relationship with his American colleague reflects the ups and downs of overall relations from the Mexican standpoint.

Every Mexican President since Luis Echeverría, who took office in late 1970, has begun his term with solid pro-American credentials and with the firm desire to improve Mexico's relations with the United States. Echeverría started with a staunch anti-Communist background of cooperation with the United States intelligence and security branches from the Ministry of the Interior, where he worked for twelve years at the highest levels. Although Echeverría had perhaps less affinity or sentimental and cultural attachment to the United States than his successors, he was bent on undertaking a comprehensive negotiation with Mexico's neighbor and reaching a grand understanding. He named a Foreign Minister, Emilio Rabasa, who spoke perfect English, whose mother was from Brooklyn, and who had been sent previously as ambassador to Washington to familiarize himself with—and become familiar to—the U.S. foreign policy establishment.

José López Portillo became President in December 1976, in the midst of a major economic upheaval and a significant crisis in U.S.-Mexican relations. As a former Finance Minister, traditionally one of the most pro-American ministries in the Mexican government, López Portillo was known for his even-keeled, moderate views toward the United States. He entered the presidency absolutely intent on improving relations, deciding to eliminate sore spots, particularly Echeverría's anti-American Third World rhetoric and posturing, as well as the contentious issues which led to strains in Mexico's relations with Israel and the Jewish community in the United States. Mexico's new President once again named a pro-American Foreign Minister, a new ambassador to Washington, who had already been posted there for six years during the honeymoon period of U.S.-Mexican relations, and quickly signed an agreement with the IMF to obtain money and show his willingness to brave the fires of Mexican nationalism.

On taking office in December 1982, Miguel de la Madrid became Mexico's first modern President to have studied in the United States and to truly come from the financial side of the Mexican bureaucracy. He made clear from the very beginning that after the disputes and contentiousness over Central America, Mexico's debt, and other issues which had marked the last year of the outgoing López Portillo regime, good relations with the United States would receive a high priority. By the nature of his appointments, the content of his statements, and most importantly through the implications of his policy toward the United States, De la Madrid informed both countries that he wanted to reduce tensions, stop the bickering and nitpicking, and strengthen bilateral cooperation.

As is already apparent, by the end of their terms, none of Mexico's last three Presidents had achieved anything near his original intentions. All presided over a serious deterioration in U.S.-Mexican relations. More importantly, from a Mexican perspective, their own personal level of animosity, irritation, and disappointment with Washington had by all accounts reached extremely high levels.

They all came to feel betrayed, having bent over backwards to accommodate U.S. concerns, improve relations, and pay the domestic political costs of friendship. In exchange, they received virtually nothing in terms of concrete concessions. Almost tragically, the chief executive who least let his feelings dominate policy quite possibly also was the one who ended up harboring the strongest negative sentiments toward the United States.

All three Presidents began by thinking that a new leaf had to be turned in U.S.-Mexican relations, that Mexico had to adopt a more mature attitude, breaking with the past, not allowing every minor disagreement to transform itself into a matter of national sovereignty. Each one was convinced that this new stance was possible and that it had not emerged previously because the country was not ready and because of obsolete opinions held by over-the-hill diplomats or intellectuals whose influence was greater than warranted. The three Presidents were convinced of the need to preserve Mexico's "conflictive capability" with the United States on substantive issues truly affecting the country's national interests, leaving by the wayside minor points of contention which did not deserve the importance they traditionally received.

The three efforts ended in complete failure. By the middle of their terms, and far more categorically toward the end, Echeverría, López Portillo, and De la Madrid had picked fights with the United States over innumerable major and minor issues, resorting to the most traditional, nationalistic postures and maneuvers and listening to veteran intellectual, diplomatic, or political establishment "gringo-bashers."

On a more substantive plane, they had concluded that Washington was determined to dominate Mexico, weaken its institutions, and destabilize their particular administrations. Although they all respected the maxim that Mexico's President has to get along with the United States, and continued to let more moderate views take precedence in their policymaking process, their convictions and sentiments had come around full circle. If at the beginning of their terms, Mexico's last three Presidents truly desired better, more stable, and conflict-free relations with the United States, by the end of their six years in office they had reached the conclusion that these were not possible, and probably not even desirable.

There are important differences among Mexico's last three administrations. Relations with the United States were undoubtedly far more erratic during the De la Madrid years than before: they had practically never been as poor as they were from 1984 to late 1986; they were quite good in 1987. The fact that De la Madrid's entire term coincided with the tenure in the White House of the most conservative, most ideological President in recent American history had much to do with these excessive fluctuations. De la Madrid tried more than his predecessors to end his term with relations on a stable note; he seemed more sensitive to the need to avoid end-of-regime crises, both domestically and in Mexico's international relations.

But from a more abstract vantage point, the process seems identical. De la Madrid may have made more concessions to the United States, or may have been more accommodating to American concerns, but in the final analysis no long-lasting, meaningful improvements in relations took place during his term. The question then becomes why three Presidents, who governed Mexico under such different circumstances, ended their administrations in such similar straits. There are three explanations.

The first is a psychological one: Mexico's leaders end up fighting with the "gringos" above all because Mexican Presidents are insecure, hyper-critically nationalistic, and unstable. While this reasoning is often valid in the case of individual Presidents, it begs the question of why the country has been ruled for the last eighteen years by such individuals. In fact, this is a non-explanation; it simply reflects the political purposes, often far from altruistic, of those who espouse it.

The second, more thoughtful, though ultimately simplistic and equally mistaken, conception stresses the links between the nature of the Mexican political system and the attitudes toward the United States adopted by its Presidents. It is often believed that the nation's leaders engage in fanning anti-American sentiments among the people and embracing these feelings chiefly to stay in power. Given the undemocratic nature of the political system, and the highly arguable validity of the elections by which the nation's politicians attain office, many, particularly in the United States, claim that only through such nationalistic grandstanding, which goes against the Mexican people's true, more moderate convictions, can undemocratically chosen Presidents preserve their grip on power.

There is no question that in Mexico, as in many other countries, including the United States—Watergate and Iran-contras situations are witness—there are many ruthless, unethical politicians in high office. It is also true that the political system's capacity to project the perception that it has kept the country's sovereignty intact is one of the pillars of its strength and legitimacy. But to dismiss everything any high-level Mexican official does or says as a cynical grab for power, which he will go to any lengths to preserve, is to apply a simplistic stereotype to a more complex situation.

This vision disregards the question of why the people of Mexico put up with this state of affairs, given that the level of repression in the country is far from sufficient to impose it on them by force. In addition, this (mis)conception rests on a logical error. If Mexican Presidents are anti-American because this brings popularity and keeps them in office, then the people of Mexico support their anti-Americanism. But if this is so, Mexican Presidents are following the people's will, not bending it or betraying it.

In fact, the true reason Mexican Presidents and other politicians become involved in conflicts and tensions with the United States, and never fulfill their ambitious and utopian dreams of improved relations, lies in the very nature of the relationship. Because of its asymmetries, complexities, and history, ties between the two nations, while manageable, are not really improvable. This is perhaps the most important conclusion of any analysis of government-to-government relations. If one problem is solved, another will surface. Atmospherics cannot be dissociated from substance, personal relations from political ones, frictions from businesslike exchange. Because the relationship is the President's affair, he directly suffers its vicissitudes, becoming a victim of its attrition. The relationship, however, is the sum of all of these parts, not a menu where one picks and chooses what one wants.

Mexico's national interests and those of the United States are in the last analysis divergent and mostly contradictory. There is common ground, and of course there is a need to render existing differences tolerable. But it is the clash of interests which determines the sporadic commonality of purpose, not the other way around. Because they disbelieve this basic truth at the start of their administrations, Mexico's Presidents raise their own and the country's hopes to dizzying heights. The rulers eventually accept reality in its stark and naked light, but by then the nation and they themselves have paid a high price. If anything can truly contribute, on the Mexican side, to an improvement in binational relations, it would be for Presidents first to expect less, then more, from the United States.

Because of the tremendous importance relations with the United States represent, all Mexican leaders, intellectuals, and politicians dream of "solving" the problems, "improving" the relationship, and at the same time "defending" and "promoting" Mexico's interests. The two ambitions are incompatible, although a precarious and peaceful coexistence can be achieved. Mexico would like to have both, ends up mostly having neither, but never gives up trying or believing that the two aims are attainable. Disenchantment is never far away, and the greater the expectations, the more bitter the disappointment. This, in a nutshell, is why Mexican Presidents end their terms convinced they could not go on for another day, if only because they came to feel too strongly about the United States, too strongly even for Mexico.

4

FACING THE WORLD

U.S. Foreign Policy

—

Robert A. Pastor

Poor Mexico, so far from God, and so close to the United States." This is the famous lament of Porfirio Díaz, who ruled Mexico from 1876 to 1911. Moshe Arad of Israel is one of the few people to serve his country as ambassador to both Mexico and the United States. He is sympathetic to Díaz's lament, even as he recognizes that it is Israel's opportunity: "Perhaps the reason is that in Israel we are so close to God and so far from the United States."[1]

Arad found a curious symmetry in the behavior of Mexico and the United States. Mexicans were intrigued by Israel's reputed ability to influence U.S. policy, but strangely, he encountered few questions as to how and why Israel does it. When he was appointed ambassador to the United States, after nearly four years in Mexico, he discovered a similar eccentricity: "Senators and congressmen I would meet said they'd love to talk to me about Mexico; they were fascinated that I had served there. But seldom did they act on it." It's almost as if leaders in both countries recognize the importance of the other, but either they lack real interest or they cannot quite bring themselves to learn how to better understand the other.

To truly understand the relationship between Mexico and the United

States, one almost needs a celestial detachment or a Zen-like concentration on another object. Diplomats from other countries may hold some clues. Augusto Ramírez-Ocampo, Colombia's Foreign Minister in the early 1980s, noted that Mexico is hardly the passive object to American designs. The Mexicans play as many games that serve their interests as the Americans do, although both rarely acknowledge these games. "The relationship," according to Ramírez-Ocampo, "is essentially a marriage of convenience, and like most such marriages, it doesn't impede other affairs."[2]

A special window for understanding the relationship is the area of foreign policy—how the two nations have related to each other as each has tried to relate to the world.

It is rare that the U.S. government publicly describes its perception of Mexican foreign policy; rarer still is a candid description. Elliott Abrams, the Reagan administration's Assistant Secretary of State for Inter-American Affairs, however, left aside diplomatic indirection in his testimony before the Senate Foreign Relations Committee: "Part of the problem is a historical one—that is, Mexico has tended, to a substantial degree, to define their foreign policy in opposition to ours. You can take that back to the Mexican War. That is part of the problem . . . a desire to be distant from us in whatever policy we are taking. . . . That explains in part their kind of Third World orientation."[3]

American officials have long believed that most of Mexico's international policies are actually aimed at the United States and are intended to harass, defeat, reverse, or contain U.S. foreign policies. Since the mid-1970s, Americans have sensed that Mexico has pursued these policies more aggressively and with increasing antagonism.

Americans not only view Mexico's foreign policy differently than Mexicans do; they also view their own foreign policy differently. As seen from Mexico, U.S. foreign policy is immoral or, at best, amoral. "I discount the possibility of any sudden, newly discovered or rediscovered goodwill, sympathy, or moral consideration on the part of the United States," wrote a former Mexican Foreign Minister in the late 1970s. "The past history of U.S. policy, its present-day arrogance, its selfishness and conservative mood, will not allow for such a change."[4] Octavio Paz described the purpose of U.S. foreign policy as simply aiming to foster division within Latin American countries in order "to materially improve its own situation and to dominate."[5]

Most Americans view their efforts in the world as more generous and selfless. From the Marshall Plan through the Alliance for Progress and up to the present, the United States has provided over $325 billion in economic and military aid to the rest of the world, of which more than two-thirds was in the form of grants.[6] This does not include the even larger loans and grants that were made by the World Bank, the Inter-American Development Bank, and other development institutions, which were created on U.S. initiative and with the United States being the major contributor. The transfer of America's resources to poorer nations around the world is unprecedented in magnitude and duration.

So much aid has been given for so long that most recipients take it for granted. Mexico, for example, has expressed reluctance about receiving direct assistance from the United States, but it still accepted nearly $420 million in aid and over $3 billion in Export-Import Bank loans and credits from the United States from 1946 to 1987. More than twice as much of the economic aid were grants as were loans. This does not include the credits, swaps, and advance purchases of oil at above market prices that the United States provided to rescue Mexico from its debt crisis. That amounted to $360 million of a total package of $2.4 billion in 1976 and $4.6 billion of a total package of $9.45 billion in 1982.[7]

The United States would have provided more bilateral aid, and indeed, gave nearly four times as much to Colombia, but Mexico has preferred to obtain most of its aid from the international development banks. It received more than $10 billion from the World Bank and over $5 billion from the Inter-American Development Bank. These two institutions have been the major sources of development funds and advice to the country. Mexico complains of U.S. dominance of these institutions instead of giving it credit for being the largest contributor to these banks. In fact, the United States does not have sufficient voting authority to impose its will on either institution.

Mexicans tend to overlook the idealism and see only the realism in U.S. policy, while most Americans, some of whose taxes are sent abroad as aid, quite naturally stress the idealistic side of the policy. The truth, of course, is that U.S. foreign policies have traditionally exhibited a blend of idealism and realism, of high-sounding moralisms and prudent calculations of the balance of power. Each year, the State Department uses both sets of arguments to persuade Congress to approve aid, and Congress' habitual reluctance is proof that the case is not clear-cut that foreign aid serves American interests. The real issue is whether or not the United States should invest in the long-term development of Mexico and other developing countries even if there is no short-term political payoff. In the case of Mexico, the problem is made more difficult because Americans feel they receive aggravation rather than gratitude in return.

President James Monroe's message to Congress in 1823—the nation's first significant foreign policy initiative—spoke for the nation's idealism in its uplifting call for a new world that was distinct from and better than the old. The realism was in the goal of excluding America's rivals from the Western Hemisphere, the tacit alliance with Britain, and the cautious implementation. For most of the nineteenth century, neither the United States nor Mexico had the resources or the internal stability to pursue foreign policies beyond border defense. However, not long after the Civil War, as the U.S. economy began to industrialize, Americans opened a debate on whether to be an imperialist nation like those in Europe. The anti-imperialists largely prevailed until the Spanish-American War in 1898.

Even then, the classic tension in U.S. policy was evident, this time in two famous amendments. The declaration of war against Spain included an amendment by Senator Henry Teller proclaiming that the United States was different from the European and Japanese imperialists; it would not annex Cuba, the main Spanish prize. A second amendment, named after its sponsor, Senator Orville Platt, and subsequently imposed on Cuba, granted to the United States the right to intervene in that country's internal affairs. Together, these two amendments reflected an ambivalence by the United States about its role and responsibility in the region. The United States did not want to rule Cuba or the other nations of the Caribbean as Europe governed its colonies, but it also would not let Europe have more influence in these countries. The United States desired these countries to be independent, but it would not permit them to become insolvent or unstable as either condition could provoke European intervention.

Fearful that a European power could exploit the region's instability to gain a foothold and threaten the Panama Canal, the United States began to play a more active role and intervened in Cuba and the Dominican Republic. But President Theodore Roosevelt and his Secretary of State Elihu Root approached Central America in a very different manner. Instead of intervening, Roosevelt aimed to prevent aggression by one Central American nation against another. And instead of acting unilaterally, he decided to consult and coordinate policy with Mexico. As viewed by the U.S. government, the region's main problem was that strong dictators in Nicaragua and Guatemala, competing for regional hegemony, were supporting rival armies in El Salvador and Honduras. After consultations, Roosevelt and Porfirio Díaz issued a joint invitation on August 28, 1907, to a Central American conference. Roosevelt wanted the meeting to be held in Mexico, but Guatemala, with the support of some of the other states, insisted on Washington.

The Central Americans accepted the joint invitation, and the conference succeeded in negotiating several treaties of peace and establishing a Court of Justice for the region. The United States wanted to actively implement the treaties, and in particular to defend the neutrality of Honduras, but it deferred to Mexico, which was averse to compelling the Central Americans to stop intervening in each other's affairs. The treaties did not keep the peace because there was no effective enforcement, but also because the interests of Mexico and the United States in Central America were different. Mexico wanted to prevent both Guatemala and the United States from expanding their influence. Guatemala felt much toward Mexico as Mexico did toward the United States, for a similar reason. Mexico seized its northern province, Chiapas, and Guatemala remained suspicious that Mexico might try to take more.

The United States hoped to stabilize the entire region, and it believed the way to do that was to prevent internal "revolutions" (actually coups) and cross-border attacks. In time, Washington came to view the Nicaraguan dictator, José Santos Zelaya, as the most dangerous and aggressive leader in the region. Zelaya, however, was the Guatemalan's rival, and thus Mexico's ally. Roosevelt and Díaz overlooked these differences and worked reasonably well together, but the relationship broke down soon after William Howard Taft became President in March 1909. Taft decided to pursue his own policy because the Mexicans were unwilling to adopt more forceful actions to restrain Zelaya. Gradually, the United States became more involved in Nicaragua, and Mexico soon was convulsed by its own revolution. Thus, the first real effort at U.S.-Mexican cooperation in Central America, which began in 1906, ended in 1909; it would also be the two countries' last joint effort in the region.[8]

After 1921, the United States recalculated the costs of intervention, and despite protests by the Nicaraguan government, in 1925 U.S. troops were withdrawn from Nicaragua. Soon after that, the government began to come apart, and Nicaraguan groups sought support from outside. Washington first tried to stay out, instructing the U.S. ambassador not to align "with any group or political faction, [or] we are liable to be more deeply involved than" we should.[9] Washington, therefore, imposed an arms embargo against all parties in Nicaragua. Juan Sacasa, a Liberal leader, reportedly struck a deal in May 1926 with Mexican President Plutarco Elías Calles, who pledged arms and aid in exchange for a promise by Sacasa that if he became President he would promote agrarian reform, abrogate a canal treaty with the United States, and set up a Central American Union to be dominated by Mexico.[10] On December 1, 1926, Sacasa landed on the east coast of Nicaragua, and backed by troops armed and trained in Mexico, he declared himself President.[11]

Because of the U.S. arms embargo, the Nicaraguan government was threatened by Sacasa's forces and asked for help. Relations between the Coolidge administration and Mexico were already strained, and Coolidge justified the return of troops to Nicaragua as a necessary response to Mexico's export of its radicalism by covert arms shipments to the rebels. An equally strong reason was that the United States simply did not want to cede its dominant influence in the region to Mexico. After American protests, Mexico soon withdrew its support from Sacasa.[12]

There was little public backing for the intervention, and so Coolidge sent Colonel Henry Stimson to mediate between the two sides. Stimson promised that the marines would remain in Nicaragua only to supervise two presidential elections. All the Nicaraguan generals accepted Stimson's proposal, except for one, Augusto Sandino, a Liberal, who had worked for a U.S. oil company in Mexico during the Revolution. Sandino later said that he learned his anti-Yankee brand of nationalism in Mexico.[13] His fight against the U.S. marines attracted worldwide support, and it continued until the marines left, as promised, immediately after the inauguration of a new Nicaraguan President in January 1933.

From the turn of the century until December 1941, the United States was a world power, but aside from the period from 1917 to 1919, and with the exception of some involvement in the Pacific, it largely behaved as if it were a Caribbean Basin power. The United States intervened frequently in the region in the first two decades, and then it sought various formulas for disengagement. It promoted development by customs receiverships and "dollar diplomacy" and political stability by elections, treaties, and professional constabularies. The gradual acceptance by the United States of the principle of nonintervention culminated with Franklin D. Roosevelt's Good Neighbor Policy, which did much to restore good relations between the United States and Latin America.

President Lázaro Cárdenas nationalized the foreign oil companies in Mexico in March 1938. He was fed up with the imperiousness of the companies and judged that the United States and Britain would not retaliate because of the approaching war in Europe. When the oil companies tried to prevent Mexico from selling its oil abroad, Cárdenas turned to Germany, Italy, and Japan. Though anti-Nazi, Cárdenas, in the words of Lorenzo Meyer, "did not fail to take advantage of the [political] situation [in Europe], fanning Washington's fear of a fascist-type movement" in Mexico and of a closer relationship with Germany. Cárdenas hinted that if the United States did not provide tankers, Germany would, and when he received fifty commercial aircraft, all convertible to military use, from Germany, Washington chose not to call his bluff. The oil dispute was settled in November 1941.[14]

The most important consequence of the oil settlement was that it cleared the way for unprecedented cooperation during the war. Mexico broke relations with Japan after Pearl Harbor, and three days later with Germany and Italy. The country stopped exporting all oil and minerals to the Axis powers, and permitted U.S. military planes to overfly its territory. The United States was also allowed to build and use some air and naval facilities and radar stations in Mexico, although the Mexican government maintained ownership. Perhaps the most surprising cooperative effort was Mexico's dispatch of its air squadron to the Philippines late in the Pacific war.[15]

Soon after entering the war, President Roosevelt began to plan for the peace with the purpose of trying to avoid a return to the isolationism that followed World War I. Roosevelt's planners consulted often with Congress and U.S. allies, and as a result, strong postwar institutions were established under U.S. leadership. After the war ended, American troops were demobilized and most were withdrawn from Europe and Asia, but the United States did not turn inward politically or economically.

While the prewar period was characterized by multiple centers of power, the postwar world was divided for strategic purposes into two parts: the West, led by the United States and Western Europe, and the East, led by the Soviet Union and Eastern Europe. Washington viewed many events in the world in terms of their possible consequences for this strategic balance. Latin America, which had been the main arena of U.S. foreign policy for the first four decades of the twentieth century, was moved to the periphery of Washington's strategic concerns thereafter.

As the bearer of the security burden for the free world, the United States was often frustrated when friendly nations, particularly those protected by the "security umbrella" and aided by taxpayers' money, would not support a U.S. position in the United Nations. Mexico often found itself in this awkward position. The U.S. government sometimes viewed Mexican policy as a nuisance; at other times, when the issue was serious and support was lacking, Washington became angry with what it perceived as Mexican uncooperativeness or obduracy.

Appropriately, one of the first major issues in the postwar period to reattract U.S. attention to Latin America stemmed from Washington's perception of expanding Communist influence in Guatemala. The crisis occurred because of a confluence of three different political changes—in the world, the United States, and in Latin America. First, a perception grew among some American leaders that world Communism was on the march, having absorbed Eastern Europe and then China. Second, after twenty years out of office, the Republican Party took power in the United States. Republicans tended to see threats to U.S. national security more intensely than the Democrats they displaced. Republicans also tended to describe a wider swath of people as leftists and Communists. The third change occurred in Central America. In 1952, the Guatemalan government of Jacobo Arbenz accelerated a land reform, which expropriated a large area of unused property owned by the United Fruit Company. The company had considerable influence in Congress, and it used it to create the impression that it was a victim of a Communist threat. John Foster Dulles, Eisenhower's Secretary of State, already saw the problem in such terms. There were no gray or neutral areas in Dulles's view of the global struggle between freedom and Communism.

The United States informed Arbenz that failure to remove the Communists from his government would be interpreted as showing he was on the wrong side. Arbenz viewed the struggle in more traditional terms, as a U.S. effort to defend its companies, stymie land reform, and demand subservience. The Communists were helping him, and he therefore rejected Dulles's demand.

Mexico was sensitive to the changing perceptions in Washington. Its Foreign Minister told a State Department official that he was deeply worried that the United States "may mistake domestic reforms among our neighbors for Communism."[16] Such a mistake was made, but that was only one part of the problem. The other was the growing influence of Communists in the Arbenz government. Juan José Arévalo, who was the first democratically elected President of Guatemala after the overthrow of Jorge Ubico in 1944, supported his successor, Arbenz, but in retrospect he said:

> Arbenz made the mistake of giving a lot of importance to his Communist friends. Arbenz's government took a turn to the extreme left; it was no longer a democratic left. . . . This provoked a violent reaction from the political right, which had already grown in Guatemala, and was supported from abroad by the United Fruit Company and the CIA. . . .[17]

The Eisenhower administration publicly tried to isolate the regime while it covertly sponsored an invasion. Mexico opposed both efforts. The United States successfully attained its objectives in a short time, and therefore Mexico's opposition did not seriously affect relations.

Cuba proved an entirely different matter. Some politicians can walk into a room filled with invective and bring adversaries together; Castro's effect on U.S.-Mexican relations was precisely the opposite. He was the ultimate polarizer; he has made Americans and Mexicans more certain of their differences. The Cuban Revolution generated more problems in the relationship between the United States and Mexico over a longer period than any other foreign event. If World War II helped Americans and Mexicans to concentrate on their common interests, the Cuban Revolution evoked feelings that separated the two countries.

So much attracted Mexico to Cuba's revolution—Fidel Castro had launched his revolution from Mexico in 1956, Cuban revolutionary rhetoric sounded much like Mexico's, only it was alive, and the two revolutions seemed directed as much against the United States as against national dictators or internal enemies. Castro, however, lacked the maturity and balance that permitted Mexico to secure its independence without so antagonizing the United States as to poison the relationship and create a new dependence. Mexico enjoyed the best of both worlds: Castro's bold defiance of the United States permitted Mexico to relive its own revolution without paying the price.

At the beginning of the Cuban Revolution, there were no serious differences between the United States and Mexico. Having failed to create a "third force" in Cuba as an alternative to the dictator Batista and the radical Castro, the Eisenhower administration grudgingly accepted Castro's victory, sent a sympathetic professional as ambassador, and expressed a willingness to discuss Cuba's economic needs.

The honeymoon was short-lived. Castro was determined to pursue a thorough revolution in Cuba, and that meant he would have to contain or eliminate all centers of economic and political power that were independent of his movement. After the destruction of Batista's army, Americans constituted the largest source of independent power on the island, with about $2 billion of investments and the power of the U.S. government behind them. A collision was not long in coming. In this struggle, Castro quickly sought the Soviet Union as an ally, and this increased U.S. anxieties about the direction of his revolution.[18]

On January 25, 1960, in a meeting with his senior advisers, Eisenhower expressed great frustration and incomprehension in regard to Castro, who he thought was beginning "to look like a madman." Philip Bonsal, who had been recalled as ambassador from Havana, explained to Eisenhower that Castro "is a very conspiratorial individual who tries to create the impression that he and Cuba are beleaguered. He is an extreme leftist and is strongly anti-American."[19] Eisenhower then said that "the best course of action in the hemisphere would be if the OAS went down the line for us in trying to put some restraints on Castro." Roy Rubottom, the Assistant Secretary of State, indicated that Mexico is "a problem— probably the greatest," and that it "would be hard to get the fourteen votes" necessary to support the U.S. position in the OAS.[20]

In San José in August 1960, the United States pressed the OAS to condemn Cuba and "Sino-Soviet intervention in the Western Hemisphere." The final "Declaration of San José" condemned extracontinental intervention as a danger to the security of the hemisphere, but it did not mention Cuba. As predicted, the Venezuelans weren't helpful and the Mexicans were also "very 'soft' in this matter, principally," according to the Secretary of State's report to the President, "for internal reasons and concern of the government that other political factions" would attack them for being hostile to Castro.[21]

After the failure of the Bay of Pigs invasion in April 1961, Mexico took the lead in the United Nations to condemn the U.S. operation. The United States continued to press for OAS action against Cuba, but only gathered backing after Castro announced in December 1961 that he was a Marxist-Leninist and began to arm rebels trying to overthrow some of his neighbors. Venezuela and Colombia broke relations with Cuba after discovering Cuban support for insurgencies in the two countries. In January 1962, the Foreign Ministers met in Punta del Este, and all twenty republics—except Cuba—supported a declaration that Marxism-Leninism was incompatible with the inter-American system. Fourteen ministers agreed to a second resolution that excluded Cuba from the inter-American system. Mexico voted for the former declaration, but against excluding Cuba.

An OAS committee investigated charges against Cuba, and in early 1964 it reported that "the Republic of Venezuela has been the target of a series of actions sponsored and directed by the Government of Cuba, openly intended to subvert Venezuelan institutions and to overthrow the democratic Government of Venezuela through terrorism, sabotage, assault, and guerrilla warfare."[22] On the basis of this report, the OAS Foreign Ministers met in July 1964 and voted to impose diplomatic and economic sanctions against Cuba and to break relations. Only Mexico opposed the OAS decision, and refused to comply with it.

Although the United States had been pressing for the isolation of Cuba since 1960, in the end Cuba's subversion persuaded the rest of Latin America more than U.S. lobbying. Mexico based its rejection of the OAS action on the principle of nonintervention and on the Estrada Doctrine, which said that nations ought to maintain diplomatic relations with de facto governments regardless of their ideology.

The Cuban issue was the source of considerable strain in the U.S.-Mexican relationship, but the Presidents of both countries kept it from harming the overall relationship. One measure of their success was the omission of Cuba in the communiqués issued after three separate summit meetings between 1962 and 1966.[23] There were probably two reasons why the United States chose not to make a public issue out of the differences. First, although Mexico publicly defended Cuba's juridical rights to be in the OAS, it also took private steps to cool and contain its relationship with Cuba.[24] Second, during most of this period, Thomas Mann, a career diplomat, was either U.S. ambassador to Mexico or Assistant Secretary of State for Inter-American Affairs. Although quite conservative, he believed in private diplomacy like most career officials.

The decision to downplay the differences on Cuba in Kennedy's meeting with López Mateos in June 1962 reaped substantial benefits four months later during the Cuban Missile Crisis. The Kennedy administration sent a special envoy to brief the Mexican President, and Mexico supported the United States in the OAS.

The principal issues of concern to the United States and Mexico during most of the 1960s and the first half of the 1970s were bilateral, and many related to the border. Foreign policy only became an issue again in the 1970s as Mexico decided to play an active role as a leader in the Third World and subsequently in the Caribbean Basin. This was of some concern to the Nixon and Ford administrations, but not very much. Mexico's support for the 1975 UN resolution equating Zionism and racism provoked an indignant response by the American Jewish community but Echeverría dismissed the Foreign Minister and, in effect, repudiated the vote before it affected the relationship.

Central America moved back to the U.S. agenda in 1977, but Mexico was at first uninterested. Of the major Latin American countries in the Caribbean Basin only Mexico played almost no role in helping the United States and Panama negotiate the Canal Treaties. Eighteen heads of state attended the signing of the Canal Treaties on September 7, 1977, at the OAS; the Mexican President did not attend.

In September 1978, Nicaragua was swept by insurrection, and the United States, which opposed Somoza but did not want to see the Sandinistas inherit the government, consulted with many of the countries in the hemisphere to try to promote a peaceful democratic transition. Secretary of State Cyrus Vance sought Mexico's support for a peaceful mediation, but was rebuffed by Foreign Minister Santiago Roel, who told Vance: "You Americans created a monster [Anastasio Somoza], so you get rid of him. We don't want to be involved."[25] But at that time Mexico did get involved, providing funds to the Sandinistas and later the use of its embassy in Managua.

In February 1979, during his conversation with López Portillo in Mexico, Carter explained U.S. policy toward Nicaragua and sought his advice for a cooperative strategy. Once again, the Mexican leader rejected the request, responding with a discursive, conservative critique of Carter's human rights policy that implied that Nicaragua's old and current troubles were wholly of U.S. manufacture. This Mexican perception was based on a widespread myth that Somoza was a U.S. puppet. The three Somozas, who ruled Nicaragua from 1936 to 1979, viewed U.S. support as a source of power and tried to perpetuate the myth that they enjoyed unequivocal support from the United States. Actually, during much of the rule of the Somozas, the United States did not assist them and indeed discouraged them from remaining in power, but there were also periods when the United States provided strong support for the regime. The Mexicans were attracted to the Somoza myth in part because it confirmed their own self-image as different from and better than U.S. surrogates in the region.

Despite Carter's efforts to consult with Mexico, in May 1979 López Portillo decided to pursue an aggressive policy in Central America without even informing Washington. After conversations with Cuban President Castro and Costa Rican President Rodrigo Carazo, he broke relations with Somoza and dispatched two advisers to Latin America to encourage other governments to do the same. He also increased covert aid to the Sandinistas.

In late June 1979, the United States requested an OAS meeting to address the Nicaraguan issue. The Sandinista forces seemed strong enough to fight the National Guard to a standstill, and the issue was whether Somoza's departure could be negotiated in a manner that ended the war and increased the prospect for a democratic transition. The United States offered a three-part proposal: (1) the departure of Somoza; (2) a cease-fire between the Sandinistas and the National Guard supervised by an Inter-American Peace Force; and (3) a negotiated transition to a coalition, democratic government.

The Mexican Foreign Minister was in Europe when the OAS meeting was called and only returned because he was told to do so by his President, whose instructions were simple: block the United States.[26] In his address to the Assembly, the Mexican praised the Sandinistas for exercising "the sacred right of rebellion against tyranny, just as the Mexican people had done seventy years before." His objective was to prevent a cease-fire and help the Sandinistas gain power. Although other Latin Americans pursued a similar objective, Mexico's efforts at the OAS were interpreted as particularly hostile and anti-American by U.S. officials.

After the Sandinistas took power, Washington saw no feasible alternative but to assist the revolution and try to establish a good relationship. Although U.S. and Mexican objectives at that time were similar, Washington perceived Mexico's policy as more devoted to promoting anti-Americanism than to supporting the Nicaraguan revolution. Similarly, in Panama, on October 1, 1979, on the occasion of the Canal Treaties coming into force, and in the presence of Vice President Walter Mondale, López Portillo celebrated Panama's liberation from imperialism and hardly mentioned any U.S. role in the treaties.

In El Salvador, after the revolution in October 1979, the United States tried to support those in the new junta who promised agrarian reform and elections. Mexico judged that Central America's future was with the Marxist rebels, and López Portillo chose to reinvigorate his country's relationship with Cuba. On a visit to Havana in July 1980, while the exodus of Cuban refugees from Mariel was continuing, López Portillo affirmed Mexico's solidarity: "We will in no way allow anything to be done to Cuba because we would feel that it is being done to ourselves."[27] The statement infuriated U.S. officials, as it was made while Cuba was flagrantly violating international law and human decency by expelling more than 125,000 people, some of them criminals, to the United States.

Still, the foreign policy differences between the Carter administration and Mexico were relatively muted as compared with the gap that opened after President Reagan's inauguration. Although Carter took exception with Mexico on Central America, he supported its aspirations to play a leading role in the Third World and on North-South economic issues. In contrast, Reagan's policy was built on the premise that the pivotal struggle in the world was between Communism and freedom. "Third World" was mentioned only in quotes as an academic term of no contemporary relevance. Washington, therefore, clashed with Mexico across a much wider set of foreign policy issues, although the principal arena remained Central America.

The recognition by Mexico and France in August 1981 of the Salvadoran Marxist rebels as "a representative political force" outraged the Reagan administration, but it also provoked condemnation from eight Latin American governments, which met in Caracas the next month. Later, five other Latin American governments added their signature to the Caracas Declaration, which criticized Mexico and France for interfering in the internal affairs of El Salvador.[28] These Latin American governments—that included both the democratic governments of Venezuela, Costa Rica, Columbia, Peru, the Dominican Republic, and Ecuador, and the military governments of the southern cone—defended the Salvadoran government because it promised and held elections, the left was unquestionably Marxist-Leninist, and Latin America's ardor for revolution had cooled as the Sandinistas retreated from their promises of nonaligned democracy. After hundreds of international observers and the press reported that Salvador's elections were fair, Mexico downplayed its support for the Salvadoran guerrillas. Increasingly, the disagreement between Washington and Mexico focused on Nicaragua, where the Reagan administration was providing major support for the contras, whose goal was to overthrow the government.

In January 1983, the Foreign Ministers of Mexico, Venezuela, Colombia, and Panama met on the island of Contadora and began an effort to promote peace in Central America and preclude intervention. It was the first international effort in the region that was not led by the United States, and indeed, did not even include it. The administration viewed Mexico as the main defender of Nicaragua in the Contadora Group. They feared that Mexico wanted to negotiate a formula that would reduce U.S. influence while permitting the Sandinista government to consolidate its power. While declaring its support for Contadora, the administration tried to undermine its efforts and change Mexico's position.

By 1985, De la Madrid had stopped oil shipments and moderated Mexican support for the Nicaraguan government, but the U.S. position "hardened," according to a senior official of the U.S. embassy in Mexico at the time. "We feel," this official said, "that Mexico is continuing to pressure us to negotiate directly with the Sandinistas. But the issue has polarized. If you're not our friend, you're our enemy. We see that Mexico remains partial to Nicaragua, not totally but still more than anyone, and hostile to our position."

The Contadora Group supervised the negotiations of significant draft treaties, but it failed in the end because of the intransigence of the Reagan administration on one side and the Sandinistas on the other. More important, the Central Americans felt that their interests were directly at stake, and they lost trust in Contadora to defend them. Costa Rican President Oscar Arias proposed a variation on the Contadora proposals in February 1987. His plan focused on internal democratization, which Costa Rica and the newly established democracies of Central America—Guatemala, Honduras, and El Salvador—felt had been ignored by Contadora in part because two of its members—Panama and Mexico—could hardly insist on democracy abroad when it would not permit it at home. Arias's colleagues in Guatemala, Honduras, and El Salvador supported his plan as a way both to strengthen their positions vis-à-vis the military in their countries and to try to liberalize Nicaragua. On August 7, 1987, the five Presidents of the region endorsed the plan and began taking steps to put it into effect. The Reagan administration's foreign policy differences with Mexico virtually evaporated as the Central Americans took the initiative away from Contadora, and Mexico focused on its internal problems.

Characteristically, it was a senator—this time from the PRI in Mexico— who stated the foreign policy views of his country the clearest. In December 1985, Victor Manzanilla said bluntly that while Mexico based its foreign policy on principles, "our friends to the north are famous for having interests and not principles."[29]

No two countries seem to have as different foreign policies as the United States and Mexico. The United States resists revolutions and promotes elections; Mexico supports revolutions and derides elections. And yet a closer examination of the two foreign policies suggests that they share certain fundamental characteristics. The United States has intervened in the Caribbean Basin, but so too has Mexico, providing covert arms and funds to Nicaraguan rebels in the 1920s and the 1930s, and funds and political support in the 1970s. In the 1950s, the Mexican government allowed Fidel Castro to use Mexico as a base for training his soldiers and obtaining arms and funds. In the 1970s and 1980s, while lecturing Washington on the sanctity of the principle of nonintervention, Mexico provided political support, funds, and security in Mexico City for the Salvadoran rebels.

Alone in the OAS, Mexico refused to comply with sanctions against Cuba, and has continually defended that country, which has intervened more than any other in the region since 1960. The implication, often heard in Mexico, that Latin America bowed to U.S. pressure in deciding to isolate Cuba naturally does not endear Mexico to other Latin Americans, who draw the opposite conclusion: that the only reason Mexico did not vote with them to exclude Cuba was that it felt compelled to vote against the United States for internal reasons. That Mexico based its rejection of the OAS resolution on "principle" (the Estrada Doctrine) made it sound as if everyone else's motives were crass. But Mexico did not hesitate to violate the same doctrine when it severed relations with Somoza and with Chile after Salvador Allende was overthrown.

Mexico supported revolution in Nicaragua and El Salvador, but it drew the line south of Guatemala, where it has privately assisted the military in putting down rebel movements. Like the United States, Mexico has been worried about the spillover effects of a revolutionary regime on its borders.[30] Within the Mexican establishment, there is an affinity for Salvadoran and Nicaraguan radicals, but a much smaller—perhaps insignificant—number express support for the Guatemalan rebels. The reason is simply that no country wants an unfriendly regime on its border.

The major difference between U.S. and Mexican policy in the region is not that Washington pursues its interests and Mexico defends its principles; both pursue their interests, and one of those is a respect for principles deemed important by each nation. In the United States, those are democracy and human rights; in Mexico, they are "social justice" and liberation by revolution. The central foreign policy issue for both countries is whether the nation's interests should be defined narrowly and belligerently or broadly and with tolerance.

Both nations try to prevent the coming to power of violent groups in the region that are viewed as hostile, and they try to help those who are friendly. The principal difference between the two nations' foreign policies is that the United States has possessed much more resources over a much longer period than has Mexico. When Mexican resources increased, it too began to play a more active and expansive role in the region, trading subsidized oil for influence. Commenting on the change in Mexico's foreign policy from its "defensive attitude that for years marked its international behavior," the Mexican Foreign Minister in January 1980 said: "In order to defend its specific interests, Mexico's present situation requires it to participate more actively in international life."[31] What had changed was that Mexico had become wealthier and more confident.

Second, all nations—especially Mexico and the United States—project their national experiences. That is why Mexico tries to encourage other nations to emulate its revolution, in rhetoric if not in reality, and why the United States encourages countries to have free elections. Neither experience has much relevance for Central America, but that has not inhibited the policies; it just makes them less effective.

Except in Guatemala, Mexico's policies suggest a preference for leftist, anti-American nations in the region, perhaps because such regimes would divert American attention and make Mexico seem moderate in comparison. Cuba has served that purpose, and Mexico apparently believes that it would benefit from "more Cubas." For the same reason, the U.S. government believes that it would benefit from "no more Cubas."

The fundamental question for both governments is whether cooperation is possible. If Mexican foreign policy, as Elliott Abrams suggested, is always the opposite of U.S. foreign policy, then cooperation is logically impossible. In practice, because Mexico is a conservative country with a revolutionary posture, its foreign policy seems most comfortably positioned alongside a conservative U.S. administration. In a meeting with López Portillo at the end of the Carter administration, future Secretary of State Alexander Haig reported that the Mexican President complained of his difficulty in dealing with Carter: "A President of Mexico cannot survive by taking positions to the right of the President of the United States."[32] Mexico's ambassador later denied that López Portillo made this statement, but it nevertheless did reflect the feeling of some in Mexico that posturing against a conservative stereotype is preferable to cooperating with a sympathetic liberal.

In the past, a change in Mexico's leadership has made a difference in the relationship with the United States on international issues, but mainly in the degree of uncooperativeness. In the future, if the PRI were replaced by the left, one could expect a more hostile relationship. Those who think the PAN would cooperate with the Republican Party in Central America do not know the PAN's position, which opposes "both Soviet intervention through Cuba and U.S. intervention through the contras." This position is closer to that of the Democratic Party, but in reality, the PAN's view of Nicaragua is mainly a projection of its struggle against the PRI. Its criticism of the Sandinistas is that they have "duplicated the Mexican political system: one official party with control of the press, unions, and elections. That is not democracy. We support the rights of Nicaraguans to oppose their government."[33] If the PAN were governing, it would still have to accommodate the left and the strong nationalism in Mexico, and therefore might find it as difficult cooperating with Washington as the PRI has found it.

The change of U.S. administrations—even when it involved a shift in parties—has not had an appreciable effect on the degree of cooperation between the two governments in the area of foreign policy. It is worth recalling that the Carter administration's opposition to Somoza and its initial support for the Sandinista government coincided in its broadest outline with Mexico's policy, but requests by Washington to work together were met by either silence or insults by Mexico. Possibly, another Mexican administration at a different time might have responded more favorably.

On the vital issues, as when the United States was genuinely threatened in World War II and the Cuban Missile Crisis, Mexico cooperated. Beyond those events, there have always been problems. Annette Baker Fox, a scholar from Columbia University, compared Washington's relationship with four friends that are close and distant from a geographical and cultural standpoint—Canada, Mexico, Brazil, and Australia. Fox found that on all but the most vital issues, these middle-power nations "put autonomy over a united front." All four stressed their independence, while Washington tried to negotiate a common approach on issues where there were shared interests. None wanted to appear to be U.S. satellites.[34]

There were, of course, important differences among the four. In the period from 1945 to 1975, Fox found, Mexico's votes in the United Nations diverged most sharply from the United States. Mexico's style was also "more rigidly principled and readier for confrontation" than the others. During World War II, Canada and Australia felt most threatened, and thus cooperated most fully with the United States. In peacetime, the more distant nations—Brazil and Australia—were more cooperative. The sharpest divergence from U.S. policy consistently came from Mexico.[35] An analysis of Mexico's voting in the United Nations in the 1980s shows that little has changed. In the hemisphere, Mexico voted fewer times with the United States than all but two countries, Cuba and Nicaragua.[36]

Stepping back from the four relationships, one recognizes that the quest for better cooperation might be permanently elusive; indeed, it is probably the wrong question. The issue is not convergence but responsiveness: whether the United States and Mexico, for example, are prepared to understand and be responsive to each nation's perspective and interests.

Using this criterion, the two countries have been responsive. Although there have been important differences of policies and attitudes, both Mexico and the United States have been sensitive to each other's vital interests during the world wars and the crisis in Cuba from 1960 to 1965. In the 1980s, there has been less responsiveness on Central America, but this might reflect the fact that neither nation has genuinely vital interests at stake there now.

Responsiveness, of course, does not mean cooperativeness. Whether U.S. policy toward Latin America has been unilateral or multilateral, aggressive or sensitive, covert or open, it has not coincided with Mexican foreign policy since its revolution. The future is unlikely to differ from the past. In the area of foreign policy, there are clear limits to cooperation. The success of the relationship should be measured, not by a convergence of policies, but by a sensitivity to the divergence of interests and by a responsiveness to vital security concerns.

Mexican Foreign Policy

Jorge G. Castañeda

Mexico has a total of 104 diplomatic missions abroad, including embassies, permanent missions, and consulates. Of these, 44 are in the United States: the embassy in Washington and two missions (United Nations and Organization of American States), 12 consulates general, and 29 career consulates. In both political and diplomatic terms, Mexican-American relations continue to dominate the nation's links with the outside world in spite of an evident and recognized need for diversification. The United States is Mexico's number one priority in foreign affairs and its ties with the rest of the world are in one way or another tainted or affected by this fact.

While economic integration may be driving both countries together and the resistance of opposing trends barely holding its own, Mexico's nationalism in one domain at least has maintained the upper hand. In foreign policy, and the way both countries view the rest of the world, the differences between the two nations are not fading.

Appearances are deceiving. On specific current issues—Central America, arms control, East-West tensions in general—there would seem to be a certain convergence of public opinion on both sides of the border. The mainstream of the American body politic holds more moderate

views than the Reagan administration. Public opinion on many foreign
policy issues in Mexico is situated slightly to the right of the government.
This apparent meeting of minds, however, has more to do with short-
term considerations than with underlying attitudes. Indeed, the substantive gap between both nations is as wide as their present governments'
disputes over Central America, United Nations voting patterns, and
other matters indicate. These and other disagreements are not new; they
were evident even at the height of the Cold War, during the U.S.-
Mexican honeymoon.

Economic integration and American pressure are influencing Mexico's
policies toward, and views of, the rest of the world, nudging them away
from their previous place in the political spectrum. But the chasm between Mexico and the United States persists. Mexico has edged away
from the left, but since the United States has simultaneously shifted to
the right, the same qualitative difference remains. There are significant
reasons for this that go beyond posturing, playing for a domestic audience, or intransigent nationalism.

Many of the reasons for the contrast between the worldviews are
self-evident. The United States is one of two superpowers, with global
commitments and responsibilities, interests and ambitions. Mexico
barely aspires to be a regional midsize power, and often has doubts even
about that. In the United States, political wisdom holds that elections are
won and popularity conserved by being liberal or moderate domestically,
conservative abroad. In Mexico, largely because successive governments
after 1940 internally turned to the right, wise old politicians advise in-
cumbents to steer foreign policy to the left of their domestic course.

There is wide agreement in the United States that the Soviet Union
represents a potential threat to the country's national security. The
keystone of American foreign policy is to deal with that danger. There
is no such consensus in Mexico with regard to the Soviet Union or even
its regional allies like Cuba. Neither has ever been seriously considered
a true threat to Mexico—though "Red scares" have been used and
abused by many Presidents, from Plutarco Elías Calles in the late 1920s
to Luis Echeverría's expulsion of four Soviet diplomats in 1971. Yet
despite widespread resentment and solid historical precedent regarding
past American aggression against Mexico, there is no unanimous perception that the United States represents a present danger. Thus the unifying
external "evil" or danger is different: in lieu of the American consensus
regarding the Soviet menace, there is division in Mexico with respect to
the American peril, and scant fear of the Soviet one.

The United States' view of the world is more like that of the nations
of Western Europe, Canada, and sometimes Japan, with whom it shares

comparable levels of development and similar political systems. More often than not, these countries' governments are located to the right of the political center. For identical reasons, Mexico has greater affinity with nations it has more in common with, particularly in matters of economic development. Not surprisingly, Mexico tends to seek out friendship, even political alliances, with other Third World powers. Among these, there are far more governments situated on the left of the political spectrum than in the industrialized world. Consequently, regardless of ideological sympathies, which sometimes exist but frequently do not, there are solid reasons for seldom keeping the same company.

But other, more subjective considerations have also contributed to the abyss between the United States and Mexico on foreign affairs. The Revolution has been over for many decades, and the governments since 1940 cannot be labeled revolutionary by any stretch of the imagination. But the mark of history is nonetheless indelible. The deep-rooted antipathy and fear which revolution, with its disorder and complexities, intolerance and heroism, instills in the American psyche is less ingrained in Mexico, although memories of the turmoil between 1910 and 1920 still haunt the nation's extraordinarily conservative upper classes and even its far more progressive intelligentsia.

The further away the Revolution becomes in time, the greater the sympathy other countries' revolts evoke in the emotions of Mexico's people. Those who still remember the rebellion support revolution in principle, but fear it and oppose it as it affects them individually. Support of or affinity with revolution abroad squares the circle neatly. The Mexican Revolution constitutes a major chapter in the history of a nation which thrives on historical inspiration and fantasy. Mexico can be unfaithful to its Revolution, perhaps even seek and obtain a legal separation from it, but it cannot yet bring itself to sue for divorce. The country's perspective on world events springs directly from this lasting though fading fidelity.

This is not to say that anti-Communism has not been a factor in Mexican political and international life. Gustavo Díaz Ordaz, President from 1964 to 1970, could hold his own as a "Red-baiter" with any American conservative. But there is less enthusiasm for it within the Mexican political establishment than in other sectors of society or the United States. During the Cold War, Mexican politicians and labor leaders were quick to display their anti-Communist credentials when asked, but this was more for American consumption than out of true conviction. The Mexican upper and middle classes, particularly outside Mexico City, are rabidly anti-Communist, though their virulence tends to be limited to land and religious issues. During the 1920s and 1930s the banner under which conservatives waged their last-ditch struggle against land reform and secularization was Christian anti-Communism, closely identified with and partly linked to Spanish Falangismo, the fascist current which laid the groundwork for Franco's coup against the Republic in 1936, the Civil War, and the subsequent forty-year dictatorship in Spain. This period left its mark on sectors of Mexican society beyond its affluent and intermediate layers. Not many years ago it was still common to see signs on the country's roads and highways reading "Cristianismo sí, Comunismo no."

The Communist Party was expelled from the Mexican labor movement in the 1940s, and many Communist labor leaders were jailed and mistreated in the 1950s and 1960s, but in general, anti-Communism at home did not play a central, unifying role. The party's weakness, at least since the 1940s, largely explains this. Enmity or distaste for the Soviet Union, or later Cuba, was never a key emotion among Mexican officials, and never became a sentiment cultivated and exacerbated by the government. So when Reagan administration officials were upset over what they perceived as Mexico's "lack of understanding" or dismissal of the "Communist threat" from Central America, their frustration was comprehensible. Mexico does not "understand" the "threat" from the Soviet Union, Cuba, or Nicaragua because the country does not believe it is affected by it.

Moreover, the Mexican political establishment finds it difficult to quarrel with the past success of policies toward Latin American radical change. From the reformist movement in Guatemala in 1954 to the Salvadoran insurgency in the 1980s, and including the Cuban Revolution, Salvador Allende's Chilean Popular Unity between 1970 and 1973, and the Sandinista revolution in Nicaragua in 1979, Mexican authorities have maintained either good or frankly intimate relations with all these regimes.

This has served Mexico well: nearly every country in the hemisphere has felt the impact of the successive revolutionary impulses of the past thirty years. Every country, that is, except Mexico, which has been able to "coopt" the continent's revolutionary figures in much the way it coopts domestic opposition. The Reagan administration's entreaties and pressures on Mexico to alter this policy could result in a relative distancing by the government from Latin American left-wingers, but could not ultimately succeed. History and pragmatism, a typically Mexican combination, forbid it.

In addition to domestic considerations, for a nation like Mexico to embrace explicitly a world divided into two superpowers' spheres of influence is conceptually intolerable—though perhaps geopolitically inescapable. Contiguity is a heavy burden to bear; the history of a century and a half's relations with the United States has made it impossible to accept the corollaries of bipolarity. If it admits that the world is split in two, and that the East-West conflict is "the only show in town," then Mexico inevitably would have to resign itself to belonging to the side geography has placed it on: the West.

But it would also have to submit to that side's leadership and to comply with that leadership's desires in all critical matters. Yet Mexico's interests as a developing country are far from identical to those of the United States, the world's premier developed nation. There is little room here for common purpose. These fears and hypotheses have led Mexico never to sign a military assistance treaty with the United States, and to keep ties between its armed forces and the Pentagon at a lower level than those of any other Latin nation. Mexico has also tried to reject the East-West division of the world, and adopted a more multipolar, North-South approach, stressing the economic and social divisions of the world over and above the ideological ones.

Mexico can hope to incorporate this different division of the world, with its complexities and ramifications, into its relations with the United States, just as the United States always attempts to include *its* division of the world in *its* bilateral relations. Mexico's characteristics as a nation, as well as the implications of its geographical proximity, have led it to adopt a strategic or geopolitical view of the world which—without being diametrically opposed to Washington's—is nevertheless contradictory.

In the 1920s and 1930s Mexico had several differences of opinion with the United States over matters not properly within the binational agenda. Policy toward Nicaragua in the late 1920s, the establishment of diplomatic relations with the Soviet Union in the early part of the same decade, and then again, after a brief interruption, in 1934, were all sources of tension. By and large, however, there were few other third-country disputes, notwithstanding a relatively conflictive binational agenda including, above all, Mexico's 1938 expropriation of foreign oil companies. At that time, we barely had relations with other nations, much less an active policy toward them. As Lorenzo Meyer has put it:

> Thus, for all practical purposes, after the First World War, Mexico and the United States stood facing each other with no intermediaries. For a long time thereafter, Mexico's political and economic relations with the rest of the world could be equated with its relations with the United States, precisely the situation that Mexican rulers had traditionally tried to avoid.[1]

It was not until the postwar period that the first meaningful hints of differences between Mexico and the United States on issues regarding the rest of the world began to emerge. The first real dispute occurred in 1954, at the Caracas Conference on inter-American security. The ministerial meeting of the OAS was used by Secretary of State Dulles to obtain hemispheric backing for his successful attempts to overthrow the reformist, democratically elected government of Guatemala headed by Jacobo Arbenz. Soon after the conference a CIA-sponsored coup unseated Arbenz, but Dulles preferred to tint his campaign against "Communism in our hemisphere" with the fictions of Latin American solidarity and collective action. He proposed a resolution which called for collective response to "extra-hemispheric" forces.

Guatemala opposed the resolution, of course; Mexico and Argentina abstained. Mexico had voted against the United States on a few occasions at the UN on the Korean crisis, but this was the first time the two countries disagreed on an issue of importance for both nations. It was also the first time the United States at least indirectly used the Mexican right wing to influence the government, particularly by falsely accusing Foreign Minister Luis Padilla Nervo of Communist sympathies. Similar but more important disputes emerged over the Cuban Revolution. Fidel Castro's victory on January 1, 1959, was welcomed in Mexico. Later, in April 1961, when the United States' attempt to do away with Castro floundered at the Bay of Pigs, there was genuine rejoicing in Mexico, as well as an outpouring of support for the revolution among the nation's youth. President Adolfo López Mateos backed the Kennedy administration during the Cuban Missile Crisis in late 1962—the only occasion when U.S. security was truly threatened, in Mexico's view—yet sympathy for Castro remained high. Hence, it was not surprising that Mexico refused to back American efforts to expel Cuba from the OAS or to sever relations. From 1964 through 1970, Mexico was the only nation in the hemisphere to maintain ties with Havana. Relations, though hardly friendly, were never interrupted.

Another parting of ways arose in 1965, when Lyndon Johnson ordered the invasion of the Dominican Republic. Although he secured hemispheric support for his venture after the fact, Mexico abstained on the OAS resolution introduced by the United States on the grounds of continental collective self-defense in the face of "Communist aggression." Mexico's strongly pro-American Foreign Minister played down the importance of his government's refusal to support the United States, but months later Díaz Ordaz himself publicly denounced the American intervention during a border summit with President Johnson.

Another disagreement emerged in relation to the Allende era in Chile.

The United States opposed the Allende regime, and did everything short of direct military action to unseat it. Mexico's rulers established close personal and political ties with the Chilean President. Before the military coup which overthrew and assassinated Allende, Mexico, after Cuba, became the Latin nation that most closely identified itself with the Popular Unity regime.

Part of the explanation of these differences lay in Mexico's deep-rooted respect for the principles of international law embodied in the United Nations Charter, particularly for those concerning nonintervention in the internal affairs of other nations and the right of self-determination. The former has a long Latin American and Mexican tradition, having been raised to the level of a "doctrine" by President Venustiano Carranza during the Revolution. The second principle, while not new, acquired greater importance during the decolonization process in Africa and Asia during the 1940s, 1950s, and early 1960s, and in the course of many UN debates.

Self-determination meant the right of a colonized people to choose freely between independence and colonization or other forms of association with the colonial power. The colonized peoples should express their choice directly, and not through the will, desires, or impositions of the colonizing state. The principle's application, however, was soon extended to situations which, although they resembled colonial status, weren't identical to it: domination by a great power, military occupation, and so forth.

As in the case of many developing countries, Mexico's diplomacy made its first major excursions into the arena of truly international affairs at the United Nations. Its envoys would dominate Mexico's foreign endeavors in the decades to come. They were profoundly imbued with the political value of international law—and the principles of nonintervention and self-determination in particular—for small and poor countries in their conflicts with the major powers. Understandably, those principles, anchored in Mexican legal and diplomatic tradition, were rapidly transformed into valued tools for dealing with the United States or third-country issues involving it.

By constantly reaffirming Mexican belief in and compliance with the principles of nonintervention and self-determination, the country feels it is strengthening its hand in dealing with its northern neighbor. If Mexico were seen in the rest of the world as a consistent upholder of these principles, it could use them to counter the United States. And it did so, not only in relation to African or Asian decolonization at the UN and concerning Guatemala at the OAS, but in its own everyday affairs with the United States. In this way Mexico showed that by disagreeing with

Washington when disagreement was unavoidable, it was defending not only principles and friends but its own independence and interests.

A final cause for U.S.-Mexican discord was of domestic origin. Mexico took the positions it did on hemispheric ideological and political issues largely because internal political opinion wanted it that way and because the workings of the political system required it.

Organized and articulate public opinion in Mexico is, and has been since the Revolution, essentially leftist and nationalistic on foreign affairs. It is undoubtedly difficult, if not impossible to ascertain the true sympathies of the Mexican masses with respect to such issues. Yet there is no question as to where the opinion of the politically active sectors of society lies. Intellectuals, the press, labor unions, many government officials, students, and artists are on the left in Mexico and have been since the 1930s.

The definition of what constitutes the left and determining who is on the left in Mexico are not simple tasks. Boundaries shift over time, as do litmus tests and political affiliations. Suffice it to say that from the 1930s on and for the purposes of this analysis the term "the left" can be taken to designate the political continuum ranging from the extreme left, Trotskyist, Maoist or Castroist, including intellectuals (Diego Rivera), political parties (presently the Revolutionary Workers' Party), and armed groups (the Genaro Vázquez and Lucio Cabañas guerrillas in the early 1970s), through the Communist Party and its successors (the Unified Socialist Party in the early 1980s, the Mexican Socialist Party today) to progressive and nationalistic intellectuals (from Pablo González Casanova to Carlos Fuentes), as well as labor leaders and politicians who have belonged to the PRI, have served in government, or have considered themselves part of the ruling political elite but have emphasized the political system's revolutionary heritage. The Cárdenas legacy (father and son) is the most representative and important segment of this last group but not the only one.

Many Mexican writers, such as Alfonso Reyes, Octavio Paz, Carlos Fuentes, and others less known outside Mexico, have been diplomats, and many diplomats have been intellectuals, precisely because both occupations neatly dovetail on the left. Mexico's most distinguished painters, writers, and poets have nearly all belonged on the left of the political spectrum although José Vascancelos and Manuel Gómez Morín are notable, dated exceptions. Even Paz, the inventor of Mexico's own brand of *nouvelle philosophie,* in his youth and middle age was of the left. His conversion to different beliefs had the impact it did precisely because it was a conversion, and an uncommon one, making Paz the first true contemporary Mexican intellectual of the right.

While this state of affairs may have begun to change in the mid-1980s, it certainly lasted until then. Those who might have disagreed with the left's positions on foreign affairs were either silent, indifferent, or impotent. They surfaced on occasion, but never really made the government feel their weight on these matters. The reason was that on many other matters, they carried the day.

The right's triumph on most domestic issues after 1940 made progressive stances on international affairs an important component of the political system. Since 1940, succeeding Mexican governments have shifted to the right on economic, political, social, agrarian, and even cultural and educational issues. They did so while keeping the system's progressive constituencies and spokesmen on board, and maintaining the Revolution's coalition intact, avoiding both splits and bloodbaths. This was largely achieved by conserving many of the left's most cherished symbols, without paying much attention to the context in which they operated. Land reform and the *ejido* land tenure system, the existence of a large state-owned sector of the economy, and a progressive foreign policy were key features in this skillful strategy.

It has often been said that Mexico's highly nationalistic foreign stances are pure grandstanding, which the country's people are indifferent to and which the left is too weak to deserve. Whatever the accuracy of this statement, it misses the point. As elsewhere in the world, the natural constituency for Mexico's foreign positions was never meant to be the majority of the country's inhabitants. Nor was it designed for the revolutionary, extreme left, but rather for the more progressive sectors of the traditional, institutional, political establishment, which were left out in the cold in 1940. The number of Mexican intellectuals, politicians, and labor leaders who would have broken with the system and ventured into the opposition because of their disagreement with a conservative foreign profile is impossible to determine. In the past, the country's leaders never undertook the risk of finding out, and if the Cárdenas split of the PRI is any indication, they were right in not doing so.

But it would be injudicious to attach excessive weight and coherence to the nation's foreign activities during this entire period. As Mario Ojeda, a well-known Mexican student of the country's foreign policy, has explained:

During those years Mexico was concentrating on the promotion of its internal development and consequently felt that getting involved in external problems was a distraction from domestic effort. Furthermore, the rigidity of a bipolar world, in addition to the intolerance of the Cold War era, left few countries the possibility of an active and independent foreign policy. Hence, Mexico's foreign policy at the time was essentially passive, defensive, and legalistic.[2]

Indeed, it would not be inaccurate to say that in lieu of a true foreign *policy,* in the full sense of the word—with clear objectives, strategy, and tactics, and the political support and resources to back these up—Mexico had set forth a series of international *stands.* These undoubtedly had a clear and consistent internal logic; above all, though, they added up to a set of principled positions at little cost and with virtually no consequences or responsibilities. It was only by the middle of the 1970s that the contours of a true foreign policy began to emerge; only since the end of the same decade has Mexico actually started to assume commitments and acquire responsibilities on the international scene. Several trends converged to make this possible, one of which was the discovery of immense oil reserves in the latter half of the 1970s, together with the self-confidence and ambition that this engendered.

But other factors, chiefly external, probably were of greater consequence. They ensured that even without oil Mexico would have assumed a more active and broader international role for itself. The first was the process of negotiations and disagreements over international economic issues that took place in numerous multilateral forums during the decade, from the International Monetary Fund and the United Nations Conference on the Law of the Sea to the North-South Conference on International Cooperation in Paris and the special sessions of the UN General Assembly on the New International Economic Order. With some exceptions, the United States and the industrialized nations in general attached only marginal importance to these negotiations, but for Mexico they meant a great deal. Practically every official who would later play a role in Mexico's diplomacy—including three future foreign ministers, five undersecretaries, and many ambassadors—participated actively in one or another of these conclaves.

The larger developing countries were seeking to change the nature of economic relations with the industrialized nations. They wanted more stable and better terms of trade, higher prices for the basic commodities and raw materials they exported, and lower costs for the intermediate and capital goods they purchased from the developed world. They sought greater access to Northern markets for their incipient manufactured exports, increases in aid, and expanded lending on more favorable terms from the wealthier nations, as well as a broader transfer of technology.

These nations were striving to achieve greater control over their natural resources by taking over the foreign oil, mining, and agricultural companies which in many cases had owned or exploited those resources for several decades. Since Mexico had nationalized its oil thirty-five years earlier, it obviously did not fit into all of these categories, but several of the goals did apply to Mexico. It took up the banners relevant to its situation and supported or sympathized with those that were not.

While few concrete results emerged from the often interminable meetings and discussions, the process proved decisive for countries such as Mexico. It forced Mexico to acknowledge the existence of dozens of nations like itself, to cut deals with them, to acquire commitments, and to establish alliances. These meetings became, in a way, Mexico's coming-out party. Because of the country's involvement with the Third World effort to restructure the existing economic order, its leaders were obliged to travel to Africa and Asia, to adopt positions on third-country issues concerning the Middle East and South Africa, and to step back from Mexico's face-to-face, decades-old relationship with the United States. Conversely, those leaders' ambitions to move the nation away from its one-on-one match with Washington were reinforced by the ongoing gatherings.

The main objective sought by Luis Echeverría, the first President to lead the country in this direction, was a substantial diversification of Mexico's economic links with the rest of the world. This effort, and similar ones by his two successors, failed: the share of Mexican trade, investment, and tourism held by the United States has, if anything, increased. But the political diversification which came of these attempts to strengthen the country's independence wrought a major alteration in Mexico's standing in world affairs, particularly among the developing nations.

Mexico adopted stances on issues which did not directly affect it, often entailing negative consequences vis-à-vis the United States, but which became a necessary element in its increasingly "international posture." And when circumstances entirely beyond Mexico's control brought to the fore an international issue which did affect the country directly, it was better prepared—and more important, had greater international stature—to deal with it. That issue was the Sandinista revolution in Nicaragua that toppled Anastasio Somoza in 1979 and brought on a major regional crisis when the United States, though formally accepting the revolutionary fait accompli, sought to reverse it. Central America, an area Mexico knew little of and cared even less about, propelled it to a center-stage role in world affairs. It subsequently provoked the sharpest and most enduring dispute with the United States over relations with the rest of the world.

The greater intensity was understandable. For the first time, Mexico's interests, as opposed to only its principles and sympathies, were directly involved in a region too close to home to be indifferent to. Mexico would no longer be able to simply enunciate its principles and limit its foreign policy to defending them. Although those principles could guide Mexico's action, giving it a domestic and international legitimacy which it might not otherwise possess, there would be times when interest and principle would clash, when mere principle would not suffice.

Unknowingly perhaps, and against the dominant trend in Mexican official opinion, by truly getting involved in international affairs Mexico lost the option of altruistically and systematically choosing principle over interest. From then on, Mexico would undoubtedly weaken its brief if it strayed away from its traditional principles, but would put itself in a straitjacket when it reduced the nation's foreign policy to the mere defense of those principles.

Mexico did not encourage or foresee the dramatic drive for radical change which shook the Caribbean Basin in the 1970s. The clamor for a major overhaul of the region's basic structures, however, created a golden opportunity to establish a foothold and wield influence in an area where otherwise it would have been unwelcome. As early as the beginning of the decade Echeverría had established a close relationship with Michael Manley, the reformist Prime Minister of Jamaica. He had also traveled to Cuba in 1975, the first Mexican chief of state to do so.

But the door truly opened for Mexico when revolutionary tremors began to seize the Central American isthmus toward the end of the 1970s. Only governments and political organizations on the left of the political spectrum would view Mexico's appearance on the scene with any sympathy; those on the right, and particularly the region's military, would use the latent anti-Mexican nationalism of many of these countries to reject Mexican overtures and maintain their predominant ties with the United States.

The Central American crisis fit Mexico's needs neatly. It was close enough to make a role possible and realistic, yet sufficiently removed not to constitute any serious danger to the country's stability. Because of its "left-right" configuration, it allowed Mexico to take sides in conformity with its traditional sympathies; due to American involvement, it permitted Mexico to raise high the banners of nonintervention and self-determination.

Central America was, in a nutshell, the perfect bridge between Mexico's previous stands in foreign affairs and its new assertive and ambitious foreign policy. By late 1978, when the Sandinista National Liberation Front began to threaten the forty-year-old rule of the Somoza family, Mexico was ready to launch itself into the fray. It did so first with discretion, then with a vengeance. Absent during the initial stages of the regional effort to mediate the crisis, by late 1978 it had consolidated ties with the Sandinistas through the PRI and the Ministry of the Interior, above all with their political arm known as the Group of 12.

The Mexican embassy in Managua, headed by a highly competent Foreign Service officer, became a haven for Sandinista militants and leaders. Money, messages, people, and other goods entered and left the embassy, and traveled to and from Nicaragua on Mexican government aircraft. Pressure from mid-level Foreign Ministry officials and from public opinion sensitized to the Somoza tyranny by extensive Mexican television coverage, together with the need to make up for previous hesitation, convinced López Portillo by the spring of 1979 that Mexico should break relations with the Somoza regime. He simply awaited the right moment.

It came that May. López Portillo went ahead with a dramatic public shift in Mexico's foreign posture, giving it the activist regional impulse which characterized it in the following years. In less than a month, López Portillo met with Fidel Castro on the island of Cozumel—the first time Castro had visited Mexico since 1956—replaced his pro-American Foreign Minister with a career diplomat and intellectual known for his nationalistic views, broke relations with the Somoza government, and saw Mexico play a leading role in the Latin effort to thwart a last-ditch attempt by the United States to stop the Sandinista triumph. Despite its reluctance to save Somoza, the Carter administration still tried to dispatch an inter-American peacekeeping force under OAS auspices. According to the Latin American specialist on the State Department policy planning staff:

The Mexican Foreign Minister took the lead in dissenting from the U.S. position. Whereas [Secretary of State Cyrus] Vance saw only a dark "war of national destruction" [the Mexican Foreign Minister] praised "el pueblo de Nicaragua" for exercising "the sacred right of rebellion against tyranny, just as el pueblo Mexicano had done seventy years before." . . . Mexico and the Andean States carried the day.[3]

When the new Sandinista government flew from Costa Rica to Managua on July 19, it did so in the company of the Foreign Ministers from several Latin nations, but on a Mexican presidential plane with a senior Mexican government official on board.

From that point on, Mexico became a key actor in the Central American and Caribbean region. It strengthened its ties with the area's left, having its highest officials, including the President, travel to Managua and Havana, and receiving Cuban and Nicaraguan leaders in Mexico. Soon after François Mitterand's election to the French presidency in May 1981, Mexico proposed joint action in the region by both governments. The result was the Franco-Mexican Declaration on El Salvador, conceived by Mexico and calling for negotiations between the U.S.-backed regime and the left-wing guerrillas of the FMLN-FDR, giving the latter an international legitimacy and standing they would never have achieved otherwise. Despite negative U.S.-inspired reaction in Latin America, mainly among the Southern Cone dictatorships (Argentina, Chile, Uruguay, Paraguay), the initiative consolidated Mexico's position as a principal actor on the Central American scene. While Mexico always maintained that none of the region's revolutionary or even reformist regimes were truly viable if they did not reach a modus vivendi with the United States, which seemed possible under the Carter administration, the country nonetheless pursued its policy when this hope became futile—that is, after Ronald Reagan's inauguration in 1981.

It also upgraded its activism in the United Nations. For the first time since 1946, Mexico was elected to the UN Security Council, something it had avoided previously, given the obligation of adopting stances on various issues which membership imposed. It took a leading role in promoting the developing countries' efforts to engage the industrialized nations in global economic negotiations. With the support of Austria and Canada, in October 1981 Mexico convened the Cancún summit on International Economic Cooperation, bringing together heads of state or government from twenty-two rich and poor nations, including the United States.

When originally conceived, in late 1979, the Cancún project had received understanding, if not sympathy, from the Carter administration, and its prospects seemed encouraging. The election of Ronald Reagan undermined its importance, since it was evident that his administration would never entertain any notion of economic development and cooperation other than through private flows of investment and trade. Nevertheless, Mexico's effort brought it prestige among developing countries who saw that it was willing to commit itself and spend political capital on issues close to their hearts.

By mid-1982 the Reagan era, together with economic crisis and personal unpopularity, made it impossible for the lame-duck López Portillo regime to sustain this policy. Mexico consequently shifted to a more mediating, evenhanded stance, emphasizing the need for coexistence between regional revolutionaries and the United States. In February 1982, López Portillo proposed in Managua a multifaceted peace plan for the region. In subsequent meetings between his Foreign Minister and Secretary of State Alexander Haig, Fidel Castro, and Daniel Ortega, a number of trade-offs and demands were clearly identified. In August 1982, together with Venezuela, Mexico issued a call for negotiations between Nicaragua, Honduras, and the United States. Six months later, newly elected President Miguel de la Madrid joined in creating the Contadora Group, named after the island resort where the Foreign Ministers of Colombia, Mexico, Panama, and Venezuela first met.

The Contadora Initiative would eventually lead to a substantive change in Mexico's Central American policy, but during its early years it enhanced the nation's regional influence, remaining consonant with its traditional sympathies and principles, as well as with its newly discovered responsibilities and ambitions. Contadora preserved one of the new policy's most redeeming virtues: the introduction of third-country issues to the bilateral U.S.-Mexican agenda, making of Mexico a valid, if not particularly welcome negotiating partner for the United States on issues no longer limited to the binational domain. In short:

> [Mexico and the United States'] disagreement over Central America had become the most prominent feature of the relationship. It brought important adjustments on both sides: Mexico was no longer simply using a foreign policy issue to exhibit its independence from the United States; and Washington for the first time reluctantly came to accept Mexico as a valid interlocutor on a problem of strategic importance to the United States.[4]

Even the Reagan administration—perhaps more so than its predecessor—was forced to deal with Mexico on Caribbean Basin issues, introducing for the first time a lasting non-bilateral element into relations. For whatever reasons, always with a certain arrogance and *a priori* dismissal of Mexican views, the United States nevertheless felt obliged at least to go through the motions of taking Mexico's wishes and requests into account.

Thus at the Cancún summit, in the course of his fourth meeting that year with Ronald Reagan, López Portillo asked the American President to authorize a secret meeting later that month in Mexico City between Secretary of State Haig and Cuban Vice President Carlos Rafael Rodríguez. Reagan replied affirmatively, emphasizing that "he accepted only because his friend López Portillo had asked him to do so." The meeting, held at the home of Mexico's Foreign Minister, was the first by a Secretary of State with a top-level Cuban official since the 1960s.

Similarly, Reagan agreed to De la Madrid's recommendation in 1984 that he send Secretary of State George Shultz to Managua to meet with Daniel Ortega and then undertake talks with the Sandinistas in Mexico. These conversations, held in the Mexican Pacific resort of Manzanillo, were the last instance of high-level contacts between Nicaragua and the United States. The fact that both demarches produced scant results was less important from the Mexican perspective than their taking place under Mexican auspices. The government gave up little in exchange and showed its people, as well as the rest of the world, that it had real influence in Washington, and that its positions were taken seriously there.

As Mexico's bilateral difficulties with the United States mounted and as the country's economic problems grew, the Contadora Initiative became the centerpiece—if not the only substantive piece—of its foreign policy. Leaders and the makers of foreign policy invested an immense amount of time and energy in Contadora, hoping both to bring peace to Central America and to have Mexico play a principal role in the process. Talks between Central American governments were promoted; a comprehensive series of negotiating points, trade-offs, and mechanisms for verification and enforcement were thrashed out. A draft treaty was drawn up and negotiated, resting on the premises that the post-1979 status quo in the region be maintained and that external military force was unacceptable and ineffective as a solution to the region's problems. It rejected the Reagan view that turmoil in the area sprang from Soviet, Cuban, and Nicaraguan subversion, emphasizing instead economic and social dimensions.

But in the Reagan era, Contadora's effectiveness was doomed to be limited in the best of cases. True, as its staunchest defenders argued, it did contribute to the strengthening of the opposition within the United States to direct American intervention against Nicaragua. Contadora was an undeniable expression of Latin American opposition to Reagan administration support for the contras and aggression against the government of Nicaragua. Moreover, it gave American critics of Reagan's policy the semblance of a policy alternative: a negotiated, hemispheric solution which would address most of the United States' main concerns with regard to Nicaragua, particularly on security issues. But Contadora's real tragedy went beyond its incapacity to bring peace in Central America, a goal probably beyond its means.

From a Mexican viewpoint, the diplomatic undertaking had been originally conceived as a way out of an apparently untenable situation. Given its deepening economic crisis and constant need of U.S. support for debt rescheduling and fresh credit, and because of growing domestic opposition to its activist posture, Mexico perceived that Central America was causing excessive damage to its relations with Washington. Meaningful political opposition to this Central American role emanated essentially from the business community, and from those sectors of the bureaucracy most directly in touch with the private sector.

This opposition, as opposed to ideologically motivated and marginal criticism from the political and journalistic right, stemmed from one consideration. They believed that Central America was not worth fighting over with the United States, and that Mexico could get a far better deal with the United States on bilateral matters if it simply gave in on Central America, or in any case stopped meddling in the region. In addition, for both generational and ideological reasons, the De la Madrid administration had far less affinity or sympathy with the Sandinistas than the previous government. In the words of a *New York Times* correspondent formerly stationed in Mexico: "In contrast to the unwavering support given to the Sandinistas by his predecessor . . . Mr. De la Madrid has adopted a more 'evenhanded' position in Central America."[5]

Yet Mexico was unable and unwilling to pull back completely from its previous commitments. The halfway solution was Contadora: a policy which toned down support for the Sandinistas and distanced Mexico from Cuba and from the insurgents in El Salvador. Simultaneously it shored up the nation's peace-seeking role by joining other Latin American nations, often on their terms, in that endeavor.

Mexico and the other Contadora nations sought and received widespread—if somewhat shallow—support from all quarters. The European Economic Community, the Pope, the Socialist International, the Movement of Non-Aligned Countries, the United Nations, and the Organization of American States all approved resolutions backing the Contadora process and calling on everyone to support it. None of this cooperation was disinterested.

In some cases it helped certain nations make a point on Central America without getting involved or opposing the United States. In others, particularly among the African and Asian nations, it allowed them to extend favors to Latin America which they would later call in on matters of more direct concern. Although Mexico has never become a full member of the Movement of Non-Aligned Countries—having traditionally considered membership to be a needless anti-American gesture—it nonetheless had the longest experience in the multilateral arena. It consequently played the most active role in lining up this type of support.

During the first two years of this exercise in diplomatic acrobatics, things went well. Mexico maintained good relations with the regional left and at the same time showed the United States that it was willing to moderate its previous stances. By late 1984, however, this situation began to change, and Mexico started suffering from the worst of both worlds. The Sandinistas and the regional left started to back away from the Contadora process. The FMLN-FDR in El Salvador complained that "Contadora, as a group, has been unwilling up to now to use its good offices to work for this dialogue [between the FMLN-FDR and President José Napoleón Duarte]. It has not even directly discussed the Salvadoran case." The United States was no longer as appreciative of Mexico's newfound moderation.

Matters reached a climax in September and October 1984, when a draft Treaty for Peace and Cooperation in Central America was finally completed. Initially the so-called Group of Tegucigalpa (Honduras, El Salvador, and Costa Rica), as well as Guatemala, assented to the draft. Nicaragua, for its part, expressed reluctance to sign, given that the proposed legal instrument included a number of internal political recommendations deemed by the Sandinistas to be in violation of the principle of nonintervention. Mexico finally convinced them, however—or they convinced themselves—and they announced their willingness to accept the treaty.

The Contadora nations began circulating the draft at the UN General Assembly. When American officials understood that their Central American allies had consented to an arrangement leaving the Sandinistas in power while cutting off funds to the contras and withdrawing American military advisers from the region, they conspired to bring the agreement down. They were all the more furious when it appeared that, more than anything else, the slip-up was due to their own dismissal of the Contadora drafting exercise. The prospects of removing Cuban advisers from Nicaragua and imposing limits on regional armament levels were not enough to make the deal palatable for the Reagan administration.

The United States, through UN Ambassador Jeane Kirkpatrick, opposed the draft on the grounds that its enforcement and verification measures were insufficient, and because there was no explicit simultaneity regarding the two sides' concessions: removal of Cuban advisers and arms reductions on the Sandinistas' part, as well as a halt to their supposed aid to the FMLN-FDR; an end to contra aid, military maneuvers, and advisers in Central America on the United States' part. Mexico and the other Contadora nations faced a choice which would seal their initiative's fate.

Although they perhaps did not realize it at the time, if they took American objections at face value and reopened the lengthy and painful negotiating process, they would never again reach a viable conclusion. While American objections may have seemed reasonable or at least worthy of consideration in themselves, they were not the real reason behind U.S. opposition. By this time it was evident that Ronald Reagan would never accept any agreement that left the Sandinistas in power. Therein lay the treaty's true defect from the U.S. point of view, not its technical minutiae or lack of specificity.

But if the Contadora nations said out loud what everybody whispered behind closed doors, that despite the Sandinistas' mistakes and unreasonableness, the real obstacle to peace in the region was Reagan's obsession with overthrowing them, they would be confronting the United States head-on, precisely what they had sought to avoid in the first place. For Mexico in particular, the dilemma was painful but its outcome was predictable. The drafting process was reopened, and blame for failure to reach an agreement was not squarely placed on the United States. The State Department had already drawn up options to follow in case Mexico chose this path; they were unnecessary.

On several later occasions similar opportunities would arise. But never again would Mexico and its allies come as close to brokering a deal or bringing the mediation effort to a dignified end. The group's incapacity to deliver American acquiescence to a fair and realistic agreement had been uncovered, and its leverage with the Sandinistas also eroded considerably. By late 1985, Nicaragua was rejecting any agreement that did not explicitly call for an immediate and complete halt to aid for the contras. When subsequently the contras ceased to be a significant threat to the Sandinista regime and Ronald Reagan became a lame duck, Managua refused to consider any document which did not address aid to the contras. By then Contadora, despite the creation of the support group composed of Argentina, Brazil, Peru, and Uruguay, had lost its original impulse. President Oscar Arias of Costa Rica had replaced it as the main generator of ideas and initiatives in the region. With the designation of

Carlos Salinas de Gortari as the PRI candidate for the 1988 elections, Miguel de la Madrid became an outgoing President and Mexico was left with virtually no place to go in Central America.

The tragic paradox behind this Mexican diplomatic impasse was that it in no way diminished tensions with the United States over Central America. If anything, matters deteriorated and the existing differences widened, despite a number of steps Mexico at least implicitly made to accommodate American desires. Notwithstanding repeated Sandinista entreaties, De la Madrid refused to visit Nicaragua. And from early 1985 on, Mexico cut off heavily subsidized oil deliveries to Managua, demanding up-front cash payments for its oil even if this meant that the Soviet Union would become Nicaragua's sole supplier. The United States noticed, but just barely, as shown by Assistant Secretary of State Elliott Abrams's exchange with Senator Jesse Helms in mid-1986:

> Mr. Abrams: We have told Mexican officials on a number of occasions, publicly and privately, that we are unhappy with the Mexican role, which has largely been to support and defend the Nicaraguan position.
>
> Senator Helms: But the fact is that they have sided with Nicaragua, haven't they?
>
> Mr. Abrams: Yes.
>
> Senator Helms: They have frequent contact—maybe contracts, too—with the Nicaraguans. How about Cuba?
>
> Mr. Abrams: Let me back up a second. I would note that Mexico used to supply about 75% of Nicaragua's oil. They are distancing themselves from Nicaragua—
>
> Senator Helms: That is true.
>
> Mr. Abrams (continuing): That we view, obviously, as a positive step.
>
> Senator Helms: I grant you that.
>
> Mr. Abrams: Nicaragua's oil now comes almost entirely from the Soviet Union.
>
> Senator Helms: Maybe that's because Nicaragua can't pay for it.[6]

The problem lay in the fact that while Mexico may have stepped back from the left, the Reagan administration was moving even further to the right. As Mexico was toning down its peacemaking initiatives and muting its criticism of U.S. policy in Central America, Washington was raising the stakes and increasing its own commitment to bring down the Sandinistas. With each congressional rejection or delay of funds for the contras, and as the American people refused to succumb to President Reagan's charm on this issue, the U.S. government became far more sensitive to and angered by Latin American and Mexican opposition to its policy.

In its view, Mexico may have adopted a quasi-neutral stance—an "impartial and objective one," as De la Madrid himself phrased it[7]—but for Reagan administration ideologues, the absence of backing for the contras was as disloyal or unfriendly as continued support for the Sandinistas. Mexico could refrain from the latter, but could not bring itself to approve the former. In American conservative eyes, both were as bad; in the Mexican view, there was a world of difference between them.

Differences between Mexican and U.S. international policies reached a crisis in the second half of the decade because several factors converged simultaneously. Mexico's new Central American policy, either in its activist, assertive mode or in its moderate, mediating one, became an obstacle to American goals in the region. As formulated by the Reagan administration, U.S. aspirations there were more ambitious and sharply focused than before, and this element transformed mere disagreements with the United States into confrontation.

Mexico's economic crisis brought the country closer to and made it more reliant on the United States. Finally, for these reasons as well as domestic political considerations, foreign affairs and relations with the United States surfaced as a public and widely debated issue within Mexico, dissolving the tacit consensus which had previously prevailed. It became increasingly difficult for Mexico to disagree with the United States, yet disagreement had never seemed as unavoidable.

The quasi-unanimity which had prevailed in foreign affairs had begun to disintegrate early on in the process of Mexico's emergence on the world scene. The first instance of unequivocal and public dispute between the private sector and the government over international issues probably came in 1972, during Salvador Allende's visit to Mexico. The business community publicly repudiated his trip and declared its solidarity with the Chilean private sector. Although Mexico's early support for the Sandinistas did not provoke major clashes with the right or the business sector, after Reagan took office in the United States and John Gavin arrived as his ambassador in Mexico, things began to change.

By late 1981 it became apparent that the private sector and the United States government were at least in tacit agreement on the need for Mexico to keep its distance from Cuba, the Sandinistas, and the Salvadoran insurgents. Some—at the highest level—believed (probably inaccurately) that the first major run on the peso, in late 1981, came in response to a leak from the government to the private sector, which then transmitted the information to the U.S. embassy, concerning the Mexican government's $100 million secret loan to Cuba.

Since that time, most of the Mexican business community has opposed the government's Central American policy. It has done so for ideological reasons as well as tactical considerations. But it has also maintained that conflict with the United States over minor issues should not poison relations on important matters such as debt, trade, and investment. It disagreed both with the aggressive stance which lasted through mid-1982 and with the more moderate, evenhanded approach adopted since then. Although its disagreement has not taken it to political extremes, there is no question that its opposition has been a major factor in the government's toning down its stance. It was a constant thorn in the De la Madrid presidency's side; since the divergency appears to be as much a matter of principle as it is of interests, it is scarcely negotiable.

The United States was quick to grasp the internal Mexican complexities of the situation. The so-called Name-Calling on Namibia Affair, in January 1986, clearly illustrated this. On January 5, De la Madrid and Reagan met for their annual summit in Mexicali. Oil prices were declining, the Mexican economy was already entering a new recession, its debt dilemma was growing worse, and the Mexico City earthquake of September 19 had seriously undermined confidence in the government.

Yet the meeting between the two Presidents lasted only for a few hours, and a substantial part of that time was wasted on a half-hour lecture delivered by George Shultz to his Mexican counterpart, Bernardo Sepúlveda. The issue was Mexico's voting pattern in the United Nations, exemplified by its position on Namibia, previously known as South-West Africa.

The question had been repeatedly debated by the United Nations; increasingly, the African countries were introducing resolutions condemning the Western powers, and chiefly the United States, for not pressing South Africa to permit self-determination for Namibia. These resolutions were labeled name-calling statements, explicitly referring to the "condemned" nations, in this case the United States. Mexico, along with nearly every other country in the Third World, voted in favor, while the United States, understandably enough, opposed the resolutions.

Ostensibly, the point Shultz wanted to make was that Mexico, as a friend, neighbor, and recipient of continued American support, should not indulge in unfriendly "U.S.-bashing," especially on issues so removed from its national interests. In the view of the Mexican participants, though, he was in fact using the occasion to exploit divisions within De la Madrid's Cabinet. The State Department knew there had been bitter disagreements in Mexico City just before the summit as to what issues should be taken up.

Many in the Cabinet, particularly the Finance and Interior ministries, had wanted to put Central America on a back burner and to accede to American wishes on UN matters when transcendent issues of principle were not involved. They argued along lines familiar to all Mexican Presidents, and to which De la Madrid had proved sensitive: Mexico should defend its own interests and only pick fights with the United States on issues deemed decisive for those interests. Debt, trade, support for the Mexican political system, and the image of friendly relations between the two nations were far more deserving of attention and time than Central America and the United Nations, not to mention Namibia.

Those views were not limited to the government ministries; large sectors of the business community and the economic and financial bureaucracy shared them. The Interior Ministry, always a guardian of good relations with the United States, had its own reasons for disagreeing with Central American policy and had expressed its dissent on several occasions. In 1984, it went through complicated maneuvers—including detaining and mistreating minor Cuban officials—to expel a high-level political officer at the Cuban embassy in Mexico. Similarly, it undertook the relocation of tens of thousands of Guatemalan refugees along the southern border against their wishes and largely in response to Guatemalan army pressures.

By openly underlining the discordant issues and devoting so much time to them, Shultz, in the Mexican view, was showing those cabinet ministers present at the meeting that the United States was willing to go to the mat over Central American and UN issues. He was insinuating that there was a price to pay for Mexican divergence with the United States, and that the place to pay it would be in matters of debt, trade, and the perception of friendly ties.

Nothing ever came of the dispute, as might have been expected. The United States continued to pressure Mexico over United Nations votes. De la Madrid restated his position that while Mexico would review its UN policy, it was not voting against the United States but rather in favor of traditional principles and in the company of the overwhelming majority of UN members, including most of Western Europe. Mexican authorities continued to insist that UN votes and Central American policy were a matter of sovereignty. In addition, Mexico could hardly ask the African and Asian nations in the United Nations for their support on Central America and then turn around and abstain or vote against them on such sensitive issues as South Africa or Namibia. But behind the give-and-take, the pressure and the resistance, lurked an increasingly insoluble problem.

Foreign policy, or opinions and actions with regard to the rest of the world, had become a crucial intersection of conflicting forces in relations between Mexico and the United States. On the one hand, the tide rising from formal and informal economic integration was pulling both nations together. But on the other, Mexican nationalism, conserved through history and education and sharpened precisely by the integrationist drift, was accentuating the demand for the preservation of the nation's independence, sovereignty, and difference from the United States. If economic differentiation was no longer possible and cultural homogenization, at least with regard to the urban middle and lower middle classes, continued to grow, then a distinct worldview, together with its practical implementation, remained as one of Mexico's most distinguishing features.

At the same time, as economic pressures and social change began to question the traditional forms of political stability, the danger of doing without foreign policy became more acute. According to a current of common political wisdom which no one dared question, the constant reaffirmation of the nation's specificity and autonomy in relation to the United States constituted a necessary component of the political system's viability. Because the system assured continuity, peaceful successions, and a certain amount of prosperity, but also because it was perceived as safeguarding the country's independence, it had lasted as long and smoothly as it had. Throwing foreign policy to the winds by refraining from opposing the United States—if not aligning itself with the United States—at a time of severe strains on the system, seemed imprudent, or even suicidal.

It also appeared to be self-contradictory. Since the early 1970s successive Mexican administrations had groped for ways to inject new ingredients and introduce different factors into bilateral ties with the United States. They concluded that the honeymoon since World War II and throughout the Cold War and the 1960s had put Mexico at too great a disadvantage and made those relations increasingly unmanageable from its perspective.

Mexico's Third World economic activism during the Echeverría regime, its assertive Central American stance under López Portillo, Contadora and its search for closer relations with South America in the De la Madrid era all addressed this quest and reflected this need. If the nation's rulers, in their intuitive and uncanny wisdom, opted for the "debilateralization" of Mexico's relations with the United States *before* the onslaught of integration, how prudent could it be to stop emphasizing that search at the moment of the country's greatest weakness vis-à-vis Washington?

Moreover, American demands were simply intractable. If only complete compliance and alignment would satisfy the Reagan administration, this implied, for all practical purposes, the end of any role for Mexico on the international scene. It meant the elimination of any remaining coherence between the political system's rhetoric and the reality of its policies. On internal matters the correspondence had long ago disappeared, but on questions of national sovereignty, the state's legitimacy and credibility were largely intact. The political system could conceivably do without its classic rhetoric and mythology, but it probably could not render these internal mechanisms compatible with a pro-American, conservative foreign policy.

In the last analysis, the choice Mexico now faces lies between a foreign policy broadly shaped like the one it has followed since the end of the 1970s and no foreign policy at all. A weak but real argument could be made for the latter option, but there is little to say for a pro-American foreign policy which would align Mexico with the United States. Mexico's sympathies and convictions, its ambitions and its geographical contiguity make it virtually impossible for it to toe the U.S. line on international affairs. The Revolution faded away nearly half a century ago, but the deep sympathy which any country that stands up to the United States awakens in the Mexican psyche is as present today as ever.

Likewise, the suspicions the country has always evoked among its natural partners in South America because of its closeness to the United States cannot be dispelled by greater closeness to the United States. Mexico's ambitions to become a regional power and its rapprochement with South America may never be fulfilled, but they certainly will never come about if it is perceived as a poor relative of the United States. In the international arena, Mexico has a role to play if it is viewed as a minor but not insignificant counterweight or small-scale alternative to the United States, but not if it simply does its bidding.

Other potential or real midsize powers in the developing world (Brazil, India, Egypt, and possibly Nigeria) are sufficiently removed from the United States, both geographically and politically, to be able to ignore Washington—or to be ignored by it—on many issues. Conversely, they have at their disposal a tool which many other, wealthier nations have put to good use since World War II: using their relations with the Soviet Union for leverage in their dealings with the United States, and vice versa. Mexico, for reasons that sheer prudence and geopolitical realism dictate, cannot play the Soviet card. And unlike other, smaller Latin

American nations which can survive and prosper without feeling the need to play a role on the world stage, Mexico has felt that it must, simply to survive. Mexico—contiguity *oblige*—enjoys or suffers from being in a unique situation.

It is difficult to imagine a Mexican President, much less his Foreign Minister or other high-level politicians, touting the virtues of Ronald Reagan "freedom fighters." Nor can one see Mexico as it is today, or as it might hopefully be tomorrow, cooperating with the United States to promote two-party political systems or market-oriented economic policies in Latin America or conspiring with Washington to remove or destabilize hemispheric governments that do not cherish American interests. Mexico and the United States are still too different, even in their natural inclinations and sympathies.

In the end, there are solid grounds for believing that a foreign policy which is high-profile and assertive, always nationalistic and often contrary to American interests, constitutes a sort of shield for Mexico. Only behind such a shield can the country proceed successfully with the delicate and exceedingly difficult balancing act it must carry out—opening its windows to the world without forsaking its national integrity or losing its national soul, and changing all that is secondary to preserve what is essential. Mexico would betray itself if it did not try to build and nurture this shield, for it may well have no other.

PART III

—

CONNECTIONS

5

SLIDING TOWARD ECONOMIC INTEGRATION

The U.S. Perspective

—

Robert A. Pastor

As hundreds of American businessmen had done before them, Felix Rohatyn and Roger Altman, two New York investment bankers, diagnosed Mexico's ailment with clarity and not a little exaggeration: "Mexico's economic and political health is so frail that a crash program on domestic and foreign investment is needed now. It is difficult to overstate the crisis." Here, Mexicans should be permitted a moment to roll their eyes as the two implore Americans to stop being so passive: "The U.S. must roll up its sleeves and become an activist." And Mexico? Mexico "must initiate much bolder policy reforms to encourage private investment . . ."[1]

The specific analysis and solution have varied somewhat, but the pattern remains unchanged since Americans first began examining the economic health of the Mexican body politic at the turn of the century. Sometimes with the sympathy of a country doctor who visits his patient regularly, sometimes with the arrogance of a big-city surgeon who reads the X rays but has no time to see the patient, but always with certainty, the American diagnoses the problem and prescribes medicine in the form of four principles, five projects, or a comprehensive plan to get the patient up on his feet. Instead of trying to learn why the previous one hundred U.S. plans were not implemented, they propose a new one.

Americans are the quintessential problem-solvers, and they view Mexico as a perennial problem. Americans propose grand schemes to develop Mexico or integrate the two markets. Mexicans, who see the problem-solver as the problem, dismiss or resist the proposals. Both nations have benefited from the steady expansion of the economic relationship. But to the American *demandeur,* that expansion has been slow and frustrating; to the Mexican, it has been rapid and worrisome.

To a great extent, each government's view of the other is a projection of its own business-government relationship. The U.S. system is decentralized. Power is distributed widely, and checks and balances prevent public and private institutions from monopolizing power. Most Americans believe that the nation's economic success is due to the ingenuity and initiative of private entrepreneurs. Another widely shared belief is that the red tape and tunnel vision of bureaucrats and the reelection motive of politicians impede development. American industries insist that government stay out of their way, and as compared with most other nations, Washington allows its businessmen considerable room to work without government interference.

Warren Harding spoke for this sentiment in his vision of America as one "with less government in business and more business in government." Calvin Coolidge was characteristically more concise: "The business of the United States is business."[2]

In Mexico, one could spend a lifetime in the archives and never find such a comment. Especially since the Revolution, the Mexican government has ruled, and business has deferred. The political elite has tended to view businessmen—the "bourgeoisie"—with contempt. The nation's development, in the view of the government, is the result of the wisdom and guiding hand of the state, and the economy's decline is due to external causes and the lack of patriotism on the part of Mexico's businessmen.

The self-perceptions of the United States and Mexico are actually more extreme than the reality. The truth is that the state has played a crucial role in the development of the United States, and businessmen have played an important role in Mexico. Nonetheless, as we have seen countless times in U.S.-Mexican relations, perceptions often shape the reality more than the reverse.

When Americans look at Mexico, they tend to see its government's deep involvement in the economy and the resistance to foreign investment as the twin reasons for the country's underdevelopment. A secret State Department memorandum in 1955 summarized this American perception: "Inordinate nationalism appears to be innate in the Mexican national character and to be the basic cause of Mexico's economic problems. It is evident in Mexico's attitude toward foreign investment and in its trade policies."[3]

This perception endures. Thirty-one years later, Senator Phil Gramm of Texas explained to a Senate hearing: "The problem with the Mexican economy is a pretty easy problem to define. Since 1970, the percentage of GNP in Mexico expended by the government has doubled, from roughly 26% . . . to over 50%. During that same period, the number of industries that were nationalized and run by the government in the parastatal system has grown from 100 to over 1,000. Today, the government controls the economy of Mexico. . . . The sad reality is . . . that many of the problems in Mexico are self-produced."[4]

Like an entrepreneur offering his young apprentice some pointers, the United States wants Mexico to develop by learning from the lessons of its own success. President Dwight Eisenhower captured this well-intentioned side of the United States in a private conversation with Mexican President Ruiz Cortines in 1956:

The United States had by a combination of circumstances reached a position of great power and wealth and was anxious to do what it could to be of assistance to Mexico, not in a patronizing way but as a good friend. We want only prosperity, happiness, and a better standard of living for our friends in Mexico. We had achieved our present well-being largely through the assistance of foreign capital . . . [which] had helped develop our railroads and the insurance business. . . . What we had been able to achieve had been done in the framework of the free enterprise system.[5]

Yet Eisenhower was more sensitive about Mexico than most Americans. He told Ruiz Cortines that if he were in his place, he "would not wish to see foreign capital come in and take charge of some major service in his country." Eisenhower therefore limited his suggestion to asking the President not to hamper "certain Mexican businessmen [if they] felt that they needed additional capital to further their own development."

Since the Revolution, the most controversial economic connection between the two nations has been direct American investment in Mexico. U.S. businessmen have been seeking profits, promising development, drawing the two economies together since the latter part of the nineteenth century. The Revolution shut the door for a while, and when it began to open after World War II, Mexico left no doubt that foreigners would never again obtain the keys to its national patrimony. Since then, the principal complaints of American businessmen have been either the rules or the lack of rules.

Mexico excludes foreign investment from a wide range of industries, from petroleum and mining to radio and television, and it limits foreign ownership to 49 percent of an enterprise. Other laws on patents and trademarks regulate which technology will be permitted and on what terms. The purpose of the laws is to get proprietary technology at the lowest possible price, but their effect often has been to discourage U.S. companies from transferring their best technology. American corporations—particularly pharmaceutical and clothing manufacturers—complain that the laws do not provide protection for their patents or trademarks.[6]

Despite efforts by the De la Madrid administration to encourage foreign investment and apply the rules more flexibly, Ambassador John Gavin criticized the Mexican government for still "severely restricting ownership and investment by foreigners."[7] The American Chamber of Commerce in Mexico City agreed that Mexico's laws impeded foreign investment. Even though the Foreign Investment Commission had approved a record amount of investment ($1.8 billion) in 1985, the Chamber complained that "only 30% of the investment authorized actually gets carried out because of the long delays in getting approval. . . . Many potential investors lose interest in their projects and put their money elsewhere."[8]

Perhaps the only thing that bothers American businessmen more than the restrictiveness of the rules is the uncertainty with which they are applied. U.S. corporations dislike the fact that Mexican laws place wide-ranging powers in the hands of bureaucrats, some of whom are flexible and some of whom are hostile. Negotiations are often protracted, and not infrequently produce an agreement that is so restrictive that most businesses would simply walk away, except that they may then be informed that they need not worry because the agreements will not be strictly implemented. Other times, powerful corporations like IBM can persuade Mexico to make an exception and permit the company to be 100 percent owned. However, some businessmen are then uncertain whether the agreement will survive the incumbent's departure. Companies fear that after undertaking a large investment, they are at the mercy of the government.

A feeling lingers that the support of De la Madrid's administration for foreign investment may only represent a tactical change because of the nation's economic weakness. When the economy recovers, a future government might return to its more traditional hostility or, at best, ambivalence. In brief, signs abound that foreign investment is welcome, but not very. American businessmen are confused: should they pay more attention to those Mexicans soliciting their investment or to those complaining that there is already too much American investment? American and other foreign businessmen sense the subterranean resentment and are hesitant to commit.

Mexico's views on U.S. investment are not unique in Latin America, but an analysis of public opinion in Mexico, Argentina, Brazil, Chile, and Venezuela showed that Mexicans are the most hostile, and that the attitude extends across economic classes. Consistent with that view, Mexico has asserted a higher degree of control over foreign investment than any other country in Latin America except Cuba.[9]

Because of Mexico's large internal market and its contiguity to the United States, many more companies would invest if they sensed a deeper, more lasting change in Mexican policy. In a 1986 survey of the Fortune 500 companies, 52 percent of their presidents responded that "if Mexico would allow foreign investment on the same basis that Japan, Korea, Taiwan, and Hong Kong do, they would either institute a new investment program or they would expand their existing investment."[10]

In recent years, U.S. investment has contributed importantly to Mexico's development, although the presence is not large enough to be able to change the direction of the Mexican economy. American corporations generated over 200,000 jobs in Mexico in 1977, and *maquiladoras* alone have contributed over 100,000 jobs since 1982. Much of the investment is in the manufacturing sector, which is the economy's most dynamic, and one-fourth of all such new investment is by U.S. corporations.[11] This represented about 1.2 percent of the total labor force in Mexico at the time, but about 16 percent of all jobs in manufacturing. Moreover, since the mid-1950s, U.S. manufacturers in Mexico have been creating jobs at a much faster rate than their local counterparts.[12]

Two surveys of U.S. corporations in Mexico showed that they paid twice as much to their employees as local firms did in 1966 and the difference had increased by 1972.[13] American companies also brought technology, albeit not the state-of-the-art, and an ability to export north. American businessmen say that they would use the latest technology if they had full control over their local corporations and if patent guarantees were more secure. They recognize that success in Mexico depends on both profits and their willingness to serve the government's developmental objectives. Since the mid-1970s, Mexico has encouraged foreign businesses to purchase more of their materials in the country and export a larger percentage of their goods. American businessmen have been responsive to these new policies.

But a climate of uncertainty sometimes evokes the kind of behavior in Americans that confirms Mexico's suspicions. Off the record, Americans complain incessantly about the difficulties of doing business in Mexico. Corruption particularly rankles. One American said that if his customers cannot pay an additional 15 percent above what he would ask of their counterparts in Hong Kong or Europe, it does not pay for him to export because that is what is needed in "entertainment costs" at the border to get the products through. When asked why they bother to invest, some businessmen will say that they cannot afford to leave; others will admit that profits compensate for their frustrations. In fact, American companies obtain a much higher rate of return in Mexico than in the United States. Many say they would not consider investing in Mexico on any other terms because of the hassle and because they feel their investment is always insecure. Therefore, if they haven't made a sufficient profit at the beginning, it is not worth the risk.

The problem with obtaining a quick payoff is that it makes the host country feel exploited, a sentiment that some Mexicans carry anyway. The pattern of interaction between Mexico and U.S. businesses therefore does not add confidence and trust to a relationship that has little, if any, in reserve. The result is that Mexico keeps its foot on the brake of U.S. investment.

That such investment remains a highly charged issue is connected more to historic perceptions than to contemporary realities. American investment benefits Mexico, but it is no panacea for that nation's economic predicament, and it never will be. The United States would be wiser to give less attention to promoting business and developing Mexico, and more to whether and how to manage the expanding and increasingly complicated economic relationship. That relationship is characterized by increasing benefits and vulnerabilities due to new bonds pulling the two economies closer together in the fields of energy, finance, trade, and production sharing.

From World War II until the 1970s, the United States remained so secure in terms of its fuel needs that it did not even have a government department responsible for energy matters. During most of this period, oil imports accounted for less than 25 percent of total consumption. Due to low world prices and a depressed domestic oil industry, in March 1959 President Eisenhower instituted quotas on all oil imports, except from Mexico and Canada.

The program permitted domestic oil production to increase at twice the rate of imports, but in 1970 domestic production peaked. Consumption continued to rise, and the result was that oil imports doubled by 1973 and the source of the imports shifted from the Western Hemisphere (Venezuela and Canada) to the Middle East. This shift coincided with a war in the Middle East and an Arab OPEC oil embargo, which pushed prices up from about $2.08 a barrel in early 1973 to $10.40 in December 1974. A second "oil shock" in 1979–80 lifted prices up to $32 a barrel.

The 1970s have rightly been called "the oil decade."[14] The change in the price of a single commodity had as profound an impact on the global balance of wealth and power as a world war. Poor oil-producing, developing countries became wealthy almost overnight, and the mightiest industrial powers were humbled and forced to suffer an economic adjustment as severe as any since the Great Depression.

The United States moved slowly to reduce its dependence on energy imports, in part because almost half of the people were not even aware that the United States imported oil.[15] In 1977, Jimmy Carter proposed a comprehensive program to lower consumption and increase production of oil. While the United States was searching for an answer to the energy crisis, Mexico offered, in the words of a Rand Corporation study, "the only demonstrated potential for large increases in oil production and exports from a non-OPEC country."[16] The Rand study judged, incorrectly as it turned out, that since Canada would not be able to export much oil to the United States in the future, "Mexico is the most secure of any country that could export sizeable amounts of oil." Nonetheless, Rand concluded, as the Carter administration had, that it would be a mistake to pressure or even to encourage Mexico to develop its oil resources rapidly. "As we have seen in Iran, rapid petroleum development can create political and economic instability."

José López Portillo chose to expand oil production, but to keep it within moderate limits. Extraction tripled from 981,000 barrels per day in 1977 to 2.75 million barrels per day (mbd) in 1982, with exports of about 1.5 mbd in that year. Oil production and exports remained at approximately those levels through 1986. To avoid becoming dependent on the U.S. market, Mexico limited oil exports to the United States to 50 percent of total foreign sales.

Mexico replaced Saudi Arabia as the largest supplier of petroleum to the United States in 1982, and it maintained that position until 1986, when it slipped behind Canada and Venezuela. This was symbolic of the shift away from insecure Middle Eastern sources. In 1979, four of the five largest exporters of oil to the United States were Saudi Arabia, Nigeria, Libya, and Algeria—accounting for half of all imports. In 1985, the top four sources also accounted for half of all imports, but they were Mexico, Canada, Venezuela, and the United Kingdom. Mexico was exporting 816,000 barrels per day to the United States, accounting for over 16 percent of total U.S. crude oil imports.[17] The increase in oil production by Mexico and other non-OPEC countries, together with the decline in world consumption, had a dampening effect on the price of oil beginning in 1981 and culminating in the plunge in 1986. Mexico's oil revenues, which had increased from nearly $4 billion in 1979 to over $16 billion each year from 1982 to 1984, suddenly fell to $6 billion in 1986.[18]

The oil and gas discoveries initially promised security and development for both Mexico and the United States, but they instead delivered costly insecurity. In 1980, the United States experienced an unprecedented surge of inflation, provoked in large part by the oil price rise, which pushed up interest rates to historic levels. Mexico borrowed heavily on the international markets at rising rates, and when the oil price declined in late 1981, the government had a debt it could not pay.

Prior to the debt crisis, the United States had been hesitant about asking Mexico to sell its oil to the Strategic Petroleum Reserve. Washington thought that Mexico would view the reserve as a threat to its own bargaining power. The debt crisis, however, turned the purpose of the reserve on its head. Originally designed to reduce U.S. dependence on foreign energy imports, it was subsequently used to mitigate Mexico's dependence. In 1982, as a part of the debt package that the United States helped to assemble to bail out Mexico, Washington agreed to make advance purchases of $1 billion of Mexican oil for the reserve at above market prices. Mexico soon became the largest supplier of the reserve, accounting for more than one-third of the total by the end of 1986.[19] America and Mexico thus decided to use the reserve to try to manage their economic and energy interdependence. The reserve, however, was inadequate to the magnitude of the task. Both nations have been beset by a deep crisis in the last decade caused in substantial degree by the extreme fluctuations in oil prices. One side has reaped excessive profits while the other paid exorbitant costs; then they traded places.

Simple lessons were not learned. By 1986, U.S. gasoline prices in constant dollars sank to the level of 1949. Consumption increased along with imports, worsening an already debilitating trade deficit and raising fears of a new dependence on foreign oil. Most distressing was that the United States in 1986 had increased its oil imports from the Persian Gulf. In response to the problem, the Department of Energy sent a report to President Reagan entitled *Energy Security.* The report warned: "Growing import dependence places our national security at serious potential risk through possible disruptions of supplies."[20] While genuflecting toward the free market, the report's recommendations were mainly aimed at increasing domestic oil production by opening new public lands, providing tax incentives, and eliminating environmental regulations. Incredibly, the report did not offer a single idea on what the United States and its neighbors could do to increase their mutual security in energy. It completely ignored the need for a sensible framework for price stability that could eliminate the wide fluctuations and the tragic economic dislocations. It was barren of any proposals to develop a North American gas market.

The United States should propose a long-term energy agreement with Mexico and its other oil-exporting neighbors, Canada, Venezuela, and Trinidad and Tobago. One part of the agreement would be a contract by the United States to purchase a fixed quantity of oil for, say, five years at a negotiated price. This would not only lend stability to oil prices, but would permit the contracting countries and their businesses to make future plans with greater reliability. Any reasonable accounting of the dislocations of the 1970s and 1980s demonstrates that both sides would have been better off in the long run if neither side had benefited too much.

The most immediate and dire effect of the oil boom was the debt bomb. The announcement by Mexico in August 1982 that it could no longer service its debt placed it in the center of Latin America's debt crisis. The United States could not afford to let Mexico stop paying its debt. Its commercial banking system's exposure in Latin America equaled 119 percent of the total capital for all major banks. The nine largest money-center banks had loans to the region that were equivalent to 176 percent of their combined capital. The Joint Economic Committee of the Congress calculated that if Latin American debtors repaid only 40 percent of their outstanding debt, all nine banks would fail. If they paid 80 percent of the loans, the banks would lose more than 35 percent of their combined capital.[21]

In 1982, American banks had outstanding loans of nearly $25 billion to Mexico. A failure by Mexico to repay these loans would have shaken not only the banks and Mexico but also the entire U.S. economy. That is why the Reagan administration quickly assembled a $9.45 billion loan and credit package. The banks promised to do their part by expanding their loans by 7 percent, but in fact they gradually reduced their exposure by not renewing all short-term loans that came due. By 1986, the nine money-center banks had reduced their outstanding loans to Mexico by $3 billion to $10.4 billion.[22]

The debt burdened both the debtor and the creditors. Mexico had to service its past debt rather than invest in its future. The large U.S. banks, constrained by reduced profits and nervous about defaults, pursued cautious strategies. Free of Third World debt, regional banks grew, merged, and began to overtake some of the New York institutions. In its weakness, Mexico thus precipitated a transformation of the banking system and a change in the balance of financial power in the United States.

At regular intervals, the two governments predicted that the bottom of the debt crisis had been reached. Each time the predictions were proven wrong, the Reagan administration took the lead in helping Mexico to fashion a new rescheduling package, which other Latin American debtors then tried to replicate. In the summer of 1986, the Treasury Department helped assemble a $12.5 billion deal that involved a contingency fund if the price of oil fell further. Then, in December 1987, when inflation soared above 140 percent in Mexico and the peso plunged, U.S. and Mexican officials devised a novel plan. Banks would swap some of their loans at a discount for bonds issued by Mexico and backed by the Treasury. The choice was to wait to be fully repaid, recognizing that that might never occur, or write off a portion of the debt and receive a guarantee that the rest would be paid.

The bond proposal was innovative in two ways. Instead of getting new loans to pay old debts, Mexico would be able to retire some of its old loans. More importantly, it was the first time that Washington had ever guaranteed private loans to Mexico, and the first time Mexico ever accepted such a guarantee. The drawback of the plan was that it was not large enough—retiring only $3.7 billion of old loans in exchange for $2.6 billion of new bonds—to make a dent in the $105 billion debt.

Thus, both governments have helped each other several times to step back from the financial precipice, but neither has had the vision or the will to fashion a long-term strategy to resolve the problem. Some Reagan administration officials have criticized Mexico for spending its large loans rather than investing them, ignoring the fact that the United States went from the largest creditor to the largest debtor in the world during Reagan's reign. Moreover, the United States has used its borrowed funds just as unwisely as Mexico. Senator Daniel Patrick Moynihan commented that the real debt crisis was the result of President Reagan's borrowing a trillion dollars from foreigners in the 1980s to throw a huge party.[23]

Instead of a reactive approach, both governments should choose from numerous proposals for reducing the stock and service of Mexico's debt.[24] Instead of mortgaging the future, the time has come to invest in it.

Oil also seeped into other crevices of the U.S.-Mexican economic relationship. Besides energy insecurity and the debt crisis, Mexico's new oil wealth altered the bilateral trading equation. Prior to the boom, trade between the United States and Mexico had stagnated at low levels. As recently as 1975, Mexican exports to the United States amounted to $1.7 billion or less than 3 percent of Mexico's gross domestic product, and U.S. exports to Mexico totaled $5.1 billion or 0.3 percent of U.S. gross national product. By 1980, Mexico's exports to the United States had risen to $10 billion or 11 percent of its gross domestic product, and U.S. exports to Mexico were $15.1 billion or 0.6 percent of U.S. GNP. Mexico became the third-largest trading partner of the United States behind Canada and Japan.

When the debt balloon burst in 1982, however, Mexico was compelled to reduce its imports, expand its exports, and use the surplus to pay the banks. U.S. exports to Mexico suffered, declining from $17.8 billion in 1981 to $9 billion in 1983.[25] This meant that the United States lost 227,040 jobs within two years as a direct result of Mexico's debt crisis.[26] To take just one sector, in 1980 the United States exported $2.5 billion of agricultural products to Mexico, but by 1986 the amount was less than $500 million. The contraction of the foreign agricultural market precipitated a financial crisis among farmers and the banks that had lent them money. Harold Ford of the Southeastern Poultry Association said that poultry exports to Mexico dropped from $31.1 million in 1982 to $11.7 million the next year. "The Mexicans just could not pay, and we had to stop exporting."[27]

The debt crisis contracted Mexico's market for U.S. goods, but it also forced Mexico to export more than ever before. Continuous peso devaluations made exports to the United States competitive, and they increased sharply. The United States and Mexico exchanged places on trade in the 1980s, with the United States first benefiting from a surplus and then paying the price of a sizable deficit. But this shift should not obscure the leap in the level of overall trade between the two countries—from a total of $8 billion in 1975 to $32 billion in 1981. Trade has since remained at about that level. The United States accepted an awesome increase of imports from Mexico without seeking commensurate access to Mexico's market because of the debt crisis. With a widening trade deficit, however, American cries for reciprocity and also some protection became louder.

The debate in Washington on trade policy has probably been as confusing and frustrating for Mexicans to understand as the debate on investment in Mexico has been for American businessmen. The U.S. policymaking process on trade is a bewildering mix of presidential statements on free trade, quasi-protectionist resolutions from congressmen, and decisions which seem to veer back and forth between opening the trading system and closing it.

Until 1934, U.S. trade policy alternated between long periods of protection and two periods—1846–60 and 1913–22—of relatively freer trade. The disastrous Smoot-Hawley Tariff Act of 1930, which raised tariffs to their highest rates in the twentieth century, represented the high-water mark of protectionism. Four years later, Congress passed the Reciprocal Trade Agreements Act, ushering in an era of freer trade policy. The argument for protection became one of exception rather than of principle, and that has remained the case to this day.[28]

Since 1934, trade policy has aimed to lower barriers to trade, ensure reciprocity, and protect American firms from a surge in imports or unfair trading practices. Initially, the United States pursued these goals by negotiating twenty-eight bilateral trade agreements, including one with Mexico in 1941. Tariffs fell from an average of 59.1 percent in 1932 to 28.2 percent in 1947. After World War II, the United States led in establishing a multilateral system of world trade under GATT. To gain international cooperation, Washington helped pay the dues of friendly governments until they could recover economically and assume their obligations. Thus, the U.S. financed the recovery of Europe and Japan and permitted them to maintain high trade barriers under GATT for about fifteen years.

In the 1960s, the United States helped Latin America much as it had Europe fifteen years before. It provided aid with the Alliance for Progress and loans from the World Bank and the Inter-American Development Bank, and Latin America was permitted to benefit from GATT without assuming its obligations. Although not required to do so, the United States extended to Mexico most favored nation treatment. One historian referred to the policy as giving Mexico "a free ride. Every time the United States makes a concession to a GATT member, Mexico gets it anyway."[29] Washington went even further in 1974 by unilaterally eliminating the tariffs on some of its products for Latin America and other Third World regions with a generalized system of tariff preferences (GSP). This program represented a recognition of the importance of trade for development and a departure from the most favored nation principle of GATT. The GSP was authorized for ten years initially, but in 1984 it was extended for another eight and a half years. From 1976 to 1985, the total duties saved by Mexico as a result of its exports under the GSP program amounted to $300.2 million.[30]

In the Tokyo Round of multilateral trade negotiations, which concluded in 1979, the United States encouraged the more advanced developing countries to "graduate" from the GSP, and thus provide poorer countries the opportunity to take better advantage of the American market. At the same time, the United States indirectly encouraged Mexico to join GATT so as to preclude a host of complaints that U.S.

industries were expected to lodge against Mexico for unfair trade practices. In addition, Washington felt that Mexico stood a better chance of expanding its trade with Europe and Japan within GATT. However, Mexico rejected GATT then because it thought it could get a better bilateral deal from the United States outside the treaty. The misunderstanding of each other's interests and capabilities could not have been wider or more ironic. The United States recommended the GATT framework because it could not then negotiate a bilateral agreement, and it thought that Mexico would prefer GATT as a way of reducing its dependence on the United States. Mexico wanted a bilateral agreement, but would not initiate negotiations. The result was an increase in trade disputes.

Mexico used a combination of import licenses and high tariffs to effectively bar the United States and other countries from exporting any product that could compete with its own industry or agriculture. In contrast, most of Mexico's nonpetroleum exports were subsidized and virtually all were directly competitive with U.S. products, and thus elicited from U.S. farmers or manufacturers petitions against unfair competition. American exporters complained that Washington not only failed to press Mexico to open its markets, but through the *maquiladoras* assisted Mexico to export products back to the United States.

Washington accepted a one-sided trade relationship because of the importance that it attributed to Mexico's development, but the pressures from various interests grew as Mexico's export capabilities increased. One result was the signing of an agreement in 1979 which set quotas on Mexico's exports of textiles and apparel. Despite these quotas, Mexico's textile exports rose by 69 percent from 1976 to 1985 [31] In 1984, Mexico agreed to limit steel exports to the United States in exchange for the end of investigations on unfair subsidization of Mexican steel. In addition, Mexico's fruit and vegetable exports were challenged repeatedly, albeit ineffectively, by Florida and California growers. Mexican exporters have been harassed by these restrictions or threats, but exports have continued to increase each year, and in some areas, like textiles, the growth has been very rapid.

According to the World Bank, Mexico's exchange rate policy has been much more influential than U.S. restrictions in explaining the success or failure of the country's nonpetroleum exports.[32] Until 1978, the value of Mexico's manufacturing sales to the United States exceeded petroleum exports. Then López Portillo decided to emphasize oil production to stimulate the entire economy. When the peso became overvalued, nonpetroleum exports suffered. Beginning in 1983, when oil prices declined along with the value of the peso, nonpetroleum exports became competitive again, and they increased. In 1986, nonpetroleum exports grew more than 30 percent and exceeded the value of oil exports, which had fallen.[33]

Mexico's success in expanding its exports is cause for both optimism and concern. It proves that a change in the nation's economic policy can hasten growth and trade between the two countries, but too much or too rapid success could create a protectionist firebreak in the United States. When Mexico is weak, it is easier for Washington to sacrifice a specific U.S. interest for the sake of the general interest in Mexico's development. If Mexico's economy recovers, and its exports begin to threaten a wider range of U.S. industries, then the pressures for protection or, more accurately, reciprocity will grow. The unfortunate irony is that Mexico's bargaining power is greatest when it is weakest.

More trade will create more, not less friction. This is because of the decentralized policymaking process and the U.S. perception that its trading partners are not playing by the same rules. De la Madrid took some bold steps to preclude a wave of protectionism from washing out Mexico's gains. In 1985, his government negotiated an agreement that would phase out Mexico's export subsidies in exchange for an "injury test" that the United States accepted to reduce the number of trade complaints against Mexico. This was followed by Mexico's entry into GATT in 1986, and a "U.S.-Mexico Framework Agreement" signed in 1987, which provides a basis for predictability and improved access to the American market.

The "framework agreement" contains a bilateral procedure for consultations on trade and investment matters. If agreement is not reached within thirty days, either party may seek to bring the issue to GATT or another forum. The stilted title of the "framework agreement" demonstrates how small and fragile a step it is toward bilateral negotiations. In comparison, the U.S.-Canadian Free Trade agreement, which was signed by President Reagan in 1988, is a giant leap, sweeping in its scope. In 1986, the two countries traded $150 billion in goods and services, the largest exchange by far of any two nations in the world. The treaty with Canada eliminates tariffs and almost all nontariff barriers, including those limiting U.S. ownership of Canadian companies. Canadian opposition was stiff, based on the same concerns that have kept Mexico from considering such an agreement—the fear of being subordinate and dominated. But the stimulus for the Canadian treaty was the same one that moved the Mexicans to accept the framework agreement—the worry that if a step is not taken forward, then there might be larger steps backward.

Since 1934, the trade policy debate in Washington has followed an unwavering pattern. A congressman, who represents a district where workers, companies, or farms are losing the competition to cheaper imports, introduces a bill calling for protection. If the free trade lobbyists and legislators believe that the bill is serious, they mobilize their forces to defeat it. As long as the administration and legislators can point to genuine efforts by Mexico to play by the same trading rules, the protectionists will remain on the defensive.

Since the signing of the framework agreement, Mexico and the United States have successfully negotiated the reciprocal reduction of tariffs on numerous products, including steel, beer, and wine. In addition, the two countries signed a four-year textile agreement that gives Mexico a 6 percent annual increase in textile and apparel import quotas to the United States in exchange for greater access by Americans to the Mexican market. These agreements represent the first swath of decisions by Mexico to lower its barriers to products that can compete directly with local industries. If these agreements can be maintained and expanded into other areas, the prospects are good for increasing economic integration and preventing the erection of new barriers to trade in the United States.

The United States and Mexico have established a unique "production-sharing" model on the border, the *maquiladoras,* to exploit the comparative advantages of both countries. Since the mid-1960s, U.S. companies have built factories in Mexico and imported components from the United States to be assembled by cheaper Mexican labor. A U.S. tariff provision permits the manufacturer to pay duty only on the "value-added" part of the final product—that is, the amount of labor and the value of the materials added to the product on the Mexican side.

As the peso began to fall in 1982, and wages on the Mexican side of the border dropped sharply in relationship to those on the U.S. side, *maquiladoras* expanded in number and size along the border. There were 588 *maquiladora* plants in Mexico in December 1982, but five years later there were 1,200 plants, which exported $6.6 billion of products.[34] In addition, Japanese, Korean, and Taiwanese manufacturers were investing in *maquiladoras* to export to the U.S. market.

A continued expansion of *maquiladoras* will inevitably engender a reaction in the United States. Labor already views *maquiladoras* as a device to export jobs and undermine unions in the United States and exploit lower-cost labor in Mexico. To American corporations, they preserve some jobs rather than lose all of them. The companies argue that their choice is between closing all their factories or just half and using the remaining half to export components to Mexico. "If it weren't for the fact that we save $400 million through our Mexican operation," claimed Zenith chairman Jerry Pearlman, "we'd be out of business."[35]

One suspects that there might be some truth to both self-serving arguments; how much truth depends on the individual case.

As the number of *maquiladoras* increased, their effect extended considerably beyond the border. A Commerce Department study found that *maquiladora* plants in Ciudad Juárez, Mexico, were supplied by 5,714 companies in 44 U.S. states; only 38 percent were in states on the border.[36] Since World War II, many U.S. corporations have internationalized their operations. This process accelerated and became more specialized in the early 1980s when the dollar was overvalued. Overseas plants were used to export to third markets and also to produce components for their U.S.-based manufacturing facilities. By 1987, 88 percent of American manufacturers were using foreign components, often from these offshore plants.[37] Mexico was on the cutting edge of the trend toward international production-sharing, which is restructuring U.S. industry while connecting the two economies.

Both sides are benefiting from this new area of interdependence, but neither is planning for a future disruption. Many of the *maquiladoras* are quite mobile; if the peso becomes overvalued again, or there is instability, a major exodus of companies to another country could occur. U.S. businesses could adjust more easily than Mexico. Planning to avoid such an eventuality ought to be a high priority.

The economies of the United States and Mexico are stumbling toward a more complex interdependence. Each benefit includes a cost; each opportunity, an accident; and each advantage, a new vulnerability. This is true of foreign investment, the new trade in energy, the debt crisis, the increased trade and investment, production-sharing—each has brought development but also insecurity to both sides.

As long as one of the economies grows, integration will continue. The fundamental question is whether both governments want to continue on the path of ad hoc integration with all of its dislocations and problems or whether they can plan a new economic relationship that can maximize the benefits of comparative advantage, expand productivity and development, and reduce vulnerability. As a result of changes in both countries, a new opportunity is emerging.

Since the end of World War II, the United States has been the motor behind global integration; its transnational corporations have integrated markets throughout the world, standardized consumer tastes, and delivered the goods more rapidly and cheaply than ever before in history. In the last decade, the rest of the world began to reach into the United States.

By 1980, the United States was not only the single largest source of foreign investment, it was also the largest destination. There is now not only more foreign direct investment in the United States than in Mexico, but it exceeds Mexico's gross domestic product. The expansion of such investment in the 1980s has been rapid, but it does not compare with the explosion of foreign portfolio investment in stocks and especially bonds, which is estimated at a trillion dollars.[38] By the mid-1980s, foreign investors were purchasing one-third of new Treasury bond issues. The mere rumor that the Japanese had stopped acquiring these bonds was reportedly one of the reasons that the stock market crashed on October 19, 1987, pulling Mexico's stock market even further down. (Mexico's stocks lost three-quarters of their value.) A former official of the Federal Reserve System estimated that if the Japanese reduced their purchases of the T-bonds by just half, that would probably add at least one point to U.S. interest rates, which in turn would add about $800 million per year to Mexico's debt service.[39] In short, increasing U.S. dependence on the world is no consolation to Mexico.

As in Mexico, some Americans have sounded alarms about the rising vulnerability that comes with large inflows of foreign capital. "We are a dependent nation that is beginning to lose control of its fate," Senator Dale Bumpers said during a Senate debate. "I can foresee a time when . . . our foreign creditors and foreign owners will demand concessions from us. . . . These concessions will undermine our independence."[40]

While the words sound like Mexico's, they fell on deaf ears. In that debate, Congress voted down an amendment requiring major foreign investors to disclose their identities and holdings. The United States not only does not have a committee to examine applications for foreign investment, it does not even have a procedure for identifying who is investing.

As America begins to feel the weight of the world, however, it may become more sensitive to Mexico's concerns about dependency. To the extent that both nations recognize how changes in their economic relationship and in the world economy have provided them opportunities and risks, a common approach becomes conceivable. The new dependencies could be a motive for both nations to develop a joint approach to cushion each other from adverse international developments.

Both sides are vulnerable as economic integration occurs, although not in the same way or to the same degree. Mexico's trade with the United States amounts to almost two-thirds of its total, whereas U.S. trade with Mexico is 5–7 percent of its exchange. Because of that asymmetry and because the U.S. economy is so large and adaptable, it can more easily absorb Mexico's downturn than Mexico can adjust to a U.S. recession.

A reduction of trade or investment barriers does not necessarily limit a nation's sovereignty or increase its vulnerability. It could permit more competitiveness, which could lower prices and improve the quality of a country's exports. In Mexico's case, this could mean that its internal and international market could expand faster than its U.S. trade. Mexico would then find its dependence on the United States reduced, not increased. To the extent that its employment increases, Mexico could also find itself less dependent on the United States to absorb its labor.

For the future, the primary economic issue facing the United States and Mexico is whether to permit or prevent further integration. This question is unlikely to be answered definitively, but for the moment, it is too costly to stop the process. The real issue is whether both sides will continue to acquiesce in a process of ad hoc, accidental integration or whether they can take a leap and negotiate a long-term arrangement for a freer trade area. Proposals have come from Americans as diverse as Ronald Reagan and former California governor Jerry Brown, but all have been rejected by Mexicans, who have viewed the proposals as "a step toward making Mexico a part of the United States rather than a partner" or as a "sophisticated provocation."[41]

The argument that might move both parties to reexamine the idea of a common market could well be the same that led to the Canadian treaty. It would grant access to both markets on a predictable and guaranteed basis, reducing the risk of disruption for businessmen on both sides. Mexico, for example, embarked on an expensive steel project in the mid-1970s without consulting the United States about a possible agreement on access to its market. If such an accord had been negotiated, the United States would not have been able to limit Mexico's steel exports as it did in 1984.

A formal agreement on integration could be structured with rules that could benefit Mexico and increase its control of its economic environment. At the present time, Mexico is the victim of decisions on the price of oil made by other governments. It bears the consequences of a rise in interest rates by New York banks, a reduction in the price of coffee, or the tightening of a marketing order by Florida farmers on tomatoes. The only way that Mexico can expand its ability to adjust to adverse effects of international prices for oil or coffee is to broaden and diversify the base of its economy. With regard to textile quotas or agricultural marketing orders, Mexico can assert greater control, but only by negotiating a package in which these items were one part.

What would the United States expect of Mexico in such a negotiation? Certainly, Washington would insist on a reduction of trade and investment barriers, but then Mexico has already acknowledged its protectionism as a liability. The United States would be agreeable to an unequal trade in which its barriers would be removed on more items sooner than would be expected of Mexico. Washington wants Mexico to accept the principle of "reciprocity," but it does not have to be precisely symmetrical.

The overall U.S. economic interest is to promote growth in both countries, and an important way to do that is to lower its own trade barriers and facilitate a fuller use of the comparative advantage of both countries. But specific interests in the United States—whether tomato growers in Florida, textile companies in North Carolina, or automobile manufacturers in Detroit—can pull U.S. policy in a contrary direction. The best way to counter a specific interest is within the context of a general agreement that benefits more interests than it costs. Such an agreement would reinforce the internationalist tendencies in each country.

Taking into account political sensitivities, a partial arrangement might be more advantageous. There are four possibilities: (1) an expansion of the *maquiladoras;* (2) a sectoral agreement, e.g., on automobiles; (3) the expansion of a free-trade zone on or near the border; or (4) increasing Mexico's quotas under the various voluntary export restraint agreements.

The *maquiladoras* can and should be expanded in number and quality, but because of the ease with which a company can move to another location, a special adjustment fund—with contributions from business and government—should be established to help communities that are harmed because of such a relocation.

The worldwide experience with free-trade arrangements for sectors such as agriculture or automobiles offers mixed lessons. In the Andean Pact, efforts to reach agreement on such plans created so much tension that the organization became paralyzed. Both the United States and Canada have been dissatisfied with the automotive agreement, feeling that the other side obtained the better part of the deal, but the experience may have helped both governments to contemplate a free-trade treaty, just as the European Coal and Steel Community may have led to the European Community. With the increased two-way trade in automobile parts, a limited sectoral agreement in this area might prove a productive experiment.

The inherent problem with any free-trade zone is that it adds a layer of bureaucracy when the objective is to eliminate red tape. A 200-mile-wide border zone, for example, would require the relocation of customs and immigration authorities 200 miles from the present border, or alternatively, the creation of a third, "governmentless" country in between.

A fourth option would be for the two governments to renegotiate existing voluntary export restraint agreements that affect Mexico so as to increase the country's quota every year at an 8 percent rate of growth above that permitted for other parties to the agreement. This would mean, for example, that if the arrangements on steel and textiles permitted an annual rate of growth of imports of 4 percent, then Mexico's exports to the United States would be permitted to rise each year by 12 percent. This would logically require a reduction by other countries, but that is consistent with U.S. interests in promoting employment in Mexico. In addition, Washington should try to alter its policy on marketing orders that would permit a similar rate of increase of Mexico's fruit and vegetable exports to the United States.

Sidney Weintraub argues that sectoral arrangements or "timid integration formulas and complex schemes such as freeing trade in certain territories are likely to fail."[42] A more generalized formula might look more difficult, but could actually be easier to negotiate and implement than a partial agreement. A comprehensive concord should address and reduce trade and investment barriers as well as impediments to the free flows of labor, capital, and technology. The pact need not lower all barriers at the same time, and indeed, that would probably be too disruptive. One could focus first on reducing the barriers that constrain the most, and implement a plan gradually over an extended period of time.

The theoretical debate as to whether such an agreement is in the interest of both countries has divided those who believe in the divergence theory, that the poor get poorer from a free-trade arrangement and the rich get richer, and those who believe in the convergence theory, that the poor grow faster than the rich. The weaker partner generally believes the divergence theory, but the empirical data substantiates the convergence theory.

In the case of the U.S.-Mexican relationship in the thirty years from 1950 to 1980, the period when integration between the two countries proceeded at its most rapid pace, Mexico's rate of growth greatly exceeded that of the United States. If Mexico's population had been stable, its per capita growth rate would have been two or three times higher.

William Baumol, a professor of economics at Princeton, examined data on productivity and growth among dozens of nations over a hundred-year period. He found that the productivity patterns have been converging—the "laggards" have grown faster than the "leaders" because of the innovations they have acquired from the leaders. "The laggards have a good deal more to learn from the leaders than the reverse. Thus, the balance of trade in ideas inherently favors the laggards, and this has led to convergence in the 19th and 20th centuries, an era of innovation explosion."[43] Returning migrants and foreigners are often the agents of change, bringing with them projects or businesses—from supermarkets to seat belts—that succeeded in the richer country. A Los Angeles entrepreneur could spend a week in Mexico City and think of dozens of ideas that had already been developed in L.A. that could make money for him and deliver a new product or service to Mexicans. The costs of transferring technology are much less than those of research and development, and the risk of failure is obviously less after a project has already succeeded.

The southern United States also stands in eloquent dissent of the divergence theory: industry has been marching South for the last fifteen years, and the rate of growth of many of the states in the region has exceeded that of the richer North. Georgia and Tennessee have attracted many out-of-state corporations by "advertising their liabilities," the large labor force and low wages.

These are Mexico's "liabilities" as well, and there is no doubt that a reduction in trade barriers between the two governments would lead many foreign companies—from the United States and all over the world—to take advantage of them. Mexico would still control which firms could invest and under what conditions. The difference is that it would have more choices. Let's assume for a moment that because Mexico is so much poorer than the United States, the adjustment process would either be inadequate or unusually delayed. In the European Community, the nations established a fund to assist those regions that were lagging behind. A similar "revolving" fund should be part of any long-term agreement between the United States and Mexico. Concessional loans or grants should be provided by regions benefiting from the integration to compensate Mexico or particular regions in the United States that might be injured by integration.

Mexico can steer the integration process in a way that permits its objectives to be attained, or it can step on the brakes of the integration process. In one way, the Mexican government has as much influence as Washington in defining the parameters and the pace of the economic relationship, since economic agreements can be attained only as fast as the more reluctant partner permits. Americans have often sought to expand the economic relationship, but they have been compelled to accede to Mexico's desire to move more slowly and in a manner that would not reduce its sense of control.

One could argue that the United States has more to fear from lowering its barriers to a Third World nation on its border than Mexico has to fear from the United States. In the short term, such an arrangement could stimulate a mass exodus of U.S. companies and lead to a large job transfer. In the long run, such a shift might serve both nations, but politicians run for election in the short term.

This might be the concluding irony of the great debate on integration. The United States will press for it at every opportunity because it is a confident nation of problem-solvers. Mexico, the weaker and defensive partner, will resist it. However, if a decision is made to drop the barriers and create a free-trade area, within five years the two nations may reverse roles. American labor would complain about an increase in unemployment and a flood of cheap goods from Mexico, and Mexico would insist that the barriers keep coming down and that the United States not succumb to interest-group pressures and short-term anxieties.

The Mexican Perspective

Jorge G. Castañeda

In late 1986 *The New York Times* printed one of the first all-encompassing and rigorous opinion surveys ever made public in Mexico. The poll contained many questionable results and suffered inevitably from difficulties which had previously dissuaded others from attempting similar studies. There is no polling tradition in Mexico, and when questioned by a stranger, many inhabitants prefer to invent an opinion or deny that they have one. Mexican census figures are barely reliable at publication; midway through their ten-year intervals they represent educated guesses at best, given the speedy movement of demographic, sociological, and economic trends. Public opinion surveys must be viewed as broad descriptions of attitudes, not precise measurements.

Nonetheless, the *Times*'s poll provided a wealth of data. Among the more enlightening results were those concerning the population's opinion on American involvement in the national economy.[1] Sixty-nine percent of those interviewed thought that "United States interests run the Mexican economy"; only 29 percent stated that "Mexicans run their own economy." Behind this answer, based more on impressions than on economic analysis, looms one of most daunting challenges of U.S.-Mexican relations in the coming years: a significant majority of Mexico's inhabitants feel that their economy is undergoing a process of gradual but certain integration with that of the United States, bringing together two unevenly matched economies.

This conclusion, if evidently unscientific, is not groundless. The asymmetrical economic integration of Mexico can be defined as: (1) a high and growing degree of concentration of Mexico's international economic relations—i.e., foreign trade, investment, and credit—with the United States beyond previously existing levels; (2) the steadily increasing relative weight of these external factors in relation to GNP and their extension to other areas of the economy; and (3) an increasingly unimpeded, though not necessarily formalized, flow of capital, labor, and other goods and services between the two nations. The term does not overstate the current and foreseeable state of affairs.[2]

The Mexican economy is not a particularly open one, but it is far from closed. In 1985, its foreign trade (exports plus imports) amounted to 20 percent of the gross domestic product.[3] Mexican foreign trade statistics generally underestimate reality; the true figure is probably higher, for reasons outlined below. Other nations with similar levels of development had comparable GDP/foreign trade ratios: Brazil, approximately 22 percent. Some developing countries have a higher number: South Korea, 71 percent; others, a lower figure: Argentina, 16 percent, India, 15 percent. Nations with a higher level of development—France, Italy, the United Kingdom—all have ratios between 40 and 50 percent. For the United States the corresponding figure is lower: around 15 percent.[4] Mexico does not possess an outwardly oriented economy and its share of world trade or the degree of openness of its economy in relation to its size (the Mexican economy ranks fifteenth in the world) is undeniably insufficient. But neither is Mexico by any stretch of the imagination an autarkical nation.

The reasons for this moderate openness of the economy are understandable. In the late nineteenth century, the country's rulers, under the aegis of Porfirio Díaz, attempted to modernize the country by embracing foreign investment, trade, and influence. Mexico received more American investment than any other country.[5] During this same period, it became the world's second-largest oil exporter; all of the petroleum industry was in foreign hands—mostly British and American. The Mexican Revolution did not take place as a direct consequence of these processes, but they were a factor. More importantly, the economic strategy devised by Díaz's advisers—mainly the group of European-oriented positivist thinkers known as *los científicos*—produced widespread discontent. With the exception of limited mining, oil, and to a lesser extent agricultural enclaves, as well as railroads, the standard of living of most Mexicans declined, and national dignity was blemished.

The revolutionary backlash against the Díaz dictatorship and its economic policy inevitably influenced the leadership that emerged from the Revolution. President Plutarco Elías Calles, and above all Lázaro Cárdenas favored a more inward-looking development approach, based on state-sponsored industrialization, domestic demand, and formal constraints on foreign economic involvement. As Mexico emerged from its revolutionary epic and later from the Great Depression and began to grow again in the late 1930s, it followed this path. After ten years of revolution, and twenty more of continuing mass movements, radical social change, and institutional ground-laying, it could hardly have been otherwise.

Together with this moderate openness with regard to foreign trade, the Mexican economy has also traditionally sought (indeed required) a significant transfer of foreign savings. This has compensated for relatively low domestic savings, particularly given the high levels of investment that the country has achieved—never below 20 percent of GDP since 1965, as high as 30 percent in 1981—and that it desperately needs to keep up with population growth. Between 1965 and the mid-1970s, Mexico's aggregate savings rate averaged approximately 17 percent of its gross domestic product. Foreign savings represented between 15 and 20 percent of Mexico's total savings, not an insignificant share. The aggregate savings rate rose in the late 1970s and in the early 1980s, reaching nearly 22 percent by 1982. After the debt crisis erupted in August 1982, Mexico experienced negative foreign savings: it was transferring up to 4 or 5 percent of GDP to its foreign creditors.[6]

The external complement to Mexico's low savings rate came in various forms: in the 1950s and 1960s, mainly foreign investment, tourism, and loans from multilateral financial agencies such as the World Bank and the Inter-American Development Bank. Mexico, together with Brazil and India, has been a major recipient of World Bank loans over the past thirty years. After 1974 the principal channel became foreign credit, not so much because the other sources dried up—they continued to increase in absolute terms—but because taken alone they were simply insufficient, given the greater size of the economy and its growing needs.

The United States has held an imposing position in the Mexican economy since the turn of the century. This standing has often been exaggerated by parts of the Mexican political spectrum who have inaccurately made the case that most or all of the national economy is under

American control. But the fact that, today, several of its decisive sectors—oil, steel, mining, banking, fertilizers, railroads, telephone and electric utilities—are in national hands does not diminish the importance of the U.S. role. Since the late nineteenth century American participation in the Mexican economy has dwarfed that of every other nation. Moreover, as the economy has opened further to foreign involvement, the relative size of the overall American stake (trade, investment, debt, tourism, in-bond industries, taken together) has grown, giving rise to the belief that economic integration between two grossly unequal economies lies in the medium- or even short-term future.

Through most of the nineteenth century, Europe received more of Mexico's exports and supplied a greater share of its imports than the United States. By 1885 the United States had become the chief market for Mexico's exports, and these levels grew with the coming of the twentieth century. The United States represented 79 percent of Mexico's exports and 54 percent of its imports in 1900. Trade between the two countries jumped from $9 million in 1870 to $117 million in 1910, on the eve of the Revolution. An artificial peak in the American share of Mexico's commerce abroad was reached during World War II because of the physical impossibility of exchange with the European economies. But even by 1950 the United States was purchasing 86 percent of Mexico's exports and supplying the country with 84 percent of its imports.[7] It was virtually Mexico's only real trading partner.

With new oil discoveries in the early 1970s and Mexico once again becoming a net exporter in 1977, some degree of diversification was achieved. By 1985, 63 percent of Mexico's exports went to its northern neighbor, with 68 percent of its imports coming from the United States.[8] It must be noted, however, that these figures do not include *maquiladora* exports, which reached a net $1.5 billion in 1986, all to the United States. In addition, there is a wide discrepancy between Mexican figures and U.S. Department of Commerce statistics for binational trade. According to American data, trade in 1985 totaled $32.4 billion, whereas Mexico's numbers show $22.2 billion.[9] The difference involves contraband, over-invoicing of imports and under-invoicing of exports for fiscal purposes and capital flight, and different accounting methods.

All of the *maquiladora* trade and most contraband is U.S.-bound or U.S.-originated. Despite some routing of Mexican exports to Europe through the United States, one can safely estimate that approximately 75 percent of Mexico's real foreign trade is with the north, and the present trend is toward a greater proportion of both exports and imports in that direction. The country's next-largest partner is Japan, accounting for 8 percent of Mexico's trade. Few countries in the world have such a degree of concentration in their foreign trade. Brazil, the other large Latin American economy, is in a markedly different situation. The United States continues to be its biggest market, but only received 27 percent of its exports and supplied only 19 percent of its foreign purchases in 1985.[10]

The situation in foreign investment is comparable. Although American foreign investment was minimal through most of the nineteenth century, by 1911 the total value of U.S. holdings in Mexico had reached $646 million. American capital was found mainly in railroads (41 percent), mining (36 percent), and by 1910 oil.[11]

Between the mid-1920s, when American investment in Mexico reached its historic high point of more than $1 billion, and 1940, when American holdings fell to approximately $300 million, foreign investment in general and U.S. investment in particular played a minor role. But by 1944 this trend was reversed and foreign direct investment began to acquire greater relevance. Legal provisions were enacted to regulate foreign ventures and to reduce constraints on foreign ownership of assets in Mexico.

From the end of World War II through the mid-1970s, foreign investment, while important, never represented more than 5–6 percent of the total investment in any given year, and averaged 4 percent. This figure somewhat underestimates the truth, though, since domestic investment by many formally Mexican companies with high levels of foreign participation is not included. In addition the low level misrepresents the weight of the foreign component in Mexico's annual investment, since by the early 1970s foreign credit, as opposed to investment, had become the main route for channeling external savings into the economy. In addition, it is worth noting that in 1987, for example, as a result of high levels of foreign investment due to the debt-equity swap program, later suspended, and low levels of domestic private investment, foreign investment represented 34 percent of total private investment, a large share by any account. Nonetheless, on the surface American investment in Mexico has not held an overpowering function in the economy. But the situation is more complex.

According to Mexican figures, by 1986 the total value of direct foreign investment had reached $14.6 billion, of which $9.6 billion was of American origin. The United States' share of the total had declined since 1973, when it reached 78 percent, but remains high: 67.3 percent in 1985.[12] The drop in American participation was taken up chiefly by West Germany, which occupied second place with 8 percent, and Japan, with 6 percent. (For a contrasting view, see pages 81–82.) The great majority of all foreign investment is in manufacturing. Thus the relatively low aggregate statistics are overshadowed by the proportional importance of American investment and by its concentration in the manufacturing sector as well as in certain key subsectors: automobiles and trucks, tires, food processing, pharmaceuticals, among others.

The situation is not unlike Mexico's debt, by far the most important vehicle for obtaining foreign capital since the first years of the previous decade. This was not an unprecedented experience: during most of the nineteenth century, Mexico had a foreign debt, and a foreign debt problem. On several occasions it was forced to suspend payments to England, France, and Spain, often suffering varying forms of retaliation, from asset seizures to armed intimidation and intervention. At the close of the century foreign investment overtook credits from abroad as a resource transfer channel; then, from 1913 until 1941, Mexico was unable to raise any funds on the international market, mainly because of previous defaults, pending litigation from the Revolution, and lack of creditworthiness. The war modified this standing; during the 1950s and 1960s the country regained access to foreign credit, but on a moderate scale and largely from sources such as the World Bank, the Export-Import Bank, and suppliers' credits. Even then, though, in relation to GDP, Mexico's absorption of foreign savings was relatively high.

It grew higher from 1973 on. Mexico's publicly held foreign debt jumped 39 percent, rising from $7 billion to $9.9 billion. Its growth has not stopped since, and by mid-1988 the total foreign debt topped $105 billion, representing well over 60 percent of its GDP. By the mid-1980s the net resource transfer involving the debt had become negative because of its heavy service, but Mexico continued to receive substantial credits from abroad, though none of a truly voluntary nature. Its creditworthiness was virtually nil, but its need for further loans remained undiminished.

The United States has been a central player in Mexico's debt dilemma. Approximately one-third of Mexico's outstanding debt to commercial banks is owed to American institutions. Of the ten largest individual lenders, six are U.S.-based: Citicorp, Bank of America, Manufacturers Hanover, Chase Manhattan, Chemical Bank, Morgan Guaranty.

The non-U.S. bank with the biggest Mexican exposure is the Bank of Tokyo, ranking sixth. As a result of this concentration, the thirteen-bank Steering Committee which has negotiated Mexican restructuring arrangements on behalf of the country's more than 500 creditor banks, holding the key to many decisions concerning Mexico's debt, has seven American members. No other country is represented by more than one bank, the other six members being one each from Japan, Great Britain, Canada, France, West Germany, and Switzerland.

Moreover, Mexico in 1988 owed approximately $8.1 billion to the World Bank and Inter-American Development Bank, and $5.1 billion to the International Monetary Fund. The United States is not only the majority shareholder and largest donor in each of these agencies; it holds virtual veto power in the first two, and through the appointment of a U.S. national as World Bank president and IMF deputy managing director, wields enormous influence. Hence it comes as no surprise that the U.S. government and in particular the chairman of the Federal Reserve Board and the Secretary of the Treasury have played a decisive role in the Mexican debt crisis ever since 1982.

Mexico's real negotiations have essentially been held with U.S. authorities, who, through varying degrees of arm-twisting, then persuade both the multilateral agencies and the banks to accept whatever agreement was originally reached by the two governments. This has on many occasions facilitated Mexico's negotiating task, but it has also underscored the great importance the United States has acquired in a relatively new economic domain in Mexico. To a considerable extent, Mexico's foreign debt has become an issue between the two governments, basically ceasing to form part of a classic debtor-creditor relationship.

Washington repeatedly bailed Mexico out essentially for political reasons; likewise, Mexico did not unilaterally suspend payments on its foreign debt for fear of the political reprisals the United States government would take, although in public Mexican authorities always stressed the negative economic consequences a moratorium would entail. While its debt may be one of Mexico's main bargaining chips with the United States, it is so only at a political level. The debt is no longer an economic or financial matter; it is a political one.

This has grown increasingly true since 1986, when a significant number of European and American regional banks began to wash their hands of the debt imbroglio. Many institutions became convinced that lending Mexico more funds for it to pay interest on outstanding debt was nonsense. Banking regulations, which in Europe differ from those in the United States, were a major factor. In addition, the balance-sheet soundness of European banks allowed them to absorb Mexican (and Latin American) debt losses, whereas for many large American money-center banks this was not the case. Together with the Europeans' and American regional banks' indifference to the political implications of Mexico's debt travail—always viewed as essentially an official American concern, not a legitimate banking or European preoccupation—these motives led many creditors to write down or write off their Mexican loans, or to sell them at a considerable discount on the secondary market.

Other banks refused to extend new loans to Mexico, as called for by the rescheduling package put together in 1986. Thus Mexico's debt became further concentrated in American hands, both in a strict sense (fewer banks holding more debt) and in a broader one. The European and Japanese banks, together with their smaller U.S. counterparts, reluctantly acquiesced to what the American authorities and mega-banks wished, but on the understanding that Mexico's foreign debt was above all a United States problem. This did not apply to other Latin American debtors. The opposition in Mexico and among Latin nations as well as in the international financial community, however, to any debtor "collective bargaining" strengthened this trend. All parties involved were inadvertently but no less surely encouraging the drift toward integration. Tighter economic ties between the United States and Mexico and looser ones between Mexico and the rest of the world in such a domain could not fail to have this effect.

The agreement by the Treasury Department to back the issue of $2 billion in zero-coupon bonds which Mexico would exchange for part of its existing debt is a clear demonstration of the extent to which Mexico's foreign debt has become a U.S. government matter. While the Treasury is not actually putting up any money, its backing was central to the entire scheme.

With regard to Mexico's other international economic links, the importance of the United States is even greater. Since the 1950s, tourism has been a significant source of hard currency; in 1986, after oil exports, it was the economy's largest foreign exchange earner. And 84 percent of Mexico's visitors from abroad that year came from the United States. Geography is obviously a factor; yet in an age of modern communications, geographical proximity should not necessarily be an overriding consideration. In the case of foreign tourism in Mexico, it is.

A large share of the $2.27 billion tourism brought Mexico in 1987 originated in the United States. For practical purposes, the United States is Mexico's only significant source of tourism. And as is frequently the case for single-market industries, it is extremely vulnerable to that market's whims. On several occasions during the last twenty years, Mexico has suffered severe drops in its tourism receipts due to noneconomic or only partly economic factors affecting the tourist trade. In late 1975, after the government voted favorably on a UN General Assembly resolution condemning "Zionism as a form of racism," American Jewish organizations mounted a boycott of travel to Mexico. The Mexican peso was overvalued at the time, pricing Mexico out of a segment of the travel market, but the boycott did unquestionable damage.

Likewise, in 1985, after the kidnapping and subsequent assassination of DEA agent Enrique Camarena Salazar and the reported deaths of several American travelers—presumed but never proven to be drug-related—Mexico received substantial negative publicity in the United States. Despite the continuing downward spiral of the peso, total revenue generated by travel from abroad dropped 12 percent, partly because of the earthquake, partly because of public threats of a State Department travel advisory. Geographical propinquity has its advantages, but the excessive concentration of tourism from the United States is not one of them. This is all the more true since closeness to the United States has been an enormous incentive for Mexican foreign travel, which on occasion has nearly taken more hard currency out of the country than tourism from abroad has brought in. Finally, despite its geographical location and largely because it has catered to upper-income vacationers, Mexico is not yet a world leader in tourism. Spain receives nearly ten times more visitors than Mexico every year.

If the United States' role in Mexico's traditional economic interchange with the world has been sizable, its place in the country's more recent international economic ties looms larger still. This is particularly true of two of Mexico's most important emerging sources of foreign exchange: the *maquiladora* industry along the border and the automotive export industry in northern Mexico. Both of these relatively new sectors of the economy possess the same characteristics as the country's older external economic links, but to a much greater degree. The American factor in these cases is overwhelming.

Inaugurated in 1965, the *maquiladora* program consists of mainly American-owned assembly plants set up on the Mexican side of the border. Mexico authorizes the firms to import finished, ready-to-assemble components and raw materials in-bond, without being subject to any local import restrictions or duties as long as the finished products are reexported to the United States. The program also allows 100 percent foreign ownership of the Mexican subsidiary as well as exemption from export taxes. For its part, the United States allows these terminal goods to be imported while paying duties only on the value added south of the border, principally Mexican labor. Many corporations have set up component-manufacturing plants on the American side of the dividing line; they then ship inputs across the border to the terminal assembly plant in Mexico and reimport the finished goods for shipment to U.S. markets.

The program has made it possible for American corporations to benefit from low Mexican wages. In 1975 dollar-converted wages in Mexico were $0.69 an hour against $4.54 in the United States; Mexican wages have never amounted to more than 15 percent of American hourly salaries. In 1987, the ratio was nearly ten to one. At the same time, the *maquiladora* program has suited Mexican needs by creating jobs in modest amounts and earning considerable foreign exchange (part of which is lost through employee purchases north of the border), without affecting Mexican-based industry through unfettered competition.

In 1975, ten years after its inception, the industry employed 67,000 workers. But the devaluation of the Mexican peso in 1976 gave it new life, and by 1981, 600 plants along the border provided jobs for 132,000 workers. A second and much steeper devaluation of the national currency brought a new spurt of growth, and by mid-1987, over 1,000 assembly plants were employing over 279,000 workers. They generated $1.5 billion in earnings, making the *maquiladora* program Mexico's third-largest single source of hard currency.[13]

But behind these impressive statistics lurk a number of problems. First, in spite of their rapid growth, the assembly plants' job-creation potential is limited. In 1984, the year of the greatest rise in *maquiladora* employment, approximately 45,000 jobs were created under the program. But Mexico requires 1 million new jobs per year between now and the turn of the century just to keep up with the population explosion it experienced in the 1960s and 1970s. Furthermore, the traditional "seven dependents for every job" ratio in Mexico does not hold for the *maquiladora* industry: the great majority of employees are young single women who support only themselves.

The *maquiladora* industry is not only merely a proverbial drop in the bucket; it is a doubly limited one: the secondary or indirect job-creating effects of the plants are practically nil, since they use minuscule quantities of Mexican inputs:

> The share of materials and supplies provided by the domestic economy is an important indicator of the linkages that foreign assembly activities have for the Mexican economy. That percentage has been exceedingly small . . . it hovered around 1.5% of the total use of components and supplies.[14]

The highest percentage of total inputs produced locally is in furniture, where the Mexican share reaches 15.9 percent, and in food, with 13.3 percent. But these two groups represent only 3.7 percent of total value added. Conversely, in the largest sectors—electric and electronic equipment, devices, and articles and apparel and other products made with textiles, which amount to 40 percent of all *maquiladora* output—local inputs make up only 0.3 percent and 0.1 percent of the total, respectively.

Furthermore, if hundreds of thousands of jobs were to be created under the *maquiladora* program, the growing opposition to the plants in the United States would become insurmountable. Already, American labor and "rust belt" legislators are questioning the wisdom of a program based on transferring jobs from the United States to Mexico. In late 1986 Congress forbade the Department of Commerce from sponsoring or funding a *maquiladora* promotional fair held in Acapulco, and further restrictions are undoubtedly bound to surface.

If the number of jobs and plants remains modest, or grows only moderately, American opposition will in all likelihood not hinder the program. Fewer jobs actually leave than many believe, and those jobs which emigrate to Mexico as opposed to the Pacific Basin make it possible for other, component-manufacturing plants to maintain operations in the United States, chiefly in the border areas.

Another obstacle to further rapid growth by the industry is the strain it is already placing on infrastructure in the Mexican border region. The concentration of the plants in certain cities is creating a bottleneck which imposes limits on the program in the coming years. Electrical power, industrial parks, phone lines, public transportation, housing, and border bridges are all being severely taxed. In 1983 more than half of the existing plants were located in only three cities: Ciudad Juárez, Tijuana, and Mexicali. All three, as well as most of the other cities where substantial increases in the number of factories have occurred, are situated along the prosperous western half of the border from El Paso–Ciudad Juárez to San Diego–Tijuana. The eastern half, mainly southern Texas on the United States side, is traditionally poorer and presently mired in economic depression because of the fall in oil prices. Hence, concentration in the already overburdened *maquiladora* havens in the west will probably continue.

Efforts to relocate plants or diversify the installation of new ones have yet to bear fruit. In 1983 the *maquiladora* regulations were extended to every state in Mexico, but by 1986 well over 90 percent of all such plants were still found along the border. The western state of Jalisco had attracted a small number of firms, chiefly in the computer industry, but moving the *maquiladoras* out of the border perimeter is proving difficult. Many regions which have actively sought assembly plants, such as Yucatán, lack either the infrastructure and social conditions or the geographical proximity, or both. Over 70 percent of all *maquiladora* employees are women:[15] this might not occur as easily in more backward areas of the country. Above all, there is no consensus in Mexico in favor of a widespread extension of the program beyond the border zones.

Once again, the difficulty lies in the "integrating" effect the industry has on the Mexican economy. The plants, by definition, export all of their output to the United States, although in theory they now can sell up to 20 percent of their output in Mexico. True, a modest number of European and Japanese companies have established facilities on the U.S. border for the same reasons that have led their American counterparts to do so.[16] But even the non-American firms export their entire production to United States markets. Consequently, the jobs, foreign exchange, and very slight technology transfer (83.1 percent of the *maquiladora* jobs are blue-collar; only 10.8 percent are technical) which the industry brings are tied to the American economy. With the exception of the peso-dollar exchange rate, the main economic indicators which affect the industry are all U.S.-oriented.

The number of plants and their output and employment respond essentially to American incentives: demand for certain products, U.S. wage scales, imports to the United States from other nations. Since the physical installations are cheap and easy to build and remove, any shift in the American business cycle can bring sudden and dramatic changes in the plant economy. Many firms simply pack up and leave, literally overnight, as they have been quitting Asia for Mexico in recent years. The fact that during the four-year period between 1982 and 1986, when the Mexican economy had a negative growth rate of nearly -4 percent, the *maquiladora* industry increased by more than 10 percent annually is less proof of its dynamism than of its very "un-Mexican" nature. For all these reasons, and many more, it has been said in Mexico that the United States' economic policy is rapidly becoming a major national security issue . . . for Mexico.

Instead of an outward-looking sector of the Mexican economy, the *maquiladoras* seem to be an extension of the American economy on Mexican soil. A welcome extension because of the badly needed dollars it brings, but a reluctantly accepted one because of its contribution to the rampant integration of two unequally matched economies.

More than extending southward in its present form, the *maquiladora* may spread to the rest of the country by adapting itself. This is what several computer manufacturers, such as IBM and Hewlett-Packard, have done, commencing operations in Guadalajara on a "semi-*maquiladora*" basis. They use significant Mexican inputs, though not as much as most industries in Mexico; they sell part of their output in

Mexico, though less than most other companies. Finally, their location, though on the border, is still closer to U.S. markets than any other area in the world.

This process has mainly taken hold in the single most dynamic sector of Mexican exports as of 1983. The automobile industry has been a fixture of the economy since 1925, when Ford set up its first assembly plant. If there was ever an inefficient, protected, and dollar-devouring economic activity in Mexico, it was the production of cars and trucks, characterized by obsolete models, exorbitant prices, and shoddy quality. Multinationals took advantage of every incentive for foreign investment in a booming domestic market, and paid little heed to any of the country's restrictions or aspirations. By 1981, the industry's banner year for internal sales, Chrysler, Ford, General Motors, and American Motors (in that order in Mexico), as well as Volkswagen, Nissan, and Renault, were manufacturing more than half a million units, ranking the country eleventh in the world. Exports were virtually nil, but output grew at over 10 percent per year.

There was a downside, of course. The automobile industry had traditionally been the single largest consumer of foreign exchange. Though far more than a simple assembly operation, it was nowhere near the integrated national industry that Mexico wanted. Laws were passed in the mid-1960s and 1970s with the hope of balancing the industry's external accounts by forcing it to use a larger share of domestic inputs or increasing its exports. Neither came about, and by 1981 the sector ate up $3.5 billion in imports, but generated only $336 million in exports, mainly in auto parts.[17] Many supporters rightly insisted, however, that the country could never have imported the 529,000 vehicles produced domestically that year, even if it had saved the industry's 1981 $3 billion trade deficit.

The situation began to change in 1983. Mexico's debt crisis threw the country into a depression from which it has not yet emerged. The economy experienced zero growth in 1982, −5 percent in 1983, and has remained flat ever since. Domestic demand declined drastically, and automobile and commercial vehicle sales dropped even more precipitously. By 1983 they had fallen 48 percent in relation to 1981 and never really recovered, flattening out at approximately 350,000 vehicles in 1984 and 1985, only to plunge again in 1986 to below 250,000 units.[18] Production and sales statistics decreased to ridiculously low levels; several companies publicly wondered whether they should remain in Mexico, and in 1986 Renault/American Motors shut down operations for the domestic market.

But simultaneously another trend was emerging. In 1983 Mexican exports of automobile engines rose 84 percent and foreign sales of vehicles and parts grew 48 percent.[19] In 1984, for the first time, the automotive industry became a net exporter, and by 1985 its total gross earnings abroad amounted to $2.8 billion, making it the country's second-largest export industry.[20] The net trade balance was less impressive, but the drain on foreign exchange had been inverted. This was partly due to the dramatic fall in imports arising from the economy's downturn, but another factor was undeniably of greater significance.

In 1983 and 1984 several immense export-oriented auto-parts plants came on-stream in the north of the country. There were new Ford facilities in the city of Chihuahua in 1983 and in Hermosillo in 1986; new Chrysler and General Motors factories in Ramos Arizpe, in 1983 and 1984; new Nissan and Renault engine plants in the states of Aguascalientes and Durango during the same period. By 1984 most of these installations were exporting automobile components to a booming U.S. auto market. That year, Mexico's vehicle-related exports climbed 150 percent and have continued to grow, albeit at more modest rates. Chrysler and Ford are the leading exporters, while Nissan, Volkswagen, and General Motors have continued to concentrate on the domestic Mexican market.

The new plants turn out major automobile components such as engines, transmissions, axles, or windshields. Their physical installations resemble domestic-oriented factories more than *maquiladoras;* they consume considerable amounts of Mexican raw materials, energy, water, and intermediate goods, thereby increasing indirect employment and linkages. A small but significant part of their production is destined for the Mexican market, thus enhancing their insertion in the national economy. Yet to the extent that they are located close to the border, though not on it, that a sizable majority of their output is U.S.-bound, that with minor exceptions they are American-owned, and that the production processes, technology, quality control, and labor skills necessary to run the plants are premised on U.S. sales, these plants have much in common with the *maquiladoras,* including their shortcomings.

The automotive export plants, which have become Mexico's largest and fastest-growing export industry after oil, are more a part of the American economy than of the Mexican one. Coming on top of the high degree of concentration of the country's traditional economic ties with the United States, these recent trends are cause for worry in Mexico. The fear is not so much that the United States will come to dominate the Mexican economy but rather that through an uncontrolled and unplanned drift toward integration, the economy will become a subordinate part of the American one. Under present circumstances, the risks and ensuing consequences for Mexico are considerable.

The real challenge facing Mexico is not the present level of integration with the American economy, or the history of how this stage was reached. The issue is whether a new spurt of integration, added to the already prevalent levels, will not threaten the nation's very soul. The country has proved it can live and even prosper under the existing state of affairs if certain conditions are fulfilled. True, as the dependency theorists of the 1960s and 1970s proclaimed, the nation's greatest problems—its poverty, backwardness, and brutally unjust distribution of income—remain unresolved. But they became manageable given stable governance. In addition, as the dependency theorists did not see, the country underwent a dramatic process of change ("modernization," some called it), partly as a result of the growing dimensions of the foreign economic presence.

Perhaps without great enthusiasm, undoubtedly with important limitations on its sovereignty and autonomy, but nonetheless without severe strains imposed on its national self and pride, Mexico has learned to cope with a high degree of economic intercourse with its northern neighbor. If nothing were to change, even for the better, the present situation could remain acceptable, though certainly it is not ideal. The problem lies in the fact that the status quo is no longer the end of the road, but rather the point of departure for a new journey with an unknown destination.

Because of the unanimous belief in industrialization as the principal instrument for modernizing the country, Mexico has over the years established a complex and effective system of bureaucratic protection for industry: advance import licenses and quotas, high tariffs on imported goods; subsidies, tax breaks, and protection from labor strife through trade unions often controlled by the state; cheap governmental credits for prospering industries and rapid state assistance for those which faltered or floundered. Thanks to this system, Mexico built up a large, diversified, and profitable industrial base in less than a half century. Between 1940 and 1981 the economy grew at a yearly rate of 6 percent, more than almost any other nation during the same time span.

This inward-looking and nationalistic approach was also extended to other economic fields, particularly foreign investment. Although Mexico was a haven for Fortune 500 multinational corporations which profited from political stability, labor peace, a skilled work force, and a booming domestic market, since the late 1930s a certain reluctance has prevailed in allowing foreign investment to play a decisive role in the economy. A number of areas were declared off-limits both by the Constitution of 1917 and by subsequent laws and decrees: oil, electricity, railroads. In other cases, a limit of 49 percent foreign ownership was imposed. Foreign firms thrived in the strongly regulated environment, so the restrictions did not deter investors interested in doing business. But together with the economic philosophy they conveyed and with the bureaucratic obstacles they erected in the path of small and medium-sized firms, they probably did contribute to fixing an implicit ceiling on the total value of foreign assets in Mexico.

The limits on foreign investment in Mexico are essentially directed at the United States and their motivation is principally historical. By and large, with the exception of oil at the turn of the century, foreign investment during this century has been American investment. The country's historical experience with American interests in Mexico convinced its leaders that it was preferable to err on the side of excessive restrictions than in the direction of insufficient ones.

Once the debt crisis exploded in 1982 and Mexico no longer had unlimited access to foreign credit, the country's leaders reached a stark conclusion. In their view the only other way to obtain the foreign resources necessary for sustaining the 6 or 7 percent yearly growth rates needed to annually employ one million new entrants into the labor market is through a hefty trade surplus. Tourism, remittances from emigrants in the United States, multilateral loans, and possibly small quantities of voluntary commercial bank lending can be counted on, but the bulk of the effort will have to come from the trade balance. Even foreign investment in itself can never make a major difference, although it can stimulate exports. Nearly 75 percent of foreign investment has been locally financed, and because of royalties, profit repatriation, and their domestic-market orientation, the net external accounts of most foreign ventures are negative or negligible.

Mexico can no longer finance its traditional trade deficit through other current account income or through its capital account. It has to pay for its high levels of imports of capital goods and raw materials, necessary for industrialization and technological catch-up, with still higher levels of exports. This implies several things.

The relative importance of foreign trade and other external factors in the economy has risen and will continue to do so. The trade/GDP ratio will reach 30 or 35 percent quickly, and perhaps more, once the Mexican economy begins to grow and import again. Already in 1987, exports represented 15 percent of GDP. While this increase in trade's importance is partly a reflection of a shift of emphasis in external factors—from foreign credit to foreign trade and investment—it will also be an undeniable sign of an opening economy. Second, for Mexican industry to be competitive, it requires greater access to foreign inputs and more exposure to foreign competition than before; this entails a drastic reduction in traditional protectionist barriers. Mexico cannot indefinitely protect a local industry (including multinational subsidiaries) which generally produces poor-quality and high-priced goods, is totally unprepared for export-led growth, has developed an increasing technological lag, and has proven incapable of generating export revenues, reducing domestic costs, and supplying acceptable products for the internal market.

Third, foreign investment, not as a direct generator of foreign exchange but as a source of exporting know-how and capabilities, will acquire a far greater role as well as a new face. Along with Fortune 500 firms, a large number of small and medium-sized, high-technology and high-export-potential companies must invest in Mexico, and their conditions for investing are more demanding. During the transition from the old way of doing things to the new, export-oriented stage of economic development, Mexico will continue to require foreign credit, if only to pay interest on previously contracted obligations.

Fourth, during the transition, the country's creditors will insist that the process be "supervised" to ensure compliance with the economic tenets of the day. Thus the International Monetary Fund, but chiefly the World Bank, and behind them the U.S. administration, will occupy an ever more important function in the management of the Mexican economy, partly as a factor of real conditionality for extending new loans, partly as a useful pretext for the government in the implementation of unpopular economic policies. Structural reform, meaning an opening up of the economy, its privatization, and sharp cutbacks in the Mexican welfare state, has become a condition for new loans. These in turn are decisive in assuring the transition's success.

In 1983 President Miguel de la Madrid began an effort to modernize the economy, with no guarantee that the process would bring a return to high growth rates, nor any certainty that the ensuing political strains would not threaten the nation's stability. The jury is still out on both of these questions: modernization has gone forward significantly but slowly, and the entire De la Madrid six-year term witnessed nil or negative economic growth, for the first time in modern Mexican history. There is an emerging agreement among analysts that while the reforms are necessary because the status quo is unsustainable, they are not a solution to Mexico's economic difficulties.

But regarding the reforms' effects on economic integration, there is little doubt as to the outcome. The most important steps concerned foreign trade liberalization and focused on Mexico's accession to GATT. In 1980, President José López Portillo pursued and concluded negotiations with the GATT Secretariat in Geneva on Mexico's entry, but after a relatively open national debate, pulled back. The country's main industrial associations and labor unions, as well as the more nationalistic wing of the political establishment, opposed entry, on the grounds that opening up to foreign imports would destroy Mexican industry, throwing millions of workers out of their jobs. Supporters of GATT included the trade associations and Chambers of Commerce, part of the banking community, the U.S. embassy, and several members of López Portillo's Cabinet, including Budget and Planning Secretary Miguel de la Madrid.

It came consequently as little surprise when late in 1985 President De la Madrid announced that Mexico would once again set in motion the entry process, following through to the end this time. By then, many of the main trade liberalization steps had already been taken. The most important one involved the elimination of the bureaucratic system of advance import licensing, and its replacement with simple tariffs, which were subsequently lowered. Although in the course of its negotiations with the GATT staff Mexico obtained significant exemptions from liberalization, the dismantling of the import-licensing process signaled the beginning of the end of high protection levels for industry.

The effects did not show up immediately, largely because 1986 brought a new drop of 4 percent in GNP and 1987 as well as 1988 taken together were years of virtually negligible growth. But if and when the economy recovers, and the exchange rate appreciates moderately, GATT membership and trade liberalization will result in the disappearance of many inefficient Mexican firms, the substitution of their production by imports from abroad, and in general a large increase of imports as a share of GNP. The remaining Mexican businesses—undeniably a majority—will in principle become more competitive, thanks to lower costs and more advanced technology. This in turn will in theory stimulate exports, particularly manufactures. The 1986 and 1987 rises in non-oil exports were partly attributed to this, but were also a result of an undervalued currency and a domestic recession.

Until the economy grows again, the true effects of the reforms will remain unknown. The resistance to change is enormous, and more important, there are valid arguments against opening up the economy to foreign trade in such a drastic way. The negatives of such a program are varied and significant, whereas its hypothetical advantages are uncertain. It could preclude the development of a capital goods industry, such as Brazil's, which is the single most important transformation the Mexican economy requires. This is the main criticism left-oriented economists from abroad have made of the entire plan.[21] Likewise, if steps are not taken to protect those sectors of the population most severely affected by the reconversion, the social and political costs could become unacceptable. The wily Mexican bureaucracy will fight tooth and nail against reforms that diminish its perks and privileges. In addition, the consequences of the program are unclear: once growth begins, imports may rise long before exports do, and if no foreign credit is available to finance the ensuing deficit, the economy will simply never grow (it is still stuck at 1981 levels). Neither is there any assurance that exporters who sold abroad when domestic demand was depressed will continue to do so if and when the economy picks up.

But even if things do work out, the traditional structure of the economy has fueled fears that an eventual jump in imports, as well as a rise in exports, would be in the direction of the United States. American firms with close ties to and knowledge of Mexico would be the first to take advantage of trade liberalization. On the export side, the United States is the closest and largest market. More important perhaps, it is the only market most Mexican entrepreneurs know and the only one the nation's infrastructure is equipped to deal with.

Moreover, the reforms require the emergence of a new sector of export-oriented entrepreneurs, since a majority of Mexico's business community has thrived on the captive domestic market. But this new class of exporters—American-educated, generally fluent in English, with personal and business associations in the United States—will inevitably reproduce and accentuate the existing concentration of ties with the United States. The American share of Mexico's foreign trade will rise; in any case, there is no reason to believe that it will diminish. And the relative weight of heavily U.S.-concentrated foreign trade in the economy will increase.

Another reason why the American share will expand is that part of the export-growth burden will hopefully be borne by firms venturing into Mexico as a result of a loosening of the restrictions on foreign investment. Foreign multinationals have the greatest potential to promote a sharp climb in exports in the short run: they have the know-how, the markets, the production chains. Later, possibly, Mexican firms will join them, as the exporting mentality and capability works its way through the economy. These late-coming multinationals, like their predecessors, will be overwhelmingly U.S.-based: they will come to Mexico because it is close to the largest market in the world and to home, because they know Mexico or are associated with firms that do, and because of their greater familiarity with the business environment.

If these changes actually take place, companies investing in Mexico, as well as U.S. importers and exporters, will require banking services to ply their trade. The financial institutions willing to reenter the Mexican market will tend to be U.S. banks. They will continue to have a stake in Mexico through their previous loans and through their close links with American investors, exporters, and importers. Last, assuming that Mexico complies with the "conditionality" which the World Bank and its creditors have demanded, those banks—and investors and trade partners—will be encouraged by Washington to develop their activities in Mexico for political reasons. The United States has an overwhelming interest in its neighbor's prosperity and stability and will go to great lengths to preserve both. Europe and Japan for now do not.

It would be senseless to argue that there is anything wrong or detrimental to Mexican interests with any one of these hypothetical possibilities *taken individually.* Mexico cannot discriminate in reverse and pretend that the hoped-for increments in its foreign trade, foreign investment, and general economic activity do not favor the United States. But it is equally naïve to imagine that a substantial growth of the external sector of the economy, together with its further concentration in U.S. hands, will have no effect on the nation. It is the conjunction of both trends, as well as their accelerated pace, which is worrisome.

There is disagreement in Mexico today over the benefits of closer economic ties with the United States. But few sectors of society still argue that economic ties with the United States in themselves have impeded economic development. Most Mexicans with opinions on the subject argue that the nation's economic relationship with the United States has sharpened and perhaps amplified existing distortions, inequities, and backwardness, but did not create them per se. There are also differences as to what parts and degrees of the economic relationship help or harm Mexico. Whether this is the product of resignation in the face of geographical inevitability or sound economic analysis is open to discussion.

Despite the initial steps taken in the direction of economic restructuring during the De la Madrid years, there is still great reluctance in Mexico to open up and privatize a substantial part of the economy and cut back the nation's welfare state. With regard to the size of the public or state-owned sector of the economy, if one excludes interest payments, public sector spending and revenues (including parastatal firms) have gone from 32 percent of GNP in 1980 to 29 percent in 1986.[22] According to the World Bank:

Although the public sector's presence in economic life has been scaled back in important ways since 1982, in some respects it has continued to grow. Meanwhile the private sector has seen its relative economic position hold stationary, or even diminish. In short, a leading role for the private sector in bringing about recovery has yet to emerge.[23]

The reluctance to privatize boils down to one basic anxiety. Leaving a vacuum for the Mexican private sector to fill requires certainty that it will do so; otherwise, the gap will in all likelihood be occupied by foreign, that is to say essentially American, entities. For more than half a century, the political establishment has acquired a strong dose of skepticism and disdain for what was once called the "national bourgeoisie."

In a large measure, the suspicion that the private sector is simply not up to the task of developing the nation is grounded in its inability to have done so in the remote past and during the Depression years in the 1930s, as well as from the early 1970s on. Disinvestment, capital flight, and quick-buck, last-in first-out business practices have led many in Mexico to believe that the private sector will only thrive in a protected environment. In this view, the cocoon the state built up around the business community was an indispensable condition for its emergence and consolidation. Without it the private sector would simply wither away, leaving the state and the foreign component of the economy face to face. The private sector's repatriation of dollars in 1987 not for investment but for speculation on the stock market and its subsequent return of dollars to the United States as soon as the market crashed, thus largely contributing to Mexico's most recent economic disaster, has done nothing to dispel this view. If anything, even the most private-sector-oriented officials of the De la Madrid administration felt betrayed by the business community, believing that they had done everything in their power to create a positive business climate and that the private sector had not responded.

Although the foregoing description of the private sector may be accurate, it begs the question of why it has acquired these characteristics. Specifically, it ignores the fact that in the mid-1970s and during the present decade, the private sector has argued that if it has exported its capital abroad and not carried its share of the national load, this has been due precisely to the mistaken statist and populist economic policies applied by the successive administrations of Echeverría, López Portillo, and to a lesser extent De la Madrid, particularly during his first years in office. Business is business, and if the conditions are not right, the private sector believes it should not be expected to take risks or initiatives. Conversely, it is argued, if the business climate improves, and government policy becomes what it should never have ceased to be, the private sector will do its part.

Mexico's economic planners, public financiers, and politicians disagree. From their perspective, as of the beginning of the 1970s the state
had to step in because of the private sector's unwillingness to invest and
create jobs in the necessary volumes. By the early 1970s not enough jobs
were being created. The 1968 student movement was rightly viewed by
the government as a warning sign that something was wrong. Its reaction
was to strive for higher growth rates and more job development. When
the private sector did not respond, the state did. The result was inflation
and debt, but the system's stability lasted another twenty years. The state
did not want to take on additional responsibilities, but faced with the
choice of no investment and growth or state-sponsored development, it
could not have acted differently.

Mexico has always had a strong state-owned or -regulated sector of
the economy, from the silver mines in the sixteenth and seventeenth
centuries to the establishment of a public railroad company at this. But
with the notable exception of a handful of individual firms, the country
never had a strong business community, and the question of which came
first, the weak private sector or the strong statist tendencies, has with
time become irrelevant. It seems reasonable to fear that today's private
sector will only partly take up the slack that structural reform will create;
the rest either will remain dangling or will fall to foreign business interests. Thus another factor of economic integration comes into focus:
privatization may well turn out to be "Americanization."

If there is little doubt regarding the reality of the drift toward economic
integration, the question remains as to its desirability for Mexico. American journalist James Fallows has summed up the debate in the United
States about greater links with Japan in a way that parallels the Mexican
debate.[24] In favor of the "merger" of Japan and the United States, he
states that "our two economies are complementary, and so are our
natural resources, human talents and even our foreign policies. Everyone
in the United States feels bad about foreigners 'taking over' American
buildings and companies, but is anyone really hurt? When Japanese
investors reopen old American factories, they bring new technology and
create new jobs. Japanese investment has helped push the American
stock market to its speculative highs."

But there are also drawbacks, according to Fallows: "America would
have less independence of action, since it would have to keep foreign
investors calm and confident. Putting the U.S. on a leash might be better
for the world, but we would never choose this course ourselves. And
sometimes debt gets out of control, leading to inflation, panic, collapse."

Fallows's solution also reminds one of the Mexican debate: "Do we think there is too much foreign investment? We can limit it, as Japan has. . . . Do we worry that Matsushita . . . will keep all the high-grade manufacturing work back in Osaka . . . ? . . . Let's pass local-content laws."

The argument has been made, though not often by Mexicans, that the solution to Mexico's problems lies in greater economic intercourse with the United States.[25] If the consequences are economic integration, so be it; Mexico would not be the first or the last country to follow that road. Many nations would not dream of disdaining the possibility of virtually unlimited exchange with the richest and most productive economy in the world. Integration would, according to this view, have the same effects similar processes have had elsewhere. Economic imbalances would even out, comparative advantage would set in, and higher productivity, efficiency, and standards of living would result.

This view has given rise to a series of proposals for the future of the two neighbors' relations. The idea of a North American Common Market, including Canada, was put forth by Ronald Reagan's advisers during his 1980 presidential campaign and has been resurrected recently as a result of growing protectionist sentiment and the 1988 Free Trade Agreement between the United States and Canada. More modestly, the notion of creating a hundred-mile-wide free trade zone on the Mexican side of the border from which goods and services could be freely exported to the United States while capital and technology could be transferred to Mexico has also been mentioned. These ideas have never struck a favorable chord in Mexico. The Common Market trial balloon was shot down; none of the other suggestions have found backers in Mexico. Despite the real movement toward integration, there is little if any support or constituency for it in Mexico today. The reasons for this apparent paradox are powerful ones.

Some scholars have suggested that the backwash effect of free trade between a rich nation and a poor one does not hold in the case of Mexico and the United States.[26] But in Mexico it is generally thought that while the unfettered flow of capital, labor, and goods and services between two economies (much more than simply free trade) with moderate disparities of development, population, and size helps the weaker economy, the opposite occurs if the integrating economies are too unevenly matched.

In the former case, the lesser economy benefits from the extension of the more advanced one's greater productivity, technological progress, and capital formation. The larger economy hauls the poorer one up to its level. The traditional example is the European Economic Community, which upon its birth in 1958 included advanced economies like most of Germany, Holland, and parts of Belgium, as well as relatively backward regions like southern Italy and parts of France.

Although there were initial misgivings in France and Italy, both countries profited from the establishment of the Common Market. The leaders of Portugal, Greece, and Spain, who entered the EEC despite major inequalities between their economies and those of Northern Europe, are hoping for a similar outcome. They believe that integration will stimulate development, providing access to affluent markets as well as investment, technology, and employment. They are confident that the positive effects will outweigh disadvantages such as the bankruptcy of inefficient firms, the purchase of national enterprises by foreign ones, and the linkage of their economies to nations over whose decisions they wield scant influence.

But if the differences in overall economic development are colossal and probably widening, the risk is great that integration will consolidate or accentuate existing disparities. Many in Mexico believe that integration in one form or another not only would not bring economic modernization but would foreclose the possibility of development for the future. Mexico would risk becoming a nation of *maquiladoras,* dishwashers, U.S. welfare recipients, and hotel help, condemned to produce the few goods for which it has a significant comparative advantage. Mexican industry would not be able to take advantage of the process. Cheap wages would initially entice American firms to Mexico, but the country's low educational level would force those firms to concentrate on assembly-type, low-technology sectors. Overall wage rates might rise, but soon the number of Mexicans finding employment in the United States would flatten out.

In addition, the principal decisions regarding economic policy would not be made jointly, but rather by the United States and imposed on Mexico. If the two economies were similar, the nations' economic interests would partly coincide and this would not be a problem. It would seem, however, that the economies' large imbalances probably preclude a hypothetical common and mutually beneficial economic policy.

But if economic integration is not perceived as favorable to Mexico from a purely economic viewpoint, this is not the main focus of opposition. The decisive factors of resistance are political and cultural.

Under certain circumstances, there is no reason why economic integration should imply a drastic loss of political autonomy or cultural identity for the integrating parties. A measure of political maneuvering room is sacrificed, unquestionably, as many governments in Western Europe have learned over the years: foreign policies, defense policies, and economic policies, both domestic and external, tend to unify along the lines of the those followed by the strongest economies. The loss of national sovereignty is relatively well shared, though inevitably some nations give up more than others. Cultural identities endure, as different languages, histories, and national characters rise above economic affinities. The French are not becoming "more German" and run little risk of doing so.

In the case of two nations as disparate in size, power, and wealth as Mexico and the United States, the weight of economic superiority can be crushing and can lead to a permanent loss of significant attributes of sovereignty and cultural identity. Mexico may harbor no illusions as to the real margins of political leeway it presently possesses: there are many things it knows it cannot do. But the perception is that economic integration would eventually entail far more political subservience, in foreign policy and domestic affairs, as well as a progressive fading of the country's heretofore vigorous cultural personality. Because of the attraction that the "American way of life" holds for large sectors of Mexico's population, particularly its urban middle classes, the conservation of clear-cut barriers between the two nations is deemed of paramount cultural importance. Mexicans would not necessarily become "more American" as a result of economic integration, but might well become "less Mexican."

Opposition to formal economic integration with the United States is widespread in Mexico. Yet it rings increasingly hollow. Many Mexicans favor the changes the economy is undergoing, but fear their consequences; many support the premises of economic integration but oppose the political and cultural changes they may lead to. A substantial part of the nation's political, intellectual, and even entrepreneurial establishment is against greater economic ties with the United States, but believes the growth of such ties may be inevitable. The question for Mexico is thus changing from "Is integration desirable?" to "Is it reversible, and if not, what are its consequences for Mexico; can it be successfully administered and can Mexico get the most out of it?"

6

THE SUPPLY AND DEMAND OF DRUGS AND MONEY

The Mexican Side

—

Jorge G. Castañeda

If the formal, legal, and well-accounted-for flows of goods and services between Mexico and the United States are leading toward economic integration, the informal, sometimes illegal, and partly untraceable patterns of exchange from one nation to the other point in the same direction.

Sometimes these crosscurrents favor one country. Such is the case of capital flight, which has a devastating effect on Mexico while benefiting the United States in general and southwestern and Texan regional banks in particular. On other occasions, the flows have a marginal negative impact on one nation, but a highly undesirable effect on the other. Drug traffic, until now a local and less than top-priority matter in Mexico, but which preys on one of the United States' most serious social problems, is the best example of this.

In other instances, the informal flows have a mixed effect, affecting both countries in different ways and for different reasons. Undocumented immigration is undoubtedly a phenomenon of this nature: it alleviates Mexico's unemployment difficulties, while creating problems with the United States and forcing Mexico to do without some of its most adventurous and enterprising citizens. Likewise, migration provides the United

States with a large supply of cheap semi-skilled and unskilled labor but creates severe social tensions.

Finally, some of the flows' consequences are difficult to determine. The "information and cultural exchange," mainly from the United States to Mexico, may have little bearing on the future or could become a decisive factor of informal integration. It is already making its presence felt, though not always in the most welcome manner.

In early 1987, a Mexico City weekly reported on how some of the capital's children were spending their afternoons. Direct telephone dialing between Mexico and the United States, together with the growing use of Spanish in California and Mexican youth's increasing familiarity with the United States through friends, travel, and relatives, had adolescents running up their parents' phone bill. They did it by calling "Dial-a-Porn" in Los Angeles, which had a Spanish-language service to accommodate its Latino customers. In a single day, nearly one hundred teenage girls from the same school in northern Mexico City dialed the number north of the border. A parent complained: "There should be a law to protect our children from these things. We seem helpless in the face of this invasion of vice from the United States."[1] Teléfonos de México said there was nothing it could do about it; American toll numbers were beyond its jurisdiction.

Obscene phone conversations, undocumented immigration, illegal drug traffic and money laundering, and incalculable capital flight are all part of an increasingly unimpeded, booming, and unmanaged intercourse of goods, services, and individuals, knowledge and information, money and customs, which is removing the two nations' economic relations from their respective governments' hands without placing them under alternative forms of administration. In themselves, these flows would undoubtedly not be sufficient to impose a trend against the will of two strong governments. But on top of classical patterns of economic integration, they sketch the landscape of a situation seemingly out of control, which neither country is ready for.

Drug traffic from Mexico to the United States is probably the one facet of this runaway economic integration which has received the most attention in recent years. Since the kidnapping and murder in Mexico of DEA agent Enrique Camarena Salazar in 1985, many in the United States apparently came to believe that this issue is one of the highest priorities on the two nations' common agenda. In meetings between the two governments, through congressional hearings on Mexico and drug enforcement, in the press and on television, certain circles in the United States have clearly stated their concerns, as well as their perceptions, that drug

traffic in Mexico has gotten out of hand. The reasons for this are considered self-evident. Economic crisis, endemic corruption, and the lack of
democracy are viewed by some Americans as inevitably having led Mexico, its government, and large sectors of its population to indifference at
best, and at worst complicity with the drug trade. Only harsh, public,
and ongoing U.S. pressure and aid, it is believed, will reverse the trend
and bring the problem back under control.

The Mexican perspective is radically different. Though the drug traffic
is not a topic of much public debate or research in Mexico, there are
indications that widespread agreement throughout society prevails on
the issue. With a few exceptions, polls, opinion pages in the nation's press
(traditionally the least self-censored in the Mexican media), and positions assumed by political parties suggest that a large sector of the
country's population seems in step with the authorities' views.

Most Mexicans believe that the responsibility for the drug traffic between the two countries falls squarely on the existence of a multibillion-
dollar market in the United States. Without the demand generated by
that market, supply would wither away. According to the previously
mentioned *New York Times* poll, "drug addiction and narcotic trafficking" are seen by Mexicans as the "most negative aspect" of the United
States; similarly, 83 percent of those interviewed thought that the use of
illegal drugs like heroin and cocaine in the United States is a very serious
problem, and 87 percent believed that this use is increasing. When asked
whether drug addiction was the fault of the U.S. government for not
stopping the use of drugs, or the fault of producer-country governments
for not curtailing production and exports, opinions were more nuanced.
But 61 percent of those questioned stated that the United States was more
to blame.[2] Given the acknowledged unpopularity of the Mexican government today and the traditional tendency of many Mexicans to blame
their own authorities for every calamity under the sun, the number of
people faulting the United States is quite high.

This point of view, like many others, has historical roots. Although
marijuana has been grown and consumed in Mexico for generations,
drugs in general are not part of the traditional rural or urban culture.
There is no equivalent in Mexico of the situation prevailing in the Andean highlands. There, coca leaf predates even its consumption by workers in the silver mines as far back as Spanish colonial times. Its use by
peasants as a tonic against the effects of extremely high altitudes is still
extensive today. In fact, widespread cultivation in Mexico of heroin-
generating poppy and to a lesser extent marijuana began during World
War II at the request of the United States. The growing need for mor-
phine and hemp, together with the physical impossibility of trade with

Asia, led American authorities to ask Mexico for assistance. The state of Sinaloa, on the Pacific coast, was deemed ideally suited for poppy growth because of its climate and terrain. By 1943 it had become a major opium producer. When the war ended, Mexico began an eradication campaign; Sinaloa has nonetheless been growing poppy ever since.

Predictably, drug enforcement soon emerged as a contentious issue between the two countries. Each time the problem bursts forth, it is viewed in Mexico as a product of domestic American political factors exported south of the border. Thus in the fall of 1969, when Richard Nixon virtually closed the San Ysidro–Tijuana border for three weeks under Operation Intercept, many in Mexico considered the act not only unfriendly but demagogic and hypocritical. Drug consumption in the United States had risen as a result of the social transformations of the 1960s. "Smoking grass" had become socially acceptable among American youth. The Vietnam War, with its increase in heroin addiction picked up by soldiers in Indochina, also contributed its share. Mexico, for its part, had become a greater supplier of drugs for this expanding market, but largely because of U.S.-sponsored eradication efforts in Turkey and the Mediterranean. Since there was little the Nixon administration could do domestically to pursue its "War on Drugs," it lashed out against an easy scapegoat.

The situation—and Mexican feeling about it—is not dissimilar today. Throughout 1985 and mainly 1986, and then again in 1988, drugs resurfaced as a political issue in the United States. The 1986 congressional elections were the peak of much of the interest and concern, but clearly a part of the great "Drug Scare" extended beyond electoral considerations. Yet many in Mexico feel that by blaming its neighbor for a crisis which is largely of its own making, and by emphasizing "drug supply-side" solutions to the problem, the United States is once again acting unfairly. The fact is that a growing drug problem has materialized in the United States. It stems above all from the socialization of cocaine, which is no longer being consumed only in high-income circles but is used in all walks of society. As seen from Mexico, the United States is caught in a political bind.

In theory at least, there are only two relatively short-term policies for dealing with drug abuse: draconian, widespread repression or legalization. But white middle-class Americans would never accept the costly, repressive, and intrusive operations that a truly drastic crackdown on drug consumption and addiction would entail if it meant testing and patrolling suburban neighborhoods and schools as well as Wall Street firms. Conversely, legalization, in addition to being politically unthinkable in the present state of American public opinion, would undoubtedly

meet stiff resistance from black leaders. Because of the disproportionate
weight of the drug blight in the black community, legalization is seen by
black politicians like Charles Rangel and Jesse Jackson as a form of
resignation and acceptance of the existence of large cohorts of addicted
black urban youths, without even maintaining the pretense that something should be done to improve their lot. Since neither option is politically admissible in the United States, and something "must be done,"
Mexico becomes one place to do it. The country is turned into the
whipping boy of American legislators, self-righteously indignant enforcement agents, and conservative ideologues. They all skillfully bullied
administration officials who knew better into accepting the fiction that
Mexico was a major reason for the new American "drug crisis."

The facts differed slightly from the mainstream Mexican view, but not
dramatically. Heroin addiction and marijuana consumption in the
United States has stabilized since the mid-1970s at approximately half a
million individuals in the former category and 20 million in the latter.
Mexico has continued to supply a substantial part of both markets:
between 25 and 30 percent of the heroin consumed in the United States,
perhaps half of the marijuana. In the meantime, the United States has
itself become one of the world's largest producers of marijuana.[3]

Mexico's eradication campaigns, concentrated in the states of Sinaloa,
Durango, and Chihuahua, proved particularly effective in the 1970s,
when the entire city of Culiacán, the capital of Sinaloa, became an armed
camp and was eventually taken over by the army. But this very effectiveness led the "Mexican mafia" to move down the coast to Guadalajara, in the state of Jalisco, and branch out into other forms of endeavor.
Operation Condor, as the main eradication campaign of the late 1970s
was designated, came to a close in 1980, though fumigation continued.
The government's efforts ebbed, however, at the end of the López Portillo administration, as all things in Mexico do. This drop-off in enforcement, in addition to two other factors, contributed to an increase in
Mexican marijuana and heroin exports.

First, traditionally insufficient Colombian efforts to eradicate marijuana finally began to work, diminishing the supply of Colombian
"grass" to the United States. Mexico took up the slack, increasing its
market share. Second, the incoming government of Miguel de la Madrid
attempted to carry out a much-needed overhaul of the nation's nonmilitary security forces. It started with the Mexico City police, which had
been headed for six years by the infamous Arturo "El Negro" Durazo,
often accused of drug-trafficking links. An inevitable short-term result
was a downturn in drug enforcement effectiveness and a rise in corrup-

tion, as new senior officials upset existing compromises and previously cut deals.

In late 1984, a huge clandestine marijuana plantation was discovered at El Búfalo in Chihuahua. It revealed that far more marijuana than formerly thought was being harvested in Mexico; at least the passive complicity of the security bureaucracy was much greater than suspected. It appeared that Mexico's share of the U.S. drug market had indeed increased, though not enormously. According to State Department statistics, the rise in heroin was from 25–30 percent to 33–35 percent from 1984 to 1985, and these were necessarily only approximate figures.[4] But heroin and marijuana had not grown out of control in Mexico and, more important, there was no perceptible increase in the demand for these drugs in the United States. The same amount of heroin and marijuana was being consumed north of the border, but a greater part of the total was coming from Mexico. While this may have been cause for concern in Washington for Mexico's welfare, it certainly made no domestic social difference in the United States. Mexicans doubted how sincere the supposed concern could actually be.

The real problem was cocaine. Although the statistical evidence is murky and inconclusive, a rise in cocaine addiction did take place in the United States as of the middle of the 1970s. Consumption certainly did increase: according to figures quoted by *The New York Times,* 18 tons of cocaine were consumed in 1976; by 1985 consumption had reached nearly 100 tons.[5] The use of the drug spread from white, upper-income, trendy sectors of American society to nearly every corner of the social edifice. For drug dealers "it is the ideal drug: compact and at retail prices extraordinarily profitable. While wholesale prices have fallen from about $23,000 a pound in 1982 to as little as $7,300 in 1986, the retail price has barely changed."[6]

By the mid-1980s, the United States was clearly in the midst of a cocaine scare. Well-known athletes were using it and dying from overdoses of it; the major television networks were airing documentaries about it and devoting large segments of their nightly newscasts to it; the newsweeklies were running cover stories on it. Even if addiction was not rising as much as some believed, the public was undoubtedly convinced that it was. It was also acquiring the conviction that Mexico was part of the problem.

This was true, but in a far more complex and subtle way than many thought. To begin with, and this fact was not widely known, Mexico does not produce cocaine. Coca leaf is not cultivated in Mexico; there is no tradition and the necessary climatological and topographical requirements are simply not present. Furthermore, Mexico is not generally used by cocaine traffickers to process the drug—to transform the coca leaf into coca paste or the latter into white powder. This dubious privilege belongs to Colombia, where coca leaf cultivation was virtually nonexistent until the late 1970s and where most of the U.S. supply of cocaine is processed. Coca leaf traditionally grows in the Andean regions of Peru, Bolivia, to a lesser degree Ecuador, and more recently in Brazil. But by the mid-1980s Mexico had become the conduit through which a considerable proportion of U.S.-destined cocaine was shipped. This was an entirely new development which totally surprised Mexican and American authorities and which they were both unprepared to cope with.

Seizures of processed cocaine at the border began in the late 1970s, but the major rise came later. According to U.S. government figures, in the six-month period from October 1, 1985, to March 31, 1986, three times more cocaine was seized on the Mexico-California line than in the previous five years along the entire border.[7] The statistic probably exaggerates the real increase in volume, since it does not take into account greater surveillance, resources, and manpower devoted to drug interdiction in the United States. But it shows the magnitude of the change and points to a sizable jump in cocaine exports from Latin America to Mexico and then to the United States.

Cocaine brought high profits but was compact, light, and easy to transport. Hence former Mexican marijuana and heroin traffickers, particularly from Guadalajara, where they had been "exiled" from Sinaloa, hooked up with Colombian exporters and ventured into the cocaine trade. They had a lot to offer their Colombian colleagues: proximity to the United States, nearly unrestricted access to the United States and to its largest single market, Los Angeles, and a strong familiarity with Mexican drug enforcement procedures and vulnerabilities. Moreover, they operated in a country where coastlines, airports and airstrips, and southern border towns were completely unequipped to interdict incoming drugs.

Finally, American and Colombian authorities' efforts to shut down or at least obstruct cocaine traffic through the Caribbean and Florida, while largely unsuccessful, nonetheless constituted an incentive for a shift of operations to the Mexican "connection." In a sense, the Colombian mafia was acting on a novel and startling premise. In its view, the easiest way to introduce illegal goods into the United States was through Mexico, despite the fact that this procedure involved two international boundary crossings and a refueling stop in Central America or the Caribbean. In their own way, the traffickers realized that the porosity of the U.S.-Mexican border for illegal entries, exports, and capital transfers had made the second dividing line a tenuous one. Once a shipment had entered Mexico, access to the United States was practically ensured. There could be no more certain symptom of the degree of economic integration already reached.

Mexican authorities were consequently faced with an unprecedented situation. Accustomed to burning marijuana and poppy fields, trained in fumigation missions and destroying heroin-processing shops, all of a sudden they had to deal with a problem of interdiction as opposed to eradication. Although in many cases it meant fighting the same individuals, the struggle was a totally different one. It had to do with patrolling coastlines, airspace, airports, and border towns. The money involved was much greater; the arms, agencies, and rules for waging the struggle were all different.

Before, Mexico had to stop homegrown crops from being cultivated or exported to the United States. Now it had to prevent the entry of goods into Mexico from abroad and their continuing journey to the United States. It also found itself in a paradoxical bind. The national authorities were probably better equipped to interdict the flow of cocaine from Mexico into the United States than from Latin America into Mexico. For obvious reasons, there has historically been a much stronger federal presence—police, customs, immigration, even military—along the country's northern border than in the south or along its coasts. The northern border, while porous, is far more patrolled than the southern one, and much more so than the coast or southern airspace. But greater efficiency in not letting the drugs leave had a special disadvantage. In the short term, it created an incentive to keep the drug for longer periods of time in Mexico, while the traffickers found safer ways of reexporting it. But the longer the drug stayed in Mexico, the greater the possibilities that local addiction would begin to spread and that the corrupting influence of the trade would extend to those sectors of the Mexican security machinery and society previously untouched by drug-related corruption. The dramatic increase in drug-related problems in border towns such as Matamoros, Ciudad Juárez, and Tijuana, where drugs are stored until their cross-border transshipment, is witness to this. Given these changes and previous obstacles, it was not surprising that efforts to deal with the new phenomenon proved inadequate. Moreover, the severe economic crisis drastically lowered the threshold of official corruption.

Corruption rapidly became the key factor in one of the most contentious facets of the drug conflict. American officials increasingly complained that the sticking point was not so much the "objective difficulties" involved in drug enforcement, which everyone acknowledged. As they saw it, the root problem was that Mexican authorities simply refused to give the matter sufficient priority. Many American officials, particularly at higher levels in the Justice and State departments, believed this, in spite of Mexican denials. They attributed it to the fact that "Mexico is the only country in the hemisphere that produces significant amounts of opium-heroin with little internal abuse. . . . Mexican drug organizations pose less of an overt threat to the society of the Republic than Colombian and Peruvian criminal organizations."[8] But certain officials within the Reagan administration, such as Customs Commissioner William von Raab, directly blamed purported Mexican indifference to drug enforcement on corruption and complicity with drug traffickers. When the Camarena case brought to light both the supposed "complacency" of the government of Mexico and the drug-related corruption in a considerable part of the nonmilitary security forces, the two points of view converged.

Mexico recognizes the existence of drug-linked corruption—the government of President De la Madrid disbanded the Federal Security Directorate and dismissed a large number of agents because of their drug involvement—but also blames much of its pervasiveness on the U.S. drug market. As Samuel del Villar, at one time President De la Madrid's chief drug enforcement adviser, phrased it in an article published after his resignation: "The greatest impact the narcotization of American life has had on Mexico has been the massive export of corruption [from the United States] . . . the U.S. government's pressures on the Mexican security machinery forced the latter to expose itself massively to the international drug traffic. Inevitably, this exposure led to the corruption of its public servants, as has occurred in the United States."[9]

Concerning the effectiveness of their drug enforcement efforts, Mexican authorities recall the more than three hundred military and security men who died in the last few years in the war on drugs, a symptom of the problem's magnitude and violence. They point out that nearly one-fifth of the army is involved at any one time in drug eradication campaigns and reject charges that Mexico does not assign a high priority to the issue. But "high priority" means different things on each side of the border and that is precisely the problem.

For perhaps the first time in its relations with Mexico, the United States has suddenly encountered the "disproportionate importance syndrome," well known to generations of Mexicans involved in dealing with the country's northern neighbor. Traditionally, Mexico's views and concerns on bilateral matters have occupied a low rank in American priorities. This time, the same phenomenon is occurring, only the other way around. Whatever the reasons which led American society and the U.S. government to attach great importance to it, drug enforcement—while undoubtedly taken more and more seriously—is still less important a matter for Mexico than it is for the United States.

That there is little or no consumption of or addiction to heroin or cocaine in Mexico; that their production and/or traffic is for now limited to certain areas of the country; and that local drug lords are viewed as modern-day Robin Hoods who bring prosperity to their communities while "getting back at the gringos"[10]—all place the United States in a situation common for Mexico but totally unprecedented for American authorities. Their concerns, while heeded, are not taken as seriously as they wish, not because of corruption, negligence, or ignorance—all of which undoubtedly exist—but because of political realities which give the issue different weight in both nations. Although PRI presidential candidate Carlos Salinas de Gortari stated during his 1988 campaign that drug traffic had become a national security threat, it continues to be viewed as a regional issue more than as a national one.

This fundamental difference lies at the heart of all the misunderstandings, frustrations, and genuine indignation on either side of the border. The fact that Mexico was probably never quite conscious of how it played down the issue or that De la Madrid's government perhaps initially underestimated the problem's magnitude and its effects in the United States may have made matters worse but did not create the conflict. Mexico was facing too many other crises and difficulties to deal with a problem which, at least for the time being, was strictly a United States affair. Dire warnings about future consequences—local addiction and "Colombianization"—while justified, necessarily fell on deaf ears. Mexico is far too involved in managing today's pressing problems to worry about tomorrow's hypothetical complications.

In view of American pressure and retaliation, Mexican authorities have made greater efforts, if not to increase their drug enforcement capabilities, at least to placate Washington superficially. But their heart can never be as much in it as the United States would want, particularly with regard to prosecuting high-level corruption (possibly true but never publicly substantiated by U.S. officials) in the security forces and military ranks. Nor can they be enthusiastic about major changes in Mexican drug enforcement procedures and American drug enforcement assistance.

Perhaps the only way to bring about a substantial drop in drug exports from Mexico to the United States is by committing the armed forces to drug enforcement on a much wider scale. This implies expanding their operations from burning marijuana and poppy crops in the fields to intelligence activities, interdiction, and arrests. This is neither a viable nor a desirable proposition. Exposing the army to drug-related corruption, by no longer limiting its drug-related activities to eradication, is a risky venture. As General Félix Galván López, a former Secretary of Defense, put it: "We cannot put soldiers alongside policemen in the field of drug enforcement."[11] And involving the armed forces in areas previously foreign to them seems unwise.

Concerning U.S. aid in drug enforcement matters, major changes in its "terms of engagement" could possibly bring an improvement in Mexican capability, but at an unacceptable political cost. The difficulties involved came to light in August 1986, during De la Madrid's second visit to Washington. On that occasion, U.S. Attorney General Meese formally requested Mexican authorization for DEA aircraft to enter Mexican airspace up to a hundred miles south of the border in "hot pursuit" of drug traffickers fleeing American surveillance. This request was refused.

During the same visit, however, Victor Cortéz, an undercover American DEA agent in Guadalajara, was arrested and—according to him—tortured by Mexican police. Whatever the actual details of the incident, it highlighted the delicate nature of U.S. participation in Mexican drug enforcement activities. Cortéz was detained in possession of arms and without identification, both necessary attributes for an undercover agent, but an unacceptable condition for a foreigner in a foreign land. As long as most aspects of bilateral drug cooperation are kept private and not formalized, Mexico can probably live with many of them. But by publicizing the status quo for American domestic purposes, or actually trying to modify it, the United States creates a situation which entails excessive political liabilities for any Mexican administration.

The only increase in American aid which could make a major difference to the United States would have to come in the field of cocaine interdiction. But such assistance would probably entail U.S. participation in patrolling the Mexican side of the border and Mexican airspace and coastlines. While not guaranteeing any major degree of success—the difficulties encountered by the South Florida Task Force in interdicting cocaine shipments from the Caribbean underline the severity of the problem—American assistance in ensuring the sanctity of the Mexican border is clearly a nonstarter. This is so not only for reasons of abstract sovereignty, which in this case are weighty: a country which allows others to defend its territorial integrity begins to lose one of the first attributes of nationhood. In some cases, it has no real choice, like much of Western Europe when it formed NATO in 1948. For now at least, Mexico has a choice, and its preference is clear.

More important, however, at this juncture the "integration" effect comes into play once again. Rightly or wrongly, Colombian and Mexican cocaine traffickers have reached the conclusion that the border is somewhat less than a rigorous dividing line between two nations. As with hundreds of thousands of Central American refugees, entry into Mexico practically signifies guaranteed access to the United States. If the authorities of the two nations were also to take this view and act as if the control of Mexico's borders were both nations' responsibility, one more long informal step toward integration would be taken.

There is nonetheless room for negotiation and agreement. Without putting its own stability, traditions, and sovereignty in danger, Mexico can probably do more to accommodate American concerns. But the United States also has to understand that the issue does not have the same bearing on one side of the border as it does on the other. Mexico does not have a drug problem; the United States does. If the United States continues to believe that its self-righteousness and absolute moral imperatives are sufficient reason for Mexico to address American drug enforcement preoccupations, little progress will be made in the long term. Mexico will prove flexible and cooperative on drug enforcement matters if it is in its interests to do so, and if the United States acknowledges that by proceeding in that fashion, its neighbor is making a concession, not "doing what is right."

Drug traffic from Mexico to the United States is to a certain extent like a large *maquiladora*. One hundred percent of the producers' output is exported, and all of Mexico's drug exports go to the United States. In the case of cocaine, all "inputs" are imported "in bond," so to speak. The four thousand indentured peasants employed at El Búfalo plantation in 1984 worked in sweatshop-like conditions not unlike the worst *maquiladoras*. Although no one knows how much Mexico's drug exports represent, estimates of gross value run in the several billions.

This may not represent a disproportionate sum in relation to the country's $175 billion GNP, but it is a great deal of money under any circumstances. Yet most of the proceeds from the drug business never reach Mexico. According to all reliable accounts, the vast majority of the dollars earned by those who have learned to take advantage of Mexico's most dynamic export market remain in that market. They are "invested" in the medium-sized and small banks of the U.S. Southwest, which have received billions of dollars in Mexican deposits since the mid-1970s. American authorities are far less persevering in controlling or enforcing this aspect of the drug trade than others. This leads directly into the second aspect of informal integration: capital flight.

The flight of large amounts of money from Mexico and other Latin American nations to the rest of the world, and particularly to the United States, has become one of the most important contact points between "capital-exporting" and "capital-importing" countries. The magnitudes involved and the effects wrought by the yearly and accumulated stock of capital flight have given the issue a degree of importance barely suspected a decade ago. An end to capital flight has come to be viewed as a make-or-break condition for the recovery of the Mexican, Venezuelan, and Argentine economies. Their creditors, together with officials from the industrialized nations, consider capital flight to be a symptom of a fundamental lack of confidence in the future by the citizens of these countries. Economic planners and managers in many Latin American nations see it as a highly complex, negative economic trend which undermines their efforts to straighten out local finances, promote exports, and obtain new credits abroad.

But in addition to these considerations, capital flight is leaving a profound mark on Latin American societies, and particularly on Mexico. It is welding a direct link between small but key affluent sectors of Mexican life, as well as much broader cross sections of the urban middle classes, and the United States. For these members of Mexican society, the national currency is no longer the peso. Their locally deposited savings are no longer held in a "foreign" land but simply in banks, which just happen to be in Houston, San Diego, or Tucson.

The first problem involving capital flight has to do with its real magnitude and motivation. A torrent of inaccurate statistics and unsubstantiated arguments on this issue have recently been generated in the United States. While it is difficult to establish with complete certainty what the true facts are, some degree of accuracy is attainable, though not often attained. With regard to capital flight from Mexico, the figure most commonly quoted stems from a Morgan Guaranty publication, *World Financial Markets,* which in its March 1986 issue included a brief study: "Less Developed Country Capital Flight."[12]

According to this survey, capital flight from Mexico between 1976 and 1985 reached $53 billion. By all indications, this estimate is too high. The sum was calculated in a residual fashion—that is, as the result of the addition and subtraction of other figures. The Morgan study adds direct investment flows, changes (plus or minus) in gross external debt, the country's current account balance, and changes in "selected gross foreign assets." The result is capital flight. Although the study includes caveats regarding the accuracy of this calculation, it does not question the precision of the final tally.

There are two solid reasons for skepticism. The first—of a technical nature—was pointed out by the governor of the Bank of Mexico in a speech in Phoenix, Arizona, in 1986.[13] Mexican current account statistics include as an income item the interest earned on bank deposits held by citizens abroad, as reported to the International Monetary Fund. Since capital flight is defined by Morgan Guaranty as the difference between reported inflows and outflows, and this overestimates inflows, it skews the current account balance upward. In addition, the Morgan method neglects both private sector debt revaluation due to better reporting and undisclosed prepayment. More important, however, the accounting system used by Morgan omits contraband between Mexico and the United States, which consists mainly of unreported imports of goods into Mexico, which necessarily imply unreported transfers of money abroad.

There is an enormous amount of contraband flowing across the border, from cigarettes to personal computers, from spare parts for oil rigs to military hardware. In most countries' national accounts contraband is either not a major item or it cancels out; consequently "Errors and Omissions" principally does reflect capital flows. But this is not true in the case of Mexico, the only developing country in the world to share a land border with a highly industrialized nation. It is worth noting, for example, that in Mexico until 1988, the overwhelming majority of consumer-owned videocassette recorders were brought into the country illegally, either by individual consumers or by professional contraband merchants who peddle their wares in the black market. The underestimation of contraband—as well as of unreported border transactions—led the Morgan study to overestimate the value of Mexican-held assets abroad.

Mexican-held bank deposits in the United States totaled roughly $13.1 billion in 1987, according to the Federal Reserve Board.[14] This figure is only a part of overall capital flight, since a substantial portion is invested in real estate, securities, and other unregistered assets. Thus the true figure for aggregate capital flight from Mexico since 1976 lies somewhere between $15 and $53 billion. While some Mexican government experts have posited totals of approximately $26 billion for the 1976–85 period, American academics who have studied the issue generally accept slightly higher figures: $36 billion in one case, around $30 billion in others. It would seem that $30 to $35 billion as the total which actually *left* Mexico in the 1976–85 period is a reasonable figure. Fernando Solana, the chairman of the Mexican Banking Association and president of Mexico's largest bank, stated in early 1988 that the total value of Mexican assets in the United States had reached $40 billion. This was the highest public estimate given to date by a senior government official.[15]

It is important to note that not all Mexican-held deposits in U.S. banks represent capital flight. Some include drug money and Mexico-based corporations' dollar accounts in the United States. In September 1982, Mexican authorities estimated deposits in the United States at $8 billion and other assets at $14 billion. If the former increased some 60 percent (i.e., from $8 billion in 1982 to $13 billion in 1987), it seems plausible to assume that the latter increased at the same rate. The resulting total for 1986 would reach approximately $35 billion.

While less than the Morgan estimate, the sum is still enormous, and has become a tremendous drain on the country's resources. It constitutes a devastating question mark raised by its citizens about the state of the nation. From the point of view of the integration of the Mexican economy with that of the United States, the key statistic is not necessarily the amount of dollars which *fled* Mexico, but the amount of dollars *held* by Mexicans in the United States. The two are different. Over time, assets appreciate in value, if only through compounded interest. If the total amount of money which *left* Mexico is in the $35 billion range, the sum of Mexican-*held* assets in the United States today is certainly greater.

Yet if one were to average out over a ten-year period the approximately $30 to $35 billion which fled Mexico, the result is a yearly transfer abroad of between 2 and 3 percent of the nation's GNP. While this is undoubtedly high, and if stopped would amount to more than half the foreign savings the country has required per year over the past several decades, it is not a significant part of Mexico's wealth or capital stock. Capital flight is an extremely harmful phenomenon at the margin, but its importance should be neither underestimated nor exaggerated.

Similarly, its causes and origins should not be oversimplified. Overevaluation of the Mexican currency and lack of confidence in the economy are the main underlying reasons for capital flight, but even these factors must be nuanced. Thus the inflated value of the peso played a major role in the massive flights of 1976 and late 1981–82, but high levels of transfers continued from 1983 through 1985, when the value of the peso was kept artificially low. The "confidence" element is also only partially valid. In 1976, in 1981–82, and from 1983 to 1985, there was a generalized lack of confidence in the economy on the part of the country's private sector, the chief author of capital flight. But the money which left in 1976, for example, did not return between 1978 and 1981, when the economy was booming and when confidence in Mexico reached an all-time high, both domestically and abroad. This was the time when Mexico was exporting newly found oil reserves at a high price, when foreign investment and credit were entering the country in historic volumes, and when Mexico was being held up as a model for other developing countries.

Conversely, in 1986, when there were no indications of any rekindled confidence in the economy (it contracted 4 percent that year and the authorities were barely able to obtain new credits just to meet interest payments), there was a substantial "reflow" of money to Mexico from the United States. The reason was speculation—the narrow-based and highly speculative Mexican stock exchange underwent an extraordinary boom and an equally spectacular subsequent crash—and mainly of a purely technical nature. A dramatic credit squeeze in Mexico, brought about by a 90 percent banking reserve requirement imposed by the government, obliged firms with dollar accounts in the United States to repatriate funds just to maintain operations. Confidence had nothing to do with the reflows, but they were nonetheless considerable, probably topping $1 billion for the year. They not only stopped but reverted, as capital flight began anew in Mexico in late 1987.

In fact, the overall process is a complex one, and there are no simple, single causes which explain it adequately. Capital flight is clearly not just a "push factor" phenomenon. There is also a "pull factor." The United States has become a capital-importing country, attracting well over $100 billion a year from the rest of the world to finance its mammoth trade and fiscal deficits. The natural, market-inspired flows of capital satisfy part of this appetite, but not all of it. Draining that amount of money from other countries also requires various forms of legitimate and not so legitimate enticement. These include high real interest rates, further market incentives, and other stimuli. "To recognize that high international interest rates encourage capital flight from debtor countries is to acknowledge that the industrial countries contributed to the problem of capital flight. They need to play their part ending the problem. A first contribution they could make is to reduce real interest rates to historically normal levels."[16]

The most important enticement, in the case of Mexico at least, is that nonresident deposits in the United States are not subject to American income taxes. The Internal Revenue Service does not even impose a refundable withholding tax on nonresident bank deposits. Since there is no double taxation treaty between the two countries, American authorities do not inform Mexican fiscal collectors of Mexican-held assets in the United States which might be taxed in Mexico. Consequently, U.S.-based Mexican assets are not taxed at all. Therefore, the real yield these deposits produce is inordinately high. Needless to say, this provides a powerful impulse to capital flight from Mexico, which the United States, whatever its other concerns regarding the Mexican economy, has never felt any desire to eliminate or even contain.

In addition, many American private and governmental entities carry out activities in Mexico to promote capital flight, or "deposits and investment" by Mexican nationals in the United States. The best example of this often neglected aspect of the problem—and of a certain hypocrisy on the part of U.S. authorities who have long insisted on the need for Mexico to curb capital flight—was the Ginnie Mae, or Government National Mortage Association, affair in late 1986. This American federal agency took out large advertisements in the Mexican press promoting "dollars without headaches" and all the benefits of a U.S.-government-guaranteed investment. A phone number in the United States—which one could call collect—was provided, as well as courier services, once a customer called, to ensure the safe transfer of the sums. The Mexican government protested to the American embassy, and eventually the advertising campaign stopped for a while, although other agencies continued to run similar campaigns. But the investment and deposits did not.[17]

From a Mexican perspective the more worrisome elements of this complex process stem from the different reasons for capital flight. While the original motivation may well have been a combination of push and pull factors—overvaluation of the peso and high real interest rates compounded by tax exemption—the same depositor may continue to feed his dollar account as a matter of course, of habit, of normal economic behavior. The previously decisive considerations may disappear, but the exit of dollars from Mexico into U.S. accounts will continue.

An exceptional device used by small and medium-sized investors to protect themselves in the midst of a perceived crisis slowly becomes a custom for all seasons. The most obvious example is the down payment on a condominium, which requires monthly payments for ten or fifteen years. Since the vast majority of Mexican holders of U.S. assets do not have dollar-generating businesses or professions, most of the money to meet those payments will continue to come from Mexico, regardless of the economic conditions and the level of confidence in its economy. This is perhaps the most important aspect of capital flight. It certainly is the most relevant one in terms of the type of relationship it establishes between the two nations.

Understanding this facet of Mexican capital flight involves knowing who the Mexican holders of U.S. assets actually are. Unfortunately there is little information available in this area. Some indications, however, are available, and a certain number of conclusions can be reached.

To begin with, the link between official corruption in Mexico and capital flight is by no means a direct one. Undoubtedly many of the corrupt government officials who have plagued Mexico's governance for years have stashed their ill-gotten earnings in the United States. But the number of such corrupt officials in the Mexican government is small, and the proportion of total *sacadólares* (dollar-removers) made up of government officials is even lower. In a large measure, capital flight has been the product of two converging and mutually reinforcing trends which together have devastated the nation's finances but are far more difficult to correct than simple corruption in high places.

The first has been the private sector's tendency to withdraw capital from Mexico in massive amounts at the slightest sign of governmental policies perceived as contrary to its interests. Bank accounts, securities, real estate in Vail, Colorado, and Coronado, near San Diego, have been the favorite nest eggs of thousands of Mexican businessmen who drained their companies' assets to pad their wallets. In some instances U.S. banks that had extended loans in dollars to Mexican firms were able to go after the owners' personal assets in the United States as collateral for corporations' unpaid loans. One bank recovered up to $50 million in this way.

The best-known case of a "poor company with a rich owner" was that of Cervecería Moctezuma (CerMoc) and Alberto Bailleres, its former owner.[18] The large beer concern, known mainly in the United States for Dos Equis, had contracted a $375 million loan from a consortium of American banks. When Mexico's financial crisis struck in 1982 and dollars for private debt payments became more difficult to secure, Cer-Moc suspended payments to its creditors. The company was finally sued by the creditor banks because it could not account for the money loaned, or for large transfers from its books to other parts of the Bailleres empire, which included Industries Peñoles, the world's largest silver producer, all incorporated as a holding company named Albacorp.[19] Bailleres eventually sold Moctezuma, after the government refused to bail it out.

Until 1982 the most important conduits for capital flight were Mexico's large commercial banks, which had themselves purchased assets abroad and assisted their Mexican clients in withdrawing their money from the country. But even since then many American institutions, chiefly Texas- and California-based, have actively promoted capital flight from Mexico and Latin America by dealing directly with their customers in Mexico and other countries.[20] Many small banks in the border region have huge amounts of Mexican deposits, and often their profits depend on continuing flows of money from down south. Since there is always a strong offshore demand for pesos there is little difficulty in having Mexican currency accepted at southwestern banks or by U.S. bank representatives in Mexico. The peso seller's American account is automatically credited for the corresponding amount in dollars.

But if Mexico's business community has led the way in the capital flight parade, the nation's middle classes have followed. Capital flight has become a social phenomenon, a widespread trend which goes beyond the tycoons who took out $5 million, $10 million, or $50 million to encompass wide swaths of the country's relatively new, urban, affluent but not rich middle classes. Most estimates of the total number of Mexican accounts in the United States range from 750,000 to 1 million, though some believe it is higher, particularly if one includes Mexican border area residents' dollar deposits.[21] This is an astounding figure from any point of view, given that there are barely 8.1 million real accounts in the entire Mexican banking system and that Fernando Solana, the previously mentioned chairman of Banamex, stated in early 1988 that Mexican assets in the United States were greater than total deposits in the Mexican banking system, but it seems plausible. If the present value of Mexican assets in the United States is posited at $50 billion and the average size of each "portfolio" (which may include bank deposits, real estate, securities, etc.) is $50,000, then the number of U.S. accounts would total 1 million.

This figure does not necessarily represent the number of asset-holders, since many have several accounts. But it nonetheless shows in approximate numbers what everybody in Mexico has known intuitively as of late 1981: most individuals with peso savings have purchased dollars at one point or another since then. This does not constitute a large mass to begin with: in a country with Mexico's flagrant inequalities and injustice, the number of people who can save anything is small in relation to the total population. But the share of total savers with dollar accounts is unquestionably high, as was shown in September 1982, when the government forcibly transformed local dollar accounts totaling over $11 billion into pesos. Moreover, there are substantial, though incalculable dollar assets held in liquid form: "under the mattress" dollar savings kept in Mexican homes. Proof of this can be found in the crime sections of the newspapers. Nearly every item concerning a home robbery includes references to the amount of dollars heisted by the growing number of thieves in Mexico City's prosperous neighborhoods.

The key issue for Mexico, and for relations with the United States, concerns the social effects of the partial loss of one of the attributes of national sovereignty—a national currency. According to another Morgan Guaranty study, published in May 1986, by 1985 Mexican deposits abroad were equal to 43 percent of total deposits in the domestic Mexican banking system. The fact that in the case of Argentina the equivalent figure was 115 percent—there were more Argentine-held deposits abroad than in the Argentine banking system—was small comfort to Mexico.[22]

For Mexicans with U.S. accounts larger than a few hundred dollars, the main currency of exchange for all purposes is the dollar. Real estate deals, unregistered purchases of other goods and services, and even some business transactions are carried out in dollars or in dollar-indexed pesos. Similarly, dollar-holders' standard of living is left untouched by national economic trends. Since inflation and the fall of the peso's value in relation to the dollar have been roughly equal for nearly five years, dollar-holders are impervious to increases in local prices of domestic and foreign goods and services. This distinguishes them from the vast majority of Mexico's population, which has suffered a severe decline in purchasing power during the past few years.

It is difficult, if not impossible, to think, buy, sell, and live in another currency without somehow believing that one also lives in another country. A parallel economy is emerging in Mexico, made up of people and businesses who use the dollar as their currency, and who are literally creating a new type of enclave, far different from the banana plantations in Central America at the turn of the century. Granted, their interests are not the same as those of the banks who hold their fortunes, and it is undoubtedly unfair to label them traitors to the fatherland or denationalized renegades, as many Mexican politicians have done. But it is true that there is a natural tendency to divide one's loyalties and sympathies the moment one divides one's savings and other assets.

With their dollars, this "Taco Power" elite takes its vacations, buys its clothes and consumer goods, obtains medical care, and sends its children to prep school and college in the United States. Its members largely identify with the United States because that is where a substantial part of their life takes place, perhaps not geographically, but certainly financially. There is little doubt, for example, that the unfounded but widespread belief that Mexico's suspension of payments on its foreign debt would lead to a freeze of dollar accounts has been a factor in the government's reluctance to utilize a negotiating tactic that other nations, mainly Brazil, have put to good purpose.

In most cases, Mexican dollar-holders prefer to continue living in Mexico, because of traditional love for the country, because that is where dollars go further, and because often emigration would entail a decline in living standards and dignity. But with time they have become a group separate from other Mexicans. Their existence as a permanent fixture of the economy and society has transformed both. For the first time in recent history, there is a substantial and influential sector of society whose interests are at least as closely identified with the United States as they are with Mexico.

Most important, though, there seems to be little that can be done to reverse this trend or curb its growth. With the exception of a brief three-month period in late 1982, exchange controls have never been tried in the recent past. Most of the country's economic and financial officials believe they would not work. Their views are generally buttressed by the apparently conclusive argument of a 2,000-mile border. This is a powerful deterrent to controls, but it is also true that the government, through oil exports and other sources, controls a significant share of Mexico's foreign earnings, and thus a large part of the supply of dollars. In fact, the political outcry which it would cause among the dollar-holding or "dollar-hoping" middle classes is the main reason why strict exchange controls have not been implemented.

The confidence factor, or "caboose view," is often mentioned as a possible solution. This line of reasoning states that after confidence in the economy is restored through the application of correct policies, capital flight will cease and some of the previously subtracted money may return. This position raises obvious questions: Whose opinion of "correct policies" is the right one? Should such power over the economy be given to a small sector of society? Just what does "confidence" mean? Moreover, there are reasons for thinking that the existence of a large stock of Mexican-held assets abroad has become one of the greatest incentives for further capital flight. Hence the restoration of confidence, were it to happen, might reduce new outflows until the next economic crisis, but would not affect those flows which are motivated by "non-confidence-related" factors.

Other, more far-reaching measures have been suggested. These include a double taxation treaty with the United States, which until now the government has resisted partly because of the tax loopholes it would create for American corporations in Mexico, partly because of the inertia from the time when Mexico was a safe haven for American money. A treaty would oblige Washington to provide information about Mexican holdings in the United States; these would necessarily be taxed either in Mexico or in the United States. Some holdings would remain hidden, and perhaps other capital would flee to Europe and Canada, but the possibility of taxing Mexican assets in the United States would, at the least, enhance the Mexican government's revenues, and at best serve as a real deterrent to capital flight. For now there is no consensus within the Mexican establishment on the desirability of such a treaty, and undeniably it has its drawbacks. Other ideas focus on ways to recycle Mexican assets in the United States back to Mexico through the Federal Reserve System and the Banco de México, with the latter paying the former an interest rate differential for the deposit of those assets in the Mexican Central Bank.

Some combination of all these tools will eventually be put in place, when it becomes clear that a simple return to the past, when the Mexican currency was strong and capital flight was a marginal or nonexistent phenomenon, is simply not possible. The policy mix will furnish a degree of control over this hemorrhaging of the nation's wealth but will not stanch it. In all likelihood, Mexico will have to come to terms with a situation in which its monetary sovereignty, already gravely impaired, will never be entirely restored, although it need not be irretrievably lost either.

A certain percentage of the country's savings will continue to be sent abroad, and many depositors will reject the charge that they are placing their money "abroad"; they are simply placing it in the United States. This is just one more feature of the process of informal integration facing Mexico today. It happens to be one which seriously damages the country while benefiting the United States.

The U.S. Side

Robert A. Pastor

During the New Deal, Harry Hopkins, one of President Roosevelt's closest advisers, received an urgent report from U.S. Naval Intelligence: "Wealthy Americans, fearful of taxes and dissatisfied with low interest rates, are sending millions of dollars of speculative capital to Mexico."[1] Capital flight is no stranger to the United States. Nearly thirty years later, President John Kennedy was obsessed with the exodus of American capital and its implications for the dollar and U.S. prestige.[2] Some problems don't go away, but they do change direction.

The most frustrating problems are those that appear easy to solve and yet persistently elude one's grasp. People know that mankind has not devised a solution to war, but they expect their nation's borders to be defended. Yet it appears that the U.S. government has no more power to prevent a person from crossing the border with a kilo of cocaine or a satchel of cash than it does to contain Iran's Islamic revolution.

When a relatively insignificant cross-border problem defies solution, there is an inevitable temptation to pass the blame—from one bureaucrat to another, from one end of Pennsylvania Avenue to the other, but most commonly from one side of the border to the other. Many in Mexico claim that the U.S. demand for drugs causes the drug problem, while 46 percent of Americans, according to a survey in July 1986, believe the most effective way to deal with the drug problem is curbing the supply in Mexico.[3] Some Mexicans see the U.S. budget deficit and the high real interest rates as the cause of capital flight, whereas from the U.S. perspective it is the result of a lack of confidence by Mexicans in their own government.

Each international transaction, whether legal or illegal, whether in goods, services, drugs, or capital, has a demand in one country and a supply in the other. To argue that the problem is only one of demand or only one of supply is a modern-day variation of the chicken-and-egg debate, and just as sterile. The essence of the dilemma is that individual governments cannot solve transnational problems. Raymond Vernon captured the frustration in a trenchant phrase. Sovereignty, he wrote, is at bay.

But if people become frustrated too soon over failing to control the drug trade and capital flight, they also leap too quickly to the conclusion that these phenomena are beyond control. Governments *have* influenced the direction and the magnitude of the trade in drugs and capital. In a decade, the United States went from worrying about the export of its capital to becoming the world's largest importer of other currencies. In a shorter period, about five years, the Mexican government, with U.S. assistance, effectively shut down much of the drug operations within the country, and then, with its attention diverted, let it burgeon again.

To understand the possibilities and the constraints in affecting the trade in drugs and capital, one should heed the advice of the Chinese sage, and look closely, but with more distance.

Since the beginning of recorded history, drugs have been used for medicinal and hedonistic reasons, and they have always been traded. Nearly five thousand years ago, the Chinese used a plant that later would be called marijuana to brew a heavenly tea. Some enterprising Chinese took the plant to India, and the Indians dried and smoked it. Marco Polo returned to Europe from the Orient with these and other delicacies. The marijuana plant also was native to North America and was said to have been brought by nomadic Indians from northern Mexico into the area now known as the United States long before Europeans arrived.

The spread of drugs took a second leap in the latter part of the nineteenth century when new production processes were combined with advances in chemistry to bring mass-produced purer drugs to an expanding market. Old-time snake-oil salesmen began selling pills and tonics.

One such salesman was John Pemberton, an Atlanta dealer of opiate liver pills. In 1887, he mixed coca leaves with the caffeine from the kola nut and produced a popular drink, Coca-Cola.[4]

The drug most abused by people then and now is alcohol, but other "modern" substances spread and created new social problems. In 1906, Congress passed the Pure Food and Drug Act to protect consumers from dangerous drugs, and eight years later, the Harrison Act imposed a nationwide ban on the nonprescribed use of cocaine and heroin. After World War I, the United States successfully pressed for the negotiation of international agreements to prohibit the trade of these and other drugs. At the same time, it prohibited the production and sale of liquor, ignoring the principal lesson of these conventions—that an effective response requires international cooperation. In 1933, after a fourteen-year experiment, the United States finally accepted the failure of unilateral prohibition.

The third expansion of the drug culture occurred as a result of the explosion of demand by the affluent "baby-boomers" who came of age in the United States in the mid-1960s. Before then, drugs were used by relatively small groups of rich Americans to escape to inner peace or poor people to escape from worldly gloom. The government tried to prevent its use, but not very much. Washington's reaction was different when the children of the middle class began to use drugs. The United States, like most democracies, tends to react rapidly to middle-class preoccupations because that segment of the population has more votes than the upper class and it participates more actively in politics than the lower class. As the drugs became increasingly deadly—from marijuana to heroin and cocaine—and as their use spread during the 1970s, popular frustration was transformed into government activism, and U.S. efforts became more comprehensive and frantic.

The government has addressed the narcotics issue as both a health and education problem and a law enforcement problem since 1935, when addicts were transferred from prisons to selected hospitals. Both Democratic and Republican administrations have recognized and confronted the two sides of the problem, but Democrats have tended to give greater attention and resources to health and education, and Republicans to law enforcement.

By far, the largest proportion of federal resources has gone to law enforcement because interstate and international crime is primarily a federal responsibility, and Washington has historically played a minor role in health and education. The private and nongovernmental sectors run most of the hospitals and the various drug treatment facilities, and local—and to a lesser degree, state—governments have been principally responsible for both the funding and the direction of education.

While a citizen in a drug-producing country might feel as if his nation is the target of the U.S. drug effort, in fact the attention and resources which Washington devotes to the entire international or supply side of the drug problem are trivial as compared with what is allocated domestically. In 1979, for example, the federal government spent more than $800 million on drug control in the areas of law enforcement, treatment, and rehabilitation. The international narcotics control program accounted for only $38.5 million. Mexico was then one of the largest suppliers and received $11.7 million of U.S. aid.[5]

The debate on drugs in the United States is the opposite of the way it is perceived abroad. The voices insisting that more attention should be paid to the supply side of the problem may sound loud in Mexico, but the budget reflects that other voices prevail. Overall, the U.S. government articulates its policy in terms of addressing both the supply side and the demand side. As the Department of State noted in its 1987 report to Congress on the administration's international efforts: "The international campaign to control production of illicit narcotics is a long-term proposition, linked to the need to reduce demand and supply simultaneously and interactively."[6] Internationally, the United States has been the leader in negotiating treaties, the most important being the Single Convention on Narcotics Drugs in 1964, and in helping supplier nations eradicate their crops of poppies, cocoa, and marijuana.

Ronald Reagan was elected President on a platform promising "law and order" at home and strength abroad. In early 1981, Attorney General William French Smith appointed a Task Force on Violent Crime. Its final report stressed the seriousness of the drug problem. In December 1981, Reagan signed a law that permitted the military to cooperate with civilian drug enforcement authorities; this represented a change from a policy established after the Civil War to keep the military separate from the police. The next month, Reagan asked Vice President George Bush to coordinate a special task force to combat illicit drug traffic in South Florida. This effort, much like the drug traffic, grew rapidly. The administration's determination, however, was not diminished by repeated failures, although it has often been diverted toward creative feats of bureaucratic legerdemain. In 1983, Bush became the head of the National Narcotics Border Interdiction System. Dozens of offices in the federal government deal with different parts of the drug elephant. Every two to four years since 1968, the government has rearranged these offices or created new ones to give an appearance of an invigorated effort. Moving around bureaucratic chairs is a habitual response to an unmanageable problem.

Not to be outdone, Congress passed the Comprehensive Crime Control Act of 1984 and two years later twelve separate congressional committees held hearings and drafted portions of a massive Drug Enforcement, Education, and Control Act. This 1986 law increased penalties for drug offenses and authorized $1.7 billion of new funds for enforcement, eradication, and interdiction efforts and for education, treatment, and rehabilitation. From 1981 to 1986, overall funding for the drug program gradually doubled from $1.2 billion to $2.3 billion; the 1986 law nearly doubled the funding again. However, drug abuse prevention and treatment had been neglected until Congress reallocated nearly one-quarter of the proposed drug budget to them in 1987. The amount given to Mexico—the largest international program—for 1987 was $15 million.[7]

Legislators pushed the omnibus bill through Congress just as drugs rose to the top of the political agenda. Local communities were feeling the consequences of a crisis that was worsening and reaching as far down as elementary schools. The issue became a national one because it was pushed up from the grass roots, rather than imposed from Washington. Community groups were demanding that schools and their elected representatives do more to stop the scourge afflicting their children.

Congress focused on the demand side of the problem—law enforcement, education, drug treatment programs—but it did not ignore the supply side. It insisted that the President apply more pressure on drug-producing nations. The new law required the President to certify that a foreign nation is cooperating fully with U.S. drug efforts before that nation could receive aid or U.S. trade preferences. Mexico was in the front of the collective mind of Congress when it passed that amendment.

This was not the first time that the United States had been disturbed about illicit drug production in Mexico. Since the 1930s, Mexico had supplied about 10 percent of the heroin market in the United States. In his summit meeting with President López Mateos in June 1962, President Kennedy raised the issue, and both publicly "agreed to redouble their efforts and their cooperation to put an end" to illegal drug traffic. A similar pledge followed Lyndon Johnson's meeting with the Mexican President in February 1964.[8]

Turkey was the major supplier of heroin, but when that stopped in 1972, and the "French Connection" was severed, international traffickers looked for an alternative. They found it on the doorstep of the world's most lucrative market. By 1975, Mexico had become the source of 80–90 percent of the heroin entering the United States. It was also the major supplier of marijuana.

Mexico acknowledged that the problem was a serious one for both countries, and negotiated an agreement with the United States to eradicate poppy and marijuana fields by aerial spraying. The United States provided aircraft and aid amounting to about $67 million in the 1970s. Mexico destroyed a vast number of fields and reduced its supply and share of heroin to the U.S. market to about 25 percent in 1980. Marijuana's decline was even more precipitous—from 95 percent to 10 percent of the U.S. market in 1980. The eradication and interdiction program liquidated or seized about 7.9 metric tons of heroin in 1976 and 9.3 metric tons in 1977. The purity of the heroin fell, and prices rose. The peak of both cooperation and success in reducing the production of opium and marijuana and its flow to the United States occurred in 1980; five years later, it descended into a deep valley. Once again, Mexico became a principal supplier of drugs in the U.S. market.

Due to the Bush Task Force, the U.S. Attorney's office in South Florida increased prosecutions by 64 percent in the first year of the program. Drug smugglers, however, moved faster than the government, and by 1984 the DEA estimated that almost twice as much cocaine entered the United States as before the establishment of the Task Force. The routes of entry changed, the quality of the cocaine increased, and the price declined by 40 percent.[9] Cocaine became the major drug problem in the United States. Demand almost doubled between 1981 and 1984, and the supply stayed ahead of the demand. By 1986, the National Institute on Drug Abuse estimated that 22 million Americans had tried it.

The economics of the trade in cocaine made it the drug dealer's favored commodity. One kilogram of cocaine has the same market value as one ton of marijuana, which means that a car filled with marijuana is equivalent in value to a two-pound flour bag filled with cocaine. In contrast to South Florida's perimeter, with its aerial and coastal surveillance, Mexico's long border with the United States was very inviting. Drug traffickers did not wait for an invitation; they moved swiftly and with increasing volume. Seizures of cocaine by U.S. customs agents in Southern California leaped in 1985 and 1986 and by an incredible 700 percent in 1987 at Mexican border crossing points.[10]

The relative ease of smuggling cocaine and the deterrence of the Bush Task Force in Florida are two reasons why cocaine smugglers shifted their operations to Mexico. But these factors do not explain the increase in the production of poppies and marijuana in Mexico or the facility with which outsiders used the country. The relaxation of enforcement was due to a scarcity of government resources caused by the debt crisis and a disorderly transition from one President to another. The period of Mexican inattention to the drug issue was extended still further because of De la Madrid's decision to reorganize the police forces. While he was seeking to enhance his control over the police, the President's reorganization initially reduced his control.

In brief, Mexico's ability to stop drug traffickers declined at the very moment that they began moving their operations into the country. Because U.S. drug abuse worsened, the spotlight on the issue became brighter, and it turned to Mexico at a most inopportune time. The result was that Mexico regained the distinction as the drug capital of the world.

The DEA initiated Operation Padrino with the Mexican government to stop a heroin and cocaine smuggling ring in the Guadalajara area. When DEA special agent Enrique Camarena Salazar learned too much about it, his targets became his hunters. On February 7, 1985, he was abducted and murdered, and DEA officials accused several well-known traffickers and the Mexican police as being responsible. The incident was one of those in which the styles of the two governments made the problem worse. Mexico reacted slowly and privately, and this frustrated an already outraged U.S. government, which interpreted the unresponsiveness as an admission of complicity or guilt. *The New York Times* criticized the Mexicans for being "distressingly casual in their search for the kidnappers." Even the normally patient Secretary of State George Shultz told a Senate committee: "Our level of tolerance has been exceeded."[11]

A year later, in February 1986, as Congress began hearings on the Omnibus Drug Bill, U.S. authorities obtained a tape recording of Camarena when he was tortured, and identified the man supervising the torture as a Mexican federal police official.[12] Three months later, the Jesse Helms hearings offered the senator and administration officials an opportunity to vent their anger. What bothered them as much as the murder was the involvement of the police, the unresponsiveness of the Mexican government, the ostensible paralysis of the Mexican legal system, and the implications for the relationship. To Helms, the source of the drug problem was the same as for Mexico's other problems: "a government dominated by corruption and fraud."[13] Others at the hearings saw both the drug problem and Mexico's problems as much more complicated. The drug issue evoked from some U.S. leaders self-righteous, sweeping charges that all Mexicans were corrupt, and it produced silent anger and intransigence in Mexico.

Both Presidents sought to limit the damage from the Camarena murder and the reaction in Congress. When they met in Washington on August 13, 1986, they stressed the progress that had been made in the war against drugs. Mexico announced that it had seized 1,058 pounds of pure Colombian cocaine in its northwest. In addition, a former police commander was sentenced to four years in prison for taking a $300,000 bribe from drug dealer Caro Quintero to allow the latter to flee Guadalajara after the murder of Camarena.[14] On the same day, U.S. officials outlined Operation Alliance, a new border enforcement initiative, similar to the Florida Task Force. Undertaken in cooperation with Mexico, the operation involved 20 federal agencies and more than 500 additional federal officers. Vice President Bush was put in charge of the $266 million program.

The two governments were so determined to wear their best faces and put the recent disagreeable incidents behind them that they tried to pretend that they did not hear the figurative explosion as De la Madrid was departing. That day, newspapers reported that still another Mexican-American DEA agent in Guadalajara had been abducted by the police and tortured.[15]

The incident was almost an exact replay of Camarena. For almost a week, Mexican officials denied that the agent, Victor Cortéz, had been arrested or mistreated, and politicians angrily demanded the expulsion of all DEA agents as foreign spies. The government said it was investigating the case, but soon after charging eleven police officers, it then released them. In an interview months later, Cortéz explained that Guadalajara police officers took him to the police station and tortured him to extract, in his words, "the names, addresses, phone numbers of other DEA agents." There was no question of mistaken identity; they knew exactly who Cortéz was.

"They told me," Cortéz said, "they were going to kill me. They told me that the same thing that happened to Camarena was going to happen to me, and that they were going to take me out to the countryside once it got dark." Fortunately, an embassy official saw Cortéz picked up, traced the license plates, and arrived at the station within four hours. He waited two more hours, but finally succeeded in securing the agent's release.[16]

In the spring of 1987, the Senate reviewed the President's certification that Mexican cooperation on narcotics had improved. A majority realized that the administration's case was weak, but they felt that imposing sanctions on Mexico, as Senator Helms proposed, would only make a bad situation worse. Senator Richard Lugar, who had been chairman of the Foreign Relations Committee the previous year when the Republicans controlled the Senate, led the opposition to Helms.

"Mexico-bashing sometimes is popular," said Lugar, "but it is never a good idea."

Senator Pete Wilson of California then explained why Helms, who usually found himself alone on issues such as this, had found a growing minority in his camp: "It is not Mexico-bashing to insist upon the enforcement of U.S. law. It is not Mexico-bashing to demand the protection of American young people" from drugs. "The blackest mark of all against Mexico," said Senator Alfonse D'Amato of New York, "is its failure to bring to justice those responsible for the 1985 torture and murder of DEA special agent Enrique Camarena and those who participated in the 1986 arrest and torture of DEA agent Victor Cortéz. . . . We are now asked to pretend that a country is cooperating with us when we know it is not."[17]

Nonetheless, when the votes were tallied, Lugar and the other senators who spoke for continued cooperation with Mexico defeated the Helms amendment 49–38.

As the two nations' legal systems confront illegal drug trafficking, the difference is not between the common law and the Napoleonic Code, as some Mexicans contend. For thirty-five years, according to the House Select Committee on Narcotics Abuse, the United States has cooperated with prosecutors in seven European countries that use a system of law similar to Mexico's. The problem, the committee delicately put it, "is one of implementation, not legal conflict."[18]

To combat drug trafficking, smuggling, and other illegal transactions across the border, over 250 Mexican and American police officers worked on a special project on both sides of the border for eight weeks in 1986. At the end, Stanley Morris, director of the U.S. Marshals Service, called the project "a valuable beginning": 3,506 fugitives had been apprehended. Off the record, a senior American official called the effort "a joke" because the Mexicans had captured only three of the fugitives. The official explained the disparity by citing a Mexican Deputy Attorney General who described his police force as either corrupt or inexperienced.[19] In its 1988 narcotics report to Congress, the State Department noted that "official corruption within high levels in the Mexican government continues to present the most serious impediment to effective narcotics cooperation with Mexico."[20]

The U.S. legal system is imperfect, but the Bill of Rights and the independence of the judiciary provide a measure of security and confidence. To some North Americans living in Mexico the Mexican legal system is arbitrary and corrupt, to others it is difficult to understand, but to no one with any experience in Mexico does it offer security.

In the mid-1970s, young Americans were arrested by the Mexican government for possession of drugs, and they experienced firsthand the difference between the two legal systems. Some of the difference was due to Mexico's relative poverty and to the fact that many of these Americans had no experience with prison. But the part that Americans remember most relates to the intimidation, extortion, and, at times, torture—not by their fellow inmates, but by the police. Their friends' and parents' complaints prompted Washington to negotiate a treaty with Mexico in 1977 that permitted prisoners who received their final sentence to return to their native country to serve the remainder of their terms. Since then, 752 Americans have chosen to complete their sentences in the United States.[21] The treaty has worked well because it has kept both countries from becoming too involved in the legal system of the other.

Drugs have affected and corruption has infected both countries. To respond to the drugs and the corruption, the U.S. system has become more intrusive, with more wiretapping, surveillance, drug-testing, detentions, and even undercover police in high schools. While the Mexican government increased its surveillance and detentions, it has also been forced to be more open and to defend itself against charges of corruption and prisoner abuse. Drugs have therefore had the paradoxical effect of forcing the Mexican system to become slightly more open and the U.S. system to become more closed than they might otherwise have been.

Cooperation between the United States and Mexico has waxed and waned since drugs became a serious problem in the early 1970s. Twice— in 1969 and in 1985—the United States has closed the border as a device to pressure the Mexican government to take more seriously concerns about narcotics trafficking. Although Washington's actions were resented, "the shock treatment succeeded," according to a Mexican scholar, "and Operation Intercept was replaced by Operation Cooperation."[22] The cooperative programs developed by the United States and Mexico were among the most effective the United States has arranged with other countries.

According to K. Mathea Falco, who was Assistant Secretary of State for International Narcotics Matters from 1977 to 1981, the program's effectiveness was the result of a clear political commitment by Mexico, technical aid by the United States and a good relationship at the working level, and the Mexican government's administrative capacity and adaptability to changing strategies by opium growers and drug traffickers.[23] Mexico's backing of the program amounted to three to four times the U.S. support in terms of funds and thousands of times in terms of personnel. "The campaign was clearly a Mexican initiative." As a result of the success of the program, for about three years the drug supply was reduced, prices went up, and, naturally, consumption declined.

In the 1980s, however, the drug problem in the United States grew worse, Mexico's involvement increased, and the level of frustration among the American people steadily and ominously rose. In two surveys in March and May 1988 by *The New York Times,* Americans described drugs as the most important domestic and international issue. When asked whether it was more important for the government to stop drug smuggling than fight Communism in Central America, the public responded three to one in favor of the first.[24]

The drug issue is one of the few on which Democrats are viewed as tough; Republicans, however, are unwilling to concede machismo on any issue. The result is that each congressional debate on drugs leads to more law enforcement and stiffer penalties. The military have been drawn into assisting this effort. Enforcement must be part of any demand-control program, but other approaches should be considered.

Some states have decriminalized the possession of small amounts of marijuana, but the movement has stalled. This may be partly because the potency of marijuana is four times what it was a decade ago, and there has been a gradual decline in its use since 1979.[25] Charles Rangel, chairman of the House Select Committee on Narcotics Abuse and Control, believes that "decriminalization would suggest that marijuana is not harmful."[26] But one need not equate decriminalization with legalization and approval. No one would interpret the decriminalization of alcohol as approval for drinking.

There are two precedents for a more liberal policy to allow prescriptions for drugs like opium or cocaine, but neither—in Britain and Sweden—is encouraging. Since the 1920s, Britain has prescribed heroin for confessed addicts, and this seemed to work for a time, although a curiously underpublicized statistic suggested otherwise. The largest proportion of declared addicts became the doctors who administered the program. In the 1960s, there was a marked increase in the number of addicts, and the system broke down from abuse. Britain then changed the program to limit permissible prescriptions, end self-administration, increase the penalties for trafficking and possession, and give police greater powers to search for evidence of possession.[27]

Just when the old British system was breaking down, Sweden adopted it, and the results were more disastrous. One of the reasons for trying to liberalize the Swedish system was to eliminate the black market, but after the law was changed, illegal trafficking actually increased, as did the number of addicts. The reason is that society always has to set some rules on drugs—for example, to keep it from youth or prohibit certain particularly bad compounds. No matter how lenient the drug policy, the black market will always find an illegal crevice and fill it.[28]

Another objection to decriminalization is that even if state and federal laws prohibiting possession or selling of these drugs were changed, the United States is still a party to several international treaties barring their use. Indeed, Washington was the moving force behind these treaties. To ignore or violate these agreements would be contrary to U.S. law and to future American interests in achieving international cooperation on drugs or other matters.

Education might be a potent weapon against drugs, as it has proven against tobacco since the Surgeon General's report in 1964. Although education programs designed to discourage drug use have been short-changed in the past, their message still appears to be having an effect. Surveys of high school seniors show that in 1978 only one-third felt that regular use of marijuana posed "great risk." By 1985 seven out of ten had reached that conclusion.[29]

The spread of cocaine and the drug crack eclipsed previous concerns with marijuana, but by 1988, although the quantity of cocaine entering the country was still high, there were some signs that its use had begun to decline among youth. A disturbing side of the surveys is that the poor seem to be expanding their consumption of these drugs. Dr. David Musto, a professor of psychiatry at Yale University, noted that when the contemporary drug epidemic began in the mid-1960s, it took years for society to understand what was happening and for the government to respond.[30] Twenty years later, there are faint signs of a favorable response on the demand side of the equation.

An effective strategy needs to distinguish between the various drugs and to concentrate resources on the most dangerous. The fact that half of all drug arrests in 1985 were for marijuana possession suggests a misallocation of resources.[31] A replacement drug or a drug to ease a person's withdrawal could help addicts detach themselves from cocaine and heroin. Improved treatment centers and an expansion of Cocaine and Heroin Anonymous—modeled on the successful Alcoholics Anonymous—could be helpful. A number of students of drug abuse have suggested that cocaine and heroin addicts ought to be committed involuntarily to treatment centers for several weeks to help them withdraw from the drug. If the commitment is civil rather than criminal, and the centers are humane and effective, then people might be more willing to ask for treatment for their close friends and relatives.

A more intelligent assault on the link between drug abuse and crime is also needed. A study by the National Institute of Justice found that 50–75 percent of the men arrested in 1987 for serious crimes in twelve

major cities tested positive for the recent use of illicit drugs.[32] Programs
that focus on the treatment rather than either the incarceration or the
release of these individuals might have the triple effect of reducing crime,
prison overcrowding, and chronic drug use among a dangerous group.

A combination of innovative policies on enforcement, education, and
treatment can reduce the demand for drugs, but thus far, the effect has
been marginal. There is no panacea for ending the demand. In comparison, supplier nations like Mexico have demonstrated that they can reduce the production of drugs at relatively little cost in a short period.
That does not solve the American problem, since other suppliers fill the
shortfall, but at least the supplier nation can extract itself from the
morass. (The transshipment of cocaine through Mexico, however, is a
different and more difficult matter.)

A hard fact to face is that the drug war has assumed a life of its own
with consequences as adverse as the drugs it combats. The drug war is
the fastest consumer of scarce government expenditures; prisons are
overcrowded and the judicial system is overburdened by drug arrests and
drug-related crime; police are being suborned; drug money is tainting
local politicians—these are not the costs of drugs but of the war against
drugs. But these are insignificant compared with the costs borne by
several Latin American countries. Entire areas in Mexico, Colombia,
and Peru are run by drug warlords. The judiciary, not strong in any of
these countries, has been intimidated and paralyzed; the political system
has been compromised; corruption has spread and deepened; senior
officials in governments have been murdered; the sovereign power of
these states has eroded; recriminations have replaced diplomacy among
governments that ought to be cooperating to end the drug menace—
these are the war's casualties.

As the price of the war increases so, too, do the costs and the risks.
The benefits remain elusive. At some point, logic would argue for a
return to first questions. Is there a direct link between the use and the
abuse of drugs? If addiction is not inevitable, then shouldn't policy be
targeted to sever the tie between use and abuse? Is it possible that a
selective legalization strategy applied to certain drugs might increase
government control of the drug trade? Is it possible that alternatives to
prohibition might reduce rather than increase the number of drug users?
If the government controlled the sale, marketing, and distribution of
drugs, could that take the profit out of the drug trade and reduce the
costs of enforcement?

Despite all of the money that is pushing drugs or chasing drug merchants, these questions have simply not been answered adequately.[33] The
experience with alcohol argues for a sober and cautious approach. De-

criminalization ended the violence and corruption associated with the illicit liquor trade, but the human costs—deaths and accidents due to alcohol—today greatly exceed those related to drug abuse. The short answer to these questions is that there is no victory in the drug war, no escape from drug abuse, but there are probably many ways to improve the way society is managing the problem. The arrival of new leadership in the United States and Mexico offers an opportunity to search for joint answers to the original questions and to fashion a cooperative strategy for coping with the drug plague.

Unlike drugs, money moves in both directions, and most of the movement is legal. Money, like people, leaves one place for another either because it has been pushed or because it walks. The Naval Intelligence report suggested that Franklin Roosevelt was influencing some American capitalists to seek a better place for their money. Similarly, the decision by López Portillo to nationalize the banking industry obviously had a chilling effect on Mexican investors.

The United States will always attract investments from abroad, although the magnitude of the flow of money will depend on interest rates and other economic factors. To explain the peaks and valleys of Mexican capital flight, and to affect future capital movements, one needs to look at the U.S. demand and also to the Mexican government's policies and its people's anxieties. In the late 1970s and early 1980s, Mexican capital went north because the peso was overvalued and the government seemed distant or hostile to those Mexicans who had money but were not associated with government. In the first six months of 1987, about $1 billion per month returned to Mexico because the peso was deliberately undervalued, domestic credit was tight, and businessmen seemed to have more confidence in the government's economic policies.

Whenever Mexico allowed the peso to become overvalued—for example, by not keeping pace with inflation—Mexican capital fled north. When Mexico permitted the exchange rate to float to its correct level, money has returned or at least not left. In brief, the government's policies matter.

In a discussion of Latin America's debt problem in 1986, Howard Baker, former Senate Majority Leader and subsequently White House Chief of Staff, complained that about $100 billion in capital had fled Latin America. "Obviously," he said, "if a portion of that money could be repatriated not only to Mexico but to other countries of this hemisphere, it would improve Latin America's ability to solve its own problems." He then asked Jesús Silva Herzog, then Mexico's Minister of Finance, how this could be done. Silva Herzog answered:

278   DRUGS AND MONEY

There is no question that the return of capital to Latin America would be positive. There is no question that the only way to accomplish this objective is to achieve sound and stable growth patterns. . . . Banks could help by not trying to attract that capital, but, of course, we live in a free market system. . . . In the long term, the only way to reverse capital flight is to regain investor confidence, and such confidence is closely linked to an improvement in the economic conditions and in the economic and social prospects of the country.[34]

Restoring that confidence will be difficult. In September 1987, to discourage Mexicans on the border from keeping bank accounts in the United States, the government decided to allow Mexican banks to open accounts in dollars. Earlier, both Mexicans and foreign residents had been permitted to hold such accounts—until 1982, when the government abolished them and reimbursed the depositors at an exchange rate 40 percent below the free market rate. Given the previous experience, few felt that Mexicans would use the new accounts. "You'd have to be a fool to fall for this thing," said one businessman. "Last time, they just flat out stole our money, and I, for one, don't intend to let it happen to me again."[35]

The problem of a lack of confidence is so deep that it includes some in Mexico's political establishment. At a time when the government was roundly condemning wealthy Mexicans for capital flight, the PRI candidate for mayor of Ciudad Juárez said that he kept his money in dollars in El Paso banks because of his admiration for the United States.[36]

The choice for the United States is to find acceptable ways to help Mexico restore this confidence. Some Americans have argued that the United States should not help Mexico solve a debt crisis that Mexicans could solve themselves merely by bringing their money home. This argument is tempting but myopic. Mexico cannot fix its debt or the problem of capital flight easily or by itself any more than the United States can win the transnational war on drugs by itself.

The flight of capital and the smuggling of drugs are but two of hundreds of illegal or quasi-legal exchanges across the long border that separates the United States from Mexico. "Right now, we know there are two to three hundred palm cockatoos being held somewhere along the border, probably in Tijuana, just waiting for a chance to come over," said Jerome S. Smith of the U.S. Fish and Wildlife Service.[37]

Beside cockatoos, many other objects or commodities—illegal diet pills, guns, killer bees, cures for AIDS—lurk on one side of the border waiting for the moment to cross. If there is a demand on the U.S. side, there is a supply on the Mexican side. If there's a supply, there's a demand. It is an inescapable law, and neither side can rescind it. With more legal transactions and an income gap that is unlikely to narrow significantly if at all in the next two decades, there will be more problems, not fewer.

It sometimes seems that the United States and Mexico cannot help but convert every physical transaction into a moral allegory. To some, Mexico is the victim of U.S. demand or U.S. demands. Those Americans who believe that Mexico is trying to shift the blame for its own problems onto the shoulders of the United States also miss the point, which is that the 2,000-mile border makes absolute control of international transactions impossible. But to leap to the opposite conclusion and suggest that such transactions are beyond the ability of man to affect is equally mistaken.

Both illegal and legal transactions can be managed more effectively than they have been. A crucial first step is to recognize that unilateralism—acting as if a problem is solely a supply or a demand issue—is a prescription for less control, not more.

PART IV

—

NEW CONFIGURATIONS

7

THE BORDER

An American View

—

Robert A. Pastor

Long before reaching the line that separates the United States and Mexico, the traveler from either the north or the south may begin to suspect that he has already left the country. From the north, the traveler notices store signs that read: *Se Habla Español,* and chili is served more than grilled cheese. From the south, the signs announce: *English Is Spoken Here,* and baseball and basketball are played more than soccer.

A two-sided border area indicates to the traveler a region with an unusual identity. Chronic problems like drugs, capital flight, and stolen cars are the result of the border's porousness. However, the goods that cross the border, legally or illegally, are less important in shaping the region's identity than the people who remain on both sides.

Washington and Mexico City defend; the borders connect and sometimes conspire to protect each other from the arbitrary dictates of the capitals. This is because a Texan in El Paso and a Mexican in Ciudad Juárez view each other as less foreign than they do a Washington bureaucrat or a Mexico City official. People on the border have always found ways to ignore, circumvent, or smooth over the demands from their central governments.

The resulting configuration is difficult to interpret using the conventional language of geographical boundaries. On the U.S. side, politicians campaign in Spanish with background music provided by mariachi bands. Barrio leaders mobilize their communities to participate in rallies and vote for the right candidates. On the Mexican side, wealthy entrepreneurs, whose loyalty might be impugned by the PRI in Mexico City, run as PRI candidates using their own money to advertise their candidacies. The border is a political Cuisinart, combining Mexican-style organized demonstrations and American-style advertising for candidates who run as individuals rather than as party representatives.

One measure of the uniqueness of the border is that there is little agreement as to what it is, beyond the simple definition of a boundary between two sovereign nations. Some view it as connecting the two sides; others, as separating them. Historian Theodore S. Beardsley, Jr., offered an eclectic compromise, defining the border as "a political division that artificially bisects a single cultural unit."[1] Roger P. Brandemeuhl, a former Border Patrol chief, describes it more graphically, with the frustration of a person who tried but failed to monitor it for several decades. To him, the border was "a monster, growing, feeding on itself."[2]

If the border connects, then how far inland does it extend? A narrow definition includes those *municipios* and counties that touch the boundary on either side, but Joel Garreau, in *The Nine Nations of North America,* describes the area as extending north as far as Houston, Santa Fe, and Sacramento and south below Monterrey and Baja California.[3]

This wider definition generates excitement in a few and anxiety among many. Some imagine a new cultural-political entity that unites Mexicans and Americans. To Garreau, a chronicler of this vision, a new nation called MexAmerica is emerging in the land between Houston and Los Angeles in the north, and Monterrey and Baja California in the south. U.S. businessmen see this new entity as a giant free zone where they can sell goods and buy labor without paying tariffs or taxes. Mexican irredentists regard the "new land" as a chance to recapture the U.S. Southwest for the Spanish language and Mexican culture.

Partly in response to these two visions, disquieting sounds are heard louder and more frequently than sanguine comments. Some in the United States worry about Montezuma's real revenge—that the Southwest is slowly being reabsorbed as the thirty-second state of Mexico. Half in jest, half in warning, these anxious voices recount the story of the Sioux chief who visited Washington in the 1930s and told the Vice President: "Let me give you a little advice. Be careful of your immigration laws. We were careless with ours." Similarly, some in Mexico worry that the northern part of the country will become the fifty-first state of the United States.

The fears are real, but not well founded. Regardless of how one defines the border, there is no obscuring the fact that the two sides are different. Sovereignty is not in jeopardy. Neither nation will tolerate a loss of territory or even a blurring of the boundary.

A better place to begin is to distinguish between political division and cultural-economic connections and between a narrow and a wider definition of the border. The narrow, geographical boundary is composed of the fourteen twin cities that interact culturally and economically on both sides of a political line that divides the two nations. The wider, cultural-economic region or borderland includes the bustling, dynamic states on both sides.

The narrow border can be drawn easily on the map as a zone about twenty miles wide—ten miles on each side—and the length of the border. Trying to draw the wider region on a map misses the point: it is not an entity about to declare its independence, but rather an area in which cultures, attitudes, and markets are mixing and assuming new forms. The states of Texas, Nuevo León, California, and Chihuahua can be included within this wider area, even though portions of Texas are as redneck and Anglo as Alabama and barrios in Nuevo León are indistinguishable from those in Mexico City or Oaxaca.

A second useful point of departure is that while both sides of the border are different, they are less different from each other than they are from the rest of their countries. New Mexico and Sonora have more in common—culturally, geographically, and economically—than New Mexico has with Pennsylvania or Sonora has with Jalisco. For this and other reasons, both sides of the border are moving toward the other and away from the capitals of their countries.

Hostility from either capital will only draw the two sides closer. But even this will not foster the emergence of a new political entity, which is feared by the capitals and hoped for by the one-worlders. More likely, they will draw closer socially and economically, while Washington largely ignores the border issues raised by its residents and Mexico City maintains a firm grip on its border's politics.

The character of the United States was shaped by its first Anglo-Saxon Protestant settlers, who believed in self-government and farmed relatively small plots of land. Many arrived in the New World seeking the freedom to worship, but their tolerance did not extend to the Indians. The Native Americans who survived the wars went west, anticipating Horace Greeley's advice. In contrast, Spanish Catholics came to Mexico and South America, and they conquered—not the land, but several of the world's most advanced civilizations.

By a convoluted irony, the North American settlers were able to create a more equal and democratic society by killing the Indians or pushing them west, whereas the settlers in Mexico developed a more stratified, authoritarian system by replacing the leaders of a stationary civilization. The Spanish used the Indians to build magnificent palaces and extract great wealth for the motherland. The use of slaves in the South resulted in a similar social structure, but most of the other new Americans relied on themselves and got off to a slower but, as it turned out, a steadier start.

Octavio Paz has described how these two points of departure shaped such different political cultures in the United States and Mexico. This cultural explanation helps to show why the two governments approach problems so differently, but it assumes that both countries are monolithic, which is not the case. Visitors soon realize that the two capitals are islands, not the centers of the two countries. In the United States, politicians strike a resonant chord in the country when they campaign against Washington for being out of touch with the nation. Mexico City is Washington with New York and Chicago included. It therefore should come as no surprise that some Mexicans who live outside the capital resent those who live within it for all the reasons that Main Street Americans resent Wall Street and Pennsylvania Avenue—for deciding their fate without asking.

No region resents an old, established center of power more than one that is young, growing, and seeking recognition as the region of the future. In the United States, that region is the Sunbelt, especially the Southwest, and in Mexico, the *norteños* feel most alienated from the center and proud of their success. The people in these two regions believe their approach is different from the rest of their countrymen. Their outlook is shaped by a similar geography and a shared history.[4]

The region contains forbidding deserts, rich but rugged mountains of minerals, and vast, barren expanses that would require twentieth-century technology to transform them into verdant farms and ample grazing land. Borders have no place in Nature's design. The contours of the mountains, land, and rivers extend north into Colorado and south to Monterrey. The Rio Grande etched a small cut in the landscape and even that stopped about two-thirds of the way from the Gulf of Mexico to the Pacific. The topography, in brief, is one. The natural division between the two countries is not at the border.

At the time of the conquest, the area was unsettled, but several Indian tribes hunted game and fought each other across small parts of the territory. In the center of Mexico, the Spanish built cities on the backs of the Aztecs and Mayans, but they failed to colonize or settle the northern area because the Apaches, Navajos, and Comanches were not like the advanced civilizations. These primitive tribes would not surrender, and the Spanish judged that the price of subduing them was too high.

Spain prohibited trade between Mexico and the English settlers who were moving west across North America, but when Mexico became independent in 1821, western trappers took advantage of the change to trade at Santa Fe and Taos.[5] After the war between Mexico and the United States, the border was officially established, but neither government asserted itself in the region because of internal divisions. The few settlers who lived or traded on the border faced constant Indian raids, but, according to one scholar, "the greatest obstacle" to development was the different economic policies of the two governments.[6] At this time, the United States had few taxes and trivial tariffs on its southern border, whereas Mexico maintained high taxes and tariffs. This difference induced many Mexicans living on the border either to settle in the United States or to smuggle American or European goods—which could be shipped through the United States duty-free—into Mexico. With Mexico City distracted by political unrest, the governor of Tamaulipas decided to try to stop the emigration and the contraband by proclaiming a free zone from the border to twelve and a half miles within his state.

Like many one-sided "solutions" on the border, the free zone merely exported the problem to the other side. With Mexican tariffs eliminated, smugglers, who had previously paid off Mexican customs agents to bring American goods into Mexico without paying a duty, soon shifted to bribing U.S. customs officials. The duty-free zone invigorated Tamaulipas's border towns and weakened the U.S. side. The governors of several other Mexican states also instituted free zones, and during the Civil War, Matamoros became one of the busiest international trading centers in the world. The South exported its cotton through Matamoros and imported European arms and supplies. Subsequently, despite vigorous protests by the United States, the Mexican government declared the entire border a free zone.[7]

After the war, the fear of Indian raids replaced the more mundane problems of duties and bribes. In 1877, President Rutherford B. Hayes instructed his generals on the border to "invite cooperation" from the Mexican army, but if cooperation was not forthcoming, to pursue the Indians into Mexico. The Mexican government was furious when the directive was disclosed and orders were dispatched to its generals on the border to repel any incursion. But the U.S. and Mexican generals overlooked the obtrusive instructions and privately cooperated with one another. By 1882, however, Apache raids so terrorized border settlements that the two governments agreed informally to allow troops of either country to cross the border in hot pursuit.[8]

.   .   .

The basis for the future relationship was established in the last decades of the nineteenth century when railroads connected central Mexico to the northern border and from there to the extensive rail grid that covered much of the United States. People and goods began to move more rapidly and in greater quantities, fundamentally changing relationships between the central governments and the states and between labor and capital.

Peasants left impoverished villages by train in search of jobs either in Mexico's cities or in the United States. More pertinent, the railroads caused Mexico's northern states to look north to a more accessible and lucrative market rather than south to the center of their country. Cattle ranching spread and became more modernized in the Southwest of the United States and in northern Mexico. The internationalization of trade, finance, mining, and agriculture, according to Steven Sanderson, "connected the Mexican North with the U.S. Southwest . . . leaving earlier, fragile market links with the central and southern regions of the country to atrophy."[9]

As the two economies became more intertwined, U.S. policies exerted a more direct effect on the region. For example, the United States raised the duty on imported bulk minerals in 1890, and this created a new industry for refined metals near Monterrey. Soon the city became a center of mining and agriculture in the north, offering relatively higher wages and attracting labor.

In 1902, the narrower border area was still "little more than an unpopulated desert," according to Raul Fernandez,[10] but the economies of the American Southwest and the Mexican north had already begun to develop in complementary patterns and to connect. Massive investment in the region's infrastructure quickened the pace of internal development and international transactions. At the turn of the century, the United States established the Bureau of Reclamation, which built dams and developed extensive irrigation projects. These projects stopped the recurring floods and drought, provided the region with cheap energy and a reliable water supply, and left a solid foundation for development.

World War II grabbed the border at its two ends and pulled the region's economy into a new age. Washington injected huge amounts of money into defense facilities in San Diego and El Paso. No longer just a point of transit, the region became a magnet for labor. The U.S. and Mexican governments negotiated a labor agreement—the "bracero" program—which brought thousands of Mexicans north. Soon the border towns began to sprout like fast-growing trees, although some Mexicans resented that the growth of some towns, like Tijuana, depended upon their being watered regularly by American servicemen.

After the war, Mexico turned its attention and some resources to its north. It increased government investment in agriculture, and 75 percent of that went for irrigation projects, the vast majority being in the north.[11] The new farms in northern Mexico were large and modern, much like those on the other side. Railroads connected the two neighboring regions, and twentieth-century technology transformed a desert wasteland into a productive agricultural economy, which further separated northern Mexico from the rest of the country.

The United States ended the bracero program in 1964, but both governments acted independently to offset Mexico's loss of jobs. Washington encouraged businessmen to invest in Mexico and reexport to the United States. Using a provision of the U.S. trade law, companies would only have to pay a duty on the value-added component (the cost of Mexican labor) of the product. In order to expand jobs in the region for the returning braceros and others, Mexico decided in 1965 to modify its foreign investment laws to permit American firms to establish *maquiladoras* on the Mexican side of the border. In addition to tourism and trade, the *maquiladora* program laid the foundation for an industrial base. Migrants from Mexico's interior, who had passed through Mexico's border towns on their way to the United States, began to stay. Other Mexicans sought work there.

In the 1980s, *maquiladoras* became an important source of jobs, income, and foreign exchange. While the Mexican economy declined by 4 percent in 1986, the number of *maquiladoras* increased by 25 percent and by the end of the year employed 268,400 workers. Originally, most of the workers were young women and all the plants were on the border, but through a variety of incentives, the percentage of male workers has steadily increased, from 23 percent in 1985 to 32.9 percent in 1986, and by 1987, 15 percent of the plants were in the interior.[12] Initially, U.S. firms did not buy any Mexican components and were not permitted to sell their products locally, but the American Chamber of Commerce in Mexico City estimated that by 1987, U.S. companies had purchased nearly $300 million worth of local parts and were beginning to sell up to 20 percent of their products locally.

Turnover of local personnel has always been a major problem for *maquiladoras* as workers left their jobs for higher wages across the border. Recently, however, U.S. firms have been able to increase the stability of the work force by investing in training and motivation programs. Several companies have also assisted higher education in the Mexican border states. Chihuahua, for example, leads the nation with five technological schools. Tamaulipas is second with four.[13]

The *maquiladoras* have become the center of Mexico's border economy with an astonishing multiplier effect. One study of the workers in Ciudad Juárez, the *"maquiladora* capital," showed that each worker supported seven other people, and one-third of all households in the city received income from them.[14] Joseph Grunwald and Kenneth Flamm conducted a long-term study of the nature and distribution of benefits to the United States as a result of the *maquiladoras.* They concluded: "U.S. consumers benefit from lower costs of a growing volume of traded goods, U.S. producers benefit from broader markets for their products, and U.S. workers benefit from reduced foreign immigration."[15] The two authors attribute the loss of U.S. jobs to the normal competition of international trade. Although assembly operations might accelerate the process of industrial restructuring, they believe the long-term consequences will be beneficial.

Originally, there were few "twin plants" on the U.S. side of the border, but the numbers have recently increased, and in El Paso, Texas, one of five jobs today is tied to the *maquiladoras.* [16] U.S. border towns have benefited in other ways. Approximately 40–60 percent of the wages earned on the Mexican side have been used to purchase goods in the United States.[17] Tourism has also gained from the more solid economic base provided by manufacturing. In 1985, for example, Mexican tourists accounted for 17 percent of total spending by foreign visitors to the United States, and over half was spent at the border.[18] In Laredo, Texas, in 1982, Mexicans bought 80 percent of the goods sold by the city's retailers, accounting for half of the municipal government's revenues via the sales tax.[19] The peso devaluations led to a reduction in both sales and city services.

San Diego's growth has also depended partly on Mexico's. In 1976, Mexican citizens spent about $200 million in San Diego, and over 90 percent of the $615 million of exports passing through the city was destined for Mexico.[20] In brief, while the U.S. side is more affluent, it is not free of the dependence that characterizes the Mexican view of the relationship.

The population on the border is quite small compared with the total population of the two countries, but it has been growing at a faster rate than that of either country. Between 1970 and 1980, the population on the U.S. side grew almost four times faster than the rest of the nation— 40.7 percent for the border as compared with 11.4 percent for the nation.[21] This was part of a broader shift in U.S. population to the Sunbelt. The movement accelerated in the 1960s and 1970s, and although it seemed to slow in the early 1980s, recent statistics show the opposite—from 1980 to

1986, the Sunbelt's population increased at ten times the rate of that of the Northeast and Midwest.[22] By 1986, six of the ten most populous U.S. cities were in the Southwest.[23]

At the same time, the Mexican population was moving north. Tijuana grew faster than even Mexico City, and the entire border area expanded at a more rapid pace than any other region with the exception of the capital. Migration to the area was such that by 1970 almost one-third of the residents of the three largest border cities were migrants.[24] By 1970, Tijuana, Ciudad Juárez, and Mexicali ranked among Mexico's ten largest cities.[25] Between 1950 and 1980, the population of thirteen Mexican cities on the border increased 355 percent.[26]

The population explosion in the U.S. Southwest was the result mostly of migration, arriving from both the South and the North. Combined with the relatively higher fertility rate for Mexican-Americans, the result was an increasing homogenization on both sides of the border. In 1978, nearly 60 percent of the population of El Paso and 85 percent of that of Laredo were of Mexican origin.[27] The number of Mexican-Americans residing in the U.S. border region in 1980 amounted to 1.4 million, or 35.6 percent of the total.[28] For the entire Southwest—California, Texas, New Mexico, Arizona, and Colorado—the proportion of Hispanic legal residents nearly doubled between 1960 and 1980, from 11.8 percent of the total to 20 percent.[29] The trend is clearest in the school-age population. In Los Angeles, the second-largest school district in the United States, the ratio of Anglo to Mexican-American students reversed in just two decades: from 56 percent Anglo and 19 percent Hispanic (almost all Mexican-American) in 1966 to 18 percent Anglo and 56 percent Hispanic in 1986.[30]

The differences in income levels reveal a similar pattern. The U.S. side of the border (except for the San Diego area) is poorer on average than the rest of the United States, but richer than the Mexican side. The Mexican side is affluent by Mexican standards.[31] The minimum wage in *maquiladora* plants is considerably higher than in the rest of the country, but a small fraction of the wages on the U.S. side.[32] With some workers receiving more in one hour on the U.S. side than what they would receive in a day on the Mexican side, it is not surprising that some Mexicans stay on the border only long enough to get across.

The population on the U.S. side is younger, less educated, and poorer than the national average, but it is still older, better educated, and richer than the Mexican side. At the same time, the population on the Mexican side is older, better educated, and much better off than the Mexican national average. In brief, as one approaches the border, one begins to notice a convergence. The two regions are much closer in levels of income, education, and development than are the rest of their countries. Their people have more contact, and indeed, an increasing proportion come from Mexico.

Nevertheless, one should not exaggerate the similarity or the unity. The economic gap is wider than that between any two other nations in the world that share a border. The Los Angeles area alone produced 30 percent more goods and services in 1986 than the entire country of Mexico.[33] And one can see and smell the difference in the level of development between the two sides even before one leaves the customs facilities. Comparing Tijuana and San Diego, Richard Rodriguez simply asserted they "are not in the same historical time zone."[34]

But the border is not a glittering Trump Tower alongside a cardboard hovel. With certain exceptions, the two sides look much more like each other than they look like the rest of their countries.

Large-scale migration from Mexico in the 1980s has reshaped the visage of the Southwest. But even before the new immigrants arrived, geography, a shared history, and a congruent pattern of economic development molded similar attitudes on the border. Both sides exhibit a defiant assertiveness that seems directed at their capitals as much as at the rugged terrain. Beneath this regional pride lies a variety of southwestern personalities.

Texas and California sit like two behemoths on the flanks of the border with personalities as fully developed as nation-states. Texas, the only country ever to become a state in the Union, remains the most independent-minded state. Whether it is cattle, cotton, or football, a Texan boasts that his is the biggest and the best. In *Texas,* James Michener's novel, one of the characters proudly recommends that the state adopt a new official song to honor "the two noblest aspects of our culture, football and religion." The song: "Drop-Kick Me, Jesus, Through the Goal Posts of Life."[35]

The population of Texas has soared from fewer than 4 million in 1910 to more than 16.5 million in 1985. A study by the Population Reference Bureau (PRB) projected that Texas would overtake New York to become the second most populous state in 1990. Texas is used to growing, but it is not accustomed to the kinds of changes that follow from the new population growth. Over half of all Mexicans resident in the state migrated there since 1970, and by 1985, they made up more than one-fifth of the state's population.[36] The PRB study projected that Anglo children will cease being the majority before the turn of the century, and by 2015, young Hispanics will equal Anglos in numbers.

Politics has adjusted slowly to these demographic shifts, but there are signs of change. These include the election of Mexican-American leaders like Henry Cisneros, mayor of San Antonio, and a growing appreciation of Mexico by conservatives like Senator Phil Gramm, who has proposed a number of economic policies to improve bilateral relations. Moreover, on the border, business and political leaders are working closer with their counterparts.

Sandwiched between Texas and California are Arizona and New Mexico, sparse in population, but with a Hispanic and Indian heritage. The entry of the two states into the Union was blocked in 1903 because a leading senator toured the two territories and concluded that few New Mexicans spoke English and Arizona was dominated by a handful of rich men. Both states have been influenced by the land, their small population, and an affinity with Mexico. "Aping the manners, customs, and dress of Easterners" is a reason for ridicule.[37]

If the U.S.-Mexican region ever adopts a personality, it will probably be California's. The most populous state with 25 million people, California already contains about half of all the Mexicans in the United States. Instead of heralding the best and the biggest, a Californian is comfortable that his state is on the cutting edge of technology and culture. Experimenting with new gadgets and life forms, Californians assume these will be adopted eventually by the rest of the country. "What California is today," writes poet Richard Armour, "the rest will be tomorrow."

As in Texas, the most important change in California has been human. Between 1970 and 1980, Hispanics, blacks, and Asians increased from 22 percent of the total population to 33 percent, with Hispanics (80 percent of whom were Mexicans) accounting for one-fifth of the total by 1980.[38] Conservative projections for California are that by 2010, Anglos will account for less than half of the population and Hispanics for a third.[39]

In California, the races and cultures have been stirred together more than in any other state. The largest port of entry for new immigrants, with 85 percent coming from Latin America and Asia, California may very well have a copper-colored future. The Los Angeles area, which contains 60 percent of the state's population, has attracted more Mexicans than any other city besides Mexico City. Instead of "Tex-Mex," a harsh-sounding phrase which conjures an image of foods clashing on a cafeteria plate, the Californian personality is more relaxed and fluid. It is embodied by the movie comic Cheech Marin, who weaves the humor and the humanity of two cultures without damaging or offending anyone. He is stateless, but aimless only about half the time.

California's pursuit of the material—even in its "spiritual" quests like est or fundamentalism—affects the new immigrants as it did a previous generation from Oklahoma. The values are transmitted as fast as cable television, and the border does not slow the transmission. Both sides watch the same sports and movies, sing the latest songs, eat similar food. If discrimination diminishes and immigration continues, California could become the first "Third World" high-tech country. This personality could be a compelling adhesive joining those in northern Mexico and those in the Southwest.

To the people in the Southwest, Washington is a distant, alien government, although this view has never inhibited the region's leaders from seeking federal grants and protection. As one Southwesterner wrote, the region has consistently "elected representatives to Washington who talk individualism while voting for the expenditure of more and yet more federal funds for Southwestern projects."[40] Barry Goldwater, Republican presidential candidate in 1964 and Arizona's senator from 1953 to 1987, epitomized the dualism in his advocacy of less government and his dogged pursuit of federal aid for state projects.

In the gap between the perception and the reality of the role of government in the region's development, Southwesterners have much in common with northern Mexicans. Both tend to attribute their success to the free market, but it was due initially to government investment, and their standard of living has been maintained partly by government spending. The U.S. government share of employment in the border states was 38 percent in 1969 and 33 percent in 1976, whereas for the country as a whole, it was 20 percent in both years.[41]

Like the Southwesterners, the *norteños* consider themselves on the frontier of their nation's economy and chafe over the influence of the capital on their affairs. Jesús González Schmal, a leader of the PAN, described the political implications of this posture: "The region is more economically independent and many people have visited the United States [where they] see highways, schools, and hospitals, and most importantly, they see true democracy and respected elections."[42]

During Christmastime in 1984, thousands of PAN supporters demonstrated against electoral fraud in the border town of Piedras Negras. When police fired tear gas, they marched to the bridge across the Rio Grande and blocked it. The same tactic was used by the PAN to protest electoral fraud in subsequent years in Ciudad Juárez and other border towns in order to attract the attention of the American media and of the United States.[43] The *norteños* are proud of their role in igniting the revolution that changed Mexico. Northern leaders conspired in San Antonio and Los Angeles and attracted support for the Revolution as they rode south to Mexico City. Today, some in the north suggest that future change in Mexico will follow a similar path.

. . .

When the celebration of mutual prosperity is over, someone has to clean up. Given the rapid growth of the region, disposing of the garbage is no trivial problem. Except for the Colorado River, most of the rivers that cross the border west of El Paso pick up sewage in Mexico and empty it in the United States. Tijuana, for example, pipes 13 million gallons of raw sewage a day to San Diego's Point Loma waste-treatment plant as part of an agreement, but it also deposits 7 million gallons near the border where currents take it to San Diego's beaches. When a sewer line broke in 1984, pouring an additional 5 million gallons of sewage into the Tijuana River, which carried it to its neighbor, the San Diego mayor sounded the alarm: "This is a foreign invasion, even if the problem is sewage and not soldiers."

Mexico accepted its responsibility, but admitted it simply did not have the funds to clean up its garbage according to U.S. standards. The Reagan administration, with its own budgetary problems, rejected a proposal offered by the binational International Boundary and Water Commission (IBWC) whereby Mexico would contribute the money it would normally pay for a sewage plant in Mexico and the United States would make up the difference to have such a plant installed in California. In November 1985, Mexico decided to go ahead with "a Mexican solution," building a sewage-treatment facility itself about six miles from the border. The plant was completed in February 1987 and is expected to cope with the problem for a few years.

When the local area is the border, issues of sanitation, air or water pollution, public health, bridge maintenance, or law enforcement are international problems. Border towns and sometimes the representatives of federal agencies on both sides have managed these issues informally, trying not to involve the central governments. In a report on border management, the State Department acknowledged that "there is often the perception along the border that bureaucrats in the two capital cities are out of touch, disinterested, or not understanding of border matters." State viewed the major impediment to greater cooperation as "the Mexican government's efforts to preserve the Mexican character of its border region and to tie it more firmly to the interior."[44]

In fact, a multitude of mechanisms address every conceivable border issue. The most effective organization is the International Boundary and Water Commission, originally established in 1889. In 1933, the IBWC's mandate was expanded to mark and maintain the boundary and construct and maintain conservation and flood-control projects. The IBWC's success is due to its precise mandate and its expert technical leadership. Although the foreign offices—and sometimes the legislatures—of both countries approve the projects, IBWC engineers have considerable freedom to pursue their work.

Much less useful have been the numerous bilateral border commissions that have been established by the two governments, beginning with the U.S.-Mexico Commission for Border Development and Friendship (CODAF), established in 1966, and continuing through the Reagan administration's Border Relations Action Group (BRAG). These committees have encouraged consultations on various issues, but they have the disadvantage of extracting issues from their local context, where they are often more manageable.

Parallel to these federal efforts have been a host of cross-border cooperative efforts, including state-to-state commissions, sister-city organizations, local voluntary associations (like the Rotary Clubs), region-wide organizations (like the Organization of U.S. Border Cities and Counties, the U.S.-Mexico Border Health Association, or the Association of Borderlands Scholars), and cross-border business associations.[45] There is, in brief, a great deal of activity and problem-solving across the border at the local, state, and federal levels. These relationships are not always effective at solving the border's problems, but, by and large, technical commissions like the IBWC and local communities are better at managing these issues than are distant federal bureaucrats.

Cooperation between the American Southwest and the Mexican north is less of an issue in Washington because of a decentralized federal system than it is in Mexico because their political system is highly centralized, the opposition is strong in the north, and the idea being propagated by the north—free elections—is one that could undermine the PRI's grip. Indeed, the fears in Mexico City are less that the north could become a fifty-first American state than that it could begin a movement that could lead to instability and the PRI's defeat. These fears are not without some basis: northern Mexico does not want to secede or join the United States, but it also does not want to be instructed by Mexico City.

The southwestern United States has traditionally looked at Washington with a mixture of distance and disdain, but almost never with fear. If anything, the Southwest has more influence on Washington than vice versa. Borrowing a tactic often used by Mexico, the Southwest often complains that Washington imposes solutions without understanding its problems. Then it tells Washington what to do.

Offering a southwestern view of U.S.-Mexican relations, Peter Flawn, the president of the University of Texas, lectured policymakers in Washington for being "culturally insensitive and commonly ignorant of Mexican traditions and values." Then he told the policymakers what they should do to improve the relationship: Washington should give more attention to Mexico and coordinate its policy more effectively.[46]

Beginning in the last decade of the nineteenth century and picking up speed over the years, a land that had been unsettled and unchanged since creation suddenly experienced a surge, a burst of energy and motion. Development of the towns on both sides of the border occurred as if on a seesaw, with one side ascending because of lower tariffs while the other declined. During World War II, the border area began to develop—first due to the military installations, then because of tourism, trade, and manufacturing.

From 1954, for twenty-two years, the border benefited from the fixed exchange rate that connected the peso with the dollar. But during that time, Mexico's peso gradually became overvalued. When Mexico finally devalued in 1976, the peso dropped sharply, and the area that felt the shock most immediately, intensely, and adversely was the border. In this case, U.S. goods became prohibitively expensive, and Mexicans stopped buying. Unemployment increased on the U.S. side, as tourism declined and hotels remained empty. The economic effect was so severe that several counties qualified to receive federal economic disaster aid.[47] The Mexican side benefited, as Americans crossed the border to fill their cars with cheaper gas and U.S. tourists discovered how far their dollars took them.

Within a year, however, the seesaw began to swing back. The Mexican economy was invigorated by oil discoveries, and as the peso increased in value, Mexican consumers went north again. Unfortunately, just as before, the Mexican government was reluctant to permit the peso to devalue gradually, and so when oil prices plummeted in 1982, and Mexico's huge debts came due, the peso fell more steeply than six years before, losing half of its value in one month. The subsequent shocks of devaluations practically incapacitated the U.S. border areas. Unemployment in the major Texas border cities increased by more than 50 percent, from an average of about 10 percent.[48] As the Mexican nation grew poorer, its border grew richer; the converse held for the United States. The stronger the dollar became vis-à-vis the peso, the more an American could buy in Mexico, and the less he would spend on the U.S. side. Shopping malls that were planned for the United States were built in Mexico.

Volatile exchange rates—the formula for trading dollars for pesos— have forced the border to accept a seesaw of alternating depression and prosperity in which one side has profited at the expense of the other. Both sides should recognize their common interests in reducing the volatility in the economic relationship and establish a fund to dampen the adverse effect of future swings of the peso pendulum. The side that has the advantage could transfer some of its added revenue—for example, through a sales tax—to the side that has lost. The funds could pass from one internal revenue service to the other, and back again, as required.

Clues to the future of the border can be found in its enduring landmarks and the words its residents use to describe them. The same river that divides two-thirds of the border is called the Rio Grande by Americans and the Rio Bravo by Mexicans. The Sierra Nevadas do not stop at the border, but at that point the Mexicans call the range the Sierra Madre Occidental. The American and the Mexican names are different, but both are Spanish.

The people are drawn together by the land, a common history, an independent and sometimes rebellious spirit, language, and a practical understanding of the benefits of cooperation. One can view the two sides of the border facing each other like Siamese twins connected at the nose, but that metaphor ignores the more important bonds connecting the American Southwest and the Mexican north. The border traffic is awesome, but more significant is the emergence of a new cultural, economic, and attitudinal pattern. A cross-border economy is taking shape that is capitalistic and mobile. A new pigment and culture is visible: it contains images of Third World social realism but these are less of a guerrilla camp than of fashionable "camp"—more Cheech Marin than Che Guevara.

The new regional perspective does not add up to a new region. The border still divides, and the north is more concerned about control and regulation of labor, drugs, and sewage, while the south is more interested in access to water and the northern market. Yet the faces on both sides are looking more alike and, certainly, they are more like each other than either is like its nation. Of greater significance, however, is not today's face, but tomorrow's. The trend is unmistakable: both sides are growing faster than the two countries as a whole and are becoming more similar in their development, culture, attitudes, and vulnerability. These changes will not threaten sovereignty except by ignoring it.

A Mexican View

Jorge G. Castañeda

For young Americans from the San Diego area over fourteen or fifteen but under twenty-one, a good time on Friday or Saturday night has a very precise meaning. It is symbolized by something known as a "Tequila Popper," the Mexican version of the "Tequila Slammer." It probably could have been invented only in "TeeJay," or Tijuana, which has been catering to American tastes in entertainment and debauchery for over fifty years. In the city where Margarita Cansino became Rita Hayworth, and where nearly half the female adult population was employed in prostitution during World War II, imagination and audacity in making a dollar are strong suits.

A Tequila Popper consists of a shot glass of tequila mixed with a small dose of 7-Up. The potion, devised and prized for its effervescent properties, is slammed down one's throat by a specialized bartender who immediately proceeds to place an armlock on the lucky customer's jaw. He then literally tries to pry young American heads off their necks through rapid, jerky lateral movements. The effect is somewhere between drowning, feeling very drunk very rapidly, and whiplash. The youngsters who cross the border by the thousands every weekend thrive on it. For it is the first, cheap ($1.25) step in a long night of alcoholic abandon. More important, it cannot be done at home: age limits, the price of a drink, and local customs do not permit.

The U.S.-Mexican border is far more than a Tequila Popper, of course, and its complexities, paradoxes, and tragedies go beyond thousands of young Americans getting stone drunk on the same streets where their fathers or grandparents found the illicit alcohol, sex, and gambling unavailable at home. But the endless "spring break" that the adolescents of San Diego County enjoy south of the demarcation line is illustrative of trends the border permits and encourages.

The border is a privileged whirlpool, formed by the potent undercurrents sweeping U.S.-Mexican relations away in many new directions. If those relations are the result of powerful forces moving in opposite ways, the border is the vortex where they converge. This is where Mexican nationalism meets economic integration, where elementary school textbooks confront cross-border education, television, customs, and conveniences. Here American hunger for Mexican labor, capital (flight), and purchasing power meets the United States' classical insecurity and ambivalence over immigration.

The border is also a series of myths, preferably dispelled. The common boundary, while long and winding, is not heavily inhabited, either in absolute terms or in relation to each nation's overall population. Up-to-date, reliable Mexican figures are hard to come by: the 1980 Census is nearly ten years old. Moreover, the enormous difficulty in estimating or even counting the number of inhabitants who actually reside in the border zone, as opposed to those who are just passing through, makes any statistic questionable.

Recent calculations, based on surveys and extrapolations in several Mexican border cities, indicate that the total population of the thirty-eight border *municipios* (roughly the equivalent of American counties) is approximately 3.9 million. In relation to the larger communities, these studies suggest, previous estimates of the number of stationary inhabitants in cities such as Tijuana and Ciudad Juárez were exaggerated. The figure of nearly two million people for Tijuana, often quoted in American articles, appears far too high.[1] The 1980 figure for the twenty-five counties bordering Mexico on the U.S. side was 4,009,179, if one includes San Diego County, which partly adjoins the border. At most, then, not more than eight million people live together in the binational border region, well under 3 percent of the total combined population of both nations. Although the "border mentality" and perhaps even the border area can be considered to extend south into Mexico to include many of the northern states of the country, this is more a psychological and historical element than an economic one.

In fact, the idea of a border region itself is to a considerable extent a fallacy. Indeed, there are only four truly large communities on the Mexican side, the other twenty or so being small and medium-sized towns ranging in population from 1,400 for Hidalgo, Coahuila, opposite Webb County in Texas, to Reynosa, Tamaulipas, across the line from McAllen, with an estimated 281,000 inhabitants in 1987. The four cities of Tijuana, Mexicali, Ciudad Juárez, and Matamoros make up 75 percent of the southern frontier's population, while San Diego, El Paso, and Tucson include more than 70 percent of the total number of U.S. border area dwellers. And the only two significant cross-border or binational communities, where the cities on each side have similar dimensions, are Tijuana–San Diego and Ciudad Juárez–El Paso.

While the border may not be a never-ending conurbation stretching from the Pacific to the Gulf of Mexico, it is nonetheless a richly diverse extension. It has often been divided in two: the rich border and the poor one, the separation coming in El Paso–Ciudad Juárez, where the abstract line becomes a river. On the U.S. as well as the Mexican side, the border is rich and prosperous to the west of Ciudad Juárez–El Paso and relatively poor to the east. In California, San Diego and Imperial counties— together with Orange County just to the north—are among the most affluent zones in the entire United States and consequently in the world. But South Texas or "the Valley," as the region along the easternmost banks of the Rio Grande (Rio Bravo in Mexico) is known, has traditionally been one of the poorer areas in the United States and is presently one of the most depressed.

Similarly, Tijuana, Mexicali, and Ciudad Juárez are among Mexico's most thriving cities, where unemployment is nearly nonexistent, education and health-care levels high, and investment and jobs constantly growing. But the same cannot be said for the eastern communities, from Ciudad Acuña in Coahuila to the sea: these are poorer, more depressed regions. The problems the west faces have little in common with those of the east; the former are the travails of prosperity, the latter of destitution, although in comparison with the rest of Mexico, the eastern border is well off. The border suffers not only from a north-south division; it is also split along an east-west axis.

The absence of economic homogeneity is not the only factor which questions the ultimate validity of the notion of a border region. Enormous differences exist with regard to the way in which different border communities on both sides get along. Between Matamoros and Brownsville—or more broadly among the towns in the Valley—relations are in general quite good, whether involving the respective authorities, business sectors, or citizens at large. Most local townspeople believe the explanation lies in the small size of their communities on both sides and the Mexican origin of nearly every inhabitant of the area. Officials know each other and often meet socially; politicians, judges, and businessmen from both nations intermarry and mingle. Many of the Mexican community leaders, mainly businessmen, actually live in the United States but work on the southern bank.

The situation is far different farther west, particularly in the case of Tijuana–San Diego, and to a lesser extent Ciudad Juárez–El Paso. In California there are virtually no twin cities, in the strict sense; there is less contact with Mexico, traditionally, than there is in Texas. The consequences are varied: less discrimination in California than in Texas in the past, but less cooperation and understanding today. The sheer size of these communities sharply reduces the personal dimension and the impact of individual ties, although from an economic standpoint the western cities may have tighter links to the United States than the eastern ones. More important, the presence of Americans of Mexican origin in the San Diego area, though numerically as important as in South Texas, does not extend into positions of power and influence, as occurs in Los Angeles. Hence this factor plays a minor role: often Mexican and American Anglo authorities, as well as citizens and businessmen, find themselves face to face, with the ensuing confrontation.

The magnitude of the flows involved in the west exponentially increase the probabilities of friction and conflict. The numbers are mind-boggling: thirty-eight million people pass back and forth every year at the San Ysidro crossing just south of San Diego. The sewage of Tijuana pouring into San Diego Harbor; middle-class Americans in San Diego County's more affluent neighborhoods becoming fearful, then xenophobic and racist, over "alien criminality," which exists more in their minds than in reality; Mexican authorities trying to shake down U.S. marines and sailors from Camp Pendleton and the San Diego Naval Base in the bars and on the sidewalks of Avenida Revolución; the American sailors arrogantly overreacting: all of these potential sources of tension frequently boil over, transforming themselves into actual incidents and real binational problems.

But if the geographical and demographic realities of the border are more complex and varied than is frequently thought, its political and economic characteristics are less innovative than many believe. In recent years the idea of a "Third State" has gained currency among observers of the border in both nations, and it is an elegant and original, albeit mistaken concept. As Bill Moyers developed the notion in his CBS documentary "One River, One Country: The U.S.-Mexico Border" in September 1986, it emphasizes the economic, political, social, and cultural traits common to both sides of the border, which distinguish them from their respective hinterlands:

> Along the river that divides the U.S. from Mexico, a third country is emerging. Its inhabitants share family and economic ties, but feel isolated from the distant capitals of their two native lands. As tensions rise between Washington and Mexico over death, drugs and immigration, there are different voices to be heard here on this border. They speak in the accents of *One River, One Country.* 2

Moyers's program was in fact limited to the eastern border, the only one where there actually is a river. But the same point of view has been expressed in relation to the west, where no river serves as a divider but far greater tensions prevail between the two nations. A lengthy piece in *The New Yorker* on San Diego and Tijuana—"Twins"—formulated the same conception through a less poetic metaphor: "Lynch and Appleyard (two researchers who carried out an authoritative study on the area in the early 1970's) pointed out that the fence was an anomaly, a completely artificial imposition upon a single natural terrain and a connected social landscape as well. San Diego and Tijuana were not separate entities facing each other but a single metropolitan region."3

This theory stresses the ties which bind the two border regions and distance them from their capitals: exchange, education, language, culture, economic configuration. The border, in this view, is no longer strictly Mexican on the southern side, American on the northern one; it is no longer really part of either nation, while perhaps not yet forming a new country on its own. The border is seen as an entity unto itself; according to this point of view, the dividing line is an abstraction and an obstructive inconvenience placed artificially between two parts of one community by bureaucrats and politicians removed from its reality.

This vision is not exclusive to individual American observers. The Congress and the Reagan administration have indirectly espoused it through the "losing control of our borders" apocalyptic vision. It is also held in Mexico, where the central government's fears of political change in the north stem largely from the belief that the border is already too far removed from central authority and too close to the United States to take risks with. As one high-level Ministry of the Interior official said privately in 1986 with regard to upcoming elections in the border state of Chihuahua: "The opposition shall one day win a state governorship, but that day is not now and that state is not Chihuahua." The idea of a border state losing its moorings and adopting a pro-U.S. right-of-center form of home rule constitutes a nightmare for traditionalist members of the Mexican political system. Yet it is also the increasingly inevitable outcome of years of neglect, imposition, and economic development of the north of the country. The "electoral insurrection of the north" is a reality, albeit a slowly progressing one, so far simply translating into understandable and legitimate discontent against an archaic political system.

To a large extent the notion of a New Border Nation, while catchy and not unfaithful to the impressions one receives when visiting the area, is incorrect. One day it may resemble this "country within two countries"; the "line," with time, may perhaps fade away—in a local sense at least— becoming no more than a legal fiction and a minor nuisance. But for now, this is nowhere near the case. The two communities, however strapped together they may be by infinite bonds, dependencies, and common interests, are two very separate, very different entities. They may be converging, but the encounter, whatever its nature, lies far in the future.

The inhabitants of the Mexican side do not generally share the Third Nation view. They do not even accept the basic premise of their government's border policy since 1940—that is, to create a buffer zone where political and security considerations outrank economic factors. Mexico City views the border as an area which must be dealt with differently, because it is alongside the United States; the border itself rejects this "special treatment," essentially arguing it is as "Mexican" as the rest of the nation, and no more vulnerable to American influence than any other region. There are divisions on this issue in Mexico, and the disagreements will widen before they narrow.

For now, it is the emergence of specific and often unexpected new attributes of the region that has lent credence to the belief in "one border, one community." They are powerful, striking, and complex; these features are worth observing and studying. But they do not a new country make. If anything, the region's most dramatic characteristic is precisely the fact that it is divided; that communities with tremendously strong ties, links, and affinities are split apart by an ineradicable demarcation line. What distinguishes the border is its division, not its unity.

From an economic standpoint, the border is a succession of separate cross-boundary relatively unified markets where binational demand for particular goods and services is satisfied by an increasingly national supply. Since the massive devaluations of the peso in 1982, which transformed and sometimes reversed traditional flows of exchange, a number of cross-border consumption patterns have become consolidated. Coming after and on top of older customs, they now form a bilateral, quasi-ideal "Ricardian" type of arrangement, where comparative advantage and its derived effects—price, availability, quality—determine which side of the border will provide which products or services.

The most important markets are for labor and basic consumer goods. Labor is by definition Mexican, but it is hired on either side of the line, depending on the need. In Mexico, it is contracted by American companies through the *maquiladora* program. On the U.S. side, Mexican labor is employed in border agriculture, in domestic service, in the construction industry, and in occasional jobs for the thousands of Mexicans who cross on a daily basis. Often called "visa-abusers" by American authorities, they enter the United States legally with their Border Crossing Cards or Mexican passports with valid U.S. visas. In principle they are not allowed to obtain employment in the north; yet most do. Others have obtained residence permits (so-called green cards), but while working on the northern side, continue to live in Mexico, where life is cheaper.[4] In this way, the immediate border communities on both sides are beginning to make up one labor market, in which the border itself is not a significant division. Everyone hires Mexican labor because there is no alternative—Central Americans cannot cross on a daily basis—regardless of legal considerations, dividing lines, and the exact geographical location of the place where the demand for that labor is generated.

This is also broadly the case for basic, everyday consumer goods. Until 1982, many on both sides of the border purchased everything in the United States. A special border area legal status was established on the Mexican side, creating duty-free zones in a wide swath extending for varying distances into Mexican territory. Mexican border residents were allowed to purchase and bring into the country a number of goods normally not permitted to other citizens. The high value of the peso, together with the traditional neglect of the border area by industry, led the enormous majority of Mexican, and also American consumers, to obtain most of their supplies in U.S. supermarkets, department stores, and appliance stores.

The crisis of 1982, with its brutal and recurrent devaluations of the peso, changed matters overnight, and brought depression and devastation to merchants in much of the American border area. Sales plummeted, small stores and some malls went to the brink of bankruptcy, and real estate developments foreclosed on Mexican clients no longer able to meet payments on condominiums. The price in pesos of goods acquired in the United States increased five- and even tenfold in less than one year, and it became impossible for Mexicans with pesos to purchase American products when similar items were now available at one-third the price on the southern side. U.S. consumers soon reached the same conclusion, and they were quickly followed by Mexican suppliers who realized that the frontier market was open to conquest and profits.

Today, with the exception of certain products sometimes unavailable because of difficulties in supply, consumers overwhelmingly purchase their goods in Mexico. New malls and supermarkets have sprung up in many Mexican towns, catering both to reconverted national shoppers and to American consumers who buy nearly all their household products south of the border. In this specific instance the boundary is an artificial dividing line: Americans and Mexicans shop in the same stores because that is where the goods they need are cheaper, and they are totally indifferent to any implications their acts might have for national sovereignties.

The same is true, in the opposite sense and less so, for durable household goods and automobiles. In those Mexican communities with duty-free status, all refrigerators, ovens, washing machines, televisions, sound systems, video recorders, come either from the north or stores set up on the Mexican side for the exclusive purpose of selling American-made (or American-supplied; in many cases the actual product is Japanese or Korean) durable wares. In the non-duty-free zones with border area privileges, legal imports of goods other than automobiles are more difficult, but contraband, arrangements of convenience, and exceptions thrive.

Hence the border market for household durables is U.S.-supplied, much in the same way that the basic goods market is Mexican-supplied. Likewise, automobiles in both Mexico and the United States are almost entirely furnished by U.S.-based manufacturers, in stark contrast to the rest of Mexico, where the industry has been one of the most protected sectors of foreign investment for several decades.

The situation is similar in the case of many other goods and services, though often the degree of specialization of certain markets can be quite high. For example, automobile repairs and dentistry are Mexican-supplied markets: few American residents of the immediate border community have their cars painted or their teeth pulled in the United States. In addition to the well-known cases of Mexican medical care provided to seriously ill U.S. patients in search of remedies and treatments unavailable in their own country, most over-the-counter and prescription drugs tend to be purchased in Mexico. Americans often request that their physicians write out prescriptions in Spanish or generically so they can be filled in Mexican drugstores.

But in the case of more complicated medical care, the single-market phenomenon becomes fragmented. The Mexican rich act differently from the poor and from middle-class Americans. Whenever possible, wealthy Mexicans seek out medical care in the United States, from the centers in Houston to those at the University of California at San Diego in La Jolla. Similarly, those who can still afford it send their children to private day schools on the U.S. side and later to boarding schools throughout the country. In addition to whatever apparent pedagogic advantages these institutions of learning may have over their Mexican counterparts, they include the all-important reluctance by principals to ask indiscreet questions concerning legal residence in the U.S. or form of entry.

An important exception to these trends is capital flow. Unlike other factors of production, capital on the border flows both ways. From the north, the *maquiladoras* attract a growing volume of American investment. From the south, capital flight and its self-perpetuating mechanisms keep U.S. border banks and real estate markets solvent, even prosperous. The reasons which determine one trend are inapplicable to the other; the causes which bring ebbs and flows in *maquiladora* investment produce different effects on Mexican capital flight. There is no unified, single capital market along the border, with every participant in the market operating on the basis of the same criteria.

These patterns of consumption are far from absolute. They fluctuate with the exchange rate, the key variable in border life. Not all, perhaps not even a majority of the region's inhabitants follow the flows. Furthermore, these patterns vary with time and by location, and, at least as far as the Mexican side is concerned, by social class. Their origins are also diverse, ranging from the pull of a market or lower prices to the push of scarcity of supply or higher prices. A recent study conducted at El Colegio de la Frontera Norte, the Mexican institution which has carried out the most extensive and rigorous research on the entire border, emphasizes the diversity in question:

> The purchase of American products is a luxury even on the border. . . . Tijuana is the border city where access to American products is more democratic in that the lower classes have closer ties to the U.S. than other sectors. The reason probably lies in the fact that the Mexican national supply of basic products does not adequately satisfy popular needs. . . . The most "linked" city to the U.S. economy is Tijuana; nonetheless, Ciudad Juárez is more linked with regard to its upper classes. . . . Matamoros is the most unlinked of all border cities on the Mexican side.[5]

The characteristics of the many cross-border markets are thus varied. But in spite of their quantity and importance, even together they do not constitute a single, unified market of goods and services on both sides of the line. The obstacle to unification and the root of this fragmentation is the border itself. The determining factor for the location of each market is precisely the tremendous differences in price for the same goods or services on one side or the other of the frontier. These differences are in turn the chief consequences of the absence of a unified market and of the existence of separate markets.

The most important attribute a unified national market possesses is that anywhere within a given geographical, juridically determined perimeter, the same product or service can be as readily obtained and at approximately the same price. If the border were a single economic unit, drinks, food, labor, abortions, televisions, milk, and Laetrile would be equally available, and at the same price, in Tijuana as in San Diego, in El Paso as in Ciudad Juárez. Needless to say, this is not the case.

The existence of two countries, two currencies, two price systems, and two sets of health, customs, and entry regulations, limit the drive toward market unification. On a product-by-product, service-by-service basis, the border is possibly an abstraction. But with regard to the creation of a truly integrated, single economic continuum, with free flows of goods and services, capital and labor, in all directions, it is far from being an abstraction, but rather a decisive element in determining consumption, investment, and pricing mechanisms and patterns.

In economic terms but also from a social, cultural, and political perspective, the border is anything but an artificial creation or an abstract inconvenience. The number of obstacles to its obliteration or weakening as a dividing line is enormous, and possibly on the rise. Conversely, those factors often underlined as signs of convergence are either fictitious or waning. The Immigration Reform and Control Act of 1986, with its penchant for order and tidiness, is certainly a new impediment to the consolidation of a single border community: it will make the crossing a far more costly and possibly risky act than ever before.

Similarly, although the Mexican side of the border receives more television and possibly radio transmissions from the United States than from Mexico, the cultural difference is still great. There are exceptions: again, Matamoros and Brownsville are far more closely knit than Ciudad Juárez–El Paso, not to mention Tijuana–San Diego. Although a growing number of Mexican border dwellers speak English, Jorge Bustamante, Mexico's foremost scholar on immigration and border issues, showed in

1983 that their use of English or anglicisms is a linguistic matter, not one of national identity.[6]

The spillover of political and legal tensions into the cultural and social spheres plays a role here. The closing of the border in 1985 and 1986 led many upper-class Mexican border inhabitants to rethink their allegiances and lifestyles. If the crossing from Mexico can literally become a nightmare from one day to the next, making access to homes, bank accounts, and shopping suddenly difficult if not impossible, the attractiveness of straddling the demarcation line and having the best of both worlds quickly vanishes.

U.S. customs agents, the Drug Enforcement Administration, and the Border Patrol, while far from free of prejudice and bigotry, tend not to discriminate among Mexicans: when they want to, they are equally unpleasant with all citizens of the south, affluent or not. But the affluent are not accustomed to the treatment their servants suffer in silence. Many upper-middle-class Mexican semi-émigrés are doubting the wisdom of close ties with a country where they will always have a second-class status and where ill treatment and arrogance on the part of the authorities come and go with no apparent logic.

Paradoxically, the political importance of the border on the Mexican side is also an obstacle to the realization of "One River, One Country." Because of the traditional and ever-present asymmetry between the two nations, control of the border in the poorer country means control of access to and from the forbidden world of the richer nation. Even today, when the asymmetry has changed, border control still implies power and money.

It thus also means corruption: border authorities, from customs to immigration officials, have since time immemorial been among the most corrupt in Mexico. This is true in many countries; customs officials nearly everywhere are too close to temptation to be able to resist it forever. Each new Mexican administration makes a serious effort to eradicate corruption on the border and improve the situation; none succeeds.

During the last half of the De la Madrid administration a particularly energetic attempt to reduce border corruption was carried out by senior officials in the Ministry of the Interior and the newly created Comptroller General's office. But it barely achieved more results than before. Control over what enters and leaves Mexico is simply too great a source of enrichment and power.

In every Mexican border town, the federal authorities have far greater weight than local ones; the chief immigration official and the highest-ranking customs agency functionary, together with the military commander, are the community's most powerful figures, easily outranking the mayor, the local police chief, and other federal representatives. They oversee the border, whereas local authorities simply run the town, and other federal bureaucrats only disburse public works or money from the capital.

This symbiosis between the border and power plays a dual role in maintaining and strengthening separation. First, a strong dividing line is supported by those who have a vested interest in maintaining it. If access to and from the United States were easy and unrestricted, there would be little percentage in controlling a virtually nonexistent demarcation line. Bureaucracy, power, and corruption thrive on restrictions, requirements, and complications, which are all waived for a price or a favor. The Mexican federal authorities stationed along the border are among its staunchest defenders, though clearly in many cases for less than honorable reasons.

Second, this state of affairs does represent a form of culture shock for the Mexicans and Americans from "the other side." While no one takes seriously the view that corruption along the border is exclusive to the Mexican side, the types of malfeasance in the north among both federal and local authorities are of a different nature. Corruption at high levels of government may not be more widespread in Mexico than in the United States, but in matters of daily life, it undoubtedly is. In the United States it is less pervasive, less overt, and in the last analysis less socialized: not every member of society feels and is affected by it. The role corruption plays in Mexico is clearly distinct—by its importance in border society and the way in which it increasingly segregates American businessmen and tourists from the mainstream of Mexican life, leaving them largely unscathed.

There is a clear form of segregation on the Mexican side, extending to bars, restaurants, nightclubs, and "red-light" and "pink-light" districts, separating the natives from the tourists. Nothing is entirely rigid, of course, and as the two nations' middle classes come closer in lifestyles, tastes, and consumption patterns, on the border they converge on the same night spots and beaches. But the Mexican power structure and its least redeeming characteristics are strictly for local consumption, with the exception of minor run-ins of drunken American youths with the police.

In the last analysis, the border's importance for Mexico lies more in the changes it already represents—and may well foreshadow—in the national economy and society than in its assimilation into a "Third State."

The roots and origins of these changes rest undeniably in the link with the United States; they would be inconceivable were it not for contiguity. Yet the transformations are weighty precisely because they take place in Mexico, not in a third country that would be of lesser import. To a certain extent, changes on the border are a reflection of the country's future, indicative of its difficulties and challenges but also of *its ultimate success in maintaining its viability as a nation.* The border thus constitutes a microcosm of Mexico and its coming years, not of its ties with the United States, however transcendental these may be.

The changes are evident, the "newness" they bring is clear. Perhaps the most important social transformation is the massive entry of women into the wage-earning labor force, through the *maquiladora* industry. Nearly three-quarters of the workers employed in the assembly plants from Matamoros to Tijuana are women, generally single, usually under twenty-five. For the first time in their lives, these young women have an independent source of sustenance, not tied to their husbands', parents', or brothers' whims and prejudices. While turnover is heavy, the hours long, and working conditions are often a far cry from decent, the effects of this trend on border families and society are far-reaching. As Héctor Aguilar Camín, the editor of *Nexos,* has phrased it:

> The change is already taking place in the border areas, in the *maquiladora* industry, where the high levels of female employment are bringing a reordering of domestic culture and of urban services, with consumer and entertainment patterns tailor-made for women and family structures where the man often assumes a female role.[7]

Tijuana and other border cities have a double employment problem. There are not enough women to satisfy *maquiladora* demand, and there are not enough jobs for young men. So while the latter wait at home for an opportunity to work or to cross, their sisters find relatively well-paid jobs and spend their money on amenities, since they have no children or husbands to hand it over to. Men at home and women at work is not exactly the Mexican way; nor is the tendency of young, independent women to search out friends or lovers among older, established border executives conducive to harmonious community relations. When these same women begin to spend more time at the plant, perhaps continuing there after they do marry, and begin to be concerned about working conditions, unions, and politics, the changes will be even more substantive. They cannot be long in coming, nor can their extension to the rest of the country be considered farfetched.

The same holds true for one of Mexico's newest and most unexpected challenges, immigration from Central America. Traditionally an emi-grant nation, Mexico had in the past received only sporadic waves of immigrants for political reasons. The few significant migrations involved refugees fleeing the fall of the Spanish Republic in the late 1930s and early 1940s and a smaller contingent of Chilean, Argentine, and Uruguayan exiles in the 1970s. Both flows were small in number but high in quality: the immigrants were mainly professionals, intellectuals, and political leaders who all contributed enormously to the nation's well-being.

Since 1980, however, Mexico has been receiving an entirely different type of migration: more massive, essentially rural and peasant in origin, also politically motivated but in a less conscious fashion, and in many cases (some Guatemalan refugees in the southern state of Chiapas are the most notable exception) hoping just to pass through Mexico en route to the United States. They are fleeing military repression in the country-sides of El Salvador and Guatemala, impervious to well-meaning but irrelevant American-sponsored elections in the cities, addressed more to the U.S. Congress than to the problems of the campesinos.

Numbers are hard to come by, but serious estimates range from 100,-000 to 150,000 Guatemalan citizens in Mexico, including but not limited to those under United Nations supervision in the southern regions, and from 150,000 to 200,000 Salvadoran refugees under no protection at all and not generally recognized by Mexican authorities. Some Ministry of the Interior officials quote figures in the 500,000 to 700,000 range. Al-though the most serious problems emerging from this new migration are concentrated on Mexico's southern border, the situation in the north is almost as tense.

Often, the Central Americans who reach the U.S.-Mexican border are "undocumented," having entered Mexico without proper papers. As depicted in the movie *El Norte*, when they arrive in northern bor-der towns, nearly at the end of their journey, they become easy prey for Mexican authorities delighted to find a new source of revenue and power. Immigration officials, Federal Judicial Police as well as state and municipal police, even agricultural and health inspectors, all stra-tegically station themselves at points of entry from the interior to the border perimeter. Everything is more expensive for the Central Ameri-cans: bribes, payments to the *polleros* who take them across, the hotels reserved for them in downtown Tijuana and elsewhere, where they fre-quently receive extortionary visits by local authorities.

These "new" emigrants and refugees—the distinction is a fine one—are often more poorly treated on the U.S. side than in Mexico; deporta-tion by American authorities back to their countries entails the risk of political persecution and death. They are caught in a binational bind: the

United States prefers not to extend them a particularly warm welcome and would rather have Mexico provide decent conditions, so that they will stay in Mexico; Mexican authorities prefer to give them a shoddy reception, thus encouraging them to leave.

The United States hopes that Mexican authorities will limit their access to the border area; high-level officials in Mexico City are constrained by constitutional doubts as well as political and humanitarian considerations. If the refugees are the result of a U.S. policy of intervention, destabilization, and decades-old support for military dictatorships, why should Mexico do the Americans' dirty work? The security forces' ineffectiveness is another policy factor. Orders to stop Central Americans simply increase the tariff they are charged, not the numbers of those getting across. And the abuses committed against them extend increasingly to Mexican nationals.

One of the more recent and widespread forms of extortion employed by Mexican authorities against *Mexican* deportees from the United States is to charge them with being undocumented Central Americans. Since there is no national identity card in Mexico, and most Mexicans never carry proof of citizenship, the accused cannot disprove their "guilt." The presence of tens of thousands of Central American refugees along the northern border, en route to the United States or recently deported from the north, is a source of severe tension for Mexico. This will get worse before it gets better, for there is no end in sight to the turmoil in Central America, and consequently no possibility of a drop in the number of people fleeing that devastated region. And in time, the havoc created along the borders will begin to affect other regions.

Other features of Mexico's future are also present on the border. Several facets of the process of informal economic integration are much more accentuated along the dividing line. They range from the obvious—the use of the dollar as the currency of exchange, savings, and accounting in Mexican territory—to information exchange—the exposure of the entire Mexican population of the area to American television, radio, and to a lesser degree the press. The border is one of the meeting points of Mexican nationalism, education, and fear of intervention with the drift toward economic integration. So far the former are winning, the latter held at bay, but just barely. Indeed, the strange, disturbing, but fascinating combination of forces which the border possesses may well be a harbinger of the future for Mexico. It could represent an eclectic, middle-of-the-road solution to the nationalism-integration paradox: an acceptable, though at present apparently undesirable, response to one of Mexico's most daunting challenges.

8

CROSSING CULTURES

The Fear of Americanization
—
Jorge G. Castañeda

It is widely believed that immigration from Mexico to the United States greatly benefits the former nation and creates serious problems for the latter. There is some truth to this conviction, but not much. In fact, Mexico provides large numbers of unskilled workers who do jobs most Americans no longer wish to do. The United States economy could undoubtedly function without Mexican labor, but at a cost. Conversely, while emigration has provided an important source of income and employment for certain regions of Mexico, it has not been all positive. Mexico loses many dynamic sons and daughters. It sees many of its rural villages turn into ghost towns, and suffers the humiliation of having its people mistreated on the other side.

This particular solution to the country's chronic incapacity to generate jobs for all its inhabitants has always had its drawbacks, both internally and in relations with the United States. The new era in U.S.-Mexican immigration relations introduced by the passage of the Simpson-Rodino Immigration Reform and Control Act, in November 1986, legalizing most undocumented aliens who arrived in the United States before January 1, 1982, but imposing sanctions on whoever employs undocumented workers after November 1986, has begun to underline these disadvantages. If immigration was never as much of a *problem* for the United States as many Americans have thought, it has never been as much of a *solution* to Mexico's travails as many Mexicans have often believed.

Emigration to the United States began in the late nineteenth century and grew during the revolutionary period between 1910 and 1920. Initially concentrated in the border areas, it rapidly spread to the American industrial heartland in the Midwest. From the very beginning, two characteristics marked the process. First, while at any one time the supply-and-demand equation may favor one term or the other, over the long-haul U.S. demand for low-cost labor has been as decisive a factor in generating immigration as surplus Mexican supply.

Second, American opposition and attempts at regulation and more or less voluntary repatriation have accompanied this demand from the outset. The Border Patrol was created in 1924; during the Depression in the 1930s, hundreds of thousands of Mexicans were "invited to leave" the United States. The invitations were not always gentle, and resentment grew over poor and brutal treatment of Mexican nationals by U.S. authorities. The paradox of simultaneous demand and deportation is only apparent: those in the United States who have most benefited from Mexican workers have never been those who most oppose immigration.

During World War II, labor shortages in the United States led both nations to an agreement whereby Washington would directly hire Mexican laborers and subcontract them to American farmers, providing guarantees against discrimination. Originally the workers were destined only for the railroads and farms in the Southwest, but soon better wages attracted other Mexicans, who entered illegally and found jobs in industry and services. Discrimination surfaced rapidly under this "bracero" agreement.

The system functioned throughout the war and was renewed through successive agreements in the 1940s and 1950s. But immigration-related problems continued to grow, and culminated in the forced departure of more than one million undocumented Mexican nationals in 1953–54 and in Operation Wetback, a deportation campaign carried out in 1954–55. After the United States in 1964 terminated the "bracero" agreement, over Mexican protest an unregulated, illegal, but, in Mexico's view, mutually advantageous flow of undocumented Mexicans took hold. It has never stopped, becoming one of the key issues on the bilateral agenda, yet from an entirely different perspective for each nation.

The official, and widely shared, view in Mexico has been that the country's authorities should strive to protect its nationals' human and labor rights in the United States, defending them against exploitation and discrimination. These range from outright brutality by American local and federal authorities and employers to segregation, denial of basic labor rights, deplorable working conditions, and nonpayment of back wages after departure. But Mexico has been reluctant to enter into any further discussion of the issue with the United States. It has feared that such exchanges would inevitably open the door to suggestions and/or impositions of binational regulation of the flow of undocumented Mexican laborers.

The country's most recent governments have felt that almost at any cost they should avoid engaging in a bargaining process whose outcome might imply a Mexican obligation to restrict emigration and patrol its side of the border, hindering or discouraging exits from the country. Concerned and informed sectors of Mexican society have felt that until the passage of the new Immigration Act, the best possible situation for Mexico was the status quo, despite the humiliating abuses of undocumented Mexican nationals.

True, business as usual implied continued mistreatment of undocumented Mexican workers, as well as constant tensions and anti-American sentiment. Nonetheless, the prevailing arrangement allowed for a relatively free flow of emigrants to the United States, in various forms, durations, and capacities. No conceivable formal agreement could represent an improvement for Mexico. In all likelihood any understanding which would address Mexico's concerns would also involve some limit on emigration and shared responsibility for enforcing it.

Additionally, any agreement with Washington which called for dual regulation or control of migratory flows would have shattering political and constitutional effects in Mexico, since it would probably involve limiting access to the border perimeter. There are chapters of the Mexican Constitution of 1917 that are not, and have never been, fully complied with, but freedom of movement within the nation is one right which has been respected almost to the letter. As expressed by former President José López Portillo:

> Regarding those Mexicans who emigrate to the north searching for the jobs which despite our progress we still cannot provide, we have achieved our essential aim. We did not lend ourselves to any arrangement which restricts the constitutional freedom of all Mexicans to enter or leave Mexico. There are no walls in our country.[1]

The implications of limiting this freedom, and doing so efficiently, peacefully, and in a politically palatable fashion, have never been seriously contemplated. As a self-deprecating Mexican *boutade* puts it, who would stop those responsible for keeping Mexicans in from being the first to abandon their jobs and cross over to the other side?

The importance of emigration for Mexico stems from various factors. The first and overriding one is related to employment, summarized by the "safety valve" theory. According to this view, the nation's chronic incapacity to create enough jobs to keep up with new entrants into the labor market has been largely relieved by emigration to the United States. In fact, many studies, beginning with Jorge Bustamante's research, have shown conclusively that those who leave tend to have jobs before their departure: the unemployed and penniless do not embark on such perilous ventures. Second, at most a fraction of the aggregate job deficit is filled by emigration: less than 20 percent. Finally, the majority who leave the nation's poorer areas in search of employment do so in the direction of the country's large cities, not the United States.

Nevertheless, these caveats do not alter the overall picture, since the jobs vacated are filled by the unemployed or new entrants into the labor force. It is important to distinguish between the causes which motivate Mexicans to leave—higher wages in the United States for employed Mexicans, rather than a job for those who are unemployed—from the effects: a significant extension of the job market open to all Mexicans, employed and unemployed. Reductions in relative unemployment and underemployment were partly made possible by the emigration of significant numbers of young Mexicans to the United States. Furthermore the majority of the emigrants came mainly from Mexico's poorer regions, though not from its most destitute areas. In the final analysis, the key to emigration's importance lies in its regional impact. For many backward communities in the states of Zacatecas, Michoacán, Guanajuato, Jalisco, San Luis Potosí, Durango, and even Oaxaca, and some urban communities in Chihuahua and Baja California, emigration has been an alternative source of employment and income.

The most reliable recent estimates of the aggregate total of money sent home by Mexican workers in the United States range from $1.5 to $2 billion annually. There is little doubt that many small towns literally depend for their livelihood on these remittances. According to a peasant organization leader, the nearly $200 million sent to Zacatecas every year by emigrants represents more money than the value of its entire agricultural crop.[2] Some villages lose almost all their male workers to the city or to the United States. The aged remaining inhabitants, so well depicted by the writer Juan Rulfo, live in a daze of obsolescence, patiently awaiting next month's money order from California.

Mexico's demographics clearly have much to do with emigration, but more than rampant population growth is involved. Thanks to the introduction of even primitive medical procedures and health practices in the countryside, the death rate dropped precipitously as of 1940, from around 25 per thousand to 11 per thousand in 1960.

But the birth rate fell nowhere nearly as rapidly, and although it stopped climbing in 1930, it remained very high, at over 44 per thousand, until 1970.[3] The ensuing natural growth rate—excess of births over deaths—of 3.5 percent was one of the highest in the world. It took time for the political establishment to adopt a more modern vision of population policy: until the early 1970s Mexico had no policy at all. Opposition from the Church, fear by the government of upsetting the status quo in church-state relations, and a vague demographic nationalism—whereby more Mexicans meant a stronger Mexico—made it impossible to move forward on this front until that time.

The adoption of a population policy, as well as the country's mounting urbanization, led to a sharp drop in the birth rate, to 35 per thousand by 1980 and perhaps 30 per thousand by 1986.[4] The number of children per family has declined and is expected to decrease to slightly over two per couple by the year 2000. Population is now essentially a problem under control as far as births are concerned. But the effects of Mexico's baby boom of the 1960s and 1970s will persist for another decade or two as the number of women of child-bearing age continues to increase. The number of entrants into the labor force will rise 3.5 percent yearly until the mid-1990s. Between now and then, approximately one million young Mexicans will enter the job market every year, establishing a need for rates of job creation higher than during the years of Mexico's greatest economic growth.

Predictably, it is as difficult to determine how many Mexicans have left their country as it is to ascertain how many have entered the United States. Estimates for the latter number range from one or two million to over eleven million. A reliable, though barely meaningful, "floor" emerged from the legalization provision of the 1986 Immigration Act: 1.8 million individuals applied for "amnesty," of whom approximately 74 percent were Mexican. For now, one of the most recent and rigorous estimates comes from a Rand Corporation study carried out in 1985 which drew largely on the previous work of other specialists.

The study divides Mexican emigrants into three categories, each including documented and undocumented migrants: short-term emigrants, who enter the United States for ten to twelve weeks, then return to

Mexico; cyclical emigrants, who leave their families in Mexico but stay in the United States for longer periods and return on a fairly regular basis; finally, permanent emigrants who bring their families with them and settle in the United States. There are also the "dailies": the thousands of Mexicans who work in the United States but who live on the Mexican side of the border. Although not emigrants in a strict sense, they are part of the Mexican labor pool employed by the U.S. economy.

The Rand Corporation summarizes its description of the complex process of Mexican emigration as follows:

> Each stage of the settlement process—from attempts to enter California and thus become short-term immigrants, to the transition of some short-termers to cyclical immigrants, to the fraction of these cyclicals who decide to settle and bring in their wives and children—is influenced by different factors. Mexico's demographic structure determines the size of the potential immigrant pool. The likelihood that a member of that pool will become a short-term immigrant is determined by Mexico's political economy. The chances of moving from short-term to cyclical status are determined by California's need for temporary workers. Finally, the probability that Mexicans will settle permanently in California is determined both by California's need for low-skilled, year-round workers and by family reunification among permanent immigrants.[5]

In 1980 there were approximately 1.2 million permanent Mexican immigrants in California—300,000 actual workers, the rest consisting of families. Since by nearly all calculations California accounts for half of total Mexican immigration in the United States, the figure for permanent immigrants at that time amounted to around 2.5 million. In 1980 approximately 300,000 laborers journeyed back and forth on a cyclical basis.

The Rand study shows to what extent the process is far more complex than the simplistic vision of a "silent invasion." There are two flows of Mexican nationals—permanents and temporaries. The American perspective tends to emphasize the permanent arrivals: hundreds of thousands of Mexicans with their families coming to settle in American communities. It disregards, or neglects, the hundreds of thousands who enter the United States, do a job most Americans refuse to do, and then return to Mexico. Conversely, the Mexican viewpoint stresses the "temporary" aspect of migration, underlining the exaggerated fears of many Americans in the face of a transient phenomenon, but dismisses the

importance and volume of "permanence." The situation's complexity
and its highly emotional and politicized nature explain this divergence
of views. Both are right, but neither is complete.

This complexity also underscores the intrinsic limitations of any attempt to determine the number of undocumented Mexicans entering the
United States annually on the basis of Immigration and Naturalization
Service apprehensions and deportations. Many Mexicans who arrive
illegally are caught and deported several times before they succeed in
getting through. The volume of arrests is as much a function of Border
Patrol resources as of the number of undocumented individuals attempting to cross. In addition, deportation and arrest figures do not indicate
the type of immigrant: short-term, cyclical, or permanent.

If the "stock" of undocumented Mexicans in the United States is not
easy to calculate, the "flow" is even more difficult. A floor figure for the
number of all Mexicans (legal and undocumented) entering the United
States every year already exists. It is simply the number of Mexican
nationals who emigrate yearly with their papers in order. Between 1981
and 1985, 244,000 Mexican citizens, or approximately 49,000 per year,
became legal immigrants in the United States. In 1986, slightly over
60,000 Mexican nationals entered the United States legally.[6]

The number of undocumented emigrants, according to the best estimates, is about twice as high. Alan Nelson, the U.S. Immigration and
Naturalization Commissioner, estimated in 1987 that the total flow of all
"illegal" entries into the United States was reaching nearly half a million,
of which approximately 50 percent were Mexican. This probably overestimates the true number because it relies on apprehension statistics,
which rose mainly because of the increase in Border Patrol resources. An
independent study by the Bureau of the Census suggests more moderate
increases in the net flow of undocumented Mexicans.

The rise since Mexico's economic downturn is much lower than suggested by alarmist scenarios of a border out of control, but it is nonetheless real. Increments have to work themselves through the system and
are a function of multiple factors, both "push" and "pull." More temporary workers become cyclicals, more cyclicals become permanents, and
more permanents bring their families to join them. Thus today a total
of 150,000 to 200,000 Mexican citizens are probably leaving the country
annually: about one-third as legal emigrants and two-thirds as undocumented expatriates. Roughly two-thirds are in the labor force; thus about
15 percent of Mexico's annual job deficit is probably met today by employment in the United States.

Would more go if they could, if jobs, wages, and dignified treatment
were available to accommodate significantly larger flows? Again, the

New York Times poll provides an indication, but it must be viewed with reservations. Forty percent of those Mexicans queried said they would live in the United States if they had the opportunity to do so; sixty percent said they would not. The number is not extraordinarily high; this is the sort of question whose answer depends largely on the information those questioned possess on the subject.

In spite of the widespread reports of unacceptable treatment of un-documented Mexican workers and deep resentment among Mexicans over it, many continue to have an idyllic view of life up north, even for "illegal aliens." This is not a new phenomenon in American immigra-tion, and its implications are as evident today for Mexico as they were for other nations in earlier periods. Emigrants' views of the United States—based on the myths of life for settled Americans, not on the reality of life for just-arrived immigrants—have always played a key role in attracting cheap labor to the United States. Hypothetically, a far greater number of Mexican citizens may wish to go to the United States, but the simple desire to go is not sufficient to make it happen.

As with other migration-generating nations, emigration is not a simple plus for Mexico. From a purely economic perspective, it is a drain on the country's resources, since whatever education and training the emi-grants obtained in Mexico will benefit other nations, in this case the United States. As Mexican emigration is increasingly characterized by higher levels of education and training, the losses involved for Mexico grow also.

It is often the youngest, the most dynamic, and the most adventurous who leave. In small communities, this means those who stay frequently lack these virtues; the resulting balance is far from favorable to each community and to the nation at large. And although emigration's effect on Mexico's burden of dependency is minimal, given the extreme youth of Mexico's population, in certain villages or regions a disproportion-ately large part of the population may be maintained by an exceptionally small part.

But in the last analysis, emigration's negative consequences are more abstract and intangible. Millions of Mexicans leaving the nation in search of (better) employment represent a damning statement about the coun-try's well-being, which shames all Mexicans. The mere fact that the frequently brutal mistreatment and discrimination which they are vic-tims of in the United States is often preferable to their lot at home is something which pains and revolts all Mexicans. One of the most damag-ing blows to its pride and self-respect is the nation's incapacity to provide jobs for all its citizens; emigration is a constant and painful reminder of this. Its negative impact is incalculable, but cannot be underestimated.

It is also the underlying, deep-rooted cause which explains the contradictory, ambivalent attitudes toward emigrants and emigration. Those who leave but return loaded with dollars are praised and admired; but those who stay in the United States are sometimes frowned upon, treated as renegades, and frequently seen as no longer Mexican, having accepted humiliation and mistreatment. Yet few who leave with the intention of never coming back are criticized by friends or family: too many know that in the end emigration will constitute an improvement. Despite the resentment arising from having personal, local, and national problems solved through American auspices, Mexicans in the last instance generally do not ostracize, despise, or revile emigrants. If anything, the nation feels it has a debt to those who are forced to leave because of the country's own limitations. The debt is canceled at the border, though: there is scant real interest in Mexico for Hispanic affairs in the United States. And, of course, there is no support, other than abstract and moral, for Mexican-American causes: bilingualism, the struggle against discrimination, etc. Nor has any serious attempt ever been made to organize Mexican-Americans or Mexican nationals living in the United States as a "Mexican lobby."

This also explains the overreaction, hysteria, and contradictory responses which immediately surface when limitations on immigration seem in the offing or actually are enforced. The response to the Simpson-Rodino law was in this sense typical and extreme. Dire scenarios of massive deportations, roundups in concentration camps, and the border becoming an impenetrable wall all emerged at one point or another in the months preceding the date when the legislation went into effect. Similarly, the new law was simultaneously condemned in Mexico as unilateral, anti-Mexican, inevitably ineffective, and fundamentally ideological. These charges rang basically true, but were at odds with each other. Moreover, Mexico was rightly unwilling to do anything about them, including any negotiations with the United States.

The highest levels of the Mexican government were more restrained and prescient. President De la Madrid publicly acknowledged that although in the future there may be a decrease in the number of Mexicans leaving for the United States, there were scant probabilities of mass deportations. But public opinion, the media, and many government-sponsored entities—the Congress, the PRI, labor—all espoused the catastrophic visions to one degree or another. The contradiction is understandable. Mexico tends to downplay the importance of emigration, but whenever it seems in jeopardy, rhetoric and confusion quickly overtake reality and reason.

This was true to such an extent that most experts on Mexican immigration reached a surprising conclusion in mid-1987. The available data from the INS, but also from Mexican consulates along the border, showed that from the beginning of the year there had been a significant drop—which faded by late summer—in the number of undocumented crossings. This was clearly not due to the Simpson-Rodino law itself, since it did not take effect until midyear. The explanation was evident: potential emigrants were dissuaded from leaving, or postponed their departure, because of the outcry in Mexico over the law. Many subscribed to the ensuing belief that entry would become more difficult, that there would be no more jobs, and that repression would increase. Once it became clear that virtually none of this came true, the number of crossings regained its former levels.

Among the fears which the law aroused in Mexico was one which sounded vaguely familiar to those knowledgeable about American attitudes toward immigration. Many warned of the social and political dangers which could arise from the displacement of presently employed Mexican workers by the returnees: their jobs would be "stolen" by Mexicans coming from the United States. In fact, with some exceptions of mistreatment at the border and the Mexico City airport, the few returnees who did come back because of the new American legislation were well received. But Mexico's complex and contradictory feelings toward immigration were highlighted by the entire episode.

Beyond the limitations which the Immigration Reform and Control Act may place on new immigration, several factors qualify contemporary Mexican immigration—since the early 1970s—in contrast to the previous flow, dating back to the beginning of the century, through World War II and the fifties and sixties. To begin with for cultural reasons but also for geographical ones, Mexican emigrants conserve their "home country" roots more than most immigrants to the United States. This has been evidenced by the fact that there are fewer Mexican applicants for American citizenship, in relative terms, than from nearly any other country with a significant immigrant presence in the United States. This also partly explains why fewer Mexicans than expected applied for legalization and eventual citizenship under the provisions of the Simpson-Rodino Act; fear and bureaucratic complications are the main reasons, but a certain reluctance in the face of assimilation is also a motivation. Mexicans are an identifiable cultural group in a way that no other group is.

The strength and vigor of Mexican culture, as well as the psychological effects of geographical contiguity and the ongoing, almost permanent nature of immigration flows from Mexico, go far in explaining this

phenomenon. Leaving for "the other side," while an adventurous undertaking, is not an irreversible and decisive endeavor. Many retain the
desire, however theoretical, to return eventually and settle down in
Mexico, once they have accumulated enough money to do so prosper-
ously. Mexican emigrants can come and go, even after they have permanently settled in the United States. This opportunity, as well as the
existence of a large Mexican community in the United States, makes it
possible for emigrants from Mexico to continue speaking Spanish, eating
Mexican food, and living in a quasi-Mexican environment in ways which
were not always feasible for generations of immigrants from other countries. This results from the factor which distinguishes Mexican immigration to the United States from all others: contiguity.

Many more Mexicans might well want to go to the United States, but
on the condition that they "stay" Mexican, that they be able to come
back to the old country, and that their quality of life remain as Mexican
as possible. While this may seem like mere nostalgia, it has a clear
"integrationist" effect on Mexico and on ties between the two nations.
While the patterns of education, language, and integration are similar to
those of previous waves of immigrants to the United States, there are
some basic differences. These are complex, and cannot be reduced to the
simplistic, zero-sum equation of assimilation versus nonintegration.
Mexican immigrants are being absorbed into the American "melting
pot" in the same fashion as others before them, but they are also conserving their culture, their mores, and their language more effectively than
their predecessors.

Contiguity explains this. Mexicans continue to enter the United States,
thus regenerating the "Mexicanness" of those who came before. This is
a major contrast with preceding immigration, which in most cases came
to an end after a given duration. But it also exposes the assimilation-
integration debate to a new factor: the changing nature of mass Mexican
emigration, a reflection of the profound transformations Mexico itself
has undergone.

From being a rural, agricultural, illiterate, immensely backward and
poor country in the 1930s, Mexico has become an urban society, essentially literate and largely working and middle class. Ample sectors of
peasant life reminiscent of the turn of the century remain, of course, and
many years will pass before they become truly marginal islands in an
urban stream. But Mexico's great transformation has taken place, and
the country will never be the same again. This change has affected all
walks of national life; emigration is inevitably one of them.

Herein lies the main explanation for the differences observed in the
sociological profile of many more recent Mexican emigrants. These dif-

ferences stem from this transformation and not, as many in the United States have claimed, from the economic crisis Mexico is undergoing. The main factor explaining the "new look" is probably more permanent and substantive. Increasingly, undocumented Mexican migration—as opposed to "white-collar" entrants examined below—no longer has peasant roots. It is more and more of urban origin, with at least elementary school education and in many cases junior high school and some high school training.

Up until their journey, more and more of the newcomers were in school, held factory jobs or odd jobs in the cities. Similarly, and largely because of changes in the structure of demand for Mexican labor in the United States, they will work in factories or the service industry. Only rarely will they seek stoop labor employment, as their predecessors did: in California, only 16 percent of Mexican immigrants work in agriculture; more than half have manufacturing and services jobs.[7]

The links the "modernized" emigrants maintain with "home" are not any weaker, and are perhaps stronger. They can write home, phone home, and go home more often. Their resistance to traditional assimilation is also undampened. If anything, the greater intensity of and pride in Mexican urban culture accentuates it. The loss for Mexico is greater; the gain for the United States is greater. But the most important effect of this change probably lies elsewhere—in the "integrationist" drift it contributes to. The "new" emigrants clearly do not want to become Americans or cease being Mexicans. If anything, they seem to want to have the best of both worlds: to live as Mexicans in the United States.

They wish to come and go as often and as easily as they please, have a home to return to both in the Latino neighborhoods of large American cities and in the sprawling Mexican barrios. They bring with them not only their music and cuisine but their movie industry, their television network with its sports and soap operas, their athletic and movie stars, even their comics. They go home to their families' and friends' weddings, *quince años* (sweet sixteen) parties, Christmases and first communions. As opposed to their largely peasant precursors, they have the drive, education, and background, perhaps not always sufficient to succeed in this intent, but at least to attempt to achieve it. The largest obstacle in their path, and paradoxically a strong possible hindrance to "integration through immigration," is the Simpson-Rodino law. For in spite of the enormous discontent it has produced in Mexico, it may yet favor the country.

The lasting effects of the new American law will not be known for several years. Employer sanctions, thanks to loopholes, difficulties in enforcement, and opposition, will be imposed only in part. They will probably become a deterrent to new flows of immigration, slowing them down over time. But they will not produce significant returns to Mexico, and the legalization and guest-worker provisions of the law may well transform some undocumented flows into documented ones. However, it will be some time before the effects in Mexico and other emigration-generating nations will be felt. Several years of a stable situation in both the United States and Mexico must pass before it is known whether the bill acted as a net deterrent to further undocumented immigration or whether after an initial dip things returned to the *status quo ante.*

Most high-level Mexican officials felt that although massive deportations would probably not occur, the law might contribute to a significant drop in new emigration. The fact that this would take place at a time when the Mexican economy's job-creation capability was at its lowest point in years underlined both the importance of the "safety valve" and the country's vulnerability to unilateral American decisions. The same officials also believed, however, that while the Congress may have adopted new legislation on immigration, it had not created a new American labor market or work force. In the long run, the demand for unskilled or semi-skilled, low-wage labor from Mexico will prove greater than legislative fiat.

At present the new legislation, simply by attempting to regulate, legalize, sanction, and put order into an essentially untidy and uncontrolled process, may well break the continuum which has developed on both sides of the border, establishing strict and artifical dividing lines. Undocumented foreigners (principally Mexicans) can apply for residence only if they have not spent long periods of time out of the United States (that is, if they have not gone home too often and stayed home too long). Within the same family some may obtain legalization while others do not. The fact that employers are sanctioned for new hirings of undocumented laborers, but not for those hired before the law took effect, serves to dissuade employed "illegals" from leaving their jobs, going home, and then returning to their old jobs or finding new ones.

By rendering employment more difficult, and by increasing the Border Patrol's resources, the new law has certainly made it harder and more expensive for Mexicans to go to the United States. As is well known, few crossovers are done alone. Most *mojados* (wet ones) or *pollos* (chickens) are taken across by *coyotes* or *polleros* (chicken-runners), professional "crossers" or smugglers, who charge for their precious and valued knowledge. They know how to cross, and when, where, and how to penetrate beyond the border zone on the U.S. side and reach the hinterland, where the probability of apprehension and deportation is virtually nil. More important, the *coyotes* often serve as hiring agents for factories, farms, and the service industry.

In some cases, for one lump sum, a prospective emigrant can cross, penetrate, and obtain employment. The price the *coyotes* charge is a function of demand for their services, together with the risks they take, the chances of success, and the peso-dollar rate of exchange. The emigrants often pay in pesos, but the *coyotes* live on dollars. By exerting significant upward pressure on the fee most potential emigrants must pay, the Simpson-Rodino law probably will have at least a temporary dissuasive effect on new immigration and will accentuate the urbanization and rise in incomes of new emigrants. But it will also make it much more difficult to come and go, to bring family members north, to continue to try to have it both ways. By regulating everything, including agricultural employment through a guest-worker program, the new legislation may well weaken the "integrationist" effect immigration was having. In the Simpson-Rodino era, the gray zones, the undefined status, the symbiosis might be all tidily classified. Those Mexicans who are in the United States and want to stay must express their desire to do so, proceed accordingly, and forsake their dreams of unresolved preferences. The law forces a choice which many Mexicans in the United States would prefer not to make. Along this road, the future holds assimilation, citizenship, and the severing of the umbilical cord with Mexico, as culture becomes folklore and tradition is reduced to food and song on Independence Day, September 16.

Conversely, those Mexican nationals who are not sure they want to emigrate to the United States, who are just thinking of trying it out for a time, may have to think twice. The cost as well as the risk of not finding a job will probably be too high for the unconvinced or the "temporaries." In this sense, while the law is certainly damaging to Mexican interests in the short term, by at least slowing the integration process, it probably favors the nation in the long run. It also has an indirect negative effect on any possibilities of institutionalized integration, since it makes the free flow of capital, goods, and labor between the two countries even more remote.

Nonetheless, many Mexicans believe that the labor flow between the two nations is precisely the one form of integration which is truly to Mexico's advantage. Beyond the obvious and perhaps simplistic vision of Texas and California being "reconquered" by their previous owner, the fact is that the apparent "Mexicanization" of large parts of California and the American Southwest does seem to favor Mexican interests. Language, customs, culture in a broader sense, political and national sympathies all stem from this process. There is a strong current of opinion in Mexico which derives hope for an eventual equalization of U.S.-Mexican relations from this trend. Within the context of integration, those who espouse these views are undoubtedly correct: it is the integration chapter most favorable to Mexico. The question remains, though, whether the most advantageous facet of a disadvantageous process is in the country's favor or not.

Other new trends have surfaced recently in emigration, and many of them reinforce the "integration drift." The most talked about new development is undoubtedly the emergence of white-collar Mexican emigration. It began in 1982, has continued since, and although it does not involve quantities of people at all comparable with traditional, unskilled flows, it could become considerable with time. For now it is merely a symptom of a very real problem.

The signs pointing to its existence are still embryonic and impressionistic. Statistics on legal entries indicate, for example, that while the Mexican "third preference" entry quota was normally unfilled, since 1983 there has been a large backlog of applications.[8] Similarly, Mexican professionals have suddenly appeared in certain areas of the United States where they were simply absent before. Those who previously spent time in the United States for academic reasons are now prolonging their stays or making them more or less permanent. The figure of 100,000 professional departures from Mexico between 1982 and 1987 has been mentioned; while high, an estimate of 10,000 to 15,000 professional expatriates per year at present may not be excessive.[9]

As in the case of their far less affluent compatriots, the process of white-collar emigration involves various "push-pull" factors which cannot be reduced to dissatisfaction or frustration with the Mexican political system or a sense of hopelessness over Mexico's future. These considerations play a role, but matters are more complex.

Many of the best-known "new" emigrants, in late 1982, were businessmen joining a small group of expatriates residing in communities such as La Jolla, California, and San Antonio and Padre Island, in Texas. Their reasons for leaving were simple, and identical to those which produced the first entrepreneurial emigrants in 1976. They had contracted large debts in dollars by purchasing condominiums and other forms of real estate in the United States. In 1982, easy access to cheap dollars in Mexico became a thing of the past. Several macro-devaluations of the peso drove its value from 28 to the dollar to 150 in less than a year. It became increasingly difficult to generate the foreign exchange for private sector debt payments as well as individual obligations while living in Mexico. Many businessmen packed up, went north, and used their personal dollar holdings to settle in the United States and pay off their debts. Some maintain houses in Mexico and spend part of the year in the old country, but with time, they have made their homes in Southern California or Texas.

Another, more recent facet of middle-class emigration involves skilled individuals who also for economic reasons have left their country. These include doctors, dentists, engineers, and architects, fields in which Mexican training, often complemented by American graduate specialization, has long produced top-flight professionals. Many retain U.S. connections from their school years or from conventions and meetings. All speak English and are familiar with American ways. A good number had already been regularly spending brief periods of time in the United States, updating their training or simply working on short, fixed-term contracts.

Once the economic crisis struck, dollars became extraordinarily expensive in peso terms, and the upper middle class's standard of living dropped precipitously. Many were faced with a decision they would have preferred not to make. Either they could go to the United States, and earn more money, but suffer a definite decline in quality of life and a slippage from their previous hierarchical rung in Mexico. Or they could stay home and accept a considerable fall in their standard of living, particularly in its dollar-denominated aspect: trips abroad, contraband consumer goods, schools and medical care in the United States. Predictably, many chose to leave, although the great majority with a choice still remains in Mexico.

A third group is made up of business professionals previously employed by Mexico-based U.S. multinational subsidiaries or Mexican firms with ties to the United States. Again, many of these upper- and middle-level professionals are partly U.S.-trained and have American connections of one type or another. It is not impossible for them to obtain transfers to their multinationals' headquarters up north or to find jobs in U.S. firms through friends and former bosses or deputies. The reasons for leaving are again primarily economic. The extraordinarily high standard of living that many enjoyed in Mexico during the boom years disappeared. While they may not regain all of it in the United States, many will recover some of its benefits.[10]

They will pay a price, of course, but many do not know it before they arrive. Often they will have to accept a downgrading of their professional standing, live in cold, dark northern American cities or in Texan suburbs. In many cases they will never rid themselves of the stigma which Mexican origin and speaking English with a Spanish accent still represents in much of the southwestern United States. But in the case of this

group, ideological factors do play a role, and they make the cost acceptable or barely noticeable. A good number of these professionals believe
that Mexico is on the verge of—or already deeply wedded to—socialism.
In their view, the private sector has no future in the country, and their
perception of the public sector's corruption, inefficiency, and omnipres-
ence makes professional life in Mexico unattractive, perhaps even un-
bearable.

Finally, in a more recent development in new emigration, Mexican
scientists, academics, and intellectuals have also begun to leave. In most
cases their departure is temporary: three months per year at an American
university or research center, one year out of every two or three in the
United States teaching or writing with the full intention of returning to
Mexico. Here monetary considerations are overpowering. Few Mexican
intellectuals can live on their university salaries, which have rarely averaged over five hundred dollars monthly in the highest categories since
1982. More important, the need to moonlight and the difficulty of obtaining research material because of economic constraints have led many to
seek out American support. Money from the United States is partly
filling the void left by traditional state support for Mexican intellectuals.
The state has run out of money, and U.S. institutions and foundations
are taking its place. Eventually, some of those who receive grants and
spend quarters or semesters in the United States stay for longer periods.
They become unwilling emigrants, though perhaps unaware of their
status.

Unlike other Latin American nations such as Argentina and Chile,
and in dramatic contrast to Asian countries like India, Mexico had never
suffered a brain drain. The highly qualified professionals the country
trained year after year stayed, worked, and helped to develop Mexico.
Traditionally, Mexican quotas at international organizations such as the
United Nations remained unfilled. Mexican professionals simply did not
like to go abroad, and thanks to high salaries, they did not have to. This
has changed.

Emigration by professionals will reproduce and even accentuate some
of the traits of the previous waves. White-collar expatriates will also
come and go, sometimes sending their families to Mexico for holidays
and even school. After their initial infatuation with the American way
of life fades, they will certainly seek out and try to regain their Mexican
way of life . . . in the United States. They will live in the Mexican
emigrant community, watch Mexican television, and try to keep Mexican hours and customs. They may significantly increase Mexican-American political clout in the United States and may even contribute to forms
of political integration on both sides of the border by demanding more

favorable American policies toward Mexico and more political reform in Mexico. They will strengthen the integration effect by not severing their ties with Mexico and by only partially being assimilated into the American melting pot. They may never really cease being Mexican, while never truly becoming Americans.

If Mexican emigrants, both white-collar and traditional, attempt to take their culture with them, it is largely because the technical means of doing so are now available. While by no means limited to television, the press, and the film industry, these are the fields in which information integration between the two countries is most rapidly moving forward. The Spanish International Network, presently known as Univisión, previously owned by Mexican television magnate Emilio Azcárraga, has become the United States' fifth-largest chain. It caters to a Spanish-speaking audience of between six and ten million viewers, feeds more than three hundred stations, and is watched by more than 10 percent of the viewing population in cities such as New York, Chicago, and Los Angeles.[11]

Univisión provides soap operas produced in Mexico, Brazil, and Argentina, variety and entertainment shows beamed directly from Mexico, and sports events transmitted live from throughout Latin America. But while this and other trends of cultural integration in the United States may acquire greater relevance over time, for now the most important aspect of this area of informal integration, with the greatest impact on U.S.-Mexican relations, involves the role of the American media in Mexico and in shaping an image of Mexico in the United States.

In March 1985, an intellectual friendly with the editor and publisher of one of Mexico's leading publications learned that President De la Madrid had been informed by Ambassador John Gavin that his government suspected the son of the Minister of Defense of involvement in drug traffic. The charge was grave, particularly in a country where the Defense Minister is always a military official and the honor of the armed forces is barely distinguishable from that of its highest-ranking officers. Moreover, the episode occurred during a period of deep tensions in U.S.-Mexican relations, just months after the death of U.S. DEA agent Enrique Camarena Salazar.

When informed of this potential front-page story, the newsman, known in Mexico for his courage and independence but fully aware of the risks of publicly criticizing the armed forces or smearing their image, told his confidant: "We won't touch the story until the gringo press publishes it." And so it was: the story was spiked in Mexico until eighteen months later, when, in November 1986, *The New York Times,* in its oft-maligned series on Mexico, finally unearthed it.[12] The more independent Mexican media quickly reproduced it, but always attributing it to the *Times.* It is worth adding that although the charge was never disproved in Mexico or substantiated by American authorities, the person in question was—if anything—more a small-time pawn of drug traffickers looking for protection from the Mexican army than an active participant in the trade. Even this scant involvement was open to question.

Since the late 1970s, and much more significantly as of the middle of the present decade, the American media have assumed a key role in U.S.-Mexican affairs. They largely shape the perceptions that ordinary U.S. citizens and policymakers have of Mexican and binational matters. They have had a decisive impact on the way Mexican public opinion and officials view American attitudes and policies toward the country. Often Mexican government circles and opinion-makers attach as much importance to what the U.S. press says *about* Mexico as to what the American administration does *to* Mexico. Frequently the reason behind this apparent reversal of priorities stems from the Mexican belief that there is less distance between the press and American administrations than many in the United States think, and that American officials can do far more about the image of Mexico conveyed by the media than they often admit to. Through leaks and impressions officials in Washington and at the U.S. embassy in Mexico shape the media's perception of the country in ways they don't realize.

But the importance of the American press is not limited to its impact in the United States. As the preceding anecdotes reveal, one of the most far-reaching results of the boom in U.S. media coverage of Mexico has been the "blow-back" or "rebound" effect in Mexico itself. To a certain extent, the American press has filled the void left by an archaic, largely self-censored Mexican press, significantly lacking in resources and credibility. In the case of newspapers, government control over the supply of newsprint and a substantial share of advertising has traditionally made the Mexican press subservient to and supportive of the state.

The fact that the country's largest and most influential publication, *Excelsior,* has a paid circulation of less than 200,000, in a city of over 15 million, is both a cause and an effect of this situation. Conversely, Televisa, the privately owned, virtually monopolistic network, is powerful, wealthy, and viewed by millions of Mexicans throughout the nation. Yet its news division is even more servile, self-censored, and government-controlled than the print media: its pro-government coverage of the 1988 presidential campaign and elections was considered scandalous even by

PRI standards. With a small number of exceptions, few Mexicans believe their national press, even when it tells the truth. But fewer still disbelieve the American press, even when it doesn't.

Stories critical about the government, high officials, or the country in general are printed abroad, and then work their way back to Mexico, sometimes with a devastating political effect. On occasion, this process reaches absurd extremes, as when a foreign correspondent sends home a dispatch simply repeating what a Mexican organ had already reported. But the original source of the story gets lost in the traffic, and a minor issue suddenly acquires relevance because it was reported abroad. Similarly, discredited columnists' or regional American papers' stories on Mexico often receive far more publicity locally than they do in the United States.

They do to a large extent because the Mexican government attributes to them a degree of importance which they may not possess. Through secretiveness, indignant and indirect replies, as well as excessive attention, Mexican authorities have given the U.S. press a force beyond its true strength. Similarly, by often refusing to grant access to foreign journalists, or allowing them only controlled access to officials and information, and by frequently ignoring the difference between background and off-the-record contacts—Mexican officials say the same things on and off the record—the government has forced the foreign press corps to seek out its own sources. In many cases these sources are less knowledgeable, credible, or authoritative than government spokesmen; but they are at least available and quotable, whereas official voices seldom are.

Needless to say, few Mexican citizens read *The New York Times* or *The Wall Street Journal* or watch Dan Rather on the *CBS Evening News.* Although American newspapers do circulate in Mexico City business and government offices on a same-day basis, and cable television subscribers as well as dish antenna owners receive U.S. television news every day, both reach only a tiny minority of the population. But through reprints in the Mexican press, Xerox copies, rumor and grapevine gossip, nearly all critical or negative investigative reporting on Mexico published in the United States circulates internally. Evidently it does so in a distorted and indirect fashion, in which criticism or unearthed information is exaggerated to the point of completely obfuscating the original report. This, of course, only makes things worse.

In September 1986, while President De la Madrid was attending the UN General Assembly, CBS ran a dubious story accusing a cousin of the President's of being a notorious drug trafficker. Enough Mexicans saw the report for the government to realize that it would be the first item on the grapevine the following day. Accordingly, the Attorney General called a news conference within hours of the CBS transmission, hoping to give a prompt, credible reply to the report. Whatever doubt anybody could still harbor with regard to the speed and extension of the dissemination of U.S. news reports in Mexico was laid to rest that evening.

But this episode also confirmed many Mexican officials' and individuals' suspicions, already aroused in 1984 by the Jack Anderson affair, of American government-inspired conspiracies behind every negative story about Mexico in the U.S. press. The story obviously overshadowed De la Madrid's speeches on the same day to the United Nations and to a Council of the Americas dinner hosted by David Rockefeller. The only source CBS used for its report was a shady, disguised, and far from trustworthy individual who apparently had worked for De la Madrid's cousin at some point. This person had been made available to CBS for an on-camera interview by American officials believed to be from the U.S. Customs Service, without the knowledge or agreement of other investigative entities, notably the DEA and the FBI, who in fact doubted the informant's reliability. Later, sources inside CBS reported that traditional double-sourcing, cross-checking procedures had not been followed by the news division because of pressure to get the story on the air the day De la Madrid was in New York. CBS had simply been manipulated—probably unwittingly—by a Reagan administration hard-liner to take a below-the-belt swipe at the country's President. Nothing was ever heard again about the incident, on CBS or elsewhere.

Indeed, during most of the "Mexico-bashing" period, beginning in 1984 and lasting through late 1986, key sectors of the Reagan administration and the Republican right wing, from William von Raab to the DEA, from Constantine Menges to Elliott Abrams, from Jesse Helms to Oliver North, have used the American media to pursue their own Mexican agendas. Timely, damaging, and unsubstantiated but plausible leaks, insinuations, and unprocessed, apparently incriminating "raw intelligence," old information rehashed and presented as revelation: all of these classical tools were used by officials, and often not clearly understood or decisively confirmed by reporters.

Beyond the paradoxical effect it has in Mexico and its contradictory role in the United States, however, the underlying issue involving the American media and Mexico has to do with the dramatic rise in Mexico's importance to the United States. Together with the country's undeniable economic and increasingly political crisis, these factors have spawned a veritable explosion in U.S. press coverage of Mexican affairs. Until 1972, Europe and other regions were covered more extensively than Mexico, but the prestige media granted Mexico priority among Third World states. In 1970, Mexico received 17 minutes of network coverage. The total had reached 88 minutes by 1979. While 1979 represented a peak period in the coverage that the Washington *Post, The New York Times,* and the three television networks gave Mexico, 1985 and 1986 witnessed a dramatic rise.

Thus ABC, CBS, and NBC all devoted more than 90 minutes of airtime to Mexico-related events on their evening news programs in 1985 and 1986, but as little as 6 minutes and never more than 70 minutes during the previous five years. The Washington *Post* devoted 1,303 and 1,575 column inches to Mexico in 1985 and 1986, respectively, but an average of 500 inches from 1980 to 1984.[13] A great deal of the airtime in 1985 was devoted to drugs and to the earthquake and did not imply that the intensive coverage would last. But like the lengthy series on Mexico which *The Wall Street Journal, The New York Times,* the Chicago *Tribune,* and even smaller papers such as the Minneapolis *Star & Tribune* or the Kansas City *Star* have run, the statistic underlines the changes during the last decade.

In the mid-1970s many of the major American newspapers and magazines had reporters in Mexico, but in a good number of cases they were correspondents or stringers who had settled in Mexico for other reasons. These individuals often knew Mexico well, had lived there for long periods of time, and had grown to love and understand the country. Things began to change with the emergence of the Central American imbroglio in 1978–79, as many of the American media not previously present in the area began to send correspondents to Central America, frequently basing them in Mexico. Even at this later stage, several reporters had experience in Mexico or Latin America, spoke excellent Spanish, and viewed Mexico through sympathetic or at least unprejudiced eyes. A highly qualified core group of correspondents gave orientation and understanding to the rest of the foreign press community.

The stage was set, though, for discouraging developments. By having to cover both Mexico and Central America, which sometimes formed one single story but mostly constituted two entirely different sets of events, the news organizations were creating situations of personal and journalistic schizophrenia. Since American domestic considerations made Central America the dominant story, Mexico was covered by exhausted, frustrated correspondents resentful over too much traveling, or by stringers and free-lancers eager to leave their mark in any way they could. And even this was better than what would happen later.

By the mid-1980s Mexico City had become a post like any other. No special qualifications were considered necessary; reporters were sent down for given periods of time and were then sent off to their next assignment. Some came from other foreign slots. Others were transferred from desk jobs in the United States or from reporting on sports or state governments. With a few notable exceptions, competence and familiarity with the country and the region largely disappeared. Thus between 1985 and 1987, for example, such major publications as *The New York Times, The Wall Street Journal, Time* magazine, and the Washington *Post* had correspondents in Mexico who did not speak Spanish. This in itself was not unjustifiable or damning: if every journalist, diplomat, or banker was expected to speak the language of the country to which he is posted, there would be few applicants for a great many jobs. But for Mexico this was new.

The decline in experience and qualifications for covering Mexican matters among the major media's journalists coincided with a sharp rise in the number of lesser U.S. news organizations with correspondents or stringers. By 1986 the Mexico City Foreign Correspondents Association Directory listed 70 American members and 214 members overall. Not every one was a full-fledged correspondent, but the figure was nonetheless revealing.[14] Simultaneously, the space and time devoted to Mexican items in the local press and television affiliates' news in the United States without reporters in Mexico but connected with news chains also increased.

A large number of newspapers, chiefly but not exclusively in the West and Southwest, from the Denver *Post* to the Houston *Chronicle,* from the Sacramento *Bee* to the San Jose *Mercury News,* from the New Orleans *Times-Picayune* to the Philadelphia *Inquirer,* began sending correspondents to Mexico and Central America. Instead of using the wire services or the large news services, they began publishing in-house reporting, sometimes better than that of the large organizations but often woefully worse.

The consequences surfaced during the first instance of extensive U.S. coverage of a strictly Mexican story: the 1985 elections for governors of Sonora and Nuevo León amidst widespread claims in Mexico and abroad of electoral fraud. They are perhaps best described by an American reporter:

> Although there were individual examples of good reporting, American press coverage of Mexico's . . . election suffered from significant errors of exaggeration and distortion. Essentially, these errors stemmed from the lack of understanding of Mexico's political reality and biases on the part of U.S. reporters. Some examples:
> —The U.S. press believed that widespread discontent with the

governing PRI—because of economic troubles and corruption—
would be channeled electorally. Although that would have happened in the U.S., that is not how the Mexican system has traditionally functioned.

—The U.S. press, because of a bias toward a two-party political
system, and an attachment to the underdog, elevated the importance of the PAN, believing that it would be the primary beneficiary
of Mexican discontent, and therefore could win the election in
several states.

—Worst of all, because of an overreaction to fraud, exaggerated
by a tendency toward "pack journalism" . . . and experience with
election violence in Central America, the U.S. press helped the
PAN promote the idea that there might be major violence after the
election if the PRI won due to widespread fraud.[15]

If viewed impartially, it is often true that serious reporting on Mexico
is barely more critical—and frequently less so—than in the few Mexican
publications that keep their distance from the government. Unfortunately, the conclusions that the U.S. press has tended to draw from this
critical coverage have indeed often been exaggerated, alarmist, and sometimes downright foolish. The fact that Mexico as a country, a society,
and a government has proved totally unprepared for the avalanche of
reporters, camera crews, and "in-depth series" has not improved matters. There have been sharpened tensions, irritation, and extreme views
on both sides.

Part of the overall deterioration in the American perception of Mexico
is due to media hype and government media manipulation. Most of what
is presently, and often justly, criticized about Mexico has been true for
at least half a century, without raising many American eyebrows or
provoking much self-righteous indignation. But while the resentment,
even the outrage, many Mexicans feel and express over the treatment
their country has received in the U.S. media is sincere, official objections
and anger stem above all from the "blow-back" phenomenon. And this
is not a media problem, or even a broader "public relations in a situation
of crisis" issue. It has to do with informal information integration: the
increasingly free, unmanaged, and uncontrollable flow of information,
impressions, and opinions from one nation to the other.

The emergence of a strong and independent Mexican press and television with resources to make its independence a fixture would undoubtedly diminish the weight of the U.S. media. But it is likely that the
American press will play a greater role in Mexico, taking advantage
either of ongoing government limitations placed on the local media or

of the opening of the Mexican news scene which might follow in the future.

Similarly, over time, many Mexican news organizations' penetration into the U.S. market, either through sales or direct presence will influence their coverage back in Mexico. If U.S. earnings eventually overtake Mexican revenues, if the American division of each entity becomes more important than the Mexican parent company, the organizations' real interests will quickly outweigh whatever feelings of patriotism it may harbor.

In the final analysis, the issue of the American media's role in Mexico must be placed in the broader context of "cultural integration" or the "Americanization of Mexico." On the surface, this would appear to be the most obvious aspect of the two nations' integration. More and more Mexicans have adopted American eating, clothing, dancing, and reading habits, sexual mores, musical taste and television and movie preferences. The examples are well known and oft-quoted: U.S. advertising agencies using American-looking (white, blond, blue-eyed, and tall) models to advertise U.S. products on Mexican television; the growing number of government officials and business community executives who have studied in the United States; Mexican youth wearing American clothes, listening to American music, speaking anglicized Spanish.

From the long lines of cars queuing up in southern Mexico City when McDonald's opened its first franchise to the millions of Mexican viewers of Dallas Cowboy football games, these and many other cases of Americanization are dragged out by two apparently opposing but in fact converging schools of thought. Right- and left-wing Mexican nationalists condemn these phenomena strongly. In their opinion, they lead down the road to damnation through the loss of the nation's identity, purity, and traditional values.

The left tends to concentrate its criticisms on the American origin of the changes sweeping Mexico. They view them as a symptom or expression of other, more significant and dangerous forms of American penetration, above all economic and political. The right, in many cases led by the Church, emphasizes the "dissolution" aspect of the country's cultural or daily-life Americanization. Its chief preoccupation concerns sexual matters, extending to the weakening of family values and religion in general. The strongest opposition to the standard elementary school textbook in Mexico has come from the Church and parent associations because of sex education.

In the United States, these same trends are similarly interpreted as symbolizing the Americanization of Mexico, as a manifestation of a diluting, fading Mexican nationalism.[16] They are frequently taken for evidence that the nationalistic posturing by Mexico's authorities is out of step with the true feelings of the country's inhabitants. According to this interpretation, while the Mexican government, the political establishment, and an anachronistic "intelligentsia" oppose or resent the United States, the people of Mexico feel differently, as shown by their widespread adoption of American customs, tastes, and products. Sometimes this view is formulated with regard to certain regions of Mexico, such as the border, the north in general, the cities, or in relation to certain social strata.

These conceptions, while inaccurate, reflect an undeniable fact. Along with its strong economic presence in Mexico, the United States also wields an undeniable, overpowering influence of another sort, which can be called cultural in the absence of a better term. It is wide-ranging, multifaceted, and growing.

There are 275,000 American citizens residing in Mexico registered with the State Department; the total number is probably far higher. Many are retirees, living in places like Cuernavaca, San Miguel de Allende, and Chapala, Jalisco. But more than 100,000 live in Mexico City, not exactly a town for retirement. They largely form part of the American business community, which is widely distributed, cohesive, yet at the same time in constant communication and interrelation with Mexican society, or more correctly, with the upper layers of Mexican "high society."

In addition to this permanent American presence, tourism is another vehicle for direct cultural outreach. While some of Mexico's resorts, like Cancún, and parts of Baja California on the Caribbean, cater almost exclusively to foreign tourists, most are not enclaves in the strict sense of the word. Acapulco never was an enclave, since Mexicans have vacationed in the bay since the 1940s. The more recent sun spots—Puerto Vallarta, Manzanillo, Ixtapa-Zihuatanejo—possess a few enclave-like characteristics, but by and large there is a great deal of intercourse between Mexicans and Americans. The United States exercises its cultural and social clout through this important channel in many ways.

But the American influence in Mexico goes beyond its presence. Between 1930 and 1985, for example, a total of approximately 20,000 movies were exhibited in Mexico. Of this sum, 53 percent were American-made, 27 percent were from other foreign countries, and 20 percent were Mexican.[17] Equivalent ratios for more recent times are even more skewed in favor of the United States. In a country which once had a thriving film industry, exporting movies to the rest of Latin America, the numbers are staggering. The U.S. share of television programs is similar; moreover, many Mexican productions are often so influenced by American fads and profoundly permeated by American role models that they are barely distinguishable from U.S.-made series. Only the *telenovela,* or Mexican soap opera, truly remains as an indigenous television genre.

There is no question that consumption patterns among the urban middle class are increasingly "American": American products, fads, and mores exert an undisputed attraction over Mexican youth. Hamburgers, jeans, rock music, a certain sexual liberation, are telltale signs of the apparent growth of American influence in Mexico in recent years.

Are these processes indicative of the Americanization of Mexico or rather of the country's growing middle-class nature as a society? Similar complaints are heard in other countries: Jack Lang, the former French Minister of Culture, expressed the most eloquent one during his speech at the UNESCO Conference on Cultural Policies in Mexico City in August 1982, when he denounced "American cultural imperialism." His cry of alarm was undoubtedly a useful and important one, to the extent that it pointed out a problem and drew attention to it. And it would be false to state that many Mexican intellectuals and politicians do not share these overall views.

But is the relative uniformity of fashion, eating habits, television fare, music popularity, and movies throughout the world a symptom of Americanization, or does it simply constitute an expression of U.S. influence in an increasingly unified, global, and mainly middle-class-oriented cultural marketplace? Are blue jeans American, or middle-class? Rock music is undoubtedly American in origin, but is it so popular because it is American, or because it is tailored for middle-class consumption? Are fast-food joints a product of American hegemony, or the result of more women in the workplace with less time to cook?

Are all these trends essentially American, or did they originate in the United States because the underlying economic and social processes which gave birth to them first emerged there? There are grounds for believing that they are American only because the United States is the quintessential middle-class country, which all others are increasingly resembling, whether they like it or not. The United States is where the massification of consumption first took place. Other countries have followed: the key question is whether the ensuing trends are signs of Americanization, or of a similar massification of consumption patterns marked by their American origin.

The "Americanization" of Mexico should perhaps be seen more correctly as the "modernization" of Mexico. In some cases, the American influence is exaggerated. In 1983, there were only 1,200 registered Mexican undergraduate students in the United States, fewer than Colombia (1,600) or Venezuela (5,000).[18] For a nation of more than eighty million inhabitants, and well over one million university students, the figure is not overwhelming. The important change in Mexico is to what extent the governing elite and the business community are now sending their off-spring to private Mexican universities, and in some cases abroad for graduate studies.

It seems futile to attempt to limit or even to condemn these trends, although many in Mexico do. In most cases, they represent consumption preferences, not political choices. The Mexican teenagers who prefer hamburgers to *mole,* football to bullfights, hard rock to *boleros* or *salsa,* are not making an irreversible political or ideological decision. They are simply expressing preferences which may have underlying, long-term political effects but which cannot be mistaken for those effects. In the same way that the United States cannot keep Mexican immigrants out, Mexico cannot exclude these American influences.

The border Mexico shares with its neighbor is permeable in both directions, at all levels. The better parts of American "culture"—its democratizing, youthful, and irreverent influence—can only do Mexico good; its negative traits (blandness, disrespect for "Culture" in the strong, European sense, the total lack of a sense of history) run up against Mexico's strong suits. The country has little to fear in this realm, al-though a certain trepidation is not surprising, given Mexico's well-founded concerns in other domains: economic and political, above all. Mexico possesses an extraordinarily rich, diversified, historically well-anchored cultural personality of its own. It has its language and shapes, its rhythms and colors, its beliefs and its fantasies. All the McDonald's in the world could never submerge them.

The Fear of Mexicanization

Robert A. Pastor

Imagine long, tall American fences and aggressive, rednecked border guards inspecting documents, interrogating illiterate Mexicans in English, searching cars and trucks for secret compartments containing drugs or undeclared goods. Then consider that 192 million people entered the country from Mexico in 1986 or roughly a half million each day. On the average, 250 U.S. customs and immigration officials were on duty. That means that there were about 1.3 entries per agent for every second of the year.[1]

Late one night in 1986, I crossed from Ciudad Juárez to El Paso with two Mexican friends who did not have documents since we were only planning to have a drink. The U.S. official asked a single question, and I answered. He then signaled us across. During rush hour, guards hardly have time to wave cars through. No border in the world is crossed more routinely and often than the 1,952-mile line that separates Mexico from the United States. From 1981 to 1986, U.S. immigration officials counted 1.1 billion individuals entering the country from Mexico.

If sovereignty divides nations, migration connects them. The governments of the United States and Mexico have erected formidable barriers to defend their differences, but the tenacious bonds connecting millions of families and friends on both sides of the border may well prove more enduring and important. In every year since 1960, there have been more immigrants from Mexico than from any other country in the world—a total of 1.5 million.

Mexico is also the largest source of illegal migration into the United States. Without hope or expectation of securing a visa, or simply without patience, many Mexicans go to the United States *indocumentado,* without documents. Estimates of the total number of Mexican illegal migrants vary widely. The Census Bureau estimated that there were about 1.47 million undocumented Mexican workers in the United States. This proved to be an underestimate. As a result of the Immigration Act of 1986, 1.8 million undocumented Mexicans applied for amnesty. This represented 74 percent of the 2.4 million people who applied under the regular and the special agricultural workers provisions of the law, and it means that more Mexicans settled in the United States illegally than legally since 1960.[2]

The absolute number of legal and illegal Mexican migrants would generate less interest if it were not for the rate of increase. In 1970, the Census Bureau reported 4.2 million people in the United States of Mexican origin. In 1987, that number had increased to 11.8 million, and this was probably low since it included only a portion of the undocumented population.[3] In other words, there were more than three times as many people of Mexican origin in the United States in 1987 as in 1970. And since 1980, the Mexican-American population has grown more than three times faster than the overall population.

The migration of people is transforming the United States and its relationship with Mexico, and some in the United States have reacted with alarm. Richard Lamm, the former governor of Colorado, described the new immigration as a "time bomb . . . massive, and it is out of control."[4] Former CIA Director William Colby saw Mexico's population explosion as "the most obvious threat" to the United States. Predicting that there might be as many as 20 million migrants by the year 2000, Colby said the Border Patrol "will not have enough bullets to stop them."[5] Similarly, in 1984, CIA Director William Casey argued that if the United States failed to prevent "another Cuba in Central America, Mexico will have a big problem, and we're going to have a massive wave of migration."[6]

In February 1986, after several months in which apprehensions of illegal aliens on the Mexican border had increased by 50 percent over the previous year, officials from the INS estimated, correctly as it turned out, that total apprehensions would reach as high as 1.8 million that year. Alan Nelson, the commissioner, warned: "We are seeing the greatest surge of people in history across our southern border."[7]

On the eve of the centennial celebration of the Statue of Liberty, in the summer of 1986, a survey showed that 49 percent of the U.S. public wanted immigration reduced.[8] In the Southwest, where immigration had been highest, the reaction seemed the most fearful. In November 1986, despite the opposition of the governor and virtually all the elected officials in California, Proposition 63 to make English the state's official language was approved by 73 percent of the voters.

Immigration, a great American tradition, a source of U.S. strength, and an integrating glue with its neighbor, has become viewed by many as a serious vulnerability. In response to Mexican immigration, the United States has begun subtly to reverse roles and exchange positions with its normally more defensive, fearful neighbor. "We find ourselves suddenly threatened by hordes of . . . immigrants . . . whose progress we cannot arrest."[9] This complaint could have been made by almost any state governor today, but it was made by the last Mexican governor of California in 1846. On immigration, Americans have begun to fear being overrun.

Ambivalence, which defines so much of the relationship, is sculpted into an art form on the issue of migration. It is evident even in the terms used to describe the phenomenon. A person who crosses the border clandestinely is called an "illegal alien," though the phrase sounds as if it should apply to a creature from another planet. More sensitive Americans use the Mexican euphemism "undocumented worker," but that should apply to an American who misplaced his punch card, not to a person who has trespassed into a neighboring country, violating its first law.

Americans are of several minds as to what to do about immigration because their emotions run in different directions from their political or economic interests. Many people find themselves on both sides of the issue at the same time. Liberals are sympathetic to the plight of illegal migrants but also oppose their entry because it undermines organized labor. Conservatives favor immigration because it means cheaper labor, but they also fear losing control and diluting the Anglo culture.

Ronald Reagan articulated the immigration myth, which occupies a special place in the American self-image, when he described the nation's uniqueness: "You can go to France. But you can't become a Frenchman. You can go to Japan, and you can't become Japanese. But people from every corner of the world can come to America and become Americans." And yet Reagan also acted on both conservative impulses. He pressed for a tough new law, warning Americans that "the simple truth is that we've lost control of our own borders, and no nation can do that and survive." And he endorsed a proposal for permitting a free flow of cheap Mexican labor for U.S. farmers and to prevent Mexico's "safety valve" from being shut.[10] Conflicting emotions and interests have produced contradictory approaches, even by the same person.

Since the nineteenth century, each migration wave that has washed onto America's shores has impelled the natives—that is, the previous immigrants—to ask themselves hard questions about who they are as a nation. Each time, Americans hesitated, then reacted negatively, but eventually the nation redefined itself and found room for every new group. Mexican immigrants, like their predecessors, have raised difficult questions; some have been asked before, but many are new.

The essence of the questions is whether Mexican-Americans are similar to other hyphenated Americans or different. Will Mexican immigrants assimilate, or will they try to keep one foot in each country until their numbers are so large that they can make separatist demands? Will they advance like other immigrants, or be segregated and stranded at the bottom of the ladder of opportunity with blacks? Will they exacerbate differences in U.S.-Mexican relations or narrow the chasm of misunderstanding? Like an Aztec priest, James Fallows grabbed the heart of the matter: will "the cultural fabric . . . stretch, as it has before, or finally be torn"?[11]

"When the country was new, it might have been good policy to admit foreigners. But it is so no longer." These are the words of a congressman. They have a contemporary ring to them, but they were uttered by Representative Harrison G. Otis of Massachusetts on June 26, 1797, when the United States had but 4 million people.[12] Fortunately, he failed to persuade his colleagues, and the argument moved few of his successors. Since Otis's warning, over 53 million people have come to the United States, moved by the two most elemental human instincts, fear and hope. They have been pushed by violence, oppression, or the lack of opportunity at home and pulled by dreams and expectations.

Those who dismiss the American dream by saying that most dreams do not come true miss the point of a dream. One expects successful second- and third-generation immigrants to wax nostalgic for the dream, but what is most intriguing is the way it rivets new immigrants. Polls show that even when they do not achieve their high expectations, few are disillusioned or dissatisfied. In 1976, a survey of Mexican immigrants three years after their arrival showed a high level of satisfaction (79 percent) and a very low level of dissatisfaction (1 percent) with their lives and work in the United States. Another survey, three years later, found an overwhelming consensus that "life in America had been a positive experience," despite difficulties.[13]

Otis's misgivings have been repeated periodically through U.S. history, but they have only been taken seriously when the nation was fearful, when the economy was depressed, when foreign enemies threatened, or when the number of immigrants seemed disproportionately large and exotic. The first nativist response occurred in the middle of the nineteenth century when the level of immigration increased sharply and a large percentage was Catholic. The Know Nothing Party, a party that received the label it deserved, spoke for the reaction.

Congress, however, delayed setting any limits until 1882, the year after the arrival of a record 788,992 immigrants. Then it established qualitative standards, excluding lunatics, idiots, and "persons likely to become a public charge." These exclusions were expanded over the next two decades to discriminate against Japanese and Chinese. At the same time, the Statue of Liberty was dedicated with Emma Lazarus's inspiring poem engraved in its base: "Give me your tired, your poor, your huddled masses yearning to breathe free." Thus, ambivalence is imprinted on the national character: the myth of welcoming everyone, the reality of choosing some.

Most immigrants came from Northern Europe until the 1880s, when their origins became more diverse. In the first two decades of the twentieth century, 14.5 million immigrants arrived, and two-thirds of these were from Southern and Eastern Europe. Because of the large numbers and the "exotic" origins, Congress finally decided to set a numerical limit on immigration, but that left the more difficult decision of choosing whom to exclude. After more than ten years of debate, Congress passed two immigration laws, in 1921 and 1924, establishing the national origins quota system. The new laws tried to re-create the nation that had existed before immigrants arrived between 1890 and 1920. The quotas were based on a formula that effectively reduced immigration from Southern and Eastern Europe. The premise was that U.S. strength depended on the racial superiority of its earlier immigrants from Northern and Western Europe.

Racism permeated the entire debate, including the issue of whether to exempt Mexico from the quotas. Congress had previously spared Mexico from a "head tax" imposed on all immigrants as a positive gesture to Mexico rather than as an incentive for immigration. But in 1924, Georgia's Senator William Harris argued for a quota, insisting that as many as 100,000 Mexicans could "come in here," and, he continued, the Mexicans "are about as undesirable as any people coming into this country, and I want to get rid of them." This view had its adherents in Congress, but others were more concerned that Mexico would become a back door for illegal migrants from Europe. "Once these aliens [Europeans] land in Mexico," said Ohio Senator Frank Willis, "they proceed to the border and almost invariably fall into the hands of the professional smuggler . . . coyotes."[14]

The majority of Congress voted to except Mexico and Latin America from any quotas to show that the United States wanted good relations and would accord the region special treatment. Also, there was no reason to fear migration from the region then. As Senator Alva Adams said: "Remember Mexico is not a populous country. It is not teeming with millions of people eager to leave. Those who seek to come are few in number. There will be no great influx if the border is left open."[15] Forty years later, after Mexico's population expanded, Adams's words would sound ironic, but in 1924, the moral and practical arguments won, and migration remained unlimited from Mexico and Latin America.

Immigration from Mexico, however, increased greatly in the 1920s as a result of the pull of an expanding U.S. economy and the push of the Cristero rebellion in Mexico, which was a reaction to the government's anti-Church campaign. From 1920 to 1930, the average number of immigrants arriving from Mexico each year was 45,929, which was more than four times the average during the first two decades of the century. After the U.S. economy plunged into the Depression in 1930, Congress debated again whether to impose a quota on Mexico. The State Department had serious differences with Mexico over Central America, but it did not link the two issues, and in fact opposed quotas against Mexico because it thought they would be interpreted as an unfriendly gesture. Historian Robert Divine concluded that this argument was the "vital factor in defeating the restrictionist cause" in Congress.[16]

Nonetheless, as the Depression worsened, the flow of immigrants to the United States slowed and even reversed. As jobs became scarce, Mexicans returned home or were repatriated. Though it had tried but failed to stop emigration in the 1920s, the Mexican government helped their countrymen return in the 1930s.[17] During World War II, the two governments' views and interests converged to permit a new policy. Mexico had come to believe in the safety valve thesis, and the United States faced severe worker shortages. The two governments began the bracero program. Since farmers in northern Mexico did not want to lose their labor, Mexico recruited workers from the interior, and it discouraged them from going to a state like Texas that discriminated against Mexicans.

Both governments had reservations about the program. Mexico was embarrassed by charges from the left that the program was a substitute for genuine land reform, and Washington was constantly pressed by farmers and businessmen who opposed the labor and anti-discrimination regulations and wanted to recruit Mexican labor themselves. Nonetheless, both governments decided that the program's benefits exceeded the costs, and the agreement was renewed after the war.

Some businesses on the U.S. border conspired with immigration officials to undermine the agreement by illegally recruiting Mexicans. In 1948, Mexico protested the illegal migration; the U.S. government apologized, but businesses continued to violate the agreement. In 1951, the President's Commission on Migratory Labor reported that the illegal traffic "is virtually an invasion." The Mexican government, according to a cable from the U.S. ambassador at the time, "asked that we pass a law making it illegal for anyone in our country to employ an illegal immigrant." The ambassador explained that Mexico's request was impractical and unreasonable;[18] twenty years later, this was Mexico's view when the United States proposed the same idea. Congress rejected employer sanctions in 1951, and as a result, illegal migration worsened.[19]

In 1954, an INS official characterized illegal migration as "the greatest peacetime invasion complacently suffered by a country under open, flagrant, contemptuous violation of its laws."[20] Mexico decided to withhold its support for a new bilateral program until the United States took action against illegal aliens. Washington responded with a curveball. It let the program expire and then announced that braceros would be contracted unilaterally until a binational accord was reached. Mexico protested and exhorted its laborers to stay home. The workers ignored the warning, and Mexican police and troops tried to prevent them from crossing. After numerous violent incidents, Mexico backed down and negotiated a new agreement.[21]

President Eisenhower then accepted Mexico's request to remove the illegals. He appointed retired General Joseph Swing as INS Commissioner. Swing initiated Operation Wetback, a massive roundup and deportation of more than one million Mexican migrants. Although the paramilitary operation trampled the rights of legitimate along with illegal migrants, both the local communities and the Mexican government viewed the operation as successful and necessary to make the bracero program work. The 1955 INS Annual Report declared victory: the "wetback problem no longer exists. . . . The border has been secured."[22]

The agreement worked for a decade, but opposition grew in the United States from labor unions and Hispanic organizations concerned about the jobs being taken from Mexican-Americans. These groups succeeded in ending the program on December 31, 1964.[23] Oscar Sanchez of the U.S. Labor Council for Latin American Advancement said that his group opposed the program because it took jobs away from native workers or undercut their wages. Reverend Sal Alvarez of the United Farmworkers of America later explained that his union saw the termination of the program as "part of the civil rights movement of the early 1960s."[24] From 1942 to 1964, between 4 and 5 million farm workers from Mexico participated in the bracero program. A comparable number of Mexicans may have worked illegally during the same period.[25] Illegal migration did not stop when the program ended; some believe that it grew worse.[26]

The Mexican government tried to persuade the United States to negotiate another bracero agreement, but the constellation of political forces in the United States precluded that. Mexico therefore implemented a Border Industrialization Program—the *maquiladoras*—to absorb some of the surplus labor, but the program attracted mostly women instead of the ex-braceros, who were mostly men. Mexico finally abandoned its effort to get a new agreement in 1975 because, according to President Luis Echeverría, such agreements "have never succeeded in preventing undocumented emigration in the past."[27]

In 1965, the year after the bracero program was terminated, the United States fundamentally changed its immigration policy. A new law repealed the national origins quota system and replaced it with one that set annual limits and allotted quotas of up to 20,000 for each country, with preference for family reunification and people with special skills. The same system was extended to the Western Hemisphere in 1976. As he signed the 1965 act, President Lyndon Johnson criticized the old policy as discriminatory and "un-American."[28]

No one then foresaw how much the new law would change immigration trends or the United States itself. At the time, the 1965 law was viewed in the context of the civil rights movement, but twenty years later, the law appears more like a global rights initiative, an unintended effort by a "Northern" country to relate to the newly emerging Third World in a unique way. Unlike conventional programs of aid to the developing world, which are inherently paternalistic, the new immigration policy could be interpreted as a message of respect for Third World people by welcoming them to change the face of the United States so as to make it look more like their countries.

Between 1820 and 1960, 80 percent of all immigrants to the United States came from Europe. In 1978, ten years after the law went into effect, 82 percent of all immigrants were from Latin America and Asia.[29] Mexicans took greatest advantage of the change. Since 1965, because the numerical limitation did not apply to family reunification, the number of Mexican immigrants each year was always two to five times the 20,000 limit per country.

The new law precipitated the third major wave of immigration to the United States after a hiatus of thirty years of few immigrants. From 1960 to 1986, the United States absorbed over 11.2 million immigrants, not including 1.4 million refugees and 2 to 4 million undocumented workers.[30] Compared with earlier waves, push factors, according to Thomas Muller of the Urban Institute, "seem to be relatively more important than 'pull' ones. In the past, such as during the 1890s, immigration slowed when unemployment in this country climbed, but in the late 1970s and [early] 1980s, immigration reached a post-1920s high—the first peak to have come when unemployment was growing rapidly."[31]

During the bracero program, Mexico was preoccupied with illegal migration, and the United States was disinterested. Since 1971, when Congress first held hearings on the subject, the two countries have reversed roles with the United States seeking an effective policy to stop it and Mexico preferring the status quo. U.S. labor unions adopted Mexico's 1950s proposal for employer sanctions to remove the incentive for hiring illegal workers. That became the centerpiece of the Simpson-Mazzoli-Rodino immigration bill. The most powerful argument on behalf of the bill, and probably the one that attracted the support of three very different Presidents—Ford, Carter, and Reagan—was the legal and sovereignty issue. The federal government is responsible for defending the border and that includes regulating entry. As a nation of laws, the United States could not accept an underclass compelled to live outside the law. No one seriously questioned the need to set limits on migration; the issue was whether and how to enforce the law. The debate on the Simpson-Rodino bill was actually not about immigration, but whether to make it illegal for employers to hire illegal migrants.

Opponents included the U.S. Chamber of Commerce because of the threat of sanctions and the promise of paperwork, farmers who wanted cheap labor, Hispanic groups that feared increased discrimination and less Mexican migration, and civil liberties groups for similar reasons. Congress massaged the bill to assuage the concerns of most of the opponents. It was amended to include a liberal legalization formula and provisions to prevent discrimination (for the Hispanic organizations), to provide an alternative to an identification card system (for the civil liberties groups), and to expand agricultural labor (for farmers).

In the final bill, Congress also established a commission for the study of international migration and cooperative economic development. The purpose of the commission was to develop trade and investment proposals for Mexico and other Western Hemisphere countries that would "alleviate the conditions that lead to illegal migration." In fact, the relationship between migration and development is an exceedingly complex one, but the available research suggests that rapid development—more than underdevelopment—stimulates migration. On the other side of the equation, it appears that migration benefits the receiving country more than it does the sending nation.[32] Congress ignored this research and established the commission for a political reason—to show Hispanic groups, Mexico, and other emigrant countries that the bill also addressed the supply side of the migration issue.

Five of the eleven Hispanic congressmen changed their previous opposition to the bill, partly because conservative groups seemed to grow more vicious in their criticism of all immigrants with each congressional failure to pass legislation. Albert Bustamente, a Mexican-American congressman from South Texas, acknowledged the need "to gain control of our borders and shores. If we don't begin to do that, Hispanics will be the victims of harsh repression and discrimination." The economic collapse in many parts of Texas also caused many Mexican-American voters to complain about losing jobs to illegals. "They're all right," said Rafael Cerda, an American, pointing to a group of undocumented workers in his city, San Antonio. "There's just an awful lot of them, and they work for less."[33] In the end, the decision by Hispanic leaders to support the legislation made passage easier in October 1986.

The 1986 Immigration Act pretended to be a global policy, but it was mostly about U.S.-Mexican labor relations. Neither government, however, was prepared to negotiate this issue. Washington sought Mexico's views, but never offered a negotiable proposal; Mexico declined to comment, but protested each time the bill neared passage. This Kabuki dance was repeated many times during a ten-year period.

While many academics predicted the bill would have no effect on illegal migration, when it finally passed Mexican President De la Madrid offered his assessment: "One can expect migration to the United States to diminish. . . . That could signify a grave element in the development of Mexico, since this factor has functioned as a mechanism of adjustment in relation to employment."[34] There were many signs of illegal workers returning to Mexico and Central America. A survey one year after the law took effect by two reporters from *The Wall Street Journal* found that "job opportunities for illegals are waning," and INS Commissioner Alan Nelson announced that border apprehensions had declined over 30 percent from the previous year, and this was with a much larger Border Patrol.[35]

If the law is enforced, it will reduce the flow, but large numbers of

Mexicans will continue to make the journey, legally and illegally, for a season or forever. The basic problem is inescapable. Mexico's population will continue growing for the foreseeable future at more than two times the rate of U.S. population growth; its labor force will expand by nearly one million per year until at least the year 2000.[36] The prospects for providing jobs for this expanding labor pool are dismal. The gap in income between the two nations will remain vast and will continue to be a strong inducement pulling Mexican workers north.

People will also continue to move for non-economic reasons—to unite families and reassemble villages, which seem to be moving across the border en masse. In the movie *El Norte,* a brother and sister flee Guatemala and journey to Los Angeles, where they live in a barrio with Mexicans and Guatemalans. After several weeks there, the man finally turns to a friend and asks in puzzlement: "Where are the gringos?" These transplanted villages facilitate the trip and the subsequent adjustment for new migrants.

The debate on the immigration bill circled around the question of whether immigrants—legal or illegal—displace American workers or create jobs. Labor unions and some economists argue that immigrants displace American workers because they are willing to work harder for less. Businessmen and other economists say that immigrants take jobs that Americans do not want, and they make the economy more productive, which in turn creates more jobs. The rebuttal—that Americans would take the job if the wages were better—is met by the argument that some businesses and farms could not survive paying higher wages.

Another economic claim is that the parts of the country with the highest rates of immigration have tended also to have the highest rates of economic growth and job creation. This was certainly true during the 1970s and 1980s in Southern California, which has the highest concentration of Mexican immigrants. It is also true that those countries, notably the United States, Australia, and Brazil, that are "immigrant nations" tend to exhibit a social and economic dynamism, an optimism, and an adaptability that are rare among more closed societies or among emigrant-sending countries. Like any imports, immigrants carry something new, and the receiving nation is affected by them even while it reshapes them. Immigrants bring a sense of movement, a desire for improvement, and a willingness to take risks.

This intangible influence has practical effects. A study by Barry Chiswick, a University of Illinois economist, found that within eleven to sixteen years after their arrival, male immigrants begin to earn more than the native-born. Their children earn 5 to 10 percent more than those of native-born parents. He also found that after fifteen years working in the United States, the average Mexican immigrant earns more than the average Mexican-American born in the United States.[37] Mexicans, like other immigrants, progress, but how far and how rapidly they advance depends to some extent on their level of education and skill when they arrive. This partly explains why middle-class Cuban immigrants have done better than Mexicans. But a fascinating study comparing Mexican immigrants with two groups of Cubans—those who emigrated for economic reasons before the Revolution and those who came for political reasons afterwards—reveals a hidden factor for Cuban success: the role of the government. For foreign policy reasons, the U.S. government fashioned an elaborate program of education and welfare to help Cuban "political" immigrants assimilate, thus reinforcing their "initial advantage of social class origin." In contrast, the lack of supportive programs for Mexican and lesser-educated Cuban economic immigrants resulted in a longer assimilation process.[38] In brief, immigrants will advance, but the government can harness the immigrant's drive and multiply his contribution to society with a well-designed educational policy.

What effect do the new immigrants have on the economy of their new communities? An Urban Institute survey of Southern Californians found that most who were questioned worried that the influx of immigrants would reduce wages and job opportunities and increase demand for public services. This perception, however, did not accord with the reality. A report written by Thomas Muller found that job opportunities were not reduced, and wages in the region rose. Between 1975 and 1981, per capita income in Los Angeles grew more rapidly than in the nation as a whole, despite the arrival of 325,000 Mexican immigrants, whose initial income was only half that of the average in the state. As to taxes, Muller reported that the "average Mexican immigrant household . . . receives somewhat more than $2,000 in state services and transfer payments than it pays in taxes." This is because the new immigrant earns less with more children than the average Californian. On the other hand, Muller estimates that 52,000 low-wage jobs were created in highly competitive industries because immigrants were available. His cost-benefit analysis takes this and other "invisible" benefits into account and concludes that "there is little question that when all factors are considered, Mexican immigrants are a definite plus to the local economy."[39]

What makes the Mexican-American community both distinctive and controversial, however, is not their effect on the economy, but rather their impact on society and politics, whether they will remain different with their own language and with a closer attachment to Mexico than to their new home. Here again, former Governor Richard Lamm is at the ramparts: "The warning signs of nonassimilation are increasing and ominous. America must make sure the melting pot continues to melt: immigrants must become Americans."[40]

The foreign-born population in the United States has increased since the 1970s to 6.2 percent after a steady decline since 1920, and immigration today accounts for about one-third of the nation's population growth. Those figures, however, are less imposing when compared with the situation in 1910, when 13 percent of the population was foreign-born and immigration accounted for about 50 percent of the nation's population growth. Moreover, in comparison with Australia, where the foreign-born population in 1970 was more than 20 percent, and Canada with 15 percent foreign-born, the immigrant population in the United States is relatively small.[41]

Spanish has become the second language in the United States, but 90 percent of the people polled by the Census Bureau in 1980 spoke English in their homes; only 5 percent spoke Spanish, and 5 percent other languages. Mexican-Americans are concentrated in the southwestern states and Illinois, but in none of the major states do they amount to more than 20 percent of the population. This contrasts sharply with the French in Quebec.

There were 18.8 million Hispanics in the United States in 1987—7.9 percent of the population. They share a language and a religion but not much else. Indeed, the term "Hispanic" is a peculiarly American one, and it ignores wide differences between conservative Cubans in Florida, liberal Puerto Ricans in New York, and predominantly Democratic but apparently apolitical Mexicans in the Southwest.

But if the fears of a Quebec-type nation within a nation or a polyglot-leaning Tower of Babel are exaggerated, that does not mean that the issue of assimilation of the new immigrants is a phantom. Americans are imbued with many myths about immigration. One of the oldest is the "melting pot," that people from many cultures "melt" into Americans. Some first- and second-generation Americans—like An Wang, Michael Blumenthal, and Lee Iacocca—have risen quickly to the heights of corporate power, and by their very success are thought of as typical Americans. But many more immigrant children remain in the same neighborhoods as their parents, and instead of just Americans, they are Italian-Americans, Jewish-Americans, Polish-Americans, and others.

On the eve of World War I, Theodore Roosevelt coined the term "hyphenated Americans," as a badge of questionable loyalty. In the late 1960s, however, there was a revival of ethnicity in the United States. Instead of concealing their background, ethnic groups began to celebrate and even flaunt their heritage.[42] Ethnic groups became "minorities" and fought discrimination less than they sought "affirmative action." One measure of this change was the rapidity with which some upwardly mobile ethnics first Americanized their names to avoid discrimination and then reverted to their original names when public institutions gave preference to hiring minorities.

A new term—"salad bowl" pluralism—replaced the melting pot image, because it was clear that Italian pasta, Chinese cabbage, and Irish potatoes had not been changed by some California agronomist or alchemist into American salad powder. America, instead, had mixed its own special salad with each vegetable retaining its ethnic distinctiveness.

Yet if the melting pot metaphor exaggerated the extent of assimilation, the salad bowl idea underestimated it. An alternative way is to look at assimilation across generations. The immigrants' foreign language generally has been lost between the first and the second generation and much of the culture between the second and the third, when intermarriages increase. This pattern was initially discerned in an analysis of European immigrants in the first half of the twentieth century, but it still applies.[43]

Rather than an event, assimilation can be thought of as a process in which members of a group gradually adopt many of the characteristics of the general population.[44] There are numerous ways to measure the process. Self-definition is one clue. If a person calls himself a Mexican, he is likely to educate his children, vote, or invest his savings differently than if he defines himself as a Mexican-American or just an American. In the 1980 census, about 15 percent of those normally grouped as Mexican-Americans chose to refer to their Hispanic roots rather than their Mexican ancestry, which might reflect cultural rather than national pride. Much more significant was that second-generation Mexican-Americans were more likely than their parents to call themselves Americans.[45]

A second clue can be found in attitudes. The political views of Mexican-Americans, according to public opinion surveys, are much closer to those of other Americans of the same age, education, and income level than to those of Mexicans. Even on questions of immigration, a Gallup poll showed that 75 percent of the Hispanics supported employer sanctions and the need for identification cards, while 79 percent of the general public backed sanctions and 66 percent were in favor of identification cards.[46] A convergence occurred on whether being able to speak English is an important obligation of a U.S. citizen, with 97 percent of the general population agreeing with that, and 98 percent of the Hispanic population.[47] A 1987 survey by a company using Spanish to advertise its products also found that 98 percent of the Mexican-origin respondents thought it important for their children to read and write English fluently.[48]

On the issue of language retention, David E. Lopez found rates of attrition comparable to those of earlier European migrants. He reported that in Los Angeles 84 percent of recent immigrants from Mexico spoke mostly Spanish in their homes, but by the third generation 84 percent use mostly English, the majority of the rest being bilingual.[49] "The inescapable conclusion is that were it not for new arrivals from Mexico, Spanish would disappear from Los Angeles nearly as rapidly as most European immigrant languages vanished from cities in the East."[50]

The major factor slowing assimilation and progress and creating social tensions is the high level of new immigration. Mexican immigrants reflect the average level of education in Mexico, but that is very low by U.S. standards. A 1987 census report shows that Mexican-Americans have attended school for 10.8 years (as compared with 12.7 for the total population), and they have the lowest family income ($19,326, as compared with $29,458).[51] Immigrants who stay in the United States tend to increase their education and income, but the statistics have shown little or no improvement because new immigrants pull the averages down. The rapid increase in immigration also has worsened both residential and educational segregation, which makes it more difficult for the poor to break out of poverty even while it has the white population worrying about separatist tendencies.[52]

Despite continued high levels of poverty and segregation in the public schools, however, assimilation and social advancement are evident in the increased levels of education and income across generations.[53] Intermarriage is also widely regarded as the "clearest measure of the extent of integration." A study of Mexican-Americans in Los Angeles County found that for Mexican men, 13.3 percent of the first generation married non-Hispanic women; 23.4 percent of the second generation; and 30.2 percent of the third generation. The rates of intermarriage increased not only over time, but also with level of education, occupational status, and dispersal from the Southwest.[54]

In the 1970s, Avelardo Valdez studied intermarriages in Bexar County, Texas, which includes San Antonio and has a population of nearly one million, half of whom are Mexican-Americans. Previous studies had found a slight increase of exogamy since the 1960s. Valdez found a "steady increase in outmarriage rates" in the 1970s, and he explained this in terms of the improvement in occupational status of Mexican-Americans during this period.[55]

.   .   .

Signs of assimilation can be found on the same road as signs of increased segregation, confusing or confirming the prejudices of Anglos about Mexican-Americans. The most controversial issue, however, concerns the new immigrants' politics. The question of political identity has been asked of Mexican-Americans more than of other immigrants because historically so few have become citizens or voted, and so many have returned to Mexico.

It is interesting that Mexican-Americans only began to define their own distinct identity, according to community leaders, when the U.S. government established the Border Patrol in 1924 and began regulating entry. A largely middle-class group of Mexican-Americans established the League of United Latin American Citizens (LULAC) to articulate a "self-conscious sense of Americanness." LULAC chose to demonstrate its "Americanness" by defending Mexican-Americans against discrimination and by protesting against the arrival of new Mexican immigrants who fled the Revolution.[56]

World War II offered Mexican-Americans and other immigrant groups the chance to prove their patriotism. Mexican-Americans distinguished themselves in battle, and the labor shortage at home permitted others to advance in occupations previously denied them. The "zoot-suit" riots in Los Angeles and the activities of the *sinarquistas,* a small group sympathetic to the Nazis, marred the generally positive experience of Mexican-Americans during the war years, but these were relatively minor diversions. By the end of the war, Mexican-Americans were more determined than ever to fight local discrimination and international derision, including criticism from Mexico, where intellectuals like Octavio Paz mocked Mexican-Americans for losing their culture and representing the "worst of two worlds." Mexican-Americans distanced themselves both from the Mexican government and from all new immigrants. They strongly opposed the bracero agreement, which the Mexican government defended, and considered its demise "a significant victory for Mexican-Americans."[57]

In the late 1960s, as many American youth rebelled, Mexican-Americans did as well. While whites mainly protested the war in Vietnam, blacks and Chicanos aimed to discover their roots and nurture community pride. Their militant language was directed at their parents as much as at the Anglo establishment. Unlike the older generation, who were worried that new immigrants would jeopardize their political status and livelihood, the younger generation drew strength and confidence from the increasing numbers.

An outdoor mural in Los Angeles captured the combination of defiance and assertiveness typical of the youth of a group seeking recognition and respect. In the mural a young Latin revolutionary with the purposeful look of a Che Guevara, a brown beret, dark, impassioned eyes, and long hair and a mustache, pointed his finger in the manner of Uncle Sam recruiting marines, and said in bold multicolored letters: "WE ARE NOT A MINORITY!!" That picture was on the front page of a cover story in *U.S. News & World Report* entitled "Hispanics Make Their Move."[58]

There were other signs of protest and separateness. Some Mexican-American leaders demanded that the United States become a bilingual nation. Young Chicanos referred to the Southwest as Aztlan, the legendary homeland of the Aztecs, and christened a journal with that name. Others said, "We didn't come to the United States; the United States came to us." (That is accurate for only a fraction of Mexican-Americans, as there were few in the territories acquired by the United States, and not everyone stayed.[59])

The mural and other comments were symptoms of a generational struggle to fashion a new identity—with parents still trying to prove their Americanness and children exhibiting their *Mexicanidad*. The mural was also an expression of pride by a people who had suffered discrimination quietly for more than a century. But such expressions, of course, were interpreted differently outside the group, in large part because the wave of uncontrolled immigration added a patina of credibility to those who exaggerated the growing power of Hispanics.

Two groups had an incentive to magnify the boasts of the young Hispanic leaders. The "arrival" of a new force in the country was a favorite story of the press, which therefore highlighted the more extreme statements by leaders who promised to displace the establishment.[60] A second group was made up of leaders from state and local governments who wanted a larger share of the $50 billion of federal funds allocated each year according to the distribution of minorities and poor people. These officials insisted that the Census Bureau should count "undocumented workers." In 1980, New York filed a lawsuit against the federal government arguing that the 1980 census had undercounted Hispanics and other minorities and the state had lost a House seat and $26 to $52 million in grants.[61]

Predictably, the proclamation of new power by Mexican-Americans provoked a reaction. Forty members of Congress filed a lawsuit to force the Census Bureau to exclude illegal aliens from the 1990 census because their states would lose representation. They argued that counting illegals watered down the power of citizens and also the concept of citizenship.[62] The Federation for American Immigration Reform, a public policy group that lobbied against illegal migration, and other groups mobilized against what they perceived was an assault on the American system, different and more dangerous than was true of previous immigration. The mantle of leadership fell to a group called US English, founded by a Japanese-American former California senator, S. I. Hayakawa, and led by a Republican activist, Linda Chavez, who is Hispanic, and other first- and second-generation immigrants. Their principal complaint was that Mexicans were demanding more from the system—that is, bilingualism and government support of their culture—than any other ethnic group had demanded or received.

The debate between US English and the Hispanic groups proceeded on several levels. On the surface, the debate was about bilingualism. The old method of teaching English to immigrants was "immersion": immigrants were thrown into an English-speaking class until they learned the language. Previous generations of immigrants had survived this method, but critics were distressed that some children failed or simply dropped out. As the federal government expanded its role in the field of education, it adopted new ways to help immigrants learn English. In 1968, Congress passed the Bilingual Education Act to provide short-term aid to school districts with high concentrations of children with "limited English-speaking ability from low-income families." There were two alternatives to immersion. Using transitional bilingual education (TBE), students are taught English as a foreign language while learning other subjects in their native language until they become proficient in English. Such programs can take from three to twelve years. The third method, English as a second language, involves more intensive training by teachers who are familiar with the students' native language. After a year or so of training, students take regular classes.

Some of TBE's critics, like US English, claim it is a method that delays the learning of English and fosters a bilingual nation. They suggest that the major proponents of that method are Hispanic teachers, who use the lengthy method to foster group consciousness rather than teach English. Although a few Hispanic leaders, like Mario Obledo, a former head of LULAC, have called for all students to be taught Spanish and English, most other Hispanic leaders insist that their objective is to teach English. This, of course, does not preclude the use of the program to transmit their culture.

Some opponents of TBE have learned English by immersion, and believe it is a hard but necessary method. The opponents are also worried about the uniqueness of the challenge. Stanley Diamond, who ran the campaign for Proposition 63 in California, painted it in dire terms: "For the first time in the history of this country, one ethnic community, the

Hispanic, wants to retain their language and their culture. Their goal is a bilingual bicultural state with two official languages."[63] John Tainton, the chairman of US English, noted that unlike previous waves of migration, in which many languages were spoken, more than half of all legal and illegal immigrants today are Spanish-speaking and 75 percent of all students in bilingual education are in Spanish-speaking programs. There is an underlying fear that the bilingual program represents a surreptitious assault on the nation's language, which has been a source of strength and unity, and this assault is being financed by public funds.

James Michener gave human form to this debate in portraying a fiery bilingual schoolteacher, Enriqueta Muzquiz, in his novel *Texas*. Muzquiz used only Spanish in her class, even though "she was supposed to use [it] only temporarily as a bridge to English." Passionate and partisan, she taught her students that "they were an oppressed group, discriminated against, and obligated to lead the great social changes which would transform their portion of America into a reclaimed homeland." Her dream of a Spanish-speaking autonomous region in the Southwest was, according to Michener, "not an idle one. . . . Everything she desired was attainable through slow but persistent penetration." As Anglos suspected or discovered her plans, they fought her.[64]

The debate on bilingualism is less an argument over methods of teaching than it is a clash of symbols, and as such, it is a microcosm of the U.S.-Mexican relationship. Most Mexican-Americans want to participate in America as full citizens, to be respected and recognized, and some believe the path to recognition is to exaggerate their strength and influence. Unfortunately, they have chosen several issues—bilingual education, illegal migration, and bilingual ballots—that have raised questions in the minds of Anglos as to Hispanic intentions and loyalties.

Some Anglos take the words and the boasts seriously and are worried about their implications. Bilingual ballots were mandated by the Civil Rights Act of 1975 as a way to overcome discrimination in the Southwest, but some see it as a dilution rather than an enhancement of citizenship, which requires a knowledge of English and the Constitution. The intent of the Anglo response—for example, constitutional amendments on English—is to prevent a separate region using a different language, but its effect is to stoke Mexican-American anxieties that they are not respected or wanted. "The driving force here is not a desire to help natively Spanish-speaking people become fluent in English," said a Hispanic leader about US English, "but a desire to suppress our language and culture."[65]

Listening to the debate, one is uncertain whether Anglos are more worried about the growing political influence of Mexican-Americans or about their lack of interest in U.S. politics. Historically, Mexican-Americans have exhibited a low level of political participation. A small percentage became U.S. citizens; those who did have tended not to register; and those who registered have tended not to vote. In congressional elections, Mexican-Americans have voted at a rate about half that for Anglos and about 60 percent of that for blacks.[66] One result has been a low level of Mexican-American officeholders.

There are two theories to explain this lack of participation. One suggests that Mexican-Americans remain attached to Mexico and view their stay in the United States as only temporary. The second posits that they bring with them a political culture in which voter participation is low because elections are preordained.

Recent studies and evidence impugn these theories. One of the reasons why the level of participation by Mexican-Americans has been so low for so long is that the number of potential voters has been low until recently and discrimination against them was high until the Voting Rights Act was expanded in 1975. That act prohibited the use of literacy tests in elections and required that election materials be in languages other than English.[67] The Mexican-American Legal Defense Fund, which was established in 1968 with the help of the Ford Foundation using the NAACP as a model, joined the Southwest Voter Registration and Education Project to mobilize the community to register and vote. Between 1975 and 1984, they completed 600 voter registration drives in the Southwest, and the result was a gradual increase in participation and more Mexican-American officeholders.[68] The level was still low in comparison with Anglo voting, but this can be explained partly in terms of the lower level of education and income of Mexican Americans.[69]

The most significant change in recent years has been the rising number of Mexican immigrants who have become citizens. Historically, Mexicans and Canadians have had the lowest rates of naturalization, for the same reason. Few immigrants—as contrasted with refugees—move with the expectation that they will stay. The closer an immigrant is to his home country, the more likely he will return. Thus, immigrants from Mexico and Canada have a 9 percent rate of naturalization, whereas Korea's is 51 percent and India's, 42 percent.[70] But this has recently changed. The number of Mexicans choosing to become citizens increased to 11,423 in 1982, and within three years it had doubled to 23,042, which was nearly eight times the number of Canadians. The numbers continued to increase in 1986.[71] Whether this represents a long-term shift or merely a response to Mexico's debt and political crisis remains to be seen.

Ambivalence is compounded in the triangular relationship among the United States, Mexico, and Mexican-Americans. The Mexican government considered using Chicanos as a lobby in the United States, but apparently backed away from the idea. Some Chicanos feel a cultural affinity with Mexico but have no affection for its political system and perceive Mexican leaders as "openly hostile" to them.[72] Some Chicano leaders have sought closer ties with the Mexican government as a way to increase their influence in the United States. Others, like Rodolfo de la Garza, the director of Mexican-American Studies at the University of Texas, view such a strategy as useful in gaining public attention "otherwise unavailable," but very risky in that it could embarrass and thus anger the United States and jeopardize political gains the community has made. De la Garza offers the following observation on the approach Chicanos should take in the triangular relationship: "In view of the way the Mexican government has responded to Chicanos and its own citizens historically, Chicanos would be naive to expect Mexican policy-makers to be more sensitive to their needs than U.S. policy-makers have been."[73]

There are very few issues which concern both Mexico and Chicanos. When asked to identify their principal concerns in surveys in the 1980s, Mexican-Americans "almost never mention U.S.-Mexican relations or any issues related to domestic Mexican politics. Indeed, only in South Texas does immigration appear as an identifiable concern, and there only 11 percent raise it as an issue." Local issues dominate the concerns of Mexican-Americans; foreign policy is a very low priority.[74] Probably the only issue that would unite Mexico and Mexican-Americans would be if Washington patronized or insulted either one.

The Mexican-American impact on American politics may seem greater than the voting indicators warrant because the group is a relatively uncommitted political bloc in crucial areas being contested by Democrats and Republicans. It is easier to influence an ethnic group before it aligns with a party than it is to change voting behavior afterwards, and so both parties are concentrating on trying to attract Mexican-American voters. The community's real impact, however, will come in ten to twenty-five years, when the recent immigrants are naturalized and vote and their children come of age.[75]

In a few recent cases when Mexican-Americans came between the two governments, the opposite of what is implied by a Mexican lobby occurred. In July 1986 after the Chihuahua elections, Tony Bonilla, chairman of the National Conference of Hispanic Leadership, sent a letter to both President Reagan and President De la Madrid asking the latter to annul the elections in Chihuahua, as well as those in Durango and Baja California Norte, because of fraud. "We are not taking sides with any party," Bonilla said, "but . . . it is clear to us from visits by Mexican representatives and our own observation of documents that there was fraud." He also said that "the United States has the responsibility of pressuring Mexico for a new election because justice has no frontiers and because Mexico is part of the Americas."[76]

This example suggests that Mexican-Americans might prove as capable of "interfering" in Mexican affairs as U.S. senators. Indeed, it confirms that the gap between Mexico and Mexican-Americans is widening, not narrowing, and that even Mexican immigrants and Mexican-Americans "constitute distinct communities."[77]

In his book comparing the Mexican-American experience with that of other immigrants in the United States, Walker Connor describes the wide diversity of views on most issues by the authors who contributed to his book, but he summarizes a consensus on one key point: "Mexican-Americans are following an integrationist pattern not qualitatively dissimilar from that followed by earlier immigrant groups."[78] Their assimilation and progress in terms of jobs, income, education, and language would have been much further advanced had the immigration flow slowed.

The recent assertiveness of Mexican-Americans should be seen in the context of a new interest group in American politics seeking a larger slice of the public pie; it is fully in the American tradition; indeed, it is an affirmation of that system, not a repudiation.

The same types of fears that lurk beneath Mexican policies on foreign investment and trade can be found beneath U.S. policy on immigration. The fears seem barely rational from the other side. After all, Mexican immigration is an economic and social benefit to the United States, and a similar case can be made with regard to foreign investment's contribution to technology, jobs, and capital for Mexico. The fears, however, have little to do with a rational calculation of costs and benefits; rather, they are fears of losing control, of being overwhelmed by one's neighbor or losing one's national identity.

The fearful receiving nation has devised means to regulate and slow the flow—Mexico through its foreign investment laws and commission, the United States through the Immigration Reform and Control Act and the INS. The policies have been somewhat effective. U.S. investment in Mexico remains relatively small and responsive to Mexican concerns. The United States has been less effective in impeding the flow of people, but the immigrants have contributed economically and have demonstrated their loyalty to the United States. Still, the anxieties of the two governments seem not to have diminished.

Despite the similarity of the fear and the response, neither government has shown an awareness of the parallel behavior. Nor has either govern-

ment considered seriously a common approach to the migration problem. In the short term, there is a need for both governments to manage
the movement of people better than they have in the past. Ultimately,
individuals in both nations will determine the ebb and flow of migration,
and that is as it should be, but both governments have a responsibility
to reduce the costs of such migration to society while increasing the
benefits in appropriate ways. They also have an obligation to try to
transform migration from a point of tension in the relationship to a
bridge for communication and comprehension.

The possibility that migration could be transformed from a problem
in the relationship to a serious crisis is real. The increasing Mexican
population, the inability to create enough jobs, a political system in
uneasy transition, constant demands for cheaper labor in the United
States, and a growing Mexican-American community to ease the transition for new arrivals—all guarantee that migration will continue at a
high level. If there is violence or instability in Mexico, the flow could
quickly turn into a flood, and the United States government might be
compelled to do whatever is necessary to shut off the valve. Given the
pressures that would be felt on the border and in Washington, a police-
oriented response simply cannot be ruled out, though it would make the
problem worse and poison the relationship among people as well as
governments.

The principal responsibility for regulating immigration has to remain
Washington's, and that task must be begun by enforcing the new immigration law. Illegal migration has impelled U.S. employers to become
immigration agents, but the alternative—ignoring the problem—was
worse. Similarly, the United States was compelled to legalize the status
of about 2.2 million people who originally entered the United States
illegally, but again, the alternative—massive deportations—was much
worse. Illegal migration may eventually impel the United States to adopt
a national identity card system, against its preference, because there will
be no other way to enforce the immigration laws without lengthy judicial
complaints.

The United States should also seek the cooperation of Mexico in three
ways. First, both could outlaw *coyotes,* people smugglers, and treat them
as criminals. They prey on the innocent in the same way as pimps or
"white slavers," and their efforts have often led to terrible tragedies, such
as deaths in boxcars. Second, while Mexico need not regulate the exit of
its citizens as it did during the *bracero* program, it could join with the
United States to advertise that migration must be done legally with visas
and documents. Third, Mexico and the United States should work together to stop the illegal transit of Central Americans.

These steps of a short-term nature are not sufficient. Both nations must begin to realize that the labor market is becoming integrated, and the two economies require some longer-term planning so as to ensure that there is sufficient trained labor. Mexico needs its technocrats and entrepreneurs, and the United States requires skilled and unskilled labor. The demands and capabilities of the two populations complement each other. Sixty percent of Mexicans and 30 percent of Americans are under the age of twenty. The United States has an aging population, and Mexico one that will soon come of age. The Inter-American Development Bank estimated that Mexico's children will expand the labor force from 22 million in 1980 to 42 million in 2000. In a study of the U.S. labor force in 2000 for the Department of Labor, the Hudson Institute concluded that a growing economy will require more immigrants in the 1990s.[79]

Both governments should draft a development plan that offers a more rational approach to the gradual integration of the two labor markets. Mexico might be more amenable to a freer trade agreement if it included provisions for the freer flow of labor. This might worry some Americans just as a freer trade arrangement concerns Mexicans. Parallel reactions offer each nation a window to awareness, and complementary economies provide an avenue toward economic progress.

Migration should be viewed as a bridge between two nations that are destined to come closer despite their governments' worst intentions. Across this bridge, the Mexican culture and Spanish language will journey north, and American political attitudes and consumer tastes will go south. But the growing bonds connecting people and families in both countries will remain more significant than the ideas or commodities that are traded. These new bonds mean that, over time, the United States may be dealing with Mexico less as a neighbor and more as a relative.

9

IS COOPERATION POSSIBLE?

—

Robert A. Pastor and Jorge G. Castañeda

We have written about the differences that separate Americans and Mexicans. If we sometimes seem to overemphasize them, that is because they have grown, even as social and economic integration has increased. Some of our differences are deeply rooted; they are not due just to insensitivity or idiosyncrasy, or to transient perceptions, errors, or incidents. The misperceptions are endemic, or as some Mexicans would say, structural. Nonetheless, we still believe that awareness of past patterns and mistakes can permit us to reduce the severity and number of both, and thus improve the relationship.

The future will bring more interaction between the two nations, not less. The Mexican economy will continue to open, albeit hesitantly and with reservations. The U.S. economy, which has reached around the world the last forty years, will begin to feel the growing weight of the world inside its borders. As we approach the year 2000, the Mexican people and culture will become a powerful ethnic presence in the United States, even while American culture continues to set commercial standards in Mexico and influence its youth. In this context, the differences between our two nations are sources of strength, not evidence of weakness; they are foundations on which to build lasting cooperation and understanding, not flawed gargoyles that should be chipped at until they fade into the building on which they sit.

Mexico and the United States are nations with different histories, dreams, and aspirations. There is nothing to be gained by denying these. Those who mistake Mexico's modernization for Americanization do the same disservice to the relationship as those who would have the United States ignore its global responsibilities. Mexico will not become more like the United States even if its economy and politics open up, and for the foreseeable future, the United States will remain a superpower with interests that extend considerably beyond its relationship with its southern neighbor. A modern and mature relationship must begin with the acceptance of each as it is and has been. This is the first lesson we draw from our own experience in writing this book and the first recommendation we would make to those whose job it is to manage the bilateral relationship.

This foundation is all the more important as the two nations move into the twenty-first century. The course of the relationship will be determined by their approach to two broad issues. First, a powerful process of economic and social integration is reshaping both countries. This process is accelerating and spreading into areas that were previously unaffected by the other nation. Our calculation of the costs and benefits to both countries differs, but we agree that they should face this issue and debate it openly. The ostrichlike attitude of pretending that integration is not proceeding or that no national priorities are at stake is neither statesmanlike nor honest.

As it goes forward, integration can be ignored and left to run its course uncontrolled by either country, or it can be resisted, managed, or negotiated. It is comfortable but unrealistic to think that one side can select the slice of integration that benefits it while discarding those that do not. However, we do not agree—nor do our two governments—on which option—ignoring, resisting, managing, or negotiating integration—should be chosen. Within the United States, there seems to be greater support for negotiating and managing integration, but there is no consensus in Mexico. This issue should also be confronted by open debate within and between our two countries.

Second, regardless of what policy is chosen or accepted on economic integration, the process will generate political, cultural, and even psychological consequences. To cope with economic integration, new political instruments will be necessary, but this does not necessarily entail a diminution of sovereignty. Similarly, integration will weave new social and cultural patterns, but we still believe that this will not change the basic cultural differences between the two nations.

. . .

As we wrote at the beginning of this book, we have chosen not to negotiate our differences here or to try to develop a common blueprint or series of policy recommendations. That is the responsibility of our two governments. We have offered some policy suggestions, but here we believe that our most constructive contribution to a better management of binational ties lies in proposing new attitudes and new ways to approach issues. While some of our ideas may have been proposed by one side or the other, they have not yet been accepted.

For the relationship to improve, the two countries should reexamine the premises underlying the way each makes policy and negotiates with the other. The United States should consider the impact that its global and domestic policies might have on Mexico before deciding on these policies. Although both nations should make concessions, the United States, the more affluent and stable neighbor, can afford to and should make more. Mexico must accept that it has to make concessions if it expects to receive them.

When Mexico has been harmed by a global U.S. policy, such as the 1971 import surcharge, the United States has insisted that that was not its intention. However true, the argument missed the point. The American government should acknowledge that in many cases its domestic or foreign policies have disproportionate consequences for Mexico because of contiguity and high levels of economic integration.

Consultations should be held, and Washington should take into account Mexico's views when considering domestic U.S. policies, such as immigration reform and anti-drug campaigns, and international matters, such as oil import fees, trade legislation, or support for international development banks. Obviously, all U.S. policies cannot be governed by its relationship with Mexico, but few changes in the way that Washington deals with Mexico would be as important, or as well received over time, as considering the implications of America's global and domestic policies for Mexico.

For its part, Mexico should review its traditional rejection of "reciprocity" in its dealings with the United States. In the past, and particularly in economic negotiations, Mexico has believed that the United States should make concessions without demanding reciprocity because of the tremendous gap in wealth and levels of development. Thus, as a result of the economic imbalance, Mexico has demanded that it be given unrestricted access to the U.S. market without opening Mexico to American products. The United States accepted Mexico's position from the 1930s until the late 1970s, when oil resources permitted it to develop more rapidly and become more competitive. Since then, invoking the principle of "graduation," Washington has begun to ask for some form of reciprocity. While Mexico has claimed—and the United States has acquiesced—that precise and symmetrical reciprocity should not be a standard for negotiations between the two nations, Mexico can no longer expect something for nothing. It has to modify what it refers to as its "principle of nonreciprocity."

Thus, in exchange for negotiating trade concessions from the United States or other countries, Mexico will need to make its own concessions. If it wants greater participation in the U.S. market, Mexico will have to grant some access to U.S. products, although not at the same level. The principle of "special and differential treatment"—that Mexico, as a developing nation, should receive better trade terms than the industrialized countries—should govern the negotiations.

Furthermore, both governments must accept certain conceptual changes in their way of negotiating. In recent years, they have negotiated as if they were playing roles in an exotic play, using a false and artificial language. The United States has presented its economic demands as if they were in Mexico's interests and of merely indirect concern to Washington. This has been especially the case since 1982, when Mexico's economic crisis became an issue in bilateral affairs. Washington has claimed that it is more in Mexico's than in U.S. interests for Mexico to reduce subsidies, privatize the state-owned sector of its economy, lower barriers to trade and investment, and restructure its welfare state. Mexico's role is to protest that it never makes concessions to Washington, saying that its "structural reforms" are entirely of its own doing.

This has had the effect of limiting Mexican negotiators, who have agreed to the structural reforms and obtained new loans but who have been unable to extract major changes in U.S. policy. And it has strengthened U.S. negotiators, who have continued to insist that Mexico's reforms were in its interests and not concessions.

While there was some truth to both postures, there was also some fiction. Structural reform *was* partly a concession to the United States and the international financial community in exchange for new loans, and the United States *does* have economic and ideological interests of its own in having Mexico lower its trade and investment barriers.

Both nations would profit by putting the relationship on a more honest foundation. If the United States wants Mexico to accept a particular economic policy, it should be clear in explaining why that is in U.S. interests. Mexico alone should define and defend its own interests. At the same time, the Mexican government needs to realize that it would gain credibility and bargaining leverage if it acknowledges that it sometimes implements some policies in exchange for certain concessions or advantages from the United States. To suggest that a *quid* has not been exchanged for a *quo* is simply not credible within Mexico or internationally. Moreover, it diminishes Mexico's leverage and makes every aspect of economic policy an issue of national sovereignty, which can only impede or harm its long-term interests in an increasingly interdependent world economy.

The United States should stop speaking for Mexico, and Mexico should stop acting as if there is no foreign influence on its economic policies. In the modern world, governments should only speak for themselves, and all economic policies are interdependent and subject to negotiation. Acceptance of these basic negotiating principles by both governments would make possible a different approach to solving outstanding issues on the binational agenda.

During recent years, many U.S. and Mexican leaders have imagined a "grand understanding" or "package deal," in which concessions in one area, say immigration, are traded for concessions in another, say oil, rather than the traditional negotiation by products or within issues. Neither side has offered any specific ideas on how to achieve it, largely because the political risks of such an arrangement are great and the chances of success are small. In addition, the trade-offs essential for a package deal require the United States to separate its interests from Mexico's and for Mexico to acknowledge concessions to the United States.

With new leadership, the moment is ripe to consider a package deal that would involve major concessions and demands by both nations in trade, energy, intelligence and security, debt, capital flight, and immigration. In some cases, the package would include items already being negotiated individually; in others, it would extend to areas previously omitted from the binational agenda. It is evident that negotiating each of these items individually would be extremely difficult, if not impossible, but because there are issues that are important and desirable to the other side, it becomes at least theoretically attainable. No demand is likely to be fully accepted by the other party; all would be negotiable with the condition that each of the negotiations is linked to the others, and none would be conceded until a package was wrapped up.

Such an arrangement would entail a sizable political risk in both countries. The Mexican President would have to deal with his country's traditional nationalism. The American President would need to make a major commitment of political capital to deliver an agreement. While it is too early to assess the potential benefits of such an undertaking or know whether it would facilitate current discussions, a comprehensive negotiation is worth exploring as a way to break the logjam that has precluded real progress on the bilateral agenda in recent years.

The differences in foreign policy between the two countries have been deep. Nonetheless, the possibility of an understanding in one area—Central America—has increased with the end of the Reagan administration, which was so committed to the Nicaraguan contras, and with the emergence of the Arias Plan, which replaced Mexico's favored Contadora Initiative. As the two new administrations focus on Central America, two central principles should guide either to an agreement or at least to an understanding on the limits of disagreement.

Mexico and the region's Marxist or leftist governments and movements must recognize American geopolitical concerns in the Caribbean Basin. This is the price revolutionary regimes must pay for peaceful coexistence with the United States.

The United States, for its part, should demonstrate to the left in the region that it can live with genuine social change or revolutionary regimes. Very few on the Latin American left believe this; many think that the United States opposes social change and programs to promote a more equitable distribution of power and wealth. We disagree as to the accuracy of this perception, but we believe that clear steps by Washington to disprove it would facilitate peace in the region.

An agreement on Central America based on these two principles would entail an acceptance by the left of genuine U.S. security concerns and a demonstration by the United States of its support for social change. It would imply an ending or at least a reduction of anti-American rhetoric and actions by radicals and an American commitment to refrain from intervening in the internal affairs of these nations. Given the historical and current level of suspicion of all parties in the region, none would take the risks necessary to accept such principles unless each believed the other would comply. Therefore, an essential part of an agreement would have to include verification and compliance. We are under no illusions that negotiating such an agreement would be easy.

To cope with the future better, the United States and Mexico need to alter fundamentally the way their governments operate in the other country. The two governments' representatives—ambassadors, embassy and consular officials—sit at the intersection of the relationship. Though their job is to facilitate solutions to problems, in many cases they symbolize the reason why problems are so difficult to resolve. The difficulties stem from tradition and old attitudes; the needed changes are different in each nation. Essentially, the United States must become more discreet, and Mexico, less.

Recent U.S. ambassadors have either had excellent connections in Washington but were embarrassingly insensitive to Mexico or were well received in Mexico but lacked influence in the U.S. capital. A new U.S. President should take more seriously the appointment of the ambassador to Mexico than his predecessors have done. The ambassador should be a person of senior stature who combines substantial diplomatic experience abroad with political and bureaucratic experience in Washington.

Mexican ambassadors and representatives have generally been well connected in Mexico but politically disconnected in Washington. Mexico needs to change the way its representatives have traditionally defined their role and activities in Washington and throughout the United States. Traditionally, the Mexican ambassador and his staff have used the Office of Mexican Affairs in the Department of State as their principal, and sometimes their only, point of contact with the U.S. government. Occasionally, the ambassador will see the Secretary of State, but he infrequently has met with other cabinet members and congressmen and almost never communicated directly with the President or the White House. Mexico would find the public and private corridors to power in Washington accessible, but it needs to take the initiative.

Mexico should also take advantage of its more than forty consulates across the United States. Beyond protecting Mexican nationals in the United States, these offices can be centers for explaining Mexico and its policies and for trying to learn how and what the United States is thinking about Mexico. Its representatives can begin to shape public opinion and images of the country and thus contribute to a better environment for a more sensitive U.S. policy.

U.S.-Mexican relations will improve with more communication, provided that each government recognizes that its effectiveness depends on its ability to adapt to the different rules of the other country. This means that U.S. officials must be more private in Mexico and Mexican representatives must be more active and public in the United States.

While the growing interaction could bring out the best in both nations, it is more likely not to. If the past, and even the present, offers a guide, more exchange and integration will mean more disputes. Even if both governments were adept, tensions are unavoidable, given the increasing flows of people, goods, capital, and information.

Many recent disputes can be traced to the fear by leaders that they are losing control of at least one aspect of the relationship. Mexico feels that it has paid a high price historically for losing control of certain facets of its relationship with the United States; it cannot help worrying that repeating such mistakes would be even more disastrous in the future. And many in the United States similarly perceive that a loss of control of the border has permitted a flood of drugs that endangers American youth, illegal aliens who undermine unions, cheap goods that threaten U.S. business, and a massive wave of migration that may wash away America's monolingual unity.

Greater flows lead to greater fears, which are not easily calmed. One possible approach to this problem would be to set up alarm mechanisms, which can alert both nations to an emerging problem and permit their governments to mitigate the harsh effects of these problems while they still can be managed.

Nongovernmental mechanisms can play an important role in channeling, articulating, and addressing concerns in both countries. Many such groups and networks have emerged in recent years to review other issues or regions. For U.S.-Mexican relations, the expansion and institutionalization of such groups—perhaps including a formal, permanent national council—could help binational relations. These can serve as shock absorbers, removing the force and intensity from the bumps in the bilateral road.

A number of steps can and should be taken to improve the broader context of mutual understanding, beginning with improvements in both the amount and the quality of press coverage of the other country. Most Mexicans and Americans obtain their information about each nation from the broadcast media and newspapers, but the problems of coverage are different in both countries.

U.S. media coverage of Mexico has expanded dramatically since the late 1970s. The media, of course, cover Mexico as they cover all stories· long periods of neglect punctuated by high-intensity bursts of attention, which make serious problems seem even more tragic, or chronic, or ridiculous than they are.

Many U.S. newspapers have established bureaus and provide regular coverage of Mexico. While this is preferable to having correspondents flying in to write a story, most American reporters arrive with precious little understanding of the history of Mexico or its relationship with the United States. Many newspaper editors erroneously believe that a good journalist can cover any story with equal expertise—a fire in the Bronx, a debate among presidential candidates, or the *tapado* in Mexico. A correspondent who moves from covering the streets of Chicago to reporting politics in Mexico without learning anything about Mexico, not surprisingly will project everything he knows about Chicago on a wholly alien landscape. This might help Mexicans understand Chicago, but it does not help Americans understand Mexico. We recommend either that major newspapers send reporters with some knowledge and experience of Mexico, Latin America, or the Third World or, alternatively, that they give new correspondents time to learn about their new assignments.

Mexican coverage of the United States is confined to a few journalists, and many of these have been woefully unqualified. It is essential that there be a change in this situation. If individual Mexican newspapers or networks cannot maintain reporters in the United States, then they should pool their resources. The Mexican media must ensure that their reporters possess some knowledge of the United States and a capability of trying to understand the United States on its own terms.

Government policies in both countries are sometimes the reaction to press accounts, and major misunderstandings have been generated or exacerbated by erroneous or distorted articles. Therefore, it is important that the amount and the quality of press coverage be upgraded and that there be sustained, accurate, balanced, and fair reporting in each nation's media about events in the other nation.

A second area would be to improve the amount and quality of teaching and research. In the last decade, a number of very good Latin American studies centers at various universities in the American Southwest have decided to concentrate more of their resources specifically on the U.S.-Mexican relationship, while at the same time new centers have been established. Most notable have been the Center for U.S.-Mexican Studies at the University of California in San Diego and various institutes on Mexico, the border, and Chicano studies at the University of Texas, the University of New Mexico, and several campuses of the University of California.

In general, these centers have developed important expertise and produced valuable research on Mexico, but they have been less effective in explaining or recommending U.S. policies. Their perspective is naturally that of the border states, and as with most U.S. specialists, they sometimes adopt the view of the foreign country they are studying rather than that of the United States. Their long-term influence will depend on their ability to make their research more relevant for the policymaking community in Washington than has been the case. The United States also should support centers in other parts of the country that could take a broader and more detached view of the relationship.

Centers for studying the United States in Mexico are virtually nonexistent today. The few attempts to establish such centers in the past either dissolved in a short time or disintegrated because, given their excessive reliance on government support, they were unable to survive reductions or tolerate conditions on that support. Although there are some individuals studying the United States in Mexican universities and research institutes, the establishment of major centers for study and research would be an important long-term contribution to improving Mexico's relations with America.

The argument of this book is that the tensions, conflicts, and misperceptions which have always characterized the U.S.-Mexican relationship are rooted in history, asymmetry, and changes in each of the countries and in the relationship. These, in turn, have led to policy mistakes and misconceptions. But the fact that the basic structure of the relationship changes so slowly does not mean that nothing can be done to improve it. These proposals will not transform the relationship, but perhaps the awareness that can emerge from our exchange will yield a synthesis that might permit some modest and positive changes.

As our children grow on both sides of the border, they might relate as poorly as present and past generations have. But we hope they will understand each other better. We end this book without illusions but with hopes. Cooperation between the United States and Mexico will always be difficult but never impossible.

NOTES

1. SHAPING MINDS AND ATTITUDES
The Mexican Mind

1. *Excelsior* (Mexico City), March 4, 1947, p. 3.
2. "Alamo Flag Is Reported Unavailable," Dallas *Morning News,* April 12, 1986.
3. Carlos Monsiváis, "Muerte y resurrección del nacionalismo mexicano," *Nexos* #109, January 1987, p. 15.
4. Arthur M. Schlesinger, Jr., *The Cycles of American History* (Houghton Mifflin, 1986), p. 17.
5. *Libro de Texto Gratuito, Ciencias Sociales, Cuarto Grado,* 1973 ed. (11th printing, 1984), p. 94. The contributing authors mentioned by the Ministry of Education are: Josefina Zoraida Vázquez, Laura Barcia, Elizabeth Velázquez, Luis González, Rodolfo Stavenhagen, Victor L. Urquidi, and Francisco Estebanez.
6. Ibid., p. 95.
7. Ibid.
8. Ibid.
9. Ibid., p. 96.
10. Quoted in Josefina Vázquez de Knauth, *Nacionalismo y Educación en México* (El Colegio de México, 1970), p. 282.
11. *Libro de Texto Gratuito, Ciencias Sociales, Sexto Grado* (14th ed., 1987), p. 99.
12. As Alan Knight has put it most recently: "A distinctively Catholic conservative patriotism, Hispanophile and gringophobic, thus matured during the nineteenth century." Alan Knight, *U.S.-Mexican Relations, 1910–1940: An Interpretation* (Center for U.S.-Mexican Studies, University of California, San Diego), Monograph Series, 28, 1987.
13. The examples are taken from two of the most widely used history books in secondary schools: Carlos Alvear Acevedo, *Historia de México* (38th ed., Editorial Jus, 1986); and José Bravo Ugarte, *Compendio de Historia de México* (12th ed., Editorial Jus, 1984).
14. Josefina Zoraida Vázquez, "Los primeros tropiezos," in *Historia General de México,* Tomo 2 (El Colegio de México, 1976), pp. 735–818.

15. Ibid., p. 809.
16. Ibid., p. 810.
17. Ibid., p. 812.
18. Ibid., p. 818.
19. Berta Ulloa, "La lucha armada (1911–1920)," in *Historia General de México,* Tomo 2, p. 1122.
20. Ibid., pp. 1127–28.
21. The by now classic account of foreign meddling during the Mexican Revolution is Friedrich Katz, *The Secret War in Mexico: Europe, the United States and the Mexican Revolution* (University of Chicago Press, 1981).
22. Adip Sabag, Instituto Mexicano de Opinión Pública, *Excelsior,* August 23–27, 1986.

The American Mind

1. L. Joanne Buggey, Gerald A. Danzer, Charles L. Mitsakos, and C. Frederick Risinger, *America! America!* (2nd ed., Scott, Foresman, 1982), p. 311.
2. Frances FitzGerald, *America Revised: History Schoolbooks in the Twentieth Century* (Atlantic Monthly Press, 1979), p. 46.
3. Joel Garreau, *The Nine Nations of North America* (Avon Books, 1982), p. 1.
4. Interviews with editors from McGraw-Hill, Scott, Foresman, and Harcourt Brace Jovanovich, in June 1987. Texas was cited as the state that most frequently requests and obtains additions to the standard texts.
5. Henry Cabot Lodge and Theodore Roosevelt, *Hero Tales from American History* (The Century Company, 1895), pp. ix, 145–54.
6. *America! America!,* pp. 311–13.
7. James West Davidson and Mark H. Lytle, *The United States: A History of the Republic* (Prentice-Hall, 1984), pp. 251–53.
8. Ibid., p. 253.
9. Ibid., pp. 256–58.
10. Samuel Eliot Morison, Henry Steele Commager, and William E. Leuchtenburg, *The Growth of the American Republic,* Vol. I (Oxford University Press, 1980), pp. 550–51.
11. Allan Nevins and Henry Steele Commager, *A Short History of the United States* (Alfred A. Knopf, 1966), p. 217.
12. *The United States: A History of the Republic,* p. 258.
13. *America! America!,* p. 614.
14. Two Mexican historians confirm this account. See Josefina Zoraida Vázquez and Lorenzo Meyer, *The United States and Mexico* (University of Chicago Press, 1985), pp. 103–09. Also see Cole Blasier, *The Hovering Giant: U.S. Response to Revolutionary Change in Latin America* (University of Pittsburgh Press, 1976), pp. 34–45.
15. *The United States: A History of the Republic,* p. 496.
16. *America Revised.*
17. Ibid., p. 49.
18. *Latin America in School and College Teaching Materials,* a report of the Committee on the Study of Teaching Materials on Inter-American Subjects (American Council on Education, 1944), p. 15.
19. Ibid., pp. 27, 32, 34–35.
20. Ibid., pp. 55, 63.

21. *America Revised,* and Nathan Glazer and Reed Ueda, *Ethnic Groups in History Books* (Ethics and Public Policy Center, 1983).
22. Matías Romero, who served as Mexico's ambassador to the United States, was his nation's most effective ambassador, but his "interference" in U.S. internal affairs easily rivaled that of the most arrogant U.S. ambassadors. He not only tried to oust Secretary of State William Seward and unseat Abraham Lincoln, but he played a "peripheral but not insignificant role in the impeachment of President [Andrew] Johnson." See Thomas D. Schoonover (ed.), *Mexican Lobby: Matías Romero in Washington, 1861–67* (University of Kentucky Press, 1986), pp. 31, 115.
23. For a good description and analysis of the impact of increasing coverage of Mexican issues by the major newspapers and television networks, see John Bailey, "Mexico in the U.S. Media: Implications for Bilateral Relations," unpublished paper, April 1987, p. 13.
24. Louis Harris, "Mexico Is Friendly but Has Serious Problems," Harris Survey, 1986, #44, August 11, 1986. This survey was taken by telephone July 18–22, 1986, among a nationwide cross section of 1,253 adults, with a plus or minus error of 3%.
25. John E. Rielly (ed.), *American Public Opinion and U.S. Foreign Policy* (Chicago Council on Foreign Relations). Rielly has edited four reports, published and dated 1975, 1979, 1983, 1987, reflecting surveys done the previous year. The first had no mention of Mexico. The two most valuable indices in the other three were the "thermometer" ratings (do you feel warm or cold toward a particular country?) (1979, p. 17; 1983, p. 19; 1987, p. 18); and questions of whether the United States has a "vital interest" in a particular country (1979, p. 16; 1983, p. 16; 1987, p. 17).
26. Christine E. Contee, *What Americans Think: Views on Development and U.S.– Third World Relations,* a Public Opinion Project of InterAction and the Overseas Development Council (InterAction and the Overseas Development Council, 1987), pp. 50, 52, 54.
27. The Chicago Council on Foreign Relations commissioned the Gallup Organization to do surveys of the general public and of a leadership sample of over 350 "representing Americans in senior positions with knowledge of and influence in international affairs." They were chosen in roughly equal proportions from the national political and governmental world, the business community, communications, education, and foreign policy institutes.
28. Survey of InterAction and the Overseas Development Council.
29. "Shaking Hands Not Fists," *Time,* August 25, 1986, pp. 30–31. This survey was done for *Time* by Yankelovich in July 1986 with a 3% sampling error.
30. Harris Survey, 1986.
31. Harris Survey, 1986. In contrast, only 30% of the American people felt that differences between the U.S. and Mexican governments on Nicaragua reflected something seriously wrong with the Mexican system.
32. Memorandum to *Time* from Yankelovich Clancy Shulman, "Poll Findings on Mexico," August 1, 1986, based on a telephone survey conducted July 7–9 with 1,017 Americans 18 years of age or older. Sampling error of plus or minus 3%.
33. Survey of InterAction and the Overseas Development Council, pp. 52–54.
34. For collecting the articles and coding them, I am grateful to Amy Gottsche, an intern at Emory University's Carter Center.
35. Carlos Fuentes, "Don't Push Mexico," April 24, 1984; Jorge Castañeda, "Enough Mexico-Bashing," May 21, 1986; editorials on June 15, 1986, and July 11, 1986.

36. See the following editorial and articles in *The New York Times:* "Texas vs. Robert Kennedy," February 18, 1962, p. 8; "Texas History Sent R. Kennedy," February 20, 1962, p. 10; "Robert Kennedy Bows in 'War' with Texans," March 5, 1962, p. 12.
37. *America! America!,* p. 718.
38. This story is recounted in Josephus Daniels's memoirs, *Shirt-Sleeve Diplomat* (University of North Carolina Press, 1947), pp. 3–14.

2. INTERVENTION

From Mexico Looking Out

1. Gavin's misadventures and incursions into Mexican politics are described in Norman Kempster, "Two Ambassadors," *Los Angeles Times Magazine,* October 26, 1986, and in Carlos Ramírez, "Operación Gavin" (editorial *El Día*, Mexico City, 1987).
2. *New York Times* poll, Mexico Survey, October 28–November 4, 1986. Partial results of the poll were published in the *New York Times* editions of November 16 and 17, 1986.
3. The data concerning the official U.S. presence in Mexico were provided by the Office of Mexican Affairs, Department of State.
4. *Newsweek,* April 2, 1984, p. 21.
5. *New York Times,* May 16, 1984.
6. Héctor Aguilar Camín, "Manuel Buendía y los idus de mayo," *Nexos,* July 1984, p. 5.
7. See in this respect the articles on Oliver North's "Mexican connection" by Alfonso Chardy in the Miami *Herald,* March 27 and May 10, 1987, as well the relevant passages on Casey's Mexican obsession in Bob Woodward, *Veil: The Secret Wars of the CIA, 1981–1987* (Simon & Schuster, 1987), mainly pp. 339–46, 382–83.
8. Mexican Foreign Secretary Bernardo Sepúlveda described the hearings as "illegitimate meddling into Mexico's internal affairs." Foreign Broadcast Information Service, May 28, 1986, pp. M1–M2.
9. Adip Sabag, Instituto Mexicano de Opinión Pública, *Excelsior,* June 27–July 2, 1986.
10. *Excelsior,* February 20, 1985, p. 23-A.
11. "Void the Chihuahua Elections! An Appeal to President Miguel de la Madrid of Mexico, Paid for and Sponsored by: Council for Inter-American Security. L. Francis Bouchey, President," Washington *Post,* August 13, 1986, p. A9.
12. See note 7 above and personal conversation with Richard Nuccio, present at the meeting between Channel and Villa.

From the United States Looking In

1. Author's telephone interview with Joseph John Jova, November 30, 1987.
2. Author's interview with Constantine Menges, Washington, D.C., February 3, 1987.
3. Author's interview with Ambassador Charles Pilliod, April 6, 1987, Mexico City.
4. For President Reagan's remarks and response by President De la Madrid, see *Department of State Bulletin,* July 1984, pp. 85–86.
5. Gavin's statement is in the Helms hearings, U.S. Senate Foreign Relations Committee, June 26, 1986, p. 92.

6. For the historical statistics, see James W. Wilkie (ed.), *Statistical Abstract of Latin America* (UCLA, 1985), Table 2901. For more recent statistics, see American Embassy, Mexico, "Economic Trends Report," February 1987, p. 16. For Mexico's GDP, see Inter-American Development Bank, *Annual Report, 1987*, p. 426.

7. See Robert Pastor, *U.S. Foreign Investment in Latin America: The Impact on Employment* (Inter-American Development Bank, 1984), p. 45.

8. The letter is reprinted in *Business Mexico,* December 1987, p. 76.

9. Cited in Josephus Daniels, *Shirt-Sleeve Diplomat* (University of North Carolina Press, 1947), pp. 271–72.

10. For the best study on the nationalization, see Lorenzo Meyer, *Mexico and the United States in the Oil Controversy, 1917–1942* (University of Texas Press, 1977), pp. 185–213.

11. Douglas C. Bennett and Kenneth Sharpe, *Transnational Corporations and the State: The Political Economy of the Mexican Auto Industry* (Princeton University Press, 1985), see especially pp. 220–24.

12. Friedrich Katz, *The Secret War in Mexico* (University of Chicago Press, 1981), p. x. For an assessment of who used whom effectively, see pp. 552–78.

13. Larry Rohter, "Just Forget the Alamo! Ponder Yankees' Sins," *New York Times,* January 7, 1988, p. 4.

14. Jack Anderson, "Mexico Makes Its Presidents Millionaires," *Washington Post,* May 15, 1984, p. C15.

15. *Washington Post,* May 29, 1984.

16. Josephus Daniels tells the story of the Rivera-Rockefeller clash, *Shirt-Sleeve Diplomat,* pp. 442–47.

17. Octavio Paz, *One Earth, Four or Five Worlds* (Harcourt Brace Jovanovich, 1985), p. 137.

18. "Address by President Woodrow Wilson before the United States Congress," April 20, 1914, printed by U.S. Department of State, *Foreign Relations of the United States, 1914,* p. 474. Friedrich Katz concludes that Wilson was motivated by his "concept of missionary diplomacy" to intervene to undermine Huerta. *The Secret War in Mexico,* pp. 196, 564.

19. U.S. Department of State, *Foreign Relations of the United States, 1955–57,* Vol. VI, pp. 687–88. This was in an addendum to a letter from Ambassador Francis White to President Eisenhower, August 29, 1955.

20. Adolfo Aguilar Zinser, "Mexico and the Guatemalan Crisis," in *The Future of Central America,* p. 162.

21. *Washington Post,* July 7, 1980, pp. A1, 12.

3. FACE TO FACE

The U.S. Government

1. Josephus Daniels, *Shirt-Sleeve Diplomat* (University of North Carolina Press, 1977), pp. viii, 526.

2. Dwight D. Eisenhower, *The White House Years: Waging Peace, 1956–61* (Doubleday, 1965), pp. 517–18.

3. The quote is from Lincoln Gordon, who was an Assistant Secretary of State in the Johnson administration. See Walter LaFeber, "Latin American Policy," in Robert

A. Divine (ed.), *Exploring the Johnson Years* (University of Texas Press, 1981), pp. 63–64.

4. Friedrich Katz, *The Secret War in Mexico,* p. 562.

5. Richard J. Meislin, "Mexico Denounces a U.S. General Who Called It a Security Problem," *New York Times,* February 28, 1984, p. A4.

6. Donald L. Wyman, "Dependence and Conflict in U.S.-Mexican Relations, 1920–75," in Robert L. Paarlberg (ed.), *Diplomatic Dispute* (Harvard University Center for International Affairs, 1978).

7. The United States worked with Mexico to persuade the International Monetary Fund to change its procedures and permit PEMEX to raise its credit ceiling. Ironically, this decision contributed to Mexico's future debt problem.

8. Raymundo Riva Palacio, "El gasoduto: corrupción, chantaje, y crimenes," *Proceso,* September 5, 1977.

9. Even James Schlesinger, who was not known for his sensitivity, testified to Congress that he told the Mexicans as early as January 1977: "We understood the sensitivities of Mexico with regard to the national patrimony. The United States did not want to be in a position of pushing them with regard to oil development, [but] we stood ready to assist in any way that we could, financial or technical." He also told Díaz Serrano that "we are eager to have a long-term agreement . . . which will permit substantial volumes of gas to move if that should be their choice, but it depends upon the right price relationships." (Schlesinger recounted these conversations in testimony before the Senate Committee on Energy and Natural Resources, January 17, 1979.)

10. These two sets of meetings are described in a chronology compiled by the Senate Committee on Energy and Natural Resources, *Mexico: The Promise and Problems of Petroleum,* March 1979, p. 158.

11. There are a number of studies on the gas negotiations. See especially George Grayson, *The Politics of Mexican Oil* (University of Pittsburgh Press, 1980), Chapter 8; and Richard R. Fagen and Henry R. Nau, "Mexican Gas: The Northern Connection," in Richard Fagen (ed.), *Capitalism and the State in U.S.–Latin American Relations* (Stanford University Press, 1979), pp. 382–427.

12. For the background of Stevenson's amendment, see Fagen and Nau, pp. 404–6. Mexico's ambassador, Hugo Margain, later wrote about Stevenson's amendment: "This was the first time since the Mexican expropriation of the foreign oil companies in 1938 that the United States applied a financial boycott to Mexico." Hugo B. Margain, "Respect in Friendship," *Case Western Reserve Journal of International Law* 12, Summer 1980, p. 458.

13. George Grayson wrote that the "overwhelming majority of the newspapers, journals of opinion, industry publications, and politicians [in the United States and Mexico] addressing the subject urged the U.S. government to accept the Mexican figure and decried Schlesinger's intransigence." Grayson, however, believes that Schlesinger was proven correct in not accepting the 1977 Mexican formula, as it would have led the U.S. to pay nearly twice the amount that it finally negotiated in 1979. "The U.S.-Mexican Natural Gas Deal and What We Can Learn from It," *Orbis,* Fall 1980, p. 603.

14. In a press conference at the 19th Annual Conference of UPI Editors on October 13, 1978, López Portillo gave a brief, but confused description of the incident: "We followed through on it [the gas pipeline] despite all the economic and political risks that it entailed. . . . A few months later, we encountered opposition from the U.S.

government, and what disconcerted me even more was that the U.S. Export-Import Bank withdrew our financing. . . . They left me 'holding the bag.' . . . Under those conditions, when the rules of the game were changed, and when we realized that free trade between us no longer worked, I had to go back to the other alternative [using the gas domestically]."

15. PRM-41 has been declassified, along with some of the documents that were written in response. I will cite from these.

16. Carlos Fuentes, "Listen, Yankee! Mexico Is a Nation, Not an Oil Well," Washington *Post,* February 11, 1979.

17. At a press conference on October 13, 1978, López Portillo elaborated on this point, which he first made in February 1977: "In the past, [problems] have been dealt with in a disorganized and haphazard fashion." As a result, he proposed and Carter accepted the use of "an overall approach to dealing with our problems, considering each in its proper place and taking into account its roots and implications. Thus, whether the problems concern immigration or are financial, commercial, monetary, diplomatic or a matter of general policy, they should all be examined within this overall approach, because if we continue to deal with them in an isolated fashion, they will never be resolved. I hope that the United States will one day assign some priority to this proposal."

18. *New York Times,* October 28, 1978, p. 57.

19. James Reston, "Mexico Lectures the U.S.," *New York Times,* February 16, 1979; *Newsweek* had a special report on the trip entitled "Scolding in Mexico," February 26, 1979; *Time* had a story entitled "The Battle of Toasts: Mexico's López Portillo Welcomes Carter with Acid," February 26, 1979. For the toasts, see *Presidential Papers, 1979,* Vol. I, pp. 273–77.

20. Ambassador Hugo Margain later wrote that the Mexicans were more confused by the reaction by the American press than by the remark itself, which, he wrote, "was given no importance at all in Mexico." Margain, "Respect in Friendship," p. 459.

21. "Mexico's Macho Mood," *Time* cover story, October 8, 1979.

22. Jimmy Carter, *Keeping Faith: Memoirs of a President* (Bantam Books, 1982), p 468.

23. Reagan mentioned this in his announcement beginning his campaign. *New York Times,* November 14, 1979, p. 1.

24. Constantine Menges, "Mexican Actions in Central America: Time for a Positive Change" (The Fund for an American Renaissance, August 1986), p. 4.

25. These statistics are from the United Nations Economic Commission for Latin America and the Caribbean, *Latin American and Caribbean Development: Obstacles, Requirements, and Options,* November 25, 1986, p. 152. Because of the nationalization of the banks, the debt figures for 1982 included some of the debt of the private sector as well.

26. Interview with Ambassador John Gavin, *Time,* March 4, 1985, p. 8.

27. U.S. Senate, Subcommittee on Western Hemisphere Affairs of the Foreign Relations Committee, *Situation in Mexico: Hearings,* June 17, 1986, pp. 41–43.

The Mexican Government

1. The point concerning the system's strength as a result of the weakness of any alternative has been made by many authors. Its most updated formulation perhaps comes in one of the better books written about Mexico by a non-Mexican in recent

years, despite its Trotskyite jargon, Maxime Durand, *La Tourmente Mexicaine* (Editions La Brèche, Paris, 1987), particularly pp. 167–78.

2. Gastón García Cantú, "El dilema del presente," *Excelsior,* July 13, 1987, p. 1.
3. The relatively scant importance the Mexican armed forces have in U.S.-Mexican affairs is consonant with their small weight in national life. In terms of the number of troops per thousand population, Mexico ranks 107th globally; in defense spending as a percentage of GNP, it ranks 129th. George T. Kurion, *The New Book of World Rankings* (Facts on File, 1984), quoted in Michael J. Dziedzic, *Mexican Defense Policy* (1987).
4. Mike Tingeman, *In These Times,* February 24, 1987.
5. Since 1970 professional diplomats have held the country's top foreign affairs job for only four and a half years, in 1976 and from 1979 to 1982.
6. Eduardo Pesquieira Olea, interview with Héctor Aguilar Camín, *La Jornada,* July 27, 1987, p. 20.
7. Miguel de la Madrid, televised interview with John McLaughlin, June 16, 1986, p. 11 of transcript.

4. FACING THE WORLD

U.S. Foreign Policy

1. Author's interview with Moshe Arad, Israel's ambassador to Mexico, 1983–87, and to the United States, 1987–present; in Atlanta, Georgia, October 30, 1987.
2. Author's interview with Augusto Ramírez-Ocampo, Wye Center, Maryland, June 21, 1987.
3. Testimony before the U.S. Senate Committee on Foreign Relations, *Hearings: Situation in Mexico,* May 13, 1986, p. 28.
4. Jorge Castañeda, "Special Problems and a Not-So-Special Relationship: Mexican Foreign Policy and the United States," in Tommie Sue Montgomery (ed.), *Mexico Today* (Institute for the Study of Human Issues, 1982), p. 130.
5. Octavio Paz, "Latin America and Democracy," in *Democracy and Dictatorship in Latin America* (Foundation for the Study of Independent Social Ideas, no date), p. 9.
6. Agency for International Development, *U.S. Overseas Loans and Grants, Obligations and Loan Authorizations, July 1, 1945–September 30, 1987,* p. 4.
7. Ibid, pp. 56, 209, for the figures on U.S. aid and loans from the international banks. These do not include loans received by Mexico after 1987. The data on the 1976 package are from George Grayson, *The United States and Mexico* (Praeger, 1984), pp. 51–52; for the 1982 package, from David Mulford's testimony to the Senate Foreign Relations Committee, *Economic Development in Mexico,* June 10, 1986, p. 25.
8. Dana Munro, *Intervention and Dollar Diplomacy in the Caribbean, 1900–1921* (Princeton University Press, 1964), pp. 144–216.
9. Cited in Dana Munro, *The United States and the Caribbean Republics, 1921–33* (Princeton University Press, 1974), p. 201. For a fuller description of U.S.-Mexican-Nicaraguan relations in the 1920s, see pp. 187–242.
10. Ibid, p. 200.
11. Ibid., p. 210. Also, Donald C. Hodges, *Intellectual Foundations of the Nicaraguan Revolution* (University of Texas Press, 1986), p. 8.

12. Senior officials then wrote that "the evidence before the Department [of State] shows an unmistakable attempt on the part of Mexico to extend Mexican influence over Central America with the unquestionable aim of ultimately achieving a Mexican primacy over the Central American countries," and of setting up governments in Central America, "which will be not only friendly but subservient to Mexico and completely under Mexican domination." Cited in Bryce Wood, *The Making of the Good Neighbor Policy* (Columbia University Press), 1961, p. 15; see also pp. 15–30.

13. *Intellectual Foundations of the Nicaraguan Revolution,* pp. 7–12.

14. For this period, see Lorenzo Meyer, *Mexico and the United States in the Oil Controversy, 1917–1942* (University of Texas Press, 1977), pp. 192, 149–216; David G. Haglund, *Latin America and the Transformation of U.S. Strategic Thought* (University of New Mexico Press, 1984), p. 94; and Annette Baker Fox, *The Politics of Attraction: Four Middle Powers and the United States* (Columbia University Press, 1977), p. 48.

15. *The Politics of Attraction,* pp. 38, 48–54.

16. This reference to the Mexican Foreign Minister's views was in a memorandum to President Eisenhower. In *Foreign Relations of the United States,* Vol. IV: 1952–54, pp. 1350–51.

17. Transcript of an interview by WGBH Public Television with Juan José Arévalo, June 21, 1984, p. 15.

18. For a chronology of developments during this time as viewed from the perspective of the U.S. government, see U.S. Senate Committee on Foreign Relations, *Events in United States–Cuban Relations: A Chronology, 1957–63, prepared by the Department of State* (Washington, D.C., January 29, 1963).

19. These statements are from a memorandum of conversation of a meeting on January 25, 1960, written by the President's National Security Adviser, General Andrew Goodpaster. The "secret" memorandum was declassified on September 22, 1980.

20. Ibid.

21. "Memorandum for the Record," drafted by National Security Adviser Andrew Goodpaster on August 29, 1960, after a conversation with the Secretary of State's chief aide. The "secret" memorandum was declassified on September 22, 1980.

22. Cited in William E. Ratliff, *Castroism and Communism in Latin America, 1959–76* (American Enterprise Institute, 1976), pp. 38–39.

23. For the three communiqués, see *New York Times,* July 1, 1962, p. 2; February 23, 1964, p. 28; April 16, 1966, p. 6. Press reports suggested that the Cuban issue was raised and occasioned the biggest differences during the Kennedy visit in 1962. The press conferences of the two Presidents and the communiqué, however, did not refer specifically to Cuba. Instead, they mentioned the importance of the principle of nonintervention and the two Presidents' opposition to "totalitarian institutions and activities which are incompatible with the democratic principles they [the two Presidents] uphold."

24. For a good description and analysis of Mexico's public and private steps vis-à-vis Cuba during the early 1960s, see Henry Gill, "Cuba and Mexico," in Barry Levine (ed.), *The New Cuban Presence in the Caribbean* (Westview Press, 1983), pp. 77–79.

25. Cited in Marlise Simons, "Mexico Leads Major Regional Effort to Isolate Somoza," Washington *Post,* May 23, 1979, p. A17. For an elaboration of the policies of the United States and Mexico on Nicaragua and the rest of Central

America in the period 1977–87, see Robert Pastor, *Condemned to Repetition: The United States and Nicaragua* (Princeton University Press, 1987), especially Chapter 7.

26. See *Condemned to Repetition,* pp. 144–49.
27. Cited by Henry Gill, "Cuba and Mexico: A Special Relationship?" in *The New Cuban Presence,* p. 82.
28. For the two documents, see Robert Leiken and Barry Rubin (eds.), *The Central American Crisis Reader* (Summit Books, 1987), pp. 628–29.
29. Cited by Ron Morgan, "Sepúlveda Stresses Closer CA Ties," Mexico City *News,* December 12, 1985, p. 1.
30. See Adolfo Aguilar Zinser, "Mexico and the Guatemalan Crisis," in Richard Fagen and Olga Pellicer (eds.), *The Future of Central America* (Stanford University Press, 1983).
31. Cited in David Ronfeldt, Richard Mehring, and Arturo Gandara, *Mexico's Petroleum and U.S. Policy* (Rand Corporation, 1980), p. 64.
32. Alexander Haig, *Caveat: Realism, Reagan, and Foreign Policy* (Macmillan, 1984), p. 99.
33. Interview of Jesús González Schmal, foreign affairs spokesman for the PAN, with the Mexico City *News,* December 20, 1986, p. 7.
34. *The Politics of Attraction,* p. 196. For the comparison of the four countries' foreign policies, see ibid., Chapter 8.
35. Ibid., p. 286.
36. U.S. Department of State, *Report to Congress on Voting Practices in the United Nations* (Washington, D.C., 1985), Tables 1, 2.

Mexican Foreign Policy

1. Josefina Zoraida Vázquez and Lorenzo Meyer, *The United States and Mexico* (University of Chicago Press, 1985), p. 135.
2. Mario Ojeda, *Las Relaciones de México con los Países de América Central* (El Colegio de México, 1985), pp. 12–13.
3. Richard E. Feinberg, *The Intemperate Zone: The Third World Challenge to U.S. Foreign Policy* (W. W. Norton, 1983), pp. 52–53.
4. Alan Riding, *Distant Neighbors: A Portrait of the Mexicans* (Alfred Knopf, 1985), p. 339.
5. Alan Riding, "Beleaguered Mexico Cedes Role as Central America Power Broker," *New York Times,* October 24, 1986, p. 1.
6. Hearings before the Subcommittee on Western Hemisphere Affairs of the Committee on Foreign Relations, United States Senate, *Situation in Mexico,* May 13, June 17 and 26 (U.S. Government Printing Office, 1986), pp. 27–28.
7. John McLaughlin's *One on One,* text of televised interview with Miguel de la Madrid, June 22, 1986, p. 11.

5. SLIDING TOWARD ECONOMIC INTEGRATION

The U.S. Perspective

1. Felix G. Rohatyn and Roger C. Altman, "Confront the Mexican Problem," *Wall Street Journal,* November 26, 1986.

2. Cited in Samuel Eliot Morison, Henry Steele Commager, and William Leuchtenburg, *The Growth of the American Republic,* Vol. II (Oxford University Press, 1980), pp. 406, 413.

3. *Foreign Relations of the United States, 1955–1957,* Vol. VI: *American Republics* (Government Printing Office, 1987), pp. 650–51.

4. U.S. Senate, Committee on Foreign Relations, *Economic Development in Mexico: Hearings,* June 10, 1986, p. 7.

5. "Memorandum of a Conversation [between President Eisenhower and Mexican President Ruiz Cortines], White Sulphur Springs, West Virginia, March 27, 1956," *Foreign Relations of the United States, 1955–57,* pp. 710–15.

6. For a good factual summary of these various laws, see U.S. International Trade Commission, *The Impact of Increased United States–Mexico Trade on Southwest Border Development,* report to the Senate Committee on Finance on Investigation No. 332-223 (Government Printing Office, November 1986), pp. 39–45 (hereafter ITC).

7. John A. Gavin, "Mexico, Land of Opportunity," *Policy Review,* Winter 1987, p. 34. On the liberalization of the rules in 1984, see Sandra F. Maviglia, "Mexico's Guidelines for Foreign Investment: The Selective Promotion of Necessary Industries," *American Journal of International Law* 80, April 1986, No. 2.

8. Cited in Douglas Friedman, "Banco de Mexico Treasurer Denies Free Market Intervention," Mexico City *News,* July 24, 1986, p. 42.

9. Jorge Dominguez, "Business Nationalism: Latin American National Business Attitudes and Behavior Toward Multinational Corporations," in Jorge Dominguez (ed.), *Economic Issues and Political Conflict: U.S.–Latin American Relations* (Butterworth, 1982).

10. Cited by Senator Phil Gramm in his testimony to the Senate Foreign Relations Committee, *Economic Development in Mexico,* June 10, 1986, p. 7.

11. Office of the U.S. Trade Representative, "Report on North American Trade Agreements," transmitted to Congress by President Reagan on August 4, 1981, p. 26.

12. See Robert Pastor, *U.S. Foreign Investment and Latin America: The Impact on Employment* (Inter-American Development Bank, 1984), pp. 31, 35–39.

13. Business International Corporation, *The Effects of Foreign Investment on Selected Host Countries,* 1979, pp. 5, 22; and Obie Whichard, "Employment and Employee Compensation of U.S. Multinational Corporations in 1977," *Survey of Current Business* 62, February 1982, No. 2.

14. See Robert J. Lieber, *The Oil Decade* (University Press of America, 1986).

15. A CBS/*New York Times* poll in 1978 showed that 48% of the American public did not believe that the United States imported oil. Cited by Peter A. Iseman, "The Arabian Ethos," *Harper's,* February 1978, p. 41. In fact, in 1978 imports of petroleum accounted for 43% of consumption (*U.S. Annual Energy Review,* 1986, Table 51).

16. David Ronfeldt, Richard Mehring, and Arturo Gandara, *Mexico's Petroleum and U.S. Policy: Implications for the 1980s,* prepared for the U.S. Department of Energy (Rand Corporation, June 1980), pp. 74–76.

17. U.S. Department of Energy, *Annual Energy Review, 1986* (Government Printing Office, May 1987), Table 48, p. 107. See also U.S. General Accounting Office, *Assessment of Factors Affecting the Availability of U.S. Oil Supplies from the Caribbean,* September 13, 1985.

18. Banco Nacional de México, "Review of the Economic Situation of Mexico" 63, No. 739 (June 1987), p. 136.
19. U.S. Department of Energy, *Strategic Petroleum Reserve, Annual Report,* February 1987, p. 10.
20. U.S. Department of Energy, *Energy Security: A Report to the President of the United States,* March 1987, pp. 57, 67, 114.
21. Joint Economic Committee, Congress of the United States, *The Impact of the Latin American Debt Crisis on the U.S. Economy: A Staff Study,* May 10, 1986, p. 2.
22. Letter from Paul A. Volcker, Chairman of the Federal Reserve Bank, to Senator Bill Bradley, November 5, 1986, Appendix 2.
23. Cited in Robert D. Hershey, Jr., "Indicators Fall, but U.S. Industry Poised to Rebound," *New York Times,* January 3, 1988, p. E3.
24. For a summary and analysis of these various formulas, see Robert Pastor, *Latin America's Debt Crisis: Adjusting to the Past or Planning for the Future?* (Lynne Rienner Publishers, 1987), pp. 141–49.
25. James W. Wilkie and David Lorey (eds.), *Statistical Abstract of Latin America* (UCLA, 1986 and 1987), Vols. 24 and 25.
26. In testimony of David Mulford before the Senate Foreign Relations Committee, *Economic Development in Mexico,* June 10, 1986, p. 36.
27. The 1980 statistic is from the STR report to Congress on "North American Trade Agreements," August 4, 1981. The 1986 figure was provided by the American embassy in Mexico City, in Stephen H. Muller, "Analysis of U.S.-Mexico Trade," March 16, 1987. Telephone conversations with Harold Ford and Gary Lindsey of the U.S. Poultry and Egg Export Council, citing Department of Commerce statistics, December 14, 1987.
28. This summary of U.S. trade policy is borrowed from Robert Pastor, *Congress and the Politics of U.S. Foreign Economic Policy* (University of California Press, 1980), Part II.
29. Howard F. Cline, *The United States and Mexico* (Harvard University Press, 1963), p. 391.
30. ITC Report in November 1986, p. 57.
31. Ibid., p. xix.
32. World Bank, *Mexico After the Oil Boom: Refashioning a Development Strategy,* June 23, 1987, pp. 23–24.
33. U.S. Embassy Economic Report, February 1987, p. 2.
34. *Business Mexico,* December 1987, pp. 14–16.
35. Ibid., p. 8.
36. See Jim Kolbe, "Made in Mexico, Good for the U.S.A.," *New York Times,* December 13, 1987, p. F2. For an opposing view that sees 807 as a tax break that harms U.S. interests, see John LaFalce's article on the same page.
37. This statistic was reported in a survey by the National Association of Purchasing Management, in Louis Uchitelle, "Two Hard-to-Quit Habits Sustain Trade Deficit," *New York Times,* January 14, 1988, pp. 29, 32.
38. Martin Tolchin, "Influx of Foreign Capital Mutes Debate on Trade," *New York Times,* February 8, 1987, p. 13.
39. Letter by Joseph Scherer to *New York Times,* December 15, 1987, p. 26.
40. Cited in Martin Tolchin and Susan Tolchin, "Foreign Money, U.S. Fears," *New York Times Magazine,* December 13, 1987, p. 64.

41. For a summary of the American proposals and the Mexican rejections, see Carlos Rico, "The Future of Mexican-U.S. Relations and the Limits of the Rhetoric of 'Interdependence,'" in Carlos Vasquez and Manuel Garcia y Griego (eds.), *Mexican-U.S. Relations: Conflict and Covergence* (UCLA, 1983), pp. 129–40.

42. Sidney Weintraub, *Free Trade Between Mexico and the United States?* (Brookings Institution, 1984), p. 135.

43. A good summary of his thesis is in William J. Baumol, "America's Productivity 'Crisis': A Modest Decline Isn't All That Bad," *New York Times,* February 15, 1987, p. 2.

The Mexican Perspective

1. *New York Times* poll, Mexico Survey, October 28–November 4, 1986. The poll was done with two samples, a national one of 1,576 individuals from communities larger than 2,500 inhabitants, and one of 299 from communities with 100 to 2,500 inhabitants. Partial results of the poll were published in *The New York Times,* November 16 and 17, 1986.

2. One of the first references to the process of integration between the two nations— qualified in this case as "silent"—appeared in Clark W. Reynolds, "Mexican-U.S. Interdependence: Economic and Social Perspectives," in Clark Reynolds and Carlos Tello (eds.), *U.S.-Mexico Relations* (Stanford University Press, 1983), p. 21.

3. CIEMEX-WEFA (Wharton Econometric Forecasting Associates), *Perspectivas Económicas de México,* June 1987, p. 174; and World Bank, *World Development Report, 1986* (Oxford University Press), pp. 185 and 196.

4. All figures are taken from World Bank, *World Development Report, 1986,* pp. 184, 196.

5. *Estadísticas Históricas de México* (Instituto Nacional de Estadística, Geografía e Informática–Instituto Nacional de Antropología e Historia, 1985), Vol. II, p. 650.

6. All figures on savings are taken from CIEMEX-WEFA (see note 3 above), p. 177, and CIEMEX-WEFA, *Perspectivas Económicas de México,* June 1985, pp. 153–54.

7. *Estadísticas Históricas de México,* pp. 665–66.

8. *Revista de Comercio Exterior,* Banco Nacional de Comercio Exterior, Vol. 36, No. 4, April 1986, quoted in "This Is Mexico," Banco BCH, 1986. All figures on present-day foreign investment, trade, *maquiladoras,* tourism, and the automotive industry, in addition to the specific reference provided, were checked with the most reliable and most up-to-date Mexican source: the President's State of the Union Report to Congress. Miguel de la Madrid, Quinto Informe de Gobierno, Estadístico, 1987.

9. The American figure is taken from *Statistical Abstract of the United States,* 1987 (U.S. Department of Commerce). The Mexican statistics are taken from Direction of Trade Statistics, International Monetary Fund, *1986 Yearbook,* p. 87. Like all governmental organizations, the IMF relies on and reproduces statistics delivered to it by its member states.

10. The figures are from a paper presented by Norberto Ingo Zadrozny, chairman of the Brazilian Exporters Association, Miami Congressional Workshop, December 28, 1986.

11. Josefina Zoraida Vázquez and Lorenzo Meyer, *The United States and Mexico* (University of Chicago Press, 1985), p. 92.

12. Dirección de Inversiones Extranjeras (see note 8 above), p. 28. Other Mexican official sources give different figures; cf., for example, La Economía Mexicana en Cifras, 1986, Nacional Financiera, p. 336. The number the latter source gives for the total stock of foreign investment in Mexico in 1985 is $10.1 billion. The most recent and authoritative figures for 1986 and 1987, presented by the President of Mexico (see note 8 above), indicate stocks of foreign investment of $17.05 billion in 1986, and $19.4 billion for 1987; the U.S. share is, respectively, 64.8% and 63%. These figures are skewed by Mexico's debt-equity swap program, which brought nearly $3 billion in foreign "investment" to the country during those two years. The program was suspended in late 1987 because of the enormous subsidy (up to 50%) which Mexico was giving foreign investors on projects most of which would have taken place anyway. Thus the most realistic figure on foreign investment is still the one for 1985.

13. The data on the *maquiladora* industry is taken from sources cited in note 8 above, and also *Mexico's In-Bond Industry,* a publication included in a "press kit" distributed by the Mexican presidency during President De la Madrid's visit to Washington in August 1986.

14. Joseph Grunwald, "The Assembly Industry in Mexico," in Joseph Grunwald and Kenneth Flamm, *The Global Factory: Foreign Assembly in International Trade* (Brookings Institution, 1985), p. 161.

15. Ibid., p. 166.

16. In 1987, despite growing complaints in the United States about Japanese "penetration" of the *maquiladora* industry, there were only 15 Japanese plants (out of nearly 1,000). Larry Rohter, "Plants in Mexico Help Japan Sell to U.S.," *New York Times,* May 26, 1987, p. D6.

17. La Economía Mexicana en Cifras, p. 327.

18. Asociación Mexicana de la Industria Automotríz, *Informe Estadístico,* December 1986

19. *Informe Anual, 1983,* Banco de México, Mexico City, p. 107; and source cited in note 18 above, p. 326.

20. Miguel de la Madrid, Quinto Informe de Gobierno, 1987, Estadístico, p. 466.

21. Maxime Durand, *La Tourmente Mexicaine* (Editions La Brèche, Paris, 1987), p. 122–25.

22. World Bank, *Mexico After the Oil Boom: Refashioning a Development Strategy,* June 23, 1987, p. 30.

23. Ibid., p. 29.

24. James Fallows, "Japan: Playing by Different Rules," *Atlantic Monthly,* September 1987, p. 29.

25. Ibid., p. 4

26. Among the more recent and articulate defenses of this view is Sidney Weintraub, *Free Trade Between Mexico and the United States?* (Brookings Institution, 1984).

6. THE SUPPLY AND DEMAND OF DRUGS AND MONEY

The Mexican Side

1. "Por el Lada, el teléfono pornográfico norteamericano al alcance de los niños de México," *Proceso* #534, January 26, 1987, pp. 50–51. On April 28, 1988, President Reagan signed an education bill prohibiting the use of the telephone for porno-

graphic messages ("Reagan Signs Education Bill," *The New York Times,* April 29, 1988, p. 11).

2. *New York Times* poll, Mexico Survey, published in *The New York Times,* November 16 and 17, 1986.

3. According to some estimates the value of the marijuana crop in California was greater than any other, including cotton and grapes. *Annual Domestic Marijuana Crop Report,* 1985, published by the National Organization for the Reform of Marijuana Laws. According to *The New York Times,* "Federal authorities estimate that nearly 2,000 tons of professionally cultivated domestic marijuana was available for sale last year, in contrast to the estimated 3,000 tons from Mexico . . . . American marijuana farmers have refined their cultivation methods so that the United States now produces the world's highest-potency marijuana, forcing growers in Mexico . . . to refine their techniques to compete." Joel Brinkley, "Drug Production in U.S. Is Reported at Record Levels," *New York Times,* June 2, 1986, p. 1.

4. According to the 1984 Production Estimates published in the 1985 *International Narcotics Control Strategy Report* presented by the Bureau of International Narcotics Matters of the Department of State to the Congress, the opium crop in Mexico amounted to 17 metric tons in 1983, 21 tons in 1984, and 21 tons in 1985. Marijuana production went from 4,975 metric tons in 1983 to 5,850 tons in 1984 and 6,124 tons in 1985 (*Summary Assessment,* p. 4, February 4, 1985). The following year's report gave opium production estimates of 17 tons for 1983, 21 tons for 1984, and a "range" of 21–45 tons each for 1985 and 1986. In its explanatory note, it states: "There are no reliable estimates for Mexican opium production for 1985 and 1986." For marijuana the new numbers were 4,975 metric tons in 1983, and 2,500–3,000 tons in 1984, 1985, and 1986. The 1987 figures showed a new drop in opium production from 1985 to 1986 (from 25–45 tons to 20–40 tons) and from 1986 to 1987 (from 20–40 tons to 10–30 tons). Concerning marijuana, it raised the previous figures, but registered a serious drop in 1987 to 2,000 metric tons. If anything, the imprecision of the estimates and the changing numbers from year to year of the U.S. government's own numbers show the dubious nature of any categorical blanket statement concerning drug production in Mexico.

5. Joel Brinkley, "Experts See U.S. Cocaine Problem as Continuing Despite Big Raids," *New York Times,* August 24, 1986, p. 1.

6. Ibid.

7. Joel Brinkley, "U.S. Aides Accuse Mexico," *New York Times,* May 12, 1986, p. 4.

8. James M. Van Wert (Bureau of International Narcotics Matters, Department of State), "Mexican Narcotics Control: A Decade of Institutionalization and a Matter for Diplomacy," March 31, 1986, mimeo, pp. 2–3.

9. Samuel del Villar, "La narcotización de la cultura en los Estados Unidos," in *Mexico–Estados Unidos 1985* (El Colegio de México, 1986), pp. 78–79.

10. According to the governor of the state of Sinaloa, in 1987 there were more than forty *corridos* (ballads or odes) to Rafael Caro Quintero, the chief drug trafficker involved in the Camarena killing. Franciso Labastida Ochoa, interview with Rita Ganem, *Televisa-24 Horas,* July 25, 1987.

11. Quoted in Julio Scherer, *Los Presidentes* (Editorial Grijalbo, Mexico City, 1986), p. 61. The reasons for this reluctance are probably similar to those which led J. Edgar Hoover to keep the FBI out of drug enforcement.

12. Morgan Guaranty Trust Company of New York, "LDC Capital Flight," *World Financial Markets,* March 1986, pp. 13–15.

13. Mimeo, address by Miguel Mancera, governor of the Bank of Mexico, 64th Annual Meeting of the Bankers' Association for Foreign Trade, Phoenix, Arizona, May 1986.

14. *Federal Reserve Bulletin,* February 1987.

15. The Mexican estimate comes from Ernesto Zedillo, "Case Study: Mexico," in Donald R. Lessard and John Williamson, *Capital Flight and Third World Debt,* Institute for International Economics (IIE), Washington, D.C., 1987, pp. 174–185. A Bank of Mexico study quoted in American publications (see, for example, David Felix, "How to Resolve Latin America's Debt Challenge," *Magazine of Economic Affairs,* November–December 1985) gives a figure of $33.2 billion for the 1977–84 period. Solana's statement appeared in *La Jornada,* January 29, p. 1. John T. Cuddington, in *Capital Flight: Estimates, Issues and Explanations,* Princeton Studies in International Finance, No. 58, December 1986, quotes $32 billion for the 1974–82 period. Finally, Donald Lessard and John Williamson, in "Capital Flight: The Problem and Policy Responses," in Lessard and Williamson, *Capital Flight,* p. 206, quote a figure slightly higher than Zedillo's.

16. Ibid., Lessard and Williamson, IIE, p. 36.

17. Carlos Acosta, "El gobierno de los Estados Unidos provoca la fuga de dolares," *Proceso* #535, February 2, 1987, pp. 20–23. The advertisements started running again soon after. As late as January 20, 1988, the American Government Certificates and Funds Corp. was running ads in *Excelsior* flaunting the security of U.S. government guarantees.

18. The information regarding Alberto Bailleres and CerMoc was taken from John Crewdson and Vincent Schodolski, "Under-the-Table Government," *Chicago Tribune,* October 23, 1986, p. 13.

19. Ibid.

20. Lessard and Williamson (see note 15 above), pp. 242–43. See also Marlise Simons, "Focus on Latin Flight of Capital," *New York Times,* May 27, p. D1.

21. There are no published figures on this matter; the estimate comes from conversations, rumors, and deduction. It is not reliable, but is not far from the truth.

22. Morgan Guaranty Trust Company, "Growth and Financial Reform in Latin America," *World Financial Markets,* April and May 1986, p. 10.

The U.S. Side

1. Cited in Lloyd Gardner, *Economic Aspects of New Deal Diplomacy* (Beacon Press, 1964), p. 205.

2. Theodore Sorensen, *Kennedy* (Harper & Row, 1965), pp. 454–58.

3. The survey of American views on Mexico was done by Yankelovich, Clancy, and Shulman for *Time* magazine, based on a survey of 1,017 Americans conducted July 7–9, 1986. The memorandum summarizing the results is dated August 1, 1986.

4. In 1906, the company took the coca out of the leaves, and in 1982, it introduced a caffeine-free version of the drink. For this and a brief history of drugs, see Robert O'Brien and Sidney Cohen (eds.), *The Encyclopedia of Drug Abuse* (Facts on File, 1984), pp. ix–xxi.

5. The Mitre Corporation, *Narcotics Control in Mexico: Final Environmental Impact Statement,* report prepared for the Department of State, April 1979, p. 2-1.

6. U.S. Department of State, Bureau of International Narcotics Matters, *International Narcotics Control Strategy Report,* March 1987, p. 6.

7. National Drug Enforcement Policy Board, *National and International Drug Law Enforcement Strategy* (Washington, D.C., January 1987), pp. 185–88, for budget statistics 1981–88. The breakdown on the international side of the budget is from the Department of State's report, *International Narcotics Control Strategy Report,* March 1987, p. 52.

8. Texts of communiqués, *New York Times,* July 1, 1962, p. 2; and February 23, 1964, p. 28.

9. These are DEA estimates, as cited by James Lieber, "Coping with Cocaine," *Atlantic Monthly* 257, No. 1, January 1986, pp. 40–42.

10. "Seizures of Cocaine Soar in California as Dealers Avoid Florida," Denver *Post,* January 2, 1988, p. 5A.

11. "The Screams at the Border," *New York Times,* February 22, 1985, editorial page. Shultz was cited by Doyle McManus, "Mexican Calls Talks with U.S. 'Constructive,' " Los Angeles *Times,* March 12, 1985.

12. Ronald J. Ostrow, "Tape Connects Mexico Officer to Drug Torture," Los Angeles *Times,* February 14, 1986, p. 1.

13. U.S. Senate Foreign Relations Committee, *Hearings,* June 17, 1986, p. 41.

14. "Ex-Police Official Jailed in Mexico in Drug-Linked Bribe Case," *New York Times,* August 14, 1986, p. 4.

15. Richard J. Meislin, "Slight Discord Ends Mexican's Visit," *New York Times,* August 15, 1986, p. 4.

16. Transcript from *20/20* program, May 7, 1987, p. 9.

17. *Congressional Record,* Senate, March 17, 1987, p. S3291.

18. U.S. House of Representatives, Select Committee on Narcotics Abuse and Control, *Annual Report for the Year 1985,* December 19, 1986, p. 71.

19. Joel Brinkley, "U.S.-Mexican Border Cooperation Hampered by Politics and Inertia," *New York Times,* June 27, 1986, pp. 1, 10.

20. U.S. Department of State, *International Narcotics Control Strategy Report,* March 1988, p. 39.

21. Telephone interview with Dennis Reece, Bureau of Consular Affairs, Department of State, August 27, 1987.

22. Mario Ojeda, "The Structural Context of U.S.-Mexican Relations," in Tommie Sue Montgomery (ed.), *Mexico Today* (Institute for the Study of Human Issues, Philadelphia, 1982), p. 110. He was specifically referring to the 1969 event, but it also applies to 1985. The cooperation after the latter was even clearer than after 1969.

23. I am indebted to several conversations with Ms. Falco in September and December 1987 and to a manuscript she has written on U.S. narcotics programs with several countries.

24. Results of the March poll were printed in *The New York Times,* April 10, 1988, p. 10. The May poll was reported by E. J. Dionne, Jr., "Poll Shows Dukakis Leads Bush; Many Who Backed Reagan Shift," *New York Times,* May 17, 1988, p. 1.

25. U.S. Department of Health and Human Services, *Drug Abuse and Drug Abuse Research: Second Triennial Report to Congress* (1987), pp. 5–6.

26. Rangel's comment is in a letter to *The New York Times,* September 18, 1987, p. 30.

27. For a brief critical analysis of the British system and other alternatives, see James Lieber, "Coping with Cocaine," pp. 44–48.
28. See Nils Bejerot, *Addiction and Society* (Charles C. Thomas, 1970).
29. Department of Health and Human Services, *Triennial Report,* pp. 21, 1–3.
30. Cited by Peter Kerr, "Rich vs. Poor: Drug Patterns Are Diverging," *New York Times,* August 30, 1987, pp. 1, 17; see also Warren E. Leary, "Survey Detects Decline in the Use of Cocaine Among Young Adults," *New York Times,* January 14, 1988, pp. 1, 17.
31. "Which War on Drugs?" *New York Times,* August 31, 1987, p. 18.
32. Peter Kerr, "Crime Study Finds High Use of Drugs at Time of Arrest," *New York Times,* January 22, 1988, pp. 1, 9.
33. For a provocative exploration of some of these questions, see Ethan A. Nadelmann, "U.S. Drug Policy: A Bad Export," *Foreign Policy* 70, Spring 1988, pp. 83–108.
34. Cited in Robert A. Pastor (ed.), *Latin America's Debt Crisis* (Lynne Rienner, 1987), p. 62.
35. Cited by Larry Rohter, "Mexico Moves to Keep Savings South of Border," *New York Times,* October 5, 1987, p. 25.
36. Interview with Jaime Bermúdez, Ciudad Juárez, Mexico, July 4, 1986.
37. Larry Rohter, "Mexico Becomes Hub for Wildlife Smugglers," *New York Times,* July 26, 1987, pp. 1, 8.

7. THE BORDER

An American View

1. Theodore S. Beardsley, Jr., "The Hispanic Impact upon the United States," in Frank J. Coppa and Thomas J. Curran (eds.), *The Immigrant Experience in America* (G. K. Hall, 1976).
2. Cited by Jack Anderson and Dale van Atta, "The Mexican Time Bomb," *Penthouse,* May 1987, p. 44.
3. Joel Garreau, *The Nine Nations of North America* (Avon Books, 1982). For a contrasting view that explores the impact of Mexican cultural influence in the United States but recognizes the enduring power of sovereignty, see Lester D. Langley, *MexAmerica: Two Countries, One Future* (Crown Publishers, 1988).
4. Enrique Krauze, "Chihuahua, ida y vuelta," *Vuelta* 115, June 1986, pp. 32–43, offers a good description of the differences between the history of northern and central Mexico and the *norteños*'s concern with the Indians. For two studies of the Southwest's view of the world and of its distant capital, see Erna Fergusson, *Our Southwest* (Alfred A. Knopf, 1946), and Odie B. Faulk, *Land of Many Frontiers: A History of the American Southwest* (Oxford University Press, 1968).
5. Raul A. Fernandez, *The United States–Mexico Border: A Politico-Economic Profile* (University of Notre Dame Press, 1977), pp. 40–45.
6. Oscar Martinez, *Border Boom Town* (University of Texas Press, 1978), p. 11.
7. For a good description of the seesaw relationship of the border towns on the issue of the free trade zone, see *Border Boom Town,* and also *The United States–Mexico Border,* p. 79.
8. Paul R. Ehrlich, Loy Bilderback, and Anne H. Ehrlich, *The Golden Door* (Ballantine Books, 1979), p. 119.

9. Steven E. Sanderson, *The Transformation of Mexican Agriculture: International Structure and the Politics of Rural Change* (Princeton University Press, 1986), p. 33.

10. *The United States–Mexico Border,* pp. 79–97.

11. Thomas E. Weil et al., *Area Handbook for Mexico* (Government Printing Office, 1975), p. 296.

12. The statistics are from an unclassified cable of the American embassy, "Maquiladora Developments—1986," July 10, 1987.

13. Roberto Mena, "Maquilas Out to Change Industry Image," *Business Mexico,* December 1987, pp. 8–18.

14. Gay Young, "The Development of Ciudad Juárez: Urbanization, Migration, Industrialization," in Gay Young (ed.), *The Social Ecology and Economic Development of Ciudad Juárez* (Westview Press, 1986), p. 14.

15. Joseph Grunwald and Kenneth Flamm, *The Global Factory: Foreign Assembly in International Trade* (Brookings Institution, 1985), pp. 237–38.

16. Testimony of Alexander H. Good, Director General of the U.S. and Foreign Commercial Service, Department of Commerce, before the House Banking, Finance, and Urban Affairs Committee, November 25, 1986, cited by Cathryn L. Thorup, *The United States and Mexico: Face to Face with New Technology* (Transaction Books, 1987), p. 14.

17. Flamm, *The Global Factory,* p. 142. U.S. International Trade Commission, *The Impact of Increased U.S.–Mexico Trade on Southwest Border Development,* report to the Senate Committee on Finance on Investigation No. 332-223 (Government Printing Office, November 1986), p. 24 (hereafter ITC Report).

18. ITC Report, p. 5.

19. Ibid., p. 9.

20. Niles Hansen, *The Border Economy: Regional Development in the Southwest* (University of Texas Press, 1981), pp. 37–38.

21. ITC Report, p. 175.

22. William K. Stevens, "Census Report Finds a Return to Normal in Population Shifts," *New York Times,* October 1, 1987, pp. 1, 16.

23. "Two More Cities Reach Million in Population," *New York Times,* October 18, 1987, p. 17. The six cities in the Southwest are Los Angeles, Houston, San Diego, Dallas, San Antonio, and Phoenix (Census Bureau statistics).

24. *The Global Factory,* p. 176.

25. *The Border Economy,* p. 155.

26. From 483,029 to 2,198,460. In F. Ray Marshall and Leon Bouvier, *Population Change and the Future of Texas* (Population Reference Bureau, 1986), pp. 92–93.

27. *The Border Economy,* p. 12.

28. ITC Report, p. 176.

29. Niles Hansen, in *The Border Economy,* includes a table with statistics for 1950, 1960, and 1970 (p. 128). For the 1980 statistics, I use the Census Bureau's "1980 Supplementary Report: Persons of Spanish Origin by State," Table 7, p. 12. This was reprinted in *The Hispanic Population of the United States: An Overview,* a report prepared by the Congressional Research Service for the Subcommittee on Census and Population of the U.S. House Committee on Post Office and Civil Service, April 21, 1983, p. 186. The earlier years do not provide a breakdown of the Spanish-origin statistics. In the 1980 census, however, the Bureau reports the following for the percentage of Hispanics who are of Mexican origin: California

(80%), Texas (92.2%), New Mexico (49%), Arizona (89.9%), and Colorado (61%) (p. 183 of the report; for the numbers, see pp. 178–79).

30. Study by Gary Orfield, cited in Amy Wallace, "U.S. Hispanics Fast Becoming a Class Apart," Atlanta *Constitution,* September 30, 1987, p. 6A. The latter figure does, however, include Central Americans.

31. ITC Report, pp. 178–80.

32. U.S. embassy statistics indicated that the average *maquila* wage in January 1986 was $4.42 per day. The per-employee annual wage differential between U.S. and Mexican employees performing the same work was then reported as $15,000–$20,-000. See U.S. General Accounting Office, *Commerce Department Conference on Mexico's Maquiladora Program,* April 3, 1987, p. 12.

33. The Los Angeles area produced $250 billion in 1986 (cited by Charles Lockwood and Christopher B. Leinberger, "Los Angeles Comes of Age," *Atlantic Monthly,* January 1988, p. 34), while Mexico's gross domestic product in that year was $191.5 billion (according to Inter-American Development Bank, *Economic and Social Progress in Latin America, 1987 Report,* p. 426).

34. Richard Rodriguez, "Across the Borders of History," *Harper's,* March 1987, p. 43.

35. James A. Michener, *Texas* (Random House, 1984), p. 1288.

36. F. Ray Marshall and Leon F. Bouvier, *Population Change and the Future of Texas* (Population Reference Bureau, 1986), pp. 9, i, ii, 24.

37. *Land of Many Frontiers,* p. 323.

38. Leon F. Bouvier and Philip Martin, *Population Change and California's Future* (Population Reference Bureau, 1985), p. 4.

39. Ibid., p. 13.

40. *Land of Many Frontiers,* p. 307.

41. *The Border Economy,* pp. 54–55.

42. Cited in *Business Mexico,* December 1987, p. 28.

43. Robert J. McCartney, "Riot in Small Mexican Town Reflects Opposition's Anger," Washington *Post,* January 6, 1985; "Low Blow in Chihuahua," *Newsweek,* July 21, 1986, pp. 8–9.

44. Department of State, "U.S.-Mexican Border Cooperation and Development: Is a New Border Commission Needed?" April 18, 1984.

45. For a catalogue of these various groups, see Milton Jamail, *The United States–Mexico Border: A Guide to Institutions, Organizations, and Scholars* (Latin American Area Center, University of Arizona, 1980).

46. Peter T. Flawn, "A Regional Perspective," in Richard D. Erb and Stanley R. Ross (eds.), *U.S. Policies Toward Mexico: Perceptions and Perspectives* (American Enterprise Institute, 1979), pp. 31–39.

47. ITC Report, p. 15.

48. ITC Report, p. 18.

A Mexican View

1. "Tijuana has a million, perhaps two million people. Tijuana will double itself in twelve years. . . . Tijuana is larger than San Diego." Richard Rodriguez, "Across the Borders of History," *Harper's,* March 1987, p. 42. According to the 1987 edition of the U.S. Department of Commerce, Bureau of the Census, *Statistical Abstract of the United States,* the San Diego "Metropolitan Statistical Area" had a population in 1985 of 2.133 million inhabitants. According to an estimate produced

by the Centro de Estudios Fronterizos del Norte de México in Tijuana, that city had a stationary population in 1987 of approximately 613,000 inhabitants. This figure perhaps underestimates the real total, but not by a factor of four.

2. *CBS Reports:* "One River, One Country: The U.S.-Mexico Border," with CBS News correspondent Bill Moyers, CBS transcript, September 3, 1986.
3. William Murray, "Twins," *The New Yorker,* December 29, 1986, p. 70.
4. "All told, 150,000 to 200,000 Mexicans with green cards work on the United States side of the border but choose to live in Mexico, according to Guillermo Arámburo Vizcarra, an economist who has been studying the phenomenon for the University of Baja California." Larry Rohter, "Tijuana Journal," *New York Times,* May 19, 1987.
5. Bernardo González-Arechiga, "Vinculación fronteriza a Estados Unidos y su cambio con la crisis," *Cuadernos del Centro de Estudios del Norte de México* (Tijuana, 1985), pp. 21–23.
6. Jorge Bustamante, "Identidad nacional en la frontera norte de México: hallazgos preliminares," mimeo, Centro de Estudios Fronterizos del Norte de México, May 1983.
7. Héctor Aguilar Camín, "El canto del futuro," *Nexos* #100, April 1986, p. 19.

8. CROSSING CULTURES

The Fear of Americanization

1. José López Portillo, Sexto Informe de Gobierno, September 1, 1982, Mexico City, p. 18.
2. Héctor Hugo Olivares Ventura, *El Universal,* April 5, 1987, p. 10.
3. *Estadísticas Históricas de México* (Instituto Nacional de Estadística, Geografía e Informática–Instituto Nacional de Antropología e Historia, 1985), Vol. I, p. 54.
4. Ibid.
5. Kevin F. McCarthy and R. Burciaga Valdez, *Current and Future Effects of Mexican Immigration in California* (Rand Corporation–California Roundtable, Santa Monica, May 1986).
6. Ibid., p. 22.
7. Leon Bouvier and David Simcox, *Many Hands, Few Jobs: Population, Unemployment and Emigration in Mexico and the Caribbean* (Center for Immigration Studies, Washington, D.C., November 1986), p. 28; and *New York Times,* December 14, 1986, p. 1.
8. *Current and Future Effects of Mexican Immigration in California,* p. 35.
9. Larry Rohter, "Mexico's New Type of Immigrant: Well-to-Do, Skilled, Disillusioned," *New York Times,* November 4, 1986, p. 1.
10. Ibid. See "Mexico: Borrowed Time, Part 2," *Wall Street Journal,* September 25, 1984.
11. Frank del Olmo, "Sour Sweetheart Deal for Spanish TV?" Los Angeles *Times,* September 12, 1986; Sergio Sarmiento, "Mexican Media Magnates Explore U.S. Market," *Wall Street Journal,* April 3, 1987, p. 31.
12. Joel Brinkley, "Mexico and the Narcotics Traffic: Growing Strain in U.S. Relations," *New York Times,* October 20, 1986, p. 1.
13. John Bailey, "Mexico in the U.S. Media, 1979–1986: Implications for the Bilateral

Relation," paper delivered at the annual meeting of the International Studies Association, Washington, D.C., April 14–18, 1987.

14. Asociación de Corresponsales Extranjeros en México, AC, Directorio 1986, Mexico City.

15. William E. Buzenberg, "The 1985 Mexican Elections and the North American Press," paper presented at a conference at the Center for U.S.-Mexican Studies, University of California, San Diego, November 8, 1985, p. 1.

16. An example of the "Americanization of Mexico" perspective in the United States is Joel Garreau, "Mexican Counter-Revolt: The Americanization of the North Threatens the System," Washington *Post,* May 25, 1986.

17. The data were provided by Ignacio Durán, a leading authority on the Mexican cinematographic scene and currently the cultural attaché at the Mexican embassy in Washington. The Camara Nacional de la Industria Cinematográfica is the principal source for the data.

18. Crawford D. Goodwin and Michael Nacht, *Decline and Renewal: Causes and Cures of Decay Among Foreign-Trained Intellectuals and Professionals in the Third World* (Institute of International Education, New York, 1986), p. 28.

The Fear of Mexicanization

1. Approximately 320 million people were admitted into the United States in 1986, 60% of them came across the Mexican border, 30% across the Canadian, and 10% at other ports (including airports). U.S. Department of Justice, Immigration and Naturalization Service, *Statistical Yearbook of the INS, 1986* (Government Printing Office, September 1987), pp. 116–17. The statistics on the number of border guard personnel came from telephone conversations with Margaret Sullivan, Charles Montgomery, and Karen Hess of the INS, September 15, 1987.

2. Three good sources for estimating the illegal Mexican population are: U.S. Department of Commerce, Bureau of the Census, *Hispanic Population in the United States: March 1986 and 1987* (Advance Report), August 1987 (hereafter Census, Hispanic, 1987), Appendix A, pp. 12–13, on estimating the illegals; *INS Annual Statistical Report, 1986* (1987), p. xi; and Robert Warren and Jeffrey S. Passel, "Estimates of Illegal Aliens from Mexico Counted in the 1980 U.S. Census," paper presented for the Population Association of America, April 1983. The amnesty program concluded on May 4, 1988. For the results, see U.S. Immigration and Naturalization Service, "Provisional Legalization Application Statistics," June 24, 1988.

3. For the 1970 census on the Mexican-origin population, see the Census Bureau's Supplementary Report, "Persons of Spanish Origin by State: 1980," which is included in the back of the report of the House Subcommittee on Census and Population, *The Hispanic Population of the United States: An Overview,* April 21, 1983, pp. 170–73 (hereafter Census, Hispanic, 1980). For more recent data, see Census, Hispanic, 1987, p. 1.

4. Governor Richard D. Lamm and Gary Imhoff, *The Immigration Time Bomb: The Fragmenting of America* (E. P. Dutton, 1985), p. 1.

5. Cited by Carlos Rico in his chapter in Carlos Vasquez and Manuel Garcia y Griego (eds.), *Mexican-U.S. Relations: Conflict and Convergence* (UCLA, 1983), p. 150.

6. "CIA Chief Sees Migration, Not Mining, as Public Worry," *New York Times,* April 16, 1984, p. A8.

7. Philip Shenon, " 'Startling' Surge Is Reported in Illegal Aliens from Mexico," *New*

York Times, February 21, 1986, p. 1. The estimate proved correct. See *INS Statistical Report, 1986,* Chart L, p. xxxvi.

8. Robert Pear, "Rising Public Support for Limits on Immigration Is Found in Poll," *New York Times,* July 1, 1986, p. 1. This was a CBS/*New York Times* poll based on 1,618 telephone interviews in June.

9. Cited in Leon F. Bouvier and Philip Martin, *Population Change and California's Future* (Population Reference Bureau, 1985), p. 12.

10. His first statement came in an interview for *USA Today,* September 11, 1987, p. 11A. His border proposal was in an interview with Walter Cronkite, in *Public Papers of the Presidents, Ronald Reagan,* March 3, 1981, pp. 201–2. His endorsement of employer sanctions, etc., was incorporated in the proposal he sent to Congress. *Presidential Papers,* July 30, 1981, pp. 676–77. His comments on losing control were at a press conference on June 14, 1984. *Presidential Papers,* p. 856.

11. James Fallows, "Immigration: How It's Affecting Us," *Atlantic Monthly* 252, No. 5 (November 1983), p. 48.

12. Cited in Earl G. Harrison, *Immigration Policy of the United States* (Foreign Policy Reports of the Foreign Policy Association, April 1, 1947), p. 1.

13. Alejandro Portes and Robert L. Bach, *Latin Journey: Cuban and Mexican Immigrants in the United States* (University of California Press, 1985), pp. 270–72.

14. For the history of U.S. immigration policy as it affected Mexico and Latin America, see Robert Pastor, "U.S. Immigration Policy and Latin America: In Search of the 'Special Relationship,' " *Latin American Research Review* 19, No. 3 (1984).

15. *Congressional Record,* Senate, April 18, 1924, p. 6625.

16. Robert A. Divine, *American Immigration Policy, 1924–1952* (Yale University Press, 1957), pp. 65–67.

17. For a good study of Mexican migration to the United States from 1900 to 1964, with particular emphasis on the bracero years (1942–64) and on the contrasting and shifting positions of the two governments, see Manuel Garcia y Griego, "The Importation of Mexican Contract Laborers to the United States, 1942–1964: Antecedents, Operation, and Legacy," in Peter G. Brown and Henry Shue (eds.), *The Border That Joins: Mexican Migrants and U.S. Responsibility* (Rowman and Littlefield, 1983), pp. 49–98. For this reference, pp. 53–54.

18. *Foreign Relations of the United States, 1952–54,* p. 1343.

19. Select Commission on Immigration and Refugee Policy, *Staff Report,* April 1981, p. 473.

20. Cited by Garcia y Griego in *The Border That Joins,* p. 63.

21. Ibid., pp. 71–72.

22. Ibid., pp. 63–66.

23. Actually, they would have stopped the program in 1963, but a last-minute request by Mexico saved the program for another year. See ibid., p. 76.

24. Cited in Select Commission on Immigration and Refugee Policy, *Staff Report,* April 1981, p. 667.

25. Ibid., pp. 469–71, 673.

26. See, for example, Wayne Cornelius, *Mexican Migration to the United States* (Massachusetts Institute of Technology, 1978), p. 8.

27. Garcia y Griego in *The Border That Joins,* pp. 77–78.

28. Cited in Select Commission *Staff Report,* April 1981, p. 207.

29. Robert Pastor, "Migration in the Caribbean Basin," in Mary Kritz (ed.), *U.S. Immigration and Refugee Policy* (Lexington Books, 1983), p. 97.

30. The statistics on immigrants and refugees are from *INS Statistical Report, 1986,* Tables 1, 34, pp. 1, 54.
31. Thomas Muller, *The Fourth Wave: California's Newest Immigrants* (Urban Institute Press, 1984), p. 3. Muller's "third wave" was the migration by blacks after World War II to the northern states.
32. See Robert Pastor (ed.), *Migration and Development in the Caribbean: The Unexplored Connection* (Westview Press, 1985).
33. Cited in Lydia Chavez, "Fears Prompt Hispanic Votes in Bill's Support: Discrimination Worried Immigration Act Foes," *New York Times,* November 11, 1986, p. 8.
34. Cited in Larry Rohter, "New U.S. Immigration Law Is Taking Its Toll in Mexico," *New York Times,* April 21, 1987, pp. 1, 4.
35. Dianna Solis and Pauline Yoshihashi, "Immigration Law Cuts Illegal Border Crossing, But It's No Panacea," *Wall Street Journal,* November 6, 1987, pp. 1, 18.
36. UN International Labour Office, *Labour Force, 1950–2000,* Vol. III: *Latin America* (Geneva, 1977), p. 50.
37. Barry R. Chiswick, "The Economic Progress of Immigrants: Some Apparently Universal Patterns," in Chiswick (ed.), *The Gateway* (American Enterprise Institute, 1982), pp. 156, 138.
38. Silvia Pedraza-Bailey, *Political and Economic Migrants in America: Cubans and Mexicans* (University of Texas Press, 1985).
39. *The Fourth Wave,* pp. 12–22.
40. Richard D. Lamm, "English Comes First," *New York Times,* July 1, 1986, p. 31.
41. Select Commission, *Staff Report,* April 1981, p. 3. For the estimate that migration is one-third of population growth in the 1980s, see Vernon M. Briggs, Jr., "The Growth and Composition of the U.S. Labor Force," *Science* 238, October 1987, p. 176.
42. Joshua Fishman, "The Ethnic Revival in the United States: Implications for the Mexican American Community," in Walker Connor (ed.), *Mexican Americans in Comparative Perspective* (Urban Institute Press, 1985), pp. 311–54.
43. Joshua Fishman et al., *Language Loyalty in the United States: The Maintenance and Perpetuation of Non-English Mother Tongues by American Ethnic and Religious Groups* (Mouton, The Hague, 1966), cited in Connor (ed.), p. 286.
44. This is J. Milton Yinger's definition, in Connor (ed.).
45. Walker Connor, "Who Are the Mexican Americans? A Note on Comparability," in Connor (ed.), pp. 24, 20.
46. Cited by Walker Connor, p. 22. There was no breakdown of the Hispanic population into groups such as Mexican-Americans.
47. National Opinion Research Center Survey, February–April 1984.
48. Strategy Research Corporation, *U.S. Hispanic Market Study: 1987,* p. 199.
49. David E. Lopez, "Chicano Language Loyalty in an Urban Setting," *Sociology and Social Research* 62, January 1978, pp. 267–78.
50. Ibid., p. 276.
51. Census, Hispanic, 1987, pp. 6–7.
52. Gary Orfield, *Public School Desegregation in the United States, 1968–1980* (Joint Center for Political Studies, 1983), pp. 12–21, 48–49.
53. Donald L. Horowitz, "Conflict and Accommodation: Mexican Americans in the Cosmopolis," in Connor (ed.), pp. 70–74. Census, Hispanic, 1987.

54. J. Milton Yinger, "Assimilation in the United States: The Mexican Americans," in Connor (ed.), p. 39.

55. Avelardo Valdez, "Recent Increases in Intermarriage by Mexican American Males," *Social Science Quarterly* 64, No. 1, March 1983, pp. 136–44.

56. Harley L. Browning and Rodolfo O. de la Garza, *Mexican Immigrants and Mexican Americans: An Evolving Relation* (University of Texas Center for Mexican American Studies, 1986), pp. 5–7.

57. Leo Grebler, Joan W. Moore, and Ralph C. Guzman, *The Mexican American People: The Nation's Second Largest Minority* (The Free Press, 1970), p. 3.

58. *U.S. News & World Report,* August 24, 1981.

59. Statistics on the original Mexican-American population were very poor for many reasons. First, the population was not defined as such until well into the twentieth century. Second, Mexicans often intermarried or described themselves as Castilians rather than Mexicans. The most often cited statistics range from 13,000 to 80,000 Mexicans. See Arthur F. Corwin, "Early Labor Migration: A Frontier Sketch, 1848–1900," in Arthur F. Corwin (ed.), *Immigrants—and Immigrants: Perspectives on Mexican Labor Migration to the United States* (Greenwood Press, 1978), p. 25.

60. See, for example, *Time* cover story, "It's Your Turn in the Sun: Now 19 Million, and Growing Fast, Hispanics Are Becoming a Power," October 16, 1978; and "The Hispanic Community—A Growing Force to Be Reckoned With," *National Journal,* April 7, 1979.

61. Spencer Rich, "Adjustments Urged in 1990 Census Tally," Washington *Post,* October 20, 1987, p. A19. See also Joel Garreau, *The Nine Nations of North America* (Avon Books), p. 215. New York lost the case.

62. Linda Greenhouse, "Lawsuit Challenges Census on Illegal Aliens," *New York Times,* February 18, 1988, p. 8.

63. Stated on *MacNeil-Lehrer Newshour,* August 14, 1987.

64. James Michener, *Texas* (Random House, 1984), pp. 1223–27.

65. Cited in "Hispanic People Attack English-Language Bills," *New York Times,* August 2, 1987, p. 32.

66. This study is cited in F. Ray Marshall and Leon Bouvier, *Population Change and the Future of Texas* (Population Reference Bureau, 1986), p. 79.

67. Rodolfo de la Garza, "As American as Tamale Pie: Mexican American Political Mobilization and the Loyalty Question," in Connor (ed.), p. 229.

68. Ibid., p. 235.

69. Ibid., p. 233.

70. Department of Justice, Immigration and Naturalization Service, *Annual Report, 1986,* Chart K, p. xxxiv.

71. Immigration and Naturalization Service, *Annual Report, 1985,* p. 141. In 1986, the number of Mexicans naturalized was 27,807 (Table 45, p. 79 of 1986 Report).

72. For the best article on the subject of the triangular relationship, see Rodolfo O. de la Garza, "Chicanos and U.S. Foreign Policy: The Future of Chicano-Mexican Relations," in Carlos Vasquez and Manuel Garcia y Griego (eds.), *Mexican-U.S. Relations: Conflict and Convergence* (UCLA, 1983), p. 401. Much of this section borrows from that essay.

73. De la Garza, in Vasquez and Garcia y Griego (eds.), p. 413.

74. De la Garza, in Connor (ed.), pp. 239–41.

75. Rodolfo de la Garza and Adela I. Flores, "The Impact of Mexican Immigrants on the Political Behavior of Chicanos: A Clarification of Issues and Some Hypotheses for Future Research," in Harley L. Browning and Rodolfo de la Garza (eds.), *Mexican Immigrants and Mexican Americans: An Evolving Relation,* pp. 220–26.

76. Cited in "Hispanic Leader: Annul Elections," Mexico City *News,* July 30, 1986, p. 6.

77. Browning and de la Garza, *Mexican Immigrants and Mexican Americans,* p. 8.

78. Connor, in Connor (ed.), p. 360.

79. Inter-American Development Bank, *Economic and Social Progress in Latin America, 1987 Report,* pp. 188–89; and Hudson Institute, *Workforce 2000* (Hudson Institute, 1987), p. 112.

INDEX

A NOTE ABOUT THE AUTHORS

ROBERT A. PASTOR was born in New Jersey, in 1947. He attended Lafayette College, the John F. Kennedy School of Government, and Harvard University, where he received his Ph.D. in government. From 1977 to 1981 he served as Director of Latin American Affairs on the National Security Council. He has taught at Harvard, the University of Maryland, and El Colegio de Mexico (Mexico City), where he was a Fulbright professor in 1985–86. Currently he is a professor of political science at Emory University and Director of the Latin American and Caribbean Program at Emory's Carter Center. He is the author of several books, most recently, *Condemned to Repetition: The United States and Nicaragua.* He lives in Atlanta with his wife and two children.

JORGE G. CASTAÑEDA was born in Mexico City, in 1953. He received his B.A. from Princeton University and his M.A. and Ph.D. from the University of Paris. He has advised the Mexican government on international affairs, and was a senior associate at the Carnegie Endowment for International Peace in Washington from 1985 to 1987. Since 1978 he has been a professor of political science at the National Autonomous University of Mexico. A regular contributor to the Los Angeles *Times* editorial page, he is the author of several books, most recently, *México: El Futuro en juego.* He lives with his wife and three children in Mexico City.

A NOTE ON THE TYPE

The text of this book was set in a type face called Times Roman,
designed by Stanley Morison (1889–1967) for *The Times* (London)
and first introduced by that newspaper in 1932.

Among typographers and designers of the twentieth century,
Stanley Morison was a strong forming influence—as a typograph-
ical adviser to The Monotype Corporation, as a director of two
distinguished English publishing houses, and as a writer of sensi-
bility, erudition, and keen practical sense.

Composed, printed and bound by
The Haddon Craftsmen, Scranton, Pennsylvania
Designed by Julie Rowse-Duquet